Forging the Chain

Studies in Ethnic and Immigration Series

Gathering Place: Peoples and Neighbourhoods of Toronto, 1834-1945. Edited
by Robert F. Harney

DP: Lithuanian Immigration to Canada After the Second World War. By
Milda Danys

Defiant Sisters: A Social History of Finnish Immigrant Women in Canada.
By Varpu Lindström-Best

*Maple Leaf and Trident: The Ukrainian Canadians during the Second World
War.* By Thomas M. Prymak

Studies in Ethnic and Immigration History

Forging the Chain

A Case Study of Italian Migration to North America, 1880-1930

Franc Sturino

1990
Multicultural History Society of Ontario
Toronto

The Multicultural History Society of Ontario wishes to thank the Department of the Secretary of State, Multiculturalism Sector for its financial assistance in the preparation of this volume.

Canadian Cataloguing in Publication Data

Sturino, Franc, 1948-
    Forging the chain: a case study of Italian migration to North America, 1880-1930

(Studies in ethnic and immigration history)
Includes bibliographical references.
ISBN 0-919045-45-6 (bound) ISBN 0-919045-43-X (pbk.)

1. Immigrants — Ontario — Toronto — History. 2. Italians — Ontario — Toronto — History. 3. Immigrants — Illinois — Chicago — History. 4. Italians — Illinois — Chicago — History. 5. Italy, Southern — Emigration and immigration — History. 6. Ontario — Emigration and immigration — History. 7. Illinois — Emigration and immigration — History. I. Multicultural History Society of Ontario. II. Title. III. Series.

FC3097.9.I8S88 1990   305'.8510713541
F1059.5.T68918 1990   C90-094893-0

Front cover: "Absent Father", early twentieth century, Cosenza.
        Courtesy: Museo etnografico di San Giovanni in Fiore.

Contents

To my daughter

IDELLA JEAN

Acknowledgments

The writing of a monograph can often seem a solitary exercise, though the author is constantly aware that without the assistance of many individuals and institutions the study would never have reached completion, let alone publication.

In conducting the research over several years for this study, I am particularly indebted to the generous support provided by the Social Sciences and Humanities Research Council of Canada and to the Ontario Ministry of Colleges and Universities; and in facilitating publication to the Mariano A. Elia Chair in Italian-Canadian Studies at York University.

Among the many scholarly repositories consulted, especially helpful were the National Archives of Canada in Ottawa, the John P. Robarts Research Library of the University of Toronto, the Multicultural History Society of Ontario, the College Library of Harvard University, the Library of the University of Illinois at Chicago, and the Biblioteca Civica di Cosenza.

I owe a debt of gratitude to Anna Maria Perricone, who gave generously of her time and patience in typing the original manuscript, to Anne McCarthy for her expert word-processing skills and preparation of the index, and to Diane Mew, whose judicious editing, peppered with good humour, did much to transform a rather unwieldy manuscript into its present form.

Several individuals read the study and offered thoughtful suggestions which helped to improve it. Among others, my thanks goes to David Levine of the Ontario Institute for Studies in Education, Charles Tilly of the New School for Social Research, and Samuel Baily of Rutgers University. Along the way, advice and support was given by Harold Troper of the Ontario Institute for Studies in Education, Roberto Perin of York University, Jean Burnet of the Multicultural History Society of Ontario, Cesare Pitto of the Università della Calabria and Gianfausto Rosoli of the Centro Studi Emigrazione, Rome.

A heartfelt thank you goes to the many *paesani* who cooperated so magnificantly with a sometimes obtrusive researcher. They opened up their homes and lives so that the experience of immigration could be recorded, and I hope this volume does justice to what they had to teach me.

Finally, I should like to express my gratitude towards an individual whose contribution as adviser, colleague, and friend played a cardinal role in shaping this volume. As Professor of History at the University of Toronto, Co-director of the University's Ethnic and Immigration Studies Program, and founder of the Multicultural History Society of Ontario, he has left an indelible mark in the field of migration studies; my sincere tribute goes to the late Robert F. Harney.

THE REGIONS OF ITALY

Introduction

The movement of immigrants to North America has long been viewed
with either fascination or foreboding by the native-born and settled
population. The stranger, aside from the economic and social impact
of his presence, has often been a source of psychological unease for
the "indigenous" inhabitants. No sooner had the doors shut at the end
of the 1920s behind the last stragglers of the great immigrant tide
from Europe that had begun a century earlier, than scholars turned
their attention to documenting its history. At first, through the thirties
and forties, these studies were few, concentrated on Northern European groups, and much influenced by a frontier thesis that bestowed
upon the land itself a powerful assimilating principle. By the mid-
fifties the field of immigration history had expanded significantly to
include more recent Southeastern European immigrants and the city.
But here again old world traits were seen as dissolving upon impact
with the new world environment, though this time the stress was on
painful disintegration rather than assimilation. Almost a decade later
this view emphasizing the absorptive power of new world forces was
called into question by scholars who focused more meticulously on
the experience of individual ethnic groups.[1]

In particular, Southern Italians have been portrayed as manifesting
tenacious and significant continuities with the old world past. Though
the position stressing continuity within the discontinuity of immigration has been challenged by assimilationalist studies with respect to
"Southerners," the weight of historical research has shown that it was
the European background and not the new world environment that
predominated in shaping the experience and social forms of these
people in North America.[2] Since 1970 a series of investigations, capi-
talizing on the growing field of social history and narrowing their
subject matter to specific aspects of the Southern Italian experience,
have illustrated, for example, that the peasant practice of relying on
literate local elites to link them with the national polity shaped the
migration process,[3] that patterns of immigrant work were intimately
connected with traditional familial roles and responsibilities, and that
the associational life and aspirations of settlers had direct antecedents
in the village.

Such findings reflect a persistent theme by social historians concerned
with documenting the effect of economic structural change upon the
social life and world view of common people. The words of two recent
investigators, Joan Scott and Louise Tilly, dealing with the effect of
European industrialization on women's work, express well the contours

of this theme: "The model we use posits a continuity of traditional values and behavior in changing circumstances. Old values coexist with and are used by people to adapt to extensive structural changes. This assumes that people perceive and act on the changes they experience in terms of ideas and attitudes they already hold. These ideas eventually change, but not ... directly or immediately."[4]

In broad terms, the present study dealing with Southern Italians can be seen as fitting into such an orientation stressing social continuity in the face of structural discontinuity. The book aims to contribute to the evolving social history of Italian immigration to the new world and, tangentially, the nature of the immigrant experience more generally. Specifically, the study's frame of reference differs from those of the past in a number of interrelated ways which may provide a fresh perspective to the store of knowledge in the field.

First, my study approaches the migration process from a "village-outward" perspective. Many other studies have begun their story of immigration from the old world, but until recently the unit of investigation has usually been the nation-state, or the region. Where the small municipal level has been examined, the frame of reference has generally remained the new world experience, so that the author looked outward from the new world city to the village background, rather than the reverse. The main thrust therefore remained a new world preoccupation with questions of assimilation, integration, adjustment, pluralism, and similar sociological constructs. Such a view, which addresses itself to the minority group's relationship with the majority, is valid within its own terms, but it cannot be said to manifest a village-outward perspective. Peasant immigrants were not concerned with ethnic survival, but with much more immediate questions of individual responsibility: how to maintain family cohesion, how to provide for its security, how to arrange the setting up of offspring, and similar issues. The two levels of inquiry – the North American-based preoccupation with societal association and the village-based preoccupation with much more immediate personal interests – are, of course, interrelated, and at strategic junctures in the narrative this relationship will be addressed. But the primary purpose is to present an account of the immigrant experience from the perspective of the actors themselves. Within this, a major concern is with their *mentalità*, defined here as what was "thinkable" – attitudes, aspirations, values, and the like   by a collectivity of peasant migrants at a given time.[5]

This study departs significantly in a second way from previous scholarship. The population of Southern Italians we will be investigating did not come, as has commonly been the case, from conventional jurisdictional boundaries. Rather, the parameters placed around this group were derived from the lives of the common people who composed it. Consultation with peasant immigrants revealed that in Southern Italy they were linked by social and economic ties which spanned several communes within walking distance of each other. Here an affinity between the present study and the field of local history, which concerns itself with the setting within which commoners lived their daily lives and the ways of this life, becomes obvious. In an essay discussing the nature of local history, Pierre Goubert has outlined the boundaries of the world of most Europeans, at least until the late nineteenth century: "For a long period ... the setting of most Europeans was the parish in the country or the small town and the surrounding district – that is, roughly speaking the stretch of land covered in a day's walk, from ten kilometres to ten miles."[6] This is in striking agreement with that unit of common human interaction defined by the villager's *mentalità*. Hence, I begin the study with a consideration of the geographical setting of the villagers, given social significance by the concrete ties between individuals. While upon the phenomenon of emigration one can no longer speak of a coherent geographic entity defined by villagers, the "social space" that people occupied within this small-scale unit does not evaporate, but rather withstands the transatlantic voyage to determine the pattern of human relations in the new world. Moving outward from a geographically bound local space in the old world, then, we conclude with a socially determined space in the new, defined by the villagers' collective mentality.

This relationship between the old world and the new is mediated, of course, by the phenomenon of chain migration, defined here in the now classic sense first annunciated by the MacDonalds as "that movement in which prospective migrants learn of opportunities, are provided with transportation, and have initial accommodation and employment arranged *by means of primary social relationships with previous migrants*." The authors distinguish three basically sequential types of chains for the period between 1880 and the First World War: the migration of males through labour agents or *padroni;* the serial migration of workers through the assistance of other established lone labourers; and delayed family migration uniting wives and children with breadwinners.[7]

The concept of chain migration brings us to the third way in which the present study parts company from most others. The concept has been one of the most fruitful devised to throw light on the Italian movement and several studies exist linking places of origin with specific destinations in the new world. However, little systematic investigation has taken place to determine the parameters within which migration chains actually operated. This would seem to be a priority since a clear definition of the narrowness or broadness of chains is important for understanding many issues central to the immigration process: early padronism, immigrant residential concentrations, occupational and industrial niches, and similar themes.

Studies on Italian immigration are full of references to village, district and provincial chains, indeed, chains at almost all possible levels of association ranging from family to *regione*. For the most part these studies have depended on public records. Migration networks in the present study, however, are grounded in the local area that was home to common people and that defined their interaction. Hence, the shape of chain migration is ecologically determined, and the impact of this is felt at all stages of migration.

In addition to these important departures from the mainstream of Italian immigration studies, other themes also loom large. I give extended treatment to the family, both in its elemental and its wider meanings, since its saliency along with that of friendship in the lives of the peasant immigrants under discussion was unmistakable. In the peasant community of villagers, such primary ties of interdependency between people formed the basic organizing principle of society. As in other peasant societies, socio-economic relations in the absence of a rationalizing centre were, by default, founded along ascriptive and kinship lines.

I have attempted to describe the gradations of interdependency, the system of rights and obligations between kin and friends, their practice of mutual aid, and their etiquette. And, further, I have attempted to delineate the points of constancy as well as flexibility in the ties of interdependency as people responded to the great changes wrought upon their community by political and economic incursions from the wider world.

The world of work was intertwined with that of family, kinship, and friends, and especially with the first of these, which formed a single corporate entity. While throughout the study I am interested in the nexus between the world of work and primary ties of interdependency, I am concerned to trace changes in occupations, as a primarily peasant mode of production gave way to incorporation into an industrial order. Further, for the villagers, their immigrant experience was defined by the world of labour, so that dealing with this theme was almost indigenous to the topic of study.

Another theme running through most of the study involves the nature of the migration process. Rather than viewing this as a simple one-way population movement from Europe to North America, I am interested in documenting the evolution of a predominantly sojourning pattern of migration as it gave way to a mixed sojourn-immigrant pattern, and hence to a committed *mentalità* of immigration or settlement. The volume of outflow from Southern Italy, especially during its peak in the decade before the Great War, was impressive, and the dynamic which underlay this – what became a veritable "culture of emigration" – can best be explained through the concept of chain migration.

Finally, I am concerned with the manner in which forces outside the small society of peasant immigrants impinged on, and influenced, events in the community. Though the point of departure is a local area of peasants, these communities are not isolated and closed, a breed apart, as it were, from the wider society. Rather, the local society, while forming an entity distinct from the larger polity, nevertheless is connected, and partially defined by, the national community. Influences from the "outside," muted and transmuted by a distinct local ethos as they may be,[8] nonetheless had a real impact. The villagers were affected by the economic, political, and social forces of the wider world and their local society was subjected to increasing encapsulation by the nation-state. However, against this process, and in particular its characteristics of proletarianization and socio-cultural homogenization, peasant immigrants put up a valiant and often effective resistance, and it is this which is examined here.

CHAPTER 1

The Socio-Economic Background in Italy

The Setting

THE RENDE AREA

Geographically, the point of origin of this study is the commune or *comune* of Rende located in the southwestern part of the province of Cosenza. The province lies within the region of Calabria, the southernmost part of the Italian peninsula. The commune or municipality of Rende in 1881 consisted of four villages and the town of Rende itself. It encompassed an area of 4,806 hectares and had a total population, covering both nucleated settlements and countryside, of 5,239. As the seat of municipal government and religious life, both the town hall and the parish or "mother" church of Santa Maria Maggiore were situated within the walls of Rende. The town also acted as the judicial and electoral centre for the *mandamento* (analogous to the North American "county") of Rende which incorporated the adjacent municipalities of Marano Marchesato and San Fili as well as the town's own commune.[1] In this sense, the town acted as the local administrative seat on behalf of the provincial administration at Cosenza, which in turn was directly responsible to Rome.[2] It is clear, therefore, that Rende's administrative responsibilities would play an important role in the lives of the local population. But, in order to understand the way in which Italy's various jurisdictional units are named, a little more background is necessary.

First, it should be noted that Italian practice denoted the provincial units by the same name as their main city and capital. So, too, the Italian commune was named after the main settlement within its borders. Further, the name of the provincial capital was also the name

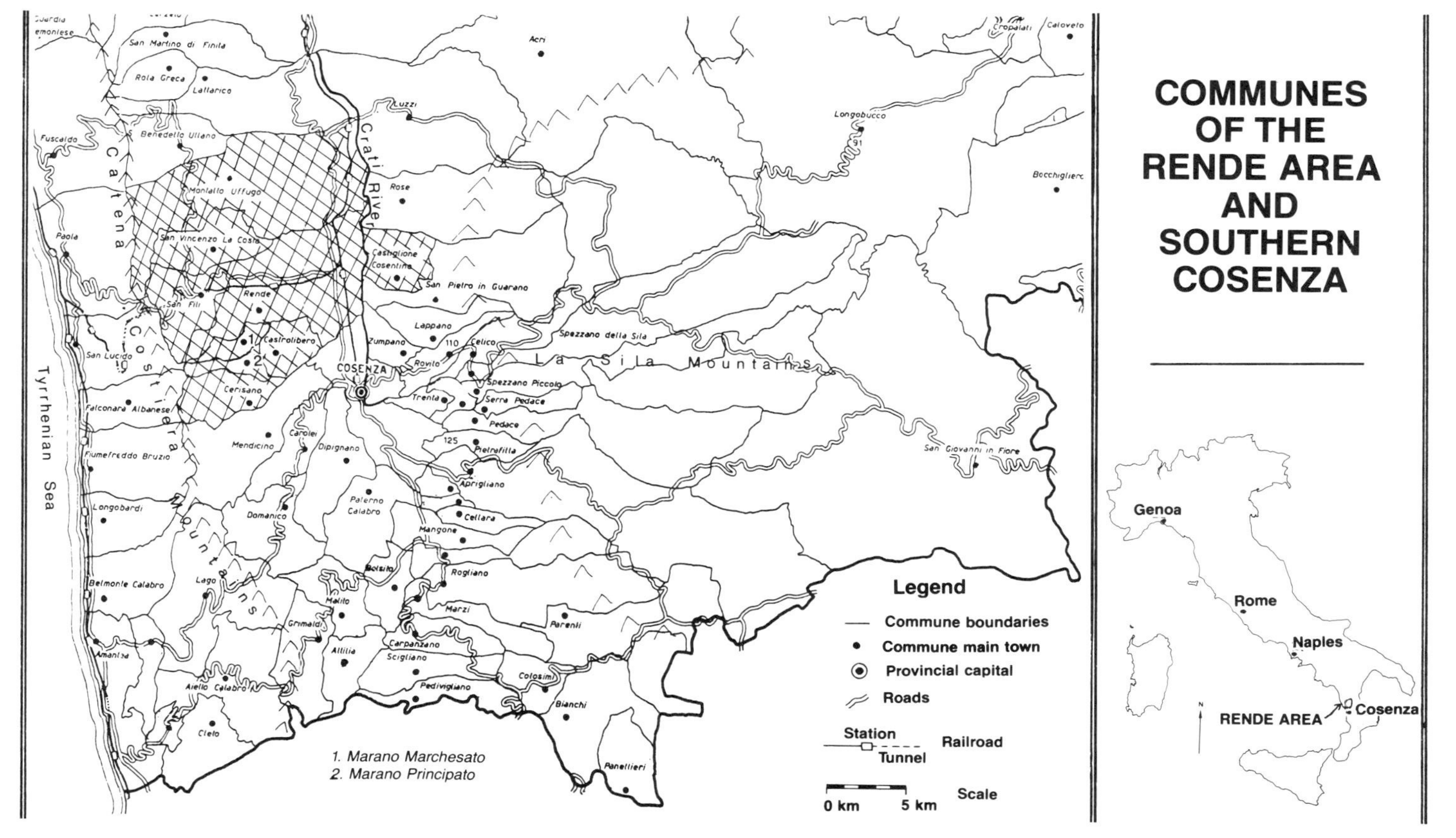

COMMUNES OF THE RENDE AREA AND SOUTHERN COSENZA
Genoa
Rome
Naples
Cosenza
RENDE AREA
N
Legend
Commune boundaries
Commune main town
Provincial capital
Roads
Station
Tunnel
Railroad
Scale
0 km
5 km
Tyrrhenian Sea
Crati River
COSENZA
La Sila Mountains
Spezzano della Sila
Catena Costiera Mountains
Caloveto
Cropalati
Bocchigliero
San Giovanni in Fiore
Longobucco
Acri
Luzzi
Rose
San Pietro in Guarano
Castiglione
Cosentino
Lappano
Celico
Spezzano Piccolo
Serra Pedace
Pedace
Pietrafitta
Aprigliano
Cellara
Figline
Zumpano
Rovito
Trenta
110
125
Mangone
Palerno
Calabro
Rogliano
Parenti
Marzi
Bianchi
Colosimi
Panettieri
Pedivigliano
Carpanzano
Scigliano
Bobbio
Dipignano
Carolei
Mendicino
Domanico
Malito
Altilia
Grimaldi
Marano Marchesato
Marano Principato
Castrolibero
Rende
San Vincenzo La Costa
Cerisano
San Fili
San Lucido
Falconara Albanese
Fiumefreddo Bruzio
Longobardi
Belmonte Calabro
Lago
Aiello Calabro
Cleto
Amantea
Montalto Uffugo
San Benedetto Ullano
Lattarico
Rota Greca
San Martino di Finita
Fuscaldo
Paola
1. Marano Marchesato
2. Marano Principato

of an intermediary unit between the city and the province, that is, the *circondario* or "provincial district." And, as has been seen, the name of the commune and its town can refer to the *mandamento*. To avoid confusion I shall employ "Cosenza," "Rende," and such to refer to their respective provincial or municipal units and shall specify when the names refer to the city/town or the intermediate *circondario/mandamento* instead. Chart 1 will help to clarify the Italian jurisdictional units found in the south after Unification.

Though the major part of the peasant immigrants in this study came from Rende, interviews revealed that for them there existed a geographic unit of socio-economic interaction that extended beyond the commune. This unit consisted of an oval-shaped area extending roughly ten kilometres north of Rende to Montalto Uffugo and an equivalent distance south to Cerisano. To the east, the watershed of the Catena Costiera Mountains narrowed the range of contact to San Fili. On the west, with the exception of the adjacent commune of Castiglione Cosentino, the unit of interaction was bounded by the Crati River, the most important waterway of Calabria.[3] This unit of socio-economic interaction consisting of Rende and its eight surrounding communes I termed the Rende area.

But a word of clarification is in order. The immigrants interviewed were linked either through networks of kinship or friendship. It was found early in the field work that a large number of the people contacted through these networks were from communes surrounding Rende rather than Rende itself. Obviously for such *paesani* who were from outside Rende but were linked to it by primary ties, the commune played an important part in their lives. For others, however, who had no such ties, Rende played a lesser role. The focal point of activity for the peasants of the other communes was often their own municipality, not Rende. For the peasants of Cerisano, for example, their area of socio-economic interaction stretched south beyond the Rende area to Mendicino. Hence, though we can speak of a "Rende area" centred on Rende, it should be noted that this commune did not hold the same importance for all *paesani,* and also that moving the locus of the study to any of the surrounding communes would skew the resulting unit of socio-economic interaction around that commune.

In 1881, within the Rende area, the administrative centres of the nine communes under study ranged in size from the village of Castrolibero with a population of 424 to the town of Montalto with 2,226. Indeed, as can be seen from Table 1 (page 252-53), three of the villages within the commune of Montalto each had populations greater than Castrolibero. It is evident that great variation existed in the size of the local administrative centres. However, the small size of some of the *comune* capitals should not detract from their importance as urban centres for the local population. As Emrys Jones points out: "Numbers

Chart I. Italian Administrative Units, Cosenza Province

Administrative unit	*Composed of:*
Comune (municipality) e.g. Rende	frazioni (hamlets, villages) i.e. Arcavacata, Nogiano citta (town) i.e. Rende rione (rural district) i.e. Surdo
Mandamento ("county") e.g. Rende	3 comuni: i.e. Rende Marano Marchesato San Fili
Circondario (provincial district) e.g. Cosenza	62 comuni: e.g. Rende, Montalto Uffugo etc., plus the capital of Cosenza
Provincia (province) i.e. Cosenza	4 circondari: i.e. Cosenza Paola Castrovillari Rossano
Regione (region) i.e. Calabria	3 provincie: i.e. Cosenza Catanzaro Reggio Calabria

alone mean very little. There are circumstances in which a numerically small settlement may have urban characteristics – like density, markets, administrative functions – and others in which a numerically large settlement ... is still obviously a village in which the vast majority of men are farmers."[4]

Generally, the Rende area, dominated by hills interspersed with small rivers flowing eastward from their source in the Catena Costiera Mountains, can be considered an extension of the Crati Valley surrounded on three sides by mountains. Immigrants from Rende and neighbouring communes spoke of the richness of this commune, which, bordering the Crati, contained a large amount of fertile land. As one man described it, "Where that Crati is, all going along that river toward the west, it's all good land ... the best you can get. Then, you know, if you go up towards Montalto, the land changes in the mountains."[5]

It was pointed out that the reasons for considering the Rende area as the unit of study grew out of the interviews themselves. But what was the exact nature of the socio-economic interaction that allows this area to be considered a distinct unit? First, although the nine communes in 1881 encompassed over two dozen towns, villages and hamlets, the geographic area is quite small, and hence personal interaction was relatively easy. It was only six kilometres from the town of Rende eastward to San Fili; northward to the farthest town, Montalto, it was about twelve kilometres. A short distance of eleven kilometres separated the town from the provincial capital of Cosenza to the southeast. And from the centre of Rende to the more distant of the neighbouring communes, it was only a few hours' walk.

Further, within the Rende area there existed considerable trading activities which served to unify the whole area. For example, peasants in the low-lying areas of Rende who specialized in intensive vegetable cultivation sold their produce in the town markets of San Fili and San Vincenzo La Costa, the higher placed communes to the east, where local production could not meet demand. In turn, the peasants of these communes exploited the abundant forests within their area and sold chestnuts and charcoal to the inhabitants of Rende.[6] Especially after the elimination of municipal levies on local area goods and produce in the 1880s, trade between the communes of the Rende area improved.[7]

The important agricultural fair of Arcavacata, held annually at the end of August just north of the town of Rende, also brought together the population of the Crati Valley in a hectic week of buying and selling. The fair dealt heavily with livestock, particularly cattle, and though much of this originated in the mountain pastures of the La Sila Mountains just east of the Rende area, agriculturalists from San Fili, San Vincenzo and western Montalto also participated as sellers. Most of the peasants of the Rende area, however, came to the fair to buy livestock – usually young animals to be fattened over the winter months for their own consumption or to be sold later in Cosenza. While the Arcavacata fair was of particular importance to the Rende area, it also attracted participants and buyers from all over the province and as far away as Crotone, Reggio Calabria and even Naples.[8]

The more powerful landlords of the area often owned estates that straddled two, three, or more communes, and this greatly facilitated economic links. In the late nineteenth century, for example, the Magdalone family, which had extensive holdings in Rende and dominated the economic life of that commune, also held land in neighbouring Marano Marchesato.[9] In such cases, the inhabitants of these communes often came into contact with each other both socially and economically. For instance, common labourers could be sent from one commune to another by the landlord, depending on his economic need, thus intermingling the municipal populations. And teamsters, while transporting the produce of their landlord's various enterprises, criss-crossed communes and played an important role as carriers of information from one commune to another.[10]

Social ties paralleled economic links in binding peasants together.

Some of these social contacts revolved around religion, which, on an intra-communal level, provided intercourse among the various sections or neighbourhoods of the individual communes. Throughout Rende, the second largest municipality after Montalto, there were about a dozen churches, half in the town itself, the rest spread throughout the countryside. Rather than adhering to a single neighbourhood church, as was common in North America, people frequented the various churches according to their preference, since different ones held mass at different times. Worshippers would also travel beyond their neighbourhood in to the various religious feasts *(feste)* for which particular churches were responsible. Hence, for example, families who regarded San Michele as a patron saint (and after whom the families' patriarch and other males would often be named) on 8 May would converge at the country church, Chiesa di Ritiro, responsible for the celebration of the saint's day and procession.[11]

Indeed, travel between communes to attend neighbouring *feste* was common and encouraged social contacts between the peasantry of the Rende area as a whole. It frequently happened, for example, that the people of Rende would travel to the neighbouring *comune* of Marano Marchesato to celebrate the important feast of the Madonna di Carmine (Our Lady of Mount Carmel). And outside the Rende area, it was usual for the peasants of the area to make an annual pilgrimage across the eastern mountains to the famous monastery of San Francesco di Paola. Then, too, on weekends and holidays young single men in couples or in small groups would walk to Castiglione, San Fili, Montalto, Cosenza, or even Paola, to pass away idle hours in the town square, perhaps buy an ice or a lemon drink, or sometimes visit relatives or friends.[12]

While such excursions could occasionally lead to the chance meeting with young women and intermarriage between communes, marrying outside one's municipality was more usually linked with internal migration within the Rende area. This migration took two forms. First, the peasants went to work harvesting in the summer or sowing in the autumn in the large wheat-growing estates of the lower-lying half of the Rende area. Often such agricultural workers would migrate eastward beyond the Rende area to the extensive wheat estates of the Crotone plain, the vineyards of Rossano, or the mountain valleys of La Sila for the sowing or harvesting of rye, potatoes, or corn.[13]

Second, and more likely to lead to intermarriage, was the movement of young single men from the more mountainous and rugged regions of the area, where land holdings were small and often fragmented, to the less congested plains where an attempt was made to rent land on a long-term basis. One peasant *fattore* or factor who worked for a medium-scale landlord, for example, married off three of his four daughters to such young men from outside Rende. One of these young men was from Marano Principato and had settled on the estate as a tenant. The second, as a boy, had followed his family which had migrated from the north and settled near the estate on the land of another landowner. The third was the nephew of the Marano settler who met his wife on one of his regular visits to his uncle's.[14]

Though intermarriage occurred mainly through the in-migration of men, instances where Rende men married outside women who then joined their husbands in the commune were not infrequent. And, of course, out-migration from Rende also occurred. One young man prospered, for example, when he left the *comune* to marry and take land as a dowry in the village of San Sisto (within the neighbouring municipality of San Vincenzo).[15] Migration and intermarriage were also facilitated by such major public works as the spur railroad line built about the time of the First World War through Rende and San Fili to connect Cosenza with the main line along the coast at Paola. The work attracted construction workers not only from the Rende area but also from neighbouring regions.[16]

While migration and intermarriage bound families throughout the Rende area together, they also influenced the various communes through the "fellow-villager" relationship. Migrants who entered a commune from the neighbouring municipalities and who married and settled there were eventually regarded as fellow-villagers, or *paesani* in its narrow municipal sense. But since these people were simultaneously still regarded as fellow-villagers in their communes of origin, they often acted to bind socially the populations of the two communes through such social contacts as attending weddings or baptisms.

Through these various connections between communes, families were known to one another throughout the Rende area. Though obviously not all individuals had personal contact with each other, people's reputations as reflected by their family membership and as transmitted through key intermediaries such as migrants or local merchants were widely known. Sometimes a family's reputation was reflected in its nickname and, commonly, the *soprannome* took the place of surnames among the peasantry.[17] As an area of common reputation, as a "moral community," an additional criterion of unity was given to the Rende area.[18]

While it has been argued that the Rende area formed one cohesive socio-economic unit, this does not mean that differences and conflict between the various communes did not exist. Each had its own municipal pride, its own patron saint, and even dress.[19] And though each tried to assert its identity positively, the reputation by which any individual commune was known often took on a humorously derogatory flavour (as was sometimes the case with family nicknames) which reflected the rivalry between them for social standing. Hence, while both Rende and San Fili had reputations for being sly, another *comune* was said to be composed of "country bumpkins" whose inhabitants walked about dumbly with open mouths *(bocche-aperti)*. Yet another commune was known by the name of the wide skirts its women wore, while the capital of Cosenza was thought to be a city of loose women.[20] Nevertheless, though conflict existed, the socio-economic links between municipalities outweighed the rivalry between them. Especially in the case of internal migration and intermarriage, the ties that were forged between people were both immediate and durable. With emigration to the new world such ties between people from the Rende area became more extensive and more manifest, and were used to help both the processes of emigration and settlement.[21]

THE POPULATION

The great bulk of the Rende area formed one easily distinguishable agricultural unit extending from 250 to 750 metres above sea level. The area was part of an intermediate agricultural zone covering half of Calabria and containing a majority of its population. This zone lies between the coastal lowlands and the mountainous interior; a 1908 study characterized it as the land of the olive and vine.[22] Within the Rende area, however, figs and grain were prime cash crops along with olives. While olive groves predominated on dry, stony areas, the growing of figs was common in the moister, richer sections of the foothills. Grain and vegetables were cultivated in the more level sections and valleys of the Rende area suitable for extensive agriculture. Whereas the olives, figs, and grain were produced for the national and international markets, vegetables were grown to meet local demand.[23]

On each side of this agricultural unit are two minor zones. On the east the lower Crati Valley forms a fertile, irrigated strip of land between 100 and 200 metres wide in which grain and vegetables were the preferred crops. On the west a mountainous strip of between 750 and 1,500 metres was characterized by forests and, to a lesser extent, pasturage.[24] The most important trees in these forests were the chestnuts, which not only provided wood for sawmills, firewood, and charcoal, but also feed for livestock, especially hogs. Further, the fruit was used by poor peasants, and in hard times by others, as a base for chestnut bread.[25]

Turning to the settlement patterns of the Rende area, a fundamental distinction can be made between what Italian sources refer to as dispersed settlement *(popolazione sparsa)* and nucleated settlement *(popolazione agglomerata)*. Such a distinction differs from the usual rural/urban dichotomy made in North America and implicitly recognizes the importance of peasant villages and agrotowns. Within the Rende area 45 per cent of the population was listed in 1911 as dispersed, that is to say, as living in the countryside, either in isolated dwellings or in small groups of houses or *casolari*.[26]

Although the proportion of peasants living in dispersed settlements was much greater for the Rende area than for Calabria as a whole, the difference was less when compared to the district of Cosenza (exclusive of the capital) in which 32 per cent of the population was similarly listed. This situation was not unique to Cosenza. In other areas of intensive agriculture – the Gerace area of Reggio Calabria, for example – similar figures of dispersed settlement were reached.[27] At any rate, the situation within the Rende area was at variance with the image of the "typical South" whereby peasants were characterized as living in villages or agrotowns from which they commuted to small plots in the countryside.[28]

Taruffi, De Nobili and Lori, authors of the voluminous 1908 study on Calabria, used the rule of thumb that dispersed rural settlements were usually found below 500 metres sea level whereas above this altitude peasants lived in nucleated settlements.[29] This rough correlation between altitude and settlement type held true for the Rende area. Most of the area was below 500 metres and the comparatively subdued topography of plains, hills, and valleys, as well as greater fertility, allowed the working of relatively large tracts of land, which made it economic to live in the countryside rather than commute from the village. In the lower-placed communes of Castiglione, Castrolibero, Marano Marchesato, and Marano Principato a dispersed rural settlement pattern predominated. In the commune of Rende itself three-quarters of the population lived in the countryside rather than in concentrated settlements.[30] Above 500 metres, in the submountainous and mountainous sections, the difficulty of amassing consolidated holdings made nucleated rural settlement the norm. Especially in San Fili and western Montalto, the typical South settlement pattern held true.

Interestingly, a comparison of the 1881 and 1911 censuses showed little change in the size of population of most municipalities except for the larger communes of Rende and Montalto, both of which had large sections of good, low-lying land bordering the Crati River able to sustain considerable increases. Since Rende had more of such land, its population grew by 2,000 in the thirty-year period to Montalto's increase of 900.[31] Although it was not possible to determine what proportion of this growth was due to in-migration rather than natural increase, oral testimony indicated that migration from the surrounding communes was common.

Migration within the Rende area was due primarily to the fact that by the late nineteenth century the population of the smaller, more rugged western communes had reached a saturation point. The division of land could not be carried on any further and still adequately support a family unit. Hence, adult sons were often forced to look outside their commune towards Rende and eastern Montalto in order to establish households.[32]

Most of the population increase was in the countryside and not in the villages and towns of the two communes. The proportion of Rende's population which lived on the land increased by 30 per cent between 1881 and 1911 and that of Montalto's by half this amount. Also, although the population of the smaller commune of Castiglione – the only other municipality bordering the Crati – remained virtually the same, it experienced a population shift of 20 per cent towards the countryside. In the rest of the Rende area, however, the proportion of people that lived in the country remained relatively static.[33]

This general population shift from the villages and towns of the Rende area to the countryside occurred throughout Calabria, though in a much more muted fashion. An Italian study on Calabria's population in the nineteenth century documented this demographic trend both for Cosenza province in particular and Calabria generally, each of which from 1871 to 1901 experienced an almost 7 per cent increase in the proportion of people on the land.[34]

Apart from demographic change (which will be discussed further in chapter 2) the increase of the agricultural population of the Rende area, as well as other parts of Calabria, was stimulated by two factors: government legislation and emigration. With respect to the former, three interrelated policies of the central state acted to encourage settlement in the countryside. First was the division and selling off of state and ecclesiastical lands between 1861 and 1881, in addition to the subsequent legislation in the early twentieth century in aid of agriculture.[35] This body of legislation had not only an economic purpose in the intensification of agriculture, but also a political purpose in encouraging the formation of a rural middle class that would act as a stabilizing force to counter the growing strength of the socialist left within Italian politics.[36] Second, and interwoven with the intensification of agriculture, was Rome's policy of encouraging the cultivation of suitable staples most in demand on the national and international markets. Within the Rende area this essentially meant olives, while in other parts of Calabria it meant vines or citrus. Such products necessitated greater labour and care than the non-intensive grain culture they often replaced, and this, in turn, encouraged settlement on the land. Lastly, the imposition of heavy state taxes on residential buildings within nucleated centres, with little regard given to their true value, hit the poor villages and agrotowns of Southern Italy particularly hard. The near exemption given to buildings in the countryside, on the other hand, made resettlement there attractive if not necessary.[37]

With respect to emigration, its opening up after 1880 gave young men the opportunity of earning the cash to rent or buy sufficient land to set up family life. Oral testimony pointed time and again to the migrations of the late nineteenth and early twentieth centuries as the means by which family plots were acquired. Moreover, as the early migration was transformed into an exodus, landlords within the Rende area were forced to offer their tenants improved conditions to discourage them from leaving for the new world. To maintain an adequate labour force landlords were often forced to offer *mezzadrie,* that is, peasant farms on which risks and profits were shared with the landlord.[38] But this effect of emigration leads to a discussion of economic life within the Rende area at the turn of the century, to which we now turn.

The Economic Background

AGRICULTURE

Until the early twentieth century the agricultural sector contained the majority of the population of the Rende area. The 1901 census shows that for the province of Cosenza 51 per cent of the population nine years of age or over was involved in agriculture. Taking into consideration the 28 per cent of the inhabitants who were listed as without a vocation (many of whom were casual agricultural labourers) or omitting the capital city from the census calculations, the agricultural population was probably more than the official figures indicate.

Throughout the nineteenth century the agricultural population of Cosenza was split into two groups: about half were linked relatively securely to the land through various forms of land tenure, while the other half were agricultural labourers living precariously from job to job.[39] Henceforth we will employ the term "peasant" or *contadino* to refer to the tenured half of the agricultural population, though both groups were part of a "peasant society." Moreover, we can take as the two main distinguishing characteristics of peasants the fact that the family farm acted as the basic unit of socio-economic organization and that traditional farming acted as the main means of livelihood, directly providing the major part of their consumption needs.[40]

Within the Rende area (and Cosenza generally) three major peasant types reflected differing systems of land tenure. First was the *colono,* or share-cropper, who was sometimes also referred to as *mezzadro.* This type was roughly equivalent to the metayer of Northern Europe.[41] Though the land tenure arrangement of the *colono* was akin to the classical *mezzadria* system of Central Italy, it differed in a significant way. Under the classical *mezzadria,* the peasant cultivated land for a landlord on condition of receiving a share (usually half) of its produce, the owner furnishing the whole or part of the capital required. Since the produce was divided on a fixed ratio, the risks of farming were split between peasant and landlord. Such a system caused the landlord to take an active interest in agriculture in order to increase productivity and hence his own return. The *mezzadria* arrangement of the South generally conformed to this picture, except for one vital difference: a substantial part of the total produce, essentially grain and vegetables, was not divided according to a fixed *ratio*, but rather according to a fixed *rent*. This hybrid land tenure system is referred to as *colonia parziaria*.[42]

Second, and more simply, was the landed peasant *(coltivatore diretto)* who owned and worked his own family plot. Third, the *affittuario*, or small tenant farmer, paid a fixed rent on the land he worked.[43] In contrast to the metayer system, here the risks of working the land fell solely on the tenant. Furthermore, *paesani* spoke of the *fattore* or peasant steward who "represented the big landlord" and oversaw the day-to-day business on many estates as well as holding for himself the best of the lord's land. Though these men were few, they held an important place in the life of peasants. People referred to the agricultural labourer as *operaio* or *bracciante*. This group was divided into two main categories: those who were employed fairly regularly throughout the year and, more numerously, those who were employed only sporadically, essentially as day-labourers or *giornalieri*.

Census figures for Cosenza from 1871 to 1901 reveal considerable fluctuation in the number of the agricultural population employed in each category. Most interesting is the doubling of peasant landowners and *mezzadri* to 18 per cent and 16 per cent respectively. This reflected the influence of emigration: on the one hand, the inflow of cash from the new world made possible the increased purchasing of family plots, while on the other hand, the exodus of young men forced landlords to offer improved land tenure conditions in order to maintain cultivated estates, thus increasing the importance of the *mezzadria* system. Conversely, the outflow of labour and consequent improvement in the bargaining power of those remaining is reflected in the decrease in the number of tenant farmers: the proportion of *affittuari* between 1871 and the turn of the century dropped by half to about 11 per cent. There was also a decrease in the number of farm labourers, placing this sector at less than half the agricultural population.[44]

We can assume that these trends in the make-up of the agricultural population of Cosenza were generally applicable to the Rende area, though both written and oral sources point to the greater importance there of the *colono* among peasant types. It should be noted, however, that the reality of socio-economic status was often more complex than the census data would lead one to believe. As both the immigrant informants and students of the *Mezzogiorno* have recognized, an agricultural worker could also simultaneously hold one or more types of peasant status. Referring specifically to the 1901 census figures for Calabria, Taruffi and his associates at the turn of the century and Izzo in recent years have pointed out that the high proportion of *giornalieri* compared to the national average must be viewed with scepticism, since many were in fact small tenant farmers who, because of the insufficiency of their plots, worked part time as day-labourers. Similarly, they warn that the relatively low Calabrian figure for tenant farmers must take account of such divided status.[45]

While the same individual might hold more than one agricultural status at any particular time, his position within society was likely to change as he progressed through life from son to husband to father. Especially with the growing popularity of emigration after 1880, an individual's position could change radically within a matter of a few years. Hence, for example, one young man who was both a small tenant farmer and *giornaliero* decided to emigrate upon the birth of his first child and, after a few years in North America, returned to the village to establish himself as a small landowner and employer, as well as maintaining his role as a small tenant.[46]

It was mentioned earlier that nearly half the population of the Rende area lived in "dispersed settlements," that is, in the countryside. But what was living on the land like? One informant gave a description of conditions, said to be common, in a peasant home rented from a large-scale landlord at the turn of the century:

> In the basement there were the animals. Upstairs there was only one room without a kitchen. There was a fireplace which they warmed up in front of. And they cooked there. You know how many beds there were in that room? Four! Four beds to sleep *cristiani* (decent people)!
>
> Above the room they made a sort of second level of cane. They used to cut and split them, then join them and place them over the beams. And there would sleep four brothers of my beloved father. His family slept downstairs, and upstairs slept his brothers on blankets, without beds .... In a house like that there lived 15-16 people ... they lived like animals in there.[47]

Such conditions – two-storey buildings with livestock in the first storey and living quarters on top composed usually of one large room with a makeshift upper level – were confirmed by contemporary observers. Dire as it was, such housing was considered relatively well placed compared to the living conditions of the mass of poorer peasants in Calabria. Poorer peasants, especially those who were forced to hire themselves out as agricultural labourers for much of the year, lived in hovels in the village and commuted to and from their work.[48] One immigrant of former *colono* status spoke of the "part-time farmers," making a clear distinction between his own "farmer" stratum and theirs:

Farmers lived in the country. They lived in the same place that
they worked .... Some lived in the town and worked out in the
country, but not many. But you don't call them farmers. They
maybe got two or three acres in the farm outside .... They go in
the morning and come home at night. But you don't call that one
a farmer ... just part-time. But the real farmers they never go
home. They got a farm; they got a house on the farm. They live
in there. They got all work to do: chickens, pigs, stuff like that.
They got to look after them night and day .... They stay there all
their life. Like us. We born and we grown and we die on the
farm.[49]

Landholdings within the Rende area ranged from small peasant
plots of only a few acres to extensive baronial estates dating back to
feudal times. One of the largest of these estates was held in emphyteusis by the Magdalone family. In the 1880s, within the commune
of Rende, Don Giovanni Magdalone presided over a domain of two
hundred hectares of fertile land and at least fifty hectares of forest.
As well he held considerable property within neighbouring Marano
Marchesato. Similar, though smaller, estates were held by the local
elite of the surrounding communes.[50]

It was from these powerful barons that the majority of peasants
rented their land. By 1914 most viable peasant farms within the Rende
area were held through *mezzadria* contracts and consisted of four to
six hectares. Similarly, though direct peasant ownership became
increasingly important as "americani" returned with newly earned cash,
these rarely exceeded six hectares (fifteen acres). On the other hand,
the average plot of *affittuari* was usually about one hectare. Lastly,
while large properties of fifty hectares or more owned by middling
landlords were relatively common, medium-scale properties ranging
from ten to fifty hectares were few.[51]

The small farm of four to six hectares was sufficient for the support
of a peasant family. Since the peasant farm was to provide self-
sufficiency and security for the family, it was labour-intensive, affording work for as many family members as possible. But it was not able
to accommodate more than one active family. Peasant farms, whether
rented or owned outright, could only be passed down to one adult
son and still remain a viable unit. Though a peasant property-owner
might choose to divide his land equally among his sons, an attempt
was made to keep the land intact. So, while the land was often formally
divided among male siblings, an arrangement was frequently worked
out whereby only one son would work the land, the other sons being
compensated through financial arrangements, the provision of
apprenticeship, or some other means. Excess sons had to move away
from the family farm and attempt to build a life for themselves on
their own.[52]

The desire for peasant self-sufficiency led to the practice of a system of mixed farming. Staple cash crops were grown for the market, but this was combined with providing for the peasant's own needs as widely as possible. It is not surprising that to the query as to what had been grown on their land in Cosenza, people at first invariably answered "everything." A rich cornucopia of vegetables – various beans, tomatoes, potatoes, peppers, broccoli, cabbage, eggplant, onions, rappini, and lettuce – as well as melons and herbs were grown. In addition, grains, primarily wheat and corn, were widely cultivated to meet the peasant family's needs, and sometimes vines also. Olives and figs required more capital outlay and land and hence, while cultivated by *coloni* and landed peasants, they were less widely grown, especially among *affittuari*. Just what crop was surplus and found its way to the marketplace depended both on the size of the peasant holdings and on the type of land farmed. For those peasants who could afford livestock, the type and quantity varied according to their means. While poultry and, to a lesser extent, goats and sheep were commonly kept, hogs and mules were less so, and horses could be afforded only by the most affluent.

With respect to rental arrangements within the Rende area, under the *colonia parziaria,* land producing herbaceous plants (mainly grains and vegetables) was paid for in produce, money, or a combination of these. In the late nineteenth century this usually meant that the *colono* paid two or three *tomoli* of grain (wheat or corn) for each *tomolata* of land rented.[53] For tree crops, however, rent was paid in a fixed ratio, again in produce, cash, or both. Generally two-thirds of the produce – usually oil or figs and sometimes chestnuts – went to the landlord and one-third to the *colono*. Wine, however, was divided half and half.

In the early twentieth century the *colonia parziaria* was substantially improved in favour of the peasant in an effort to stem widespread emigration. Informants reported that the rent in grain was now changed to one *tomolo* per *tomolata* of land cultivated; olives were often split in the reverse ratio of two-thirds for the peasant and one-third for the landlord; and figs were brought to a fifty-fifty split.[54] Heterogeneity of contract terms was often more common in the case of the *affittuario* than that of the *colono*. By and large, however, his rent payment consisted of one to two *tomoli* of grain per *tomolata* of land.

Both the *colono* and *affittuario* were usually obligated to set aside a number of days on which they worked the landlord's own holdings. Most often this work involved the preparation of new crops in the spring. Though the peasants were paid for their labour, it was at a wage much below the market rate. In addition, peasants had to pay rent on their homes, especially before the advent of widespread overseas migration when relatively few owned their own. This house rent, which was paid yearly either in produce or cash, was due, like the land rent, in the autumn (usually late August or September). Fees paid in kind for the use of the local grain mill or oil press, often owned by the chief landlord of the area, further cut into the stock of the peasant. And lastly, the peasant was under the social obligation, and often the threat of losing patronage or service, of presenting "gifts" of agricultural produce to his "betters." Landlords, as well as professionals, bureaucrats, and even important artisans, all had to be shown "respect" with gifts of vegetables, eggs, or other produce at important religious and feast days if they were to keep useful relationships alive.[55]

THE INDUSTRIAL BACKGROUND

While it is common for studies of Southern Italian immigrants to deal with their agricultural background, little mention is made of their industrial past. The industrial background of the *paesani*, though subsidiary to their agricultural experience, was nevertheless important. More accurately, we should speak here of a "rural industrial" past. As a general type, rural industry was not, of course, "modern industry." Whereas the former existed side by side with agricultural production and rhythms, was small scale, was dominated by merchant capital, and commonly left the tools and processes of production under the control of the workers, the latter was urbanized and ecologically divorced from agriculture, based on economics of scale, dominated by industrial capital, and characterized by mass employment in factories where the workers had scant control over the means and processes of production. While these differences existed, rural industry was the necessary precursor of the factory system and urban industrialization.[56] The two forms can, therefore, be seen as continuous, though within the local area under study industrial activity stopped short at the early rural stage.

It is fruitful to think of post-feudal peasant society as a "part-society," which, while agriculturally based, traditionalist, and localized, nevertheless embodied within it elements which were reflective of the wider society. In terms of the present study, the Rende area was dotted with various small factories, domestic industries and food-processing activities, thus rendering the rural industrial past of the peasant immigrants an important element which anticipated the reality of their North American experience.

In his excellent study of nineteenth-century Calabria, Izzo documents the extent of industrial activity in Cosenza. He notes how traditionally the industrial sector of Cosenza was centred on silk production. Textiles, notably of wool and cotton, and forest products were also important and widely worked. These products, as well as supplying regional demands, were linked to external markets and of considerable export value. Further, a number of other industries, such as the copper and bronze works at Dipignano just south of the Rende area or the tanneries of the city of Cosenza itself, were found spread throughout the province and had an important impact on local economies.[57]

The importance of Cosenza's industrial sector during the nineteenth century is clear from the amount of foreign capital attracted to the province. Under the aegis of restored Bourbon rule, as early as 1817 an association for the promotion of industry in the province was founded by local employers and entrepreneurs. Considerable industrial expansion followed. By 1834 the provincial output of silk had reached a respectable 300,200 *libbre,* out of which the district of Cosenza contributed 165,760 *libbre.* And by 1841 the association (Reale Società Economica della Calabria Citeriore), felt confident enough to sponsor its first industrial exposition of provincial products. Various silk and cotton goods, linen, ironworks, firearms, spinning machines, dairy products, tools, and local crafts were all displayed as examples of Cosentine industry.[58]

With Unification, Cosenza's industrial sector suffered both dislocation and decline. Removal of the Bourbon duties which had protected the important textile industry and integration into a new national market placed small producers at a disadvantage in competing with their more efficient competitors in Northern Italy.[59] The pivotal silk industry which was hit by pebrina in 1856 was further eroded with the added burden of Northern competition. In Calabria generally, out of 3,071 basinettes held by silk mills in 1876, fully 1,143 were inactive.[60] And in the textile sector of Cosenza the number of workers employed – in household industries as well as small factories – dropped from 68.1 per cent of all non-agricultural workers in 1871 to 50.6 per cent in 1901. This substantially decreased the high proportion of women employed in industry.[61]

The situation within the Rende area was the same. The silk factory of Cerisano opened at mid-century by the Lupo family had closed its doors by the turn of the century. That of Carolei, just south of Cerisano, which had earlier been updated, suffered a similar fate. Within the capital of Cosenza itself not only were the silk factories hard hit, but so too were the cotton mills which after 1865 had to contend with American competition hitherto temporarily kept at bay by the Civil War.

Up until the First World War cottage industries were a major component of Cosenza's manufacturing sector. Foremost were the household industries centring around the production of textiles. These were dominated by peasant women, craft-oriented, and family-centred with children often contributing to the household economy.[62] These industries survived to a greater extent within the Rende area than in other parts of Calabria because, being surrounded by mountains, the area was ill-served by railroad and hence less easily penetrable by Northern factory-made goods.[63] Here the wives and daughters of peasants contributed to the family's upkeep by various strategies. Some were involved in the weaving of coarse wool cloth, while others were occupied in the spinning of flax or cotton, the homespun yarn of which was then sent to weavers in nearby towns. Many, especially prior to Unification, were involved in the cultivation of silkworms and silk production. Also important was the making of charcoal, to which many peasants applied themselves during idle months.[64] The household production of various food products such as cheese and wine were destined primarily for local markets.

Such home industries both supplied for the marketplace, and provided for the family's own immediate needs. Nearly all households, for example, spun their own wool and made much of their own clothing; soap was made from the residue left over in the processing of olive oil; and a syrup made from figs acted as a substitute for the sugar few could afford.[65]

The processing of agricultural products or other primary material underlay the industrial activity carried on by Cosenza's various factories, mills and similar establishments. Though here, too, women outnumbered men, they did not dominate the scene to the extent that they did in the household industries. While textiles and food-processing were the most important sources of employment, forest industries and metallurgical works were also significant.[66]

All three types of peasants participated in the industrial sector. For some families, industrial work allowed them to buy needed food or shoes and other basic items. As one informant reported, speaking of an *affittuario* family:

> There were only five brothers, eh. They only had a little bit of farm. The one farm ... there was too many in the family. They couldn't work all in the family .... You know, they had to buy something else. They had to buy shoes, they had to buy shirts. So a few go to make a few bucks. They go here and there. They work here and there [in mills and factories] ... four or five months of the year .... In the winter-time there's very little to do anyway. Then they would go back to the farm.[67]

For other peasants, however, work outside of agriculture was more a means of accumulating cash with which to improve the family's socio-economic standing within the community. On the other hand, rich peasants avoided industrial work; having large farms, they lacked idle time, and their social position was considered above such labour.

Much industrial employment, except textiles, was of a seasonal or temporary nature. Since, like agriculture, the rural industrial base relied on harvests and weather conditions, a similarly floating work force resulted. Hence, though census figures give an estimate of the number of workers industrially employed at any one time, they fail to provide an indication of the actual, widespread frequency of extra-agricultural experience within the peasant population.

Keeping this in mind, some idea of the number of jobs available within the factories and mills of the Rende area can be had from Table 2 (see pp. 254-55), derived from the 1911 census. In that year, the two textile factories of Marano Marchesato employed a total of 132 workers while a smaller operation at Montalto employed twenty-eight. A few miles away within the city of Cosenza, thirty-three textile enterprises employed 440 workers out of a total industrial force of 1,343. Similarly, the chemical industry of San Vincenzo employed seventy-one men and the tannic acid factory of San Fili, using the nearby oak forests and producing for local tanneries, employed about one hundred men. Also important were the many small mills involved in the processing of agricultural produce. Within the Rende area (excluding Cosenza *comune*) 372 people out of a total of 950 workers were involved in such activity. While the ratio of employees involved with food-processing was even higher for the district of Cosenza, for the province as a whole it appears that textiles were the most important source of manufacturing employment.[68]

In response to the encouragement given olive production by the central government after Unification, the number of olive presses underwent considerable expansion within the Rende area. Though the work at the presses was seasonal, occurring in winter, jobs were created not only in the presses themselves but also in the transportation of produce. Olive oil had to be first collected from the various landlords and peasants and then distributed for export (especially to France and Northern Italy) as well as for local use. Further, olive presses created opportunities for the soap factories of Montalto and Cosenza, which used the residual lower grades of oil.[69]

Saw mills also increased in importance within the area as the remaining forests of the province were exploited. The number of workers in Cosenza involved in the processing of wood rose from 1.3 per cent of all workers in 1871 to 5 per cent in 1901. Rende area peasants were employed in the lumber camps of the nearby La Sila forests. Because of its harshness, and because it involved fairly extended absences from one's family, work in the lumber camps was usually undertaken by poor *affittuari* or agricultural labourers, rather than well-to-do *coloni* or landed peasants. Similarly, flour mills scattered throughout the grain-producing sections of the Rende area contributed to the employment of labour.

In the commune of Rende, the Zagarese family was probably the largest employer of industrial labour. As well as holding considerable land in the countryside, the family owned a large brick and tile works and an important liquorice concern. The liquorice factory operated year-round and in 1911 reportedly employed up to half the 164 workers involved in food-processing within the commune. Work at the factory was looked upon favourably and both men and women were employed. Further, the liquorice plant was common throughout the Crati Valley and provided employment for many peasants. An immigrant from Rende talked of this: "He (Zagarese) used to make liquorice. A liquorice factory – a lot of people used to work there. They used to go to the farm, you know, and dig up the roots with the pick and shovel. And the women used to pick them, bring them to the factory and it was manufactured, you know .... We dig roots ourselves on our own farm."[70]

Also using local produce was the fig-processing plant of the Vittoria company. Both this establishment and the liquorice factory exported their products throughout Europe, and with the advent of emigration overseas, they exported to meet the demand of former residents.

It was these factories and mills, along with household industries, that comprised the rural industrial sector of the Rende area. But there existed an additional source of extra-agricultural employment which cannot properly be called "industrial": construction work. After Unification an effort was made by the central state to improve the roads and other facilities of the former kingdom of Naples. Though the funds remained inadequate, nevertheless some improvement was made. In the Rende area, state funds were received in 1872, for example, for the building of a road connecting Marano Marchesato with Rende to the north and Cosenza to the east.[71] Although the improvement of communications throughout the South served to link the Rende area more effectively with the industrial North, thus further weakening the local economy, it also created new jobs within the construction industry.

Individual communes, too, employed construction labourers to work on local roads, aqueducts, river projects, and municipal buildings. For example, local jobs were created around 1885 when Rende undertook to restore its communal buildings. Private projects were another source of construction employment. Large landlords frequently had to have their irrigation canals cleared and better-off peasants demanded more and better housing facilities. In any case, construction employment was an important means by which the poorer peasants sought to augment their livelihood.

The temporary nature of construction work meant that peasants often had to follow projects throughout the Rende area as jobs shifted from commune to commune. In the early twentieth century, with the building of the spur rail line between Paola and Cosenza, the commune of Rende emerged as a focus for construction labourers, since the line had to be built through the difficult Catena Costiera Mountains within its borders. Indeed, the project was so large that it attracted labourers from outside Calabria. As can be seen in Table 2, according to the 1911 census 134 of Rende's 333 extra-agricultural workers were involved in construction. Most of these labourers worked with relatively small companies, the census listing ten firms in 1911 with an average of thirteen employees per firm.

However, oral testimony suggested that the censuses may underestimate the total number of people employed in construction. Here again, the statistics cannot tell us much about the "mixed status" of many of the peasants and it is likely that many men who worked temporarily on construction are hidden under peasant categories.

The economic background of the peasant immigrant was a complex one. Within the agricultural sector many were both landholders and agricultural labourers and, at the same time, many of these were also rural industrial workers. It becomes evident that a person's status, while taking on one predominant characteristic or another, was fluid. The one element that remained common throughout, however, was the peasant's desire for economic security and furtherance of socio-economic standing. It was in this same vein that he embarked upon emigration. But before turning specifically to this, let us pause to consider some important features of his social background.

The Social Background

CLASS STRUCTURE

In most discussions of the background of the Southern Italian peasant or immigrant a model of social stratification system is presented.[72] Not surprisingly, accounts differ, although such variance is probably due to the different localities studied and the different types of informants. As Lopreato found in his study of a Southern village, the social stratification system looks different to respondents of different classes. Essentially the "middle" stratum see a multi-layered system, whereas the "common people" see a simpler system of three or so classes. Interestingly, this simpler view is also shared by the local aristocracy.[73] Though such variation occurred in the present study, the fact that the informants were mainly of former *colono* or *affittuario* status resulted in a considerable measure of agreement.

Generally three main classes were mentioned. At the top of the socio-economic hierarchy people recognized an upper class commonly referred to as *pezzi grossi* ("big shots") composed of large-scale land-owners and local notables. Though many of the large landowners, such as the Magdalone and Morelli of Rende or the Miceli of San Fili, were *baroni* with pre-Unification roots, newer families of middle-class origin, such as the Giorgelli of Rende, became increasingly important as new agricultural staples replaced wheat in predominance. As well as being important landowners, these families were also major owners of housing, local industries, and town real estate.[74]

The large landlords commanded respect because of their sheer economic power. On the other hand, teachers, lawyers, priests, and other such notables did so because of their possession of specialized knowledge and capacity to do the peasant favours. For the *paesani*, however, the distinction was often superficial since, until the First World War, notables were often drawn from the large landowning families.

Within the Rende area what distinguished one's social position were the two interrelated criteria of landownership and the ability to live without engaging in manual labour. The large landlords not only did not work their land, but, moreover, because those of feudal lineage disdained modern agricultural management, they "came always more clearly to assume the figure and the characteristics of simple *rentiers* with no real function in production and in agricultural progress."[75] For their part, many of the notables of professional status were small landowners renting out to *affittuari*.

Social distance between the peasants and the *pezzi grossi,* or more properly speaking the *galantuomini* (gentlemen), was readily perceived and acutely felt in day-to-day affairs. Even in common speech social distance was maintained. As one informant put it, "over there you got discrimination of words." The pronoun "you" had three forms which varied in degree of formality and respect. The large landowners and notables were given the highest form of address, "Lei." When addressed by name, it was prefaced by "Signore" and often by "Don."[76] Though the latter was properly to be used only where lineage could be traced to landed aristocratic stock, both the priest and doctor, the most important of the professionals, were also usually addressed with "Don."

Below the *galantuomini,* people recognized a middling class composed of two strata. On the upper level they placed government functionaries, clerks and the like *(impiegati)* as well as merchants. On the lower level were "the skilled men," that is, artisans and craftsmen: tailors, shoemakers, barbers, and others. The *impiegati,* like many notables, occupied positions as strategic intermediaries between the peasantry and the institutions of the new state. As possessors of particular information or skills, these men had to be treated with respect for it was understood that without it one could not expect adequate service. Then, too, in a society of high illiteracy, one never knew when one would require the "favour" of a literate man to write a letter, translate a government notice, or such.

The middling class was addressed by the second degree "voi" form of the pronoun "you." When called by name, it was addressed with the preface *signore* in the case of functionaries and merchants or with *maestro* in the case of artisans. Many within this class were able to become small landowners.[77] For the less prosperous and prestigious *artigiano,* landownership often took the form of holding a small plot outside the town walls, which was frequently worked by the owner himself or family members.

Both the upper and middling classes generally lived in town and hence imparted a civility *(civiltà)* to town life which was perceived as lacking in the countryside.[78] Though peasant immigrants admitted their esteem for town life, which was seen as desirable and urbane, they tempered their enthusiasm by noting the presence in town of poorer peasants who, because they lacked land and the potential independence and security this denoted, were viewed as socially inferior.

Peasants were linked to the town and its representatives of *civiltà* in a myriad of ways. People went there to seek the services of professionals, landlords, or bureaucrats, and some were linked by kinship. As peasants became more integrated into the socio-economic fabric of the larger society, contact with the town and its skilled and professional inhabitants became increasingly important. With the coming of emigration, the peasant's need for educated intermediaries who would facilitate the journey on one hand, and the readiness of professionals and government bureaucrats to profit from the exodus on the other, resulted in more frequent contact both between classes and between town and country.

Following the middle class in social status, informants saw their own old world class of peasants. They saw themselves as the mass of common people, honest and hard-working. They addressed each other with the familiar form of the pronoun you, "tu," and referred to themselves as *cristiani:* common, decent, working folk. Seen as a mass by their social superiors, they were again addressed by "tu," though the context in which it was used often denoted disdain.

Though on the level of looking "outward," informants saw the peasantry as a class, on the level of looking "inward," they pointed to distinctions within it that corresponded to the three different types of peasants discussed earlier. First in social standing, owing to their relative prosperity and independence, were the landed peasants, along with the small, but important, number of *fattori.* The large mass of fairly stable *coloni* were next, followed by the *affittuari* who were seen as living the most precariously. Below the peasantry were landless labourers who were regarded as existing hand-to-mouth and as rootless.[79]

Beyond the pale and removed from the social fabric of the community were the gypsies *(zingari).* While gypsies were important middlemen at local fairs as horse and cattle traders, they were generally despised and distrusted. Seen as dishonest, lazy, and dirty, they were shunned and their very name was employed as a denigrating term to be used as an insult or in jest.

Although a well-defined scheme of social stratification was presented by *paesani*, ambiguity and fluidity existed.[80] Fluidity implied economic mobility and, except for the landless very poor, people aspired to a better future. In this connection, exogamy between strata, where it could lead to a loss of status, was censured. The name of the game was to improve, or at least maintain, one's position; and marriage, being an important avenue to potential mobility, was too crucial a matter to be left to the whims of the heart. Indeed, in a society in which virginity and the sacrament of marriage played such an important part, instances of common-law marriages or liaisons between peasant women and landlords or notables were looked upon in a surprisingly amoral and pragmatic manner. For invariably such arrangements brought the peasant families involved the patronage and favouritism of powerful men. So it was, for example, that a well-known Rende family was able to rise from *affittuario* to *fattore* status through the liaison of a daughter with a landlord of noble lineage.[81]

Mobility could occur in various other ways. The contacts of a respected peasant family with an *artigiano* might place a son in apprenticeship to be a barber or tailor. For those fortunate enough to afford schooling, the natural intelligence of a youth might come to the attention of a sympathetic priest or enable an individual to qualify as a candidate for the government bureaucracy. For most, however, aspirations of mobility took another form: migration to "America." In migrating to the bourgeoning economy of North America, peasants were willing to undertake backbreaking and dangerous work (which in many cases would have been regarded as beneath their dignity in the *paese*) in the hope that hard cash would enable them to buy another notch in the socio-economic ladder and ensure them an additional measure of security in a changing economy. For those peasants who returned wealthy enough to buy a handsome property, with time and the right deportment of civility they could come to command greater respect than others and be given a status on a par with, or even greater than, that of *artigiani*.

If mobility along the socio-economic ladder could lead upward, it could also lead downward. A peasant with too many sons or lack of occupational options for them could find himself reduced to the poverty level associated with the agricultural labourer. The transfer of land from one landlord to another or its reorganization could cost the *colono* or *fattore* the patronage he hitherto enjoyed and make an *affittuario* or worse out of him. Or the capriciousness of nature itself, which resulted in the Marano Marchesato landslide of 1877, the poor harvests of the late 1880s, and the disastrous 1905 earthquake throughout Calabria, could reduce a peasant to penury and reliance on day labour or public works for the destitute. Here, emigration could serve to regain one's position.

PEASANT-LANDLORD RELATIONSHIP

For the peasants of the Rende area, one of their most important relationships was that between themselves and their landlords who were viewed both with respect and resentment. Respect was most apparent towards landlords with whom the peasant entered into a patron-client arrangement. Usually such a relationship was carried on through an intermediary who was either closer in social status or more closely connected to the patron. Depending on the situation, a local priest, a *fattore*, a kinsman, or a friend could all supply such mediation.

Though different peasants viewed different men as their patrons, the persistence, up until the twentieth century, of large *baroni* within the Rende area whose power was much greater than other landlords meant that it was ultimately these privileged families that held the local levers of power. Hence, within the commune of Rende, though different peasants viewed the Zagarese or Quintieri or several smaller landlords as patrons, it was the powerful Magdalone that were at the apex of the socio-economic hierarchy.[82]

The relationship between the peasant and his patron was both reciprocal and dependent. Though prior to Unification the relationship was often passed from one generation to another, in the late nineteenth century the propensity of peasants to seek alternative landlord-patrons with the hope of receiving more favourable tenure terms increased.

Although what was most important for the peasant in the patron-client relationship was security of employment and sustenance, the desire to augment one's material well-being and status in life, expressed through privileges and services expected of one's landlord, became increasingly important. It was expected, for example, that the patron aid in finding work for members of one's family, that housing conditions be improved, or that the client be offered land put up for sale before any others. Then, too, the peasant often expected the patron to mediate between himself and the wider society, or put him in touch with the appropriate "connection" when the need arose. Hence the peasant might ask for help in exempting an only son from military service or in institutionalizing a chronically ill relative.

From his point of view, what was most important for the patron was the maintenance or increase of his power which ultimately rested on the loyalty of his workers. Thus, the patron expected the peasant to recruit family members to work on his estate during bottlenecks. He expected a pervasive attitude of respect expressed, for instance, in the peasant's removal of his cap in the landlord's presence. Also, loyalty could take on an overtly political form, as in the episode around 1880 when Don Giovanni Magdalone, then mayor of Rende, mobilized his peasants to intimidate the supporters of a rival mayor, the middling landowner Luigi Conforti of Marano Marchesato, for effective control of the *mandamento*. On the part of the peasant, it was expected that such loyalty would be reciprocated through political favouritism such as jobs on public works or access to public lands.[83]

After Unification there was a tendency for the patron-client relationship to decrease in significance while a similar type of relationship gained increasing importance between peasants and notables (especially professionals) and various functionaries. Though the distinction here is not completely clear because of the overlapping of landowning families and notables, it is nonetheless significant. While the post-Unification shift toward professionals and functionaries was owing largely to their growing socio-economic and political power, emigration often provided the practical necessity by which the peasant's contact with such people was promoted. It was the educated men and not the landlords – whose interests were ill served by emigration – who acted as the intermediaries facilitating the transoceanic journey. In a sense, this was part and parcel of the intermediary role professionals and functionaries played between peasant community and modern society and between local and national cultures. At any rate, the patron-client set of social expectations that characterized the landlord-peasant relationship persisted in the new relationship also. However, there was one important difference. Whereas the landlord-peasant relationship contained a component of hostility as well as respect, this resentment was more muted in the peasant's view of professionals and similar intermediaries.[84]

Oral testimony focused on the conflict between peasants and their landlords. While peasants went through the formal motions of paying respect to their "betters" in public, in private their talk was full of jokes, complaints and gossip directed against the *pezzi grossi*. Indeed, the very name *pezzi grossi* used to designate *galantuomini* was itself a disparaging term by which they gave vent to their class resentment. Conflict with landlords was expressed around two basic themes: complaints about abuse of power, and brigandage. Regarding the former, *paesani* indicated how throughout the nineteenth century effective power and the rule of law in the Rende area were invested not in an impersonal state, but in the personal rule of the large *baroni*. As a measure of this power, informants reported that up to mid-century, the large landlords still exacted the right of *la prima notte*.[85] For a society traditionally male dominant, and in which "maleness" and "honour" were synonymous with protecting the virginity of women, this perception that the *barone* had sexual access to his tenant's new bride on the wedding night was the ultimate expression of the peasant's subjection to his landlord.

Informants remarked how, at least until the fall of the Bourbons, the large landlords were empowered with the right of asylum. They reported that if a fugitive succeeded in reaching the gates of their estates, he could not be apprehended by government pursuers and the lord could deal with him at his own discretion.

Even after 1861 the exercise of personal law remained considerable. Hence, within Rende *mandamento,* the many *guardiani* and *agenti* (estate guards and agents), as well as the peasant reserves of Don Giovanni Magdalone, amounted to a veritable private army by which the family held its preponderant power, well greased by patronage, up to the twentieth century.[86] But the *gran signore* not only commanded private power, as mayor of Rende commune, he also held the reins of legal power and political patronage, a situation that was repeated by the Miceli in San Fili and by other powerful families in neighbouring municipalities.[87] While the simultaneous welding of private and public power acted to monopolize its exercise, it also reflected the inadequacy of public power alone as a means for attaining political hegemony. Legal power had to be reinforced by an extra-legal base. Then, too, from the point of view of the Magdalone or Miceli, their private power acted as an insurance against challengers who might usurp the family in the legal arena.

This failure of the central state to check the neo-feudal power of local strongmen lent itself to the perpetuation of abuses. As a *paesano* put it, during the barons' rule "might was right .... They did as they wanted."[88] As far as the peasants were concerned, effective power resided in those landlords most able to use force in seeking their ends. Hence, a man who allowed his sheep to trespass on the lord's estate or was caught poaching, or who did not show the proper reserve and diffidence, could be dealt with according to the personal inclination of the *baroni.* As late as the beginning of the twentieth century, "there were cases where they whipped people until they bled," another man said.[89]

People resented not only gross injustices but also the less explicit abuses of power. The landlord-mayor of Marano Marchesato practised widespread nepotism by appointing one nephew as the municipality's tax collector and municipal treasurer, another as one of the commune's two teachers (without being required to teach), and a brother as tax assessor. Political corruption was also common in Rende, where the mayor conveniently escaped the payment of large amounts of taxes owing the commune.[90]

The landlord's arbitrary use of power was evident in many facets of social life. Taking education as a specific example, Taruffi and his colleagues reported specifically on the Rende area. They reported how public education was grossly inadequate. Some municipalities held classes in cellars and vacated peasant hovels; others did not have any accommodation whatever. And the blame for such deplorable conditions was placed mainly on the local elite which refused to supply even surplus quarters for the education of peasant children. Public funds for education were only scantily and niggardly made available by the landlord-mayors. Instead, preference was often given to prestige projects, Rende's campaign to renovate its municipal buildings being a case in point.[91]

Paesani conceived of any concession they won vis-à-vis the large landlords as being gained through active opposition rather than as emanating from the state. Hence, some believed that *la prima notte* came to an end with the widespread introduction of firearms among the peasants which made revenge on the part of the aggrieved husband possible. Similarly, the end of the ruthless power of Miceli of San Fili was attributed to peasant violence which confronted that meted out by the landlord. From the *paesani*'s view, the diminution of the *baroni*'s personal power and abuse was traced to the late nineteenth century when peasants began "to get brains" and assert themselves – a development in which emigration played an important role.

The personal power of the *baroni* was not only undermined by increasing assertiveness on the part of peasants, but also by an ascending urban petit bourgeoisie that looked longingly at the power wielded by the large landlords. Furthermore, steady if slow progress made by the state in encouraging education, improving communications, increasing the presence of the *carabinieri* (state police), promoting peasant landownership, and progressively extending the franchise (culminating in universal male suffrage in 1912), all contributed to undermining the neo-feudal power of the landlords.

Nevertheless, through the early twentieth century, vestiges of the private power of the *baroni* remained, though its scope varied. While in San Fili the power of the Miceli seems to have been particularly tenacious, in other communes the personal rule of *baroni* was reduced to a mere relic of the past.[92]

The second theme through which informants expressed conflict with landlords, that is, brigandage, was more generalized than their complaints of abuses and reflected opposition or resentment not only against the *baroni,* but also against the state, or more specifically, the state's representatives such as tax collectors and the military. Informants told of brigandage as being endemic within the Rende area. Apparently prior to Unification, the catacombs of the town of Rende itself were inhabited by *briganti.* The local "Su Luise" hills, however, were their territorial stronghold. Here they even had their own cemetery for their dead, victims from confrontations with the authorities or frequent internecine wars between rival bands. It was claimed that at the turn of the century peasants had stumbled across secret grave sites while turning sod in the area and that gold had been found buried among the tombs.[93]

Local brigands, such as Alessandro De Pelligrini, were a powerful force within the Rende area in the late nineteenth century, commanding the respect of peasants and landlords alike.[94] It was not unknown for the informants themselves to report having ancestors who had been part of brigand gangs. By the First World War, few *banditi* remained. However, as was the case with the personal power of the *baroni*, it was not until the entrenchment of fascism in the 1920s that brigandage ceased to be a common part of the lives of *paesani*.

Though people generally expressed admiration for brigands and their deeds, this support was not unequivocal. Alongside admiration, villagers also expressed a desire for law and order, for safety on the roads, for security. The opinion held by *paesani* of the most famous of Calabrian bandits, Giuseppe Musolino, who roamed throughout the region at the close of the century, was reserved: "Poor people were scared that he was powerful .... I don't think he was giving much away because he didn't even have much for himself .... If he had nothing, he'd go to the poor and take it."

Nonetheless, the *brigante* was seen as a poor, generally honourable, man who was "forced" to turn to brigandage by some wrong meted him by powerful men or the state. Again speaking of Musolino, the sentiment was expressed: "Sure he was a bad guy, but the first time he was arrested he was innocent. He was arrested by mistake. That's why he became a bandit; he got mad, so he became a bandit."

Having turned bandit, the *brigante* was seen as a type of Robin Hood, who, if he did not actively redistribute wealth, at least usually did the peasant no harm, which was more than could be said for the landlord, tax collector and arrogant state bureaucrats. Hence public opinion towards Musolino was generally favourable: "Well, poor people spoke about him in a good way. He never did anything wrong with the poor people .... The farmers in our area, he wouldn't do nothing to them. As long as they respect him, he respect them."[95]

Lastly, the brigand's career was seen as coming to an end not as the result of the state honestly apprehending the brigand, or as "good" defeating "evil," but through treachery. Often it was a relative or a fellow band member who betrayed the *brigante*-hero. Generally, the peasant perceived the *brigante* as an honourable man fighting against oppression. As such his cause was essentially worthy; only through treachery could defeat come.

This image of the brigand stands in contrast to the *paesani*'s perceptions of another manifestation of class conflict between peasant and landlord, the agricultural union or *lega*.

Prior to the First World War the city of Cosenza was headquarters for both Catholic and Socialist leagues. The former under Father Cardona took an active role in establishing rural banks for *contadini* and in attempting to organize the peasants into a viable movement.[96] *Paesani* recalled the efforts of the Catholic party in trying to mobilize the peasants of the Rende area around the issue of improving the agricultural contracts under which they laboured. This effort was strongly opposed by the local landlords, who, supported by the state police, reportedly put an end to the organizing campaign within a few months. One informant recalled how as a young man he had attended a meeting of the league at a tavern within the town of Rende. The rally was promptly broken up by *carabinieri* who then proceeded to arrest the leaders.[97] Such state action, along with the use of intimidation by the landlords, was a major factor in the failure of the league. The less than enthusiastic response of the peasants themselves to the organizing campaign of the agricultural union also retarded the prospects for success. In any case, in contrast to this failure, *peasani* held up the action of the brigands who instilled both fear and respect on the part of landlords and the state. As one man succinctly remarked, *"briganti* counted for more than *la lega."*[98]

Conflict between peasants and landlords could also be detected in the many ways by which social distance was maintained. The "discrimination of words" divided classes of men from each other and the peasant was expected to show respect and diffidence to the *pezzi grossi.* Informants referred to the ubiquitous image of the peasant with his "cap in hand" which expressed not only respect, but also fear and insecurity. This respect was shown through the many "gifts" the peasant was obliged to give his landlord: "Every best thing was for the owner. The best thing we had, fruit, tomatoes, eggs, everything." Such "gifts" were to be delivered at appropriate intervals "right into their house, like a servant."[99]

Moreover, conflict can be detected in the very structure of the patron-client relationship. While the relationship denoted reciprocity and mutual dependency between peasant and landlord, it did not give rise to corporate cohesiveness. While peasants "went along with the game," the strategy was always to "get the most out of it."[100] Conflict here took the form of individual self-interest which masked itself under a veneer of peasant docility. But when emigration presented an alternative strategy of self-interest, then respect, obligation, and diffidence to the landlord were frequently thrown to the wind, and men, by voting with their feet, made manifest the grievances they had largely held in check.

Social distance between peasant and landlord lent itself to a dichotomous view of the social universe. As one *paesano* expressed it: "There sure was quite a gap between us and them. They were big shots and we were nothing .... They had no respect for nobody."[101] Informants frequently referred to themselves as like slaves *(schiavi)* or beasts of burden when speaking of their treatment and position. They made the distinction between themselves as those who worked and the landlords and others who did not work; between men who had calloused hands and those with long fingernails. They were quite aware of social definitions which distinguished between themselves as *cafoni* or country oafs and the *galantuomini* who embodied *civiltà*. Essentially, peasants and *galantuomini* inhabited two different social worlds. A determinant as to which world one would belong to, alongside class or wealth, though deeply interdependent with these, was education.

EDUCATION

In turning to a discussion of the educational background of the immigrants, two purposes are served. First, the state of education gives us a good indication of social conditions generally within the Rende area, especially in the fields of health, housing and social welfare. Secondly, the educational background of the *paesani* is important in determining the nature of the emigration process and the interaction with North American society.

The predominant fact regarding education in the Rende area is the high illiteracy rate, which if adjusted to reflect the situation only among the peasantry, would be even higher than official figures indicate. In 1881, for example, 85 per cent of the inhabitants of Cosenza district six years of age or older were illiterate.[102] High illiteracy rates in the late nineteenth century were common throughout the South and justifiably condemned by *meridionalisti*. In the 1908 study of Taruffi, De Nobili and Lori, it was noted that American immigration statistics for 1901-2 placed Southern Italians as the most illiterate of immigrants after the Turks – a situation the authors considered a national disgrace.[103]

A more distanced view reveals steady improvement in the new Italian state's attempt to ameliorate the illiteracy of the South after 1861. Between 1871 and 1901 illiteracy among people of school age in the province of Cosenza dropped from 89 per cent to 79 per cent. But when compared to progress in the North, which brought the illiteracy rate for the kingdom as a whole down from 69 per cent to 49 per cent in the same thirty-year period, the improvements in the South pale considerably.[104] As Table 3 regarding the Rende area reveals, even by 1911, over three decades after the introduction of compulsory education in 1877, 66 per cent of school-age inhabitants within Cosenza district were still illiterate.

To an extent, the situation within the Rende area reflected the demands of peasant agriculture and the attitudes of the peasants themselves. National compulsory education legislation had practically no effect. The need for labour, especially during sowing and harvest seasons, kept many children from class for much of the year if not altogether. Poorer children were kept away because of their parents' shame (or "pride") at not being able to dress them properly for school. Indeed, Taruffi and his associates remarked that they had never seen children so miserably dressed, in rags and shoeless, as in Calabria. Then too, books, pens and paper cost money that many could ill afford.

Other *paesani* were simply not convinced of the benefits of education and preferred to rely on the traditional folk knowledge to guide their children. Not surprisingly, because of the characteristic male dominance of peasant society, this attitude was particularly true towards girls. It was thought that their future, seen in terms of wife and mother, could make no use of formal learning. As one elderly woman from Montalto said: "I never went to school. My brothers went. They would send the boys, not the girls. They would say that school was not for girls."[105] Hence, in the district of Cosenza, while 81 per cent of school-age males were illiterate in 1871, the figure for females was 96 per cent. Indeed, as Table 3 shows, though the rate had dropped to 55 per cent for males in 1911, it was still a high 74 per cent for females.

However, while peasant agriculture and attitudes posed impediments to formal education, this should not be taken to mean that the "demand" for education fell short of its "supply," for, indeed, it far surpassed it. Especially after emigration had become a fact of life within the Rende area, peasants sought education. The migration process made it imperative that the peasant deal with the wider society and the state. Such contact necessitated literacy, and though the peasant used intermediaries who could read and write for him, it was thought preferable to have such skills oneself. In that way one would be more certain that information was transmitted accurately, more independent of *galantuomini,* and would not have to pay the go-betweens for their services. For many, emigration opened horizons of enterprise and social mobility that had hitherto remained closed. Ambition, desire and energy that had remained latent now came to the fore once emigration provided a viable strategy for their employment. An essential key to this new opportunity was literacy.

The peasant's newly acquired appreciation for education expressed itself as a demand for improved educational facilities for himself as well as his children. Evening and "holiday" schools for illiterate adolescents and adults in Cosenza were filled to capacity (by both males and females) and many of these were responding to the new opportunities presented by emigration. Interestingly, a local government official reported how one of the most successful of these evening schools, rather than being operated under government auspices, was run by the local workers' society of the provincial capital.[106]

The existing facilities for the education of peasant children and adults alike fell far short of their needs and aspirations. Time and again *paesani* expressed how, had the opportunity for education been present in their youth, they would have taken advantage of it.[107]

There were many reasons why improvements did not take place to meet the popular demand for education. Since education was primarily the responsibility of the commune, it can be argued that the poverty of the South impeded improvements in education.[108] National policy, however, aggravated the disadvantage of poverty, since state funding of education was assessed on the basis of existing schools rather than on the need for new ones, thus favouring the North. To remedy the situation conscientious Calabrian officials and *meridionalisti* called on the national government to assume directly the administration of education, which, they argued, the impoverished communes could not adequately fulfill.[109]

But the problem was not simply one of poverty or lack of capital, for a great deal of the national funds that were assigned to Calabrian municipalities somehow never found their proper purpose. Moreover, few communes took the trouble to avail themselves of state programs that were introduced to aid in the construction of new schools. And the municipalities themselves were never as helpless as many contemporaries believed. Communes that spent handsome sums on municipal facelifts, *feste*, village bands, and similar things, spent precious little, and sometimes nothing at all, on education.[110]

It is on the local elites who were responsible for the fate of the Southern municipalities and not on the "natural" poverty of the South that in large part explains the backward state of education. In the Rende area members of the local elites, especially the large landlords, were commonly of feudal origin and their power was near feudal in nature. To preserve their waning power and privilege these elites sought to retard public education, which they viewed as a threat to their position. As one Calabrian official reported to the 1908 inquiry, "the *signori* are fond of obscurantism; every progress in education makes them fear the loss of their feudal supremacy." This was echoed by a man of science who had spent much effort in the fight against malaria: "Here the men who govern, the ruling classes, have all the interest in the world in maintaining illiteracy and the status quo."[111]

Conditions within the Rende area were documented by a 1906 inquiry carried out by the office of the provincial superintendent of education. In Castiglione the inquiry found the primary education classes closed since it was impossible to find adequate accommodation for them. In Marano Marchesato a similar situation prevailed, though popular pressure was being applied to commence classes. In Marano Principato, for lack of a better location, classes were held in a cellar. The school of a village within the commune of Rende was closed because the landlord who had donated a peasant home for the purpose refused to renew permission for its use. The school had occupied the second level of the home, while the mules were housed below. To remedy the situation, education officials approached a large landlord with several hundred peasants under her but were unable to persuade her to donate even one of her many peasant homes or other premises, supposedly because she disapproved of the teacher. In the village of San Benedetto Ullano near the municipality of Montalto, the local school was closed after being destroyed by the 1905 earthquake and a year later new premises were still not found. Within the capital of Cosenza itself proper public schools were lacking and considerable rent had to be paid annually for accommodation, much of which was poor, some of it deplorable.

Contemporary observers despaired of the conditions of the few schools that were in existence within the Rende area. The provincial medical officer lamented that the concept of "public health" in the schools was non-existent and recommended many times the closing of buildings for hygienic reasons. Many schools had no heating and were damp and cold in the winter; they lacked toilets and water facilities and, not uncommonly, the premises were shared with farm animals. Often classrooms were grossly overcrowded, with many students being forced to stand. Equally lacking were school supplies of the most elementary sort. Reflecting the opposition of landlord-politicians to public funding for education, basic items such as ink, paper and blackboards were in many communes almost a luxury.[112]

As the mayors of municipalities, some landlords were able to fill educational vacancies through nepotism. Such appointed teachers and officials took advantage of their favoured positions, thus further undermining the already low level of education. Further, it seems that within Cosenza the local opponents of education were not beyond using violence and intimidation to bring to heel over-zealous teachers or their supporters when they persisted in efforts, such as establishing adult evening schools, that were seen as a threat to their position.

To be a teacher within the Rende area at the turn of the century was not a position of enviable status and the calling, frequently filled by women, was seen as probably the lowest of the professions. Consequently, many who were attracted to teaching were of relatively low intellectual calibre and sometimes of questionable character. Local supervision of teachers was non-existent; for the whole of Cosenza incorporating 152 municipalities there was only one inspector of education, which meant that these incompetent local teachers had virtually free rein.

This, then, was the state of education within the Rende area. However, it is noteworthy that the educational profile of the immigrants was considerably more accomplished than that of the inhab-

itants generally. While a majority of those going to the new world
were illiterate, the proportion was less than the home illiteracy rate –
an observation consonant with the large representation from the better-
off peasantry that contributed to emigration from the Rende area.[113]

Though we have focused on formal education and its gross deficiency
within the Rende area, it must be recognized that education, broadly
viewed, consisted of more than the literacy that schools could supply.
Especially in a peasant society yet to be completely absorbed by the
cultural and economic apparatus of the nation-state, people looked
to other avenues by which to transmit knowledge.

Of these, the system most akin to formal education was apprenticeship. Through this route some peasant sons were able to enter the
ranks of artisans and craftsmen. But this was not easy to do, for skilled
men – smiths and tailors, for example – jealously protected entrance
into their crafts. The infrequency of exogamy between classes further
blocked access into the *artigiani*. Nevertheless, it sometimes happened
that a son of a better-off peasant, through his family's connections of
clientage, friendship, or perhaps even kinship with a *maestro*, would
train as an apprentice.

A novice apprentice would usually begin training at the age of twelve
or thirteen and for the first two years be given minor tasks and remain
unpaid. In the subsequent stage of journeyman, the young man would
practise the trade proper and be given a modest wage in return. Finally,
in adulthood, the stage of *maestro* would have been reached and he
could start to think of building up his own clientele, and perhaps
training and employing his own apprentices.

Alongside the formal educational system and apprenticeship lay the
family unit as an agency for the education of the young. Naturally,
the family acted to socialize the young into the values and expectations
of the local society – an obvious function of the family everywhere.
But in contrast to modern, industrial society, within the Rende area
the family had almost exclusive control over the socialization process
since the state failed to forge an effective and universal educational
system in the South until after 1911.[114] While a detailed account of
this socialization is beyond my purpose, there are two aspects of the
family's educational role that should be noted.

First, the family taught basic skills. Though seemingly simple and
of little consequence to the *galantuomini* and townspeople, these were
in fact complex. For the boy, the skills of peasant farming were passed
on in preparation for his later livelihood. Peasant farming was a heter-
ogeneous and intricate form of agriculture. In the growing of many
crops, a complex agricultural cycle was operative in which one had to
learn when and how to plant the various crops; how to use the changing topography and soil of one's land to the best advantage; how to

prune trees and irrigate vegetable patches; how to rotate crops, dry figs or thresh wheat. Further, one had to know about livestock and how to prepare for consumption the produce of one's labour. Since the peasant often entered the marketplace, he had to know something of buying and selling, of marketing, and dealing with middlemen. He had to be aware of market conditions and of the different qualities of his crops and livestock if he was to be able to bargain with any hope of a fair return. The skill and knowledge needed by peasant farmers was not learned in the classroom; it was learned at home and the teachers were parents and often grandparents.

A similar situation prevailed for the girl. Besides having to know about some of the less arduous agricultural tasks in which she was expected to work alongside her husband – raising livestock and harvesting, for example – she had to know about the preparation and preservation of the family's produce. The skill of preserving food was particularly important lest spoilage set in and make dents in the peasant family's already precarious winter supplies. She had to know about managing the family budget, how to spin wool, knit, make clothes and soap, and much more. For example, she had to have a grasp of local botanical knowledge in the preparation of folk medicines and in order to take advantage of gleaning, which was not insignificant as a supplement to the family diet. This served the peasant families in good stead upon immigration to the new world and goes some distance in explaining the economy by which they were often able to survive depressed conditions and evoke the astonishment (whether favourable or adverse) of native observers.

The second aspect of the family's educational role worth noting involved the transmission from generation to generation of folk knowledge and beliefs via an oral tradition. Such knowledge and beliefs were generally transmitted through narratives, or through set forms like proverbs and folk songs. It seems that whereas narrative accounts, primarily of an historical nature, were passed down mainly through males, the proverbs and folk songs were more likely to be recalled by females. These latter forms of oral tradition concerned almost all aspects of life: work, the agricultural cycle, *feste*, religion, nature and relations between the sexes.[115]

Through proverbs and folk songs, the values and expectations of the society were made known to the young in readily remembered formulas. Hard work, personal effort and energy were held in high esteem and extolled as measures of the worth and social standing of *paesani*. Informants gave proverbs such as the following illustrating this view of work: "An early rise makes for a full day's work"; "Chickens do not lay eggs while chattering"; and, "He who does not work, does not eat."[116] Related to this, the hard lot of the peasant was also commonly expressed, such as in the following verse of a folk song wherein even at carnival time the peasant was reminded of harsh reality:

> Friend of carnival
> The doctor wants to be paid
> And he doesn't want excuses
> Whether you're rich or poor.[117]

With respect to the transmission of narratives, *paesani* told of how in conversations with old men, usually grandfathers or elder uncles, they would learn of the past, often with a surprising degree of factual basis. For these men, largely illiterate, the oral tradition was a real and valuable part of their educational experience. Informants knew, for example, of "a great earthquake before 1700" which hit the Rende area "and turned it into a sea." This report was almost certainly a reference to the Great Earthquake of 1638 which struck Calabria, and Cosenza in particular, causing the ruin of many settlements and the death of fifty thousand.[118] A contemporary account of the earthquake published in London under the heading of "Dreadful Newes" during the same year recorded the catastrophe and spoke specifically of the Rende area. It made mention of "the city of Castialione which is wholly destroyed." It continued:

> The famous city of Cossensa, is the one halfe ruined and destroyed, with the Countrey-houses thereabouts in the territory adjoining; also the Palace of the Prince, the famous Convent of the Jesuits, and the much noted Convent of the Capuchin Friers.
> A great part of the City of Paola.
> The Balliwicke belonging to the Knights of Malta is wholly destroied and of a place of firme land, is become a standing Lake and Water.[119]

In connection with this disaster, it was related how the survivors of the quake dedicated the feast of the Immaculate Conception to giving thanks for their good fortune, this practice being carried on by their descendants well into the twentieth century.[120]

Other informants illustrated how information about one's own family was sometimes orally transmitted across generations. One man reported how family tradition held that his clan was originally descended from Jewish or Albanian settlers in Cosenza.[121] Here the informant was harking back to the flourishing Jewish communities within Calabria before their expulsion by the Spanish crown in the sixteenth century. A Hebrew presence in the region can be traced back to Roman times and many communities were founded in the early Middle Ages. In Cosenza province the communities of Corigliano and the capital were particularly important, and within the Rende area both Montalto and Rende itself held a substantial Jewish quarter or *Giudeca*.[122] Furthermore, the informant was referring to the well-known Albanian refugees who settled in Cosenza after the Turkish invasion of the Balkans in the fifteenth century. Recent documentation, he reported, had confirmed the family story by pointing to a Jewish origin. Allegedly, records in Cosenza showed that the family had descended from two Jewish brothers who had converted and married Christian women.

In sum, it can be said that while the formal educational conditions of the Rende area were grossly inadequate, an oral tradition existed through which a variety of skills and information was transmitted to the young, making intelligible to them both their past and present. However, though folk knowledge compensated considerably for illiteracy, it could not substitute for the reading and writing peasants came to recognize as necessary for a better future.

But before proceeding to a discussion of the migration process, there remains one final element of the *paesani*'s social background of importance to their movement. This involves the question of kin coherence.

KIN COHESION

Much has been written on the quality of human relations in Southern Italy by social scientists, and although this literature is often not directly applicable to the situation existing at the turn of the century, still, the general tenor of the findings cannot be ignored. In such studies social relations have alternatively been viewed as competitive and malicious on one hand and co-operative and well-adjusted on the other. Characterizing Southern Italy as motivated by "amoral familism" – the unrelenting drive to maximize "the material, short-run advantage of the nuclear family" – Banfield has viewed social relations as marked by selfishness and distrust.[123] Two later studies on the South by Brögger and Davis, however, take issue with this interpretation. Both these authors stressed the coherence of the kindred, the importance of friends and neighbours, the practice of work parties, and the intricate system of rights and obligations binding individuals to one another.[124]

Similarly, these two perspectives are reflected in writings regarding Southern Italian immigrants in the new world. Cronin, for example, in her study of Sicilian immigrants in Australia, concurred with the familism presented by Banfield, whereas Boissevain, in his study of the primarily Southern Italian community in Montreal, showed how commitment to kindred, friends and neighbours bound the community together.[125]

My own evidence on the social conditions within the Rende area substantiates the co-operative perspective. This is not, of course, to say that competitive friction did not exist; nevertheless, I give predominance to co-operativeness over competitiveness. For not only did the informants themselves stress cohesion over friction, but the very process of chain migration by which they emigrated to the new world would have been impossible had strict familism and competitiveness been predominant.

Social cohesiveness which later facilitated chain migration was revealed through informants' reports at three levels of kinship. The unit claiming the individual's primary loyalty was the nuclear family, consisting of the father, mother and their children. Within the Rende area the word *famiglia* was used to refer both to this grouping and to the *familiari* or "family circle." *Familiari* included kindred up to (but excluding) the degree of cousin and their spouses. But not all kindred who were genealogically *familiari* were in fact so. Informants considered only those who lived relatively near one another and interacted closely as a unit as *familiari*. The members of such a family circle perceived themselves as a bounded group in distinction to other kin.

The third level of kin consisted of all remaining relatives up to second cousin. Up to this boundary one could not intermarry and significant rights and obligations existed. Beyond this, one was expected to "recognize" cousins up to the fourth degree, but here the commitment of reciprocal rights and obligations was weaker and intermarriage was permissible. All blood relations from closest to most distant taken together formed an extensive kin group referred to as *parenti*.[126]

Within the nuclear family, the father was above all the family's provider. It was his ability to maintain or improve the socio-economic position of his family – or in the words of informants to *tirare avanti*, literally to "pull forward" – through working land that was the main criterion of the father's standing within the community. The family's wealth, modest as it was, was not seen as a matter of individual ownership but rather as held in trust by the father for the benefit of his family. A father who squandered the wealth of his family was held in disrepute. Essentially, within the Rende area, the family, with the father as head, was a corporate group in which property and status were seen to be held in common.

In return for his material support, the husband held exclusive sexual rights to his wife. It was necessary for the wife to observe her obligations in order to uphold the family's honour and cohesion. She was responsible for the upbringing of children, the household, and the tending of farm animals.[127]

Children were expected to obey and respect their parents, especially the father. From the age of four or five they contributed to the economic life of the family by doing simple agricultural or household tasks. Single young men were expected to contribute directly to the family wealth either by working the land or earning a salary. They were also responsible for the good reputation of their sisters and the family honour. Unmarried female children were expected to undertake the many household and domestic tasks required by the family. Like her mother, a young woman was expected to protect her own, and hence the family's, honour.[128]

Parents judged the success of their lives primarily in terms of their children: the support they provided them with as children; the extent to which they were able to set them up at marriage; the honour they maintained intact and augmented in order to bequeath them. These obligations were pervasive and primary and, of necessity, individual pursuits and comforts were subordinated to them. It is in this sense that informants spoke of parents having "sacrificed" for their children.

The main function of the family's common wealth was to enable parents to provide their children with the means by which they could establish themselves as independent adults. This process of *sistemazione* involved both the successful marrying off of children and their adequate material provision to ensure independence, ideally within a separate household. The bilateral kinship system of Southern Italy, by which descent was traced through both parents, meant that daughters as well as sons had claim to the family's common wealth. For a son, *sistemazione* ideally meant the endowment of land and for a daughter, a dowry and complete trousseau of linen. The endowment of land and the dowry were decided upon by the father. The mother was responsible for the trousseau, in which she often invested considerable labour and money.[129]

For their part, children were to show gratitude for the sacrifice of their parents, primarily through a pervasive attitude of respect. This quality was to be manifest in numerous ways. It ranged from mere obedience in childhood to supporting aged parents in adulthood. As young adults, children were expected to contribute to the family's wealth and status. For a male, this took the form of working and turning over the whole or part of his earnings to his parents. Older sons were expected to contribute directly to the *sistemazione* of sisters and often their contribution, especially after emigration provided new means for earning cash, was critical in this setting-up process. As will be detailed later, it was the desire of young fathers and single men to fulfill their obligations and improve the social and economic standing of their families (or at least to maintain it) that was the *raison d'être* for their migration from the Rende area in the late nineteenth and early twentieth centuries.

Rights and obligations in the nuclear family were both implicit and diffuse. There was no separation between the context in which these occurred and the nuclear family itself. On the other hand, with respect to *familiari*, rights and obligations took on a more definite character and occurred within concrete circumstances. In other words, a man "lived" rights and obligations – as he breathed the air, so to speak – within his nuclear family, but he did not do so within *familiari*. Rather, there was a more conscious recognition among the family circle of rights and obligations.

It is beyond this study to delineate all the concrete circumstances under which rights and obligations between *familiari* occurred. It will suffice to consider this reciprocal relationship as it occurred within the context of the work party – the most important of co-operative forms that bound *familiari* as a group.

Within the Rende area, various work parties among *coloni* and *affittuari* formed around critical junctures in the agricultural cycle. The most important of these work parties occurred during the June grain harvest for, as one informant put it, "all had to have bread to eat."[130] In such work parties, *familiari,* in addition to some cousins and friends who also lived in the neighbourhood, were brought together. This work party varied in size depending on the total amount of grain to be harvested and the availability of kindred, but usually it consisted of one to two dozen adults. This group would work each member's field until all the grain had been harvested. It was in the participants' interest to make the work group as large as possible for, quite simply, as the above informant said, "the more people there were, the earlier we finished." Similar work parties based on reciprocal rights and obligations formed for the grape harvest and wine-making in October, and the hog slaughter and meat-processing in January. A former *colono* told of such occasions and brought forward some salient features of the work party:

> In the countryside where we lived, we got together often. We went to visit each other all the time. We were friends. Say they would kill a pig – and about a dozen people would get together. Say they would start at my house – well, wherever they finished the round, they would play the bagpipes there and drink and eat .... One time they would say they had to kill the pigs, another time they had to weigh the wheat, another time they said they had to do the threshing, and another time that they had to harvest the grain ... we did these "exchanging of hands" *(cambiare di mano)* all the time. It was worth your while to do it this way.[131]

Though these work parties had a definite economic function, they also acted as social excursions described by one informant as like *feste* and another as full of *fratellanza.* Work parties were particularly looked forward to by young single men and women who took advantage of these situations to do some courting.

At all the agricultural seasons there were objective economic conditions that facilitated co-operation. In each case, for example, the task had to be accomplished within a short period of time lest spoilage set in, and each task was labour-intensive requiring more hands than could be supplied by the nuclear family. "The olives gave you some time, but the wheat didn't. If you waited, it would ripen too much (i.e., burn) .... One family couldn't do this work. We had to work together," one woman said.[132] Co-operation, then, was not lacking within the Rende area, but it was shaped by kinship (and to a lesser degree, friendship) and the concomitant system of rights and obligations that bound *paesani*.

Reciprocity among *familiari* united through work parties was part of a wider, comprehensive network of explicit rights and obligations that bound the kindred as a whole. In this network, *parenti* were linked by dyadic relationships of mutual exchange of goods and services. There was a constant exchange between individuals and families of specialized services, of matched aid, of "samples" of domestically made products and of visiting and gifts. But at the same time there were specific occasions when many members of the kindred as a whole came together. The most important of these occasions were the rites of passage. The rites of baptism at birth, confirmation at maturity, matrimony at the assumption of full adult status, and extreme unction at the point of death, marked major watersheds in the life cycle and were given due recognition by the kindred.

Of the rites of passage, marriage was most important socially (baptism or its converse being more critical religiously). One did not truly gain independence from one's parents or truly contribute to the polity of the community until one was married. In making men providers of their own families and women mothers, marriage in the kindred's eyes bestowed upon the participants the primary criterion of adulthood. Within the Rende area the importance of marriage was attested to by the fact that not one, but several celebrations surrounded the rite.

Among the better-off peasants, the engagement, which occurred a year before the wedding, and the posting of the banns about a month before, were both occasions for celebration, bringing together from two dozen to forty *familiari* and close kin.[133] Modest, domestic gifts were brought by the guests and, in return, the hosts provided pork giblet dishes, *salumi* and wine. On the Thursday before the wedding, *"giovedì di panni"* a procession was held in which the young female relatives of the affianced would parade the bride's linen, furniture, kitchenware and other dowry items through the countryside. Joined by *paesani,* the merriment would culminate in an evening dance at which young men and women would seek future partners.

On the day of marriage itself, usually a Sunday, as many *parenti* as could be accommodated (sixty or more being common) would be invited to the festivities. Cash gifts or presents were brought by the guests and the hosts provided food, wine and music. Afterwards, on the "Tuesday of Presents" (*"martedì dei presenti"*) the newlyweds would be visited by their wedding guests and brought gitfs of poultry, eggs, sugar or liquor. This was a day of informal sociability and the new couple reciprocated with sweets, spirits, and kerchiefed keepsakes of candied almonds or *bomboniere*.

The costs of these ceremonies (except for the last) was borne by the couple's parents. The *parenti*'s gifts outweighed the costs incurred and the difference was the kindred's contribution to the *sistemazione* of the bridal couple. Generally, the extent to which one was expected to contribute to the setting-up of the new family was determined by the closeness of the kinship tie. For their part, the hosts were expected to reciprocate the kindred's gifts in the same way in upcoming marriages.

Common to all these rites of passage was the institution of *comparaggio* or ritual kinship. Through *comparaggio,* one adult conferred upon another the honour of godparenthood at baptism, sponsorship at confirmation, or witness at marriage, though in each case the individuals involved referred to each other as *compare*. A *compare* could be chosen from kin and non-kin alike. In the latter case, ritual kinship was sometimes a strategy by which *paesani* attempted to forge new, formal links with a *patrono*. Most commonly, the institution of *comparaggio* was a means by which a *de facto* close relationship could be made *de jure:* it was a means by which close non-kin were given kinship status and distant kin the status of *familiari*.[134]

Both through the rites of passage and the institution of *comparaggio* the system of rights and obligations between *paesani* was validated and the cohesiveness of the kindred and close friends reconfirmed. How these social relations were used by the people of the Rende area who undertook the journey to the new world, and how the socio-economic background generally influenced this journey, will be made clear in subsequent chapters.

CHAPTER 2

Causation and Contours of Emigration

Causes of Initial Emigration

PRIMARY CAUSES OF INITIAL EMIGRATION

The preceding chapter set out to describe the socio-economic background of the Rende area migrants. Here, much of the foregoing material will be related to the question of causation,[1] though some aspects of this material will have to wait to be drawn directly into the account of emigration. Here, too, are included a few aspects of background – in particular the whole question of population growth – which are intimately tied to the present discussion.

Emigration from the Rende area can be divided into four distinct phases: a pioneer phase between 1876 and 1881; a growth period between 1882 and 1903; a period of mass emigration from 1904 to the First World War; and a span of heavily settler emigration between the war and 1929. At this juncture we will consider the causes that lay behind the initial impetus to emigrate, though these factors no doubt influenced the decision of *paesani* well into the growth period.

Prior to the nineteenth century, the demographic trends within Cosenza can be assumed to have paralleled those of the Italian peninsula as a whole, where there had been little real expansion in its population until after the mid-seventeenth century. At that time, the absence of the plague allowed modest increases.[2] In the nineteenth century the annual rate of increase within Cosenza expanded to about 6 per thousand after 1830 and 10.5 per thousand after 1870; these ratios being roughly equal to the increases for Italy as a whole.[3] While from 1820 to 1890 the birth rate in Cosenza fluctuated between 34 and 45 per thousand, the province saw a steady diminution in its death rate from 31 to 23.7 per thousand in the same interval. This translated itself into a steady increase in population from 328,483 inhabitants in 1820 to 497,885 in 1890, or an increase of about 52 per cent.[4] Since there was no trend toward an increased birth rate, the net increase in population resulted from a lowered death rate and a reduction in the rate of infant mortality. In particular, government promotion of smallpox vaccination seems to have gone a long way in decreasing the incidence of infant deaths. Between 1863 and 1890 the province of Cosenza cut its infant mortality rate from 229 deaths per thousand to 173. Accordingly, the province experienced an increase in population density which, starting from a ratio of 49 inhabitants per square kilometre in 1820 rose to 69.6 in 1901, notwithstanding the effects of emigration after the mid-1870s.[5]

This demographic profile of Cosenza was reflected in the Rende area, though the details tended to fluctuate according to local circumstances. This is illustrated in Table 4 (see p. 257) which shows that the populations of both Rende and Castiglione – representative of the lower lying plains of the Rende area – underwent the greatest population increase, that is, 46.2 and 54.9 per cent respectively. In terms of population density this meant an increase from 74.7 to 109.2 inhabitants per square kilometre between 1820 and 1881 for Rende and an increase from 61.7 to 95.5 for Castiglione. Mountainous San Fili, whose countryside and strategic town had already reached near capacity population levels by mid-century, was less able to accommodate an increase and its population rose only by 29 per cent. This is reflected in its population density which, starting from a high of 157.9 inhabitants per square kilometre in 1820, could only expand to 203.8 in 1881. Castrolibero, with a mixed plains/mountainous geography, underwent an intermediate increase in its population of 32.9 per cent. Being the most agricultural, its density was the lowest, expanding from 58.1 to 77.2 inhabitants per square kilometre between 1820 and 1881. Not surprisingly, the nearby commune of Cosenza, whose importance as an industrial, commercial, and administrative centre increased after Unification, saw the greatest population increase, 88.4 per cent. Its density expanded from 217.4 to 409.7 people per square kilometre.

The density figures of the Rende area municipalities are illustrative of the relative richness of the area and its greater emphasis on intensive agriculture vis-à-vis the province as a whole. Hence, in the late nineteenth century the *comuni* under discussion consistently had density levels higher then the provincial average of about 70 inhabitants per square kilometre.

As the population of the Rende area increased through the early and mid nineteenth century, its economy underwent considerable growth, enabling it to absorb additional people. However, this economic expansion was so great that the level of living did not undergo a corresponding increase. Expansion in both the agricultural and industrial sectors kept up with local demand as well as contributing to extra-regional and international trade. But, with Unification, a number of economic developments took place which, alongside an acceleration in the rate of population increase, caused serious dislocations.

As we have seen, the industrial sector of the Rende area was centred on textiles, which began to decline after Unification, as the area's cottage industries and small factories were put at the mercy of more efficient Northern enterprises. Just at the time when an increased population required an expansion of this sector to create new employment, incorporation into a national market brought about a disastrous contraction of full-time employment. Many part-time jobs in the agriculturally based factories and mills that peasants relied on to supplement their livelihood also suffered decline and added to the area's unemployment and underemployment. The traditional artisan trades in the towns – coppersmiths, blacksmiths, tailors and others – were also adversely affected by incorporation into a national market, thus putting even more pressure on labour.

But it was within agriculture, which formed the economic base of the society, that the dislocations were the most serious. The policy of the new central government encouraged the growing of lucrative exportable staples which, within the Rende area, meant olives and figs. The production of wheat was also increased to meet extra-regional demand by expanding into hitherto unproductive and marginal land. A large number of peasants were involved in its sowing, harvesting and threshing on the estates of large landlords, but while grain culture produced some short-term benefits for the local economy, greater dependence upon the foreign and Northern Italian markets soon caused economic havoc for Cosenza.

In the mid-seventies American and Russian grain began to invade the European market due to the enormous progress made in long-distance transportation and the opening up of virgin land. By the early eighties Italy herself felt the effects of this new competition, which cut deeply into wheat prices and production. Between 1881 and 1894 the price of wheat in Calabria dropped from 27.2 to 19.2 lire per quintal.[6] This depression in grain prices motivated landlords to cut back their growing of wheat and demand for labour. Within the province, wheat production, which had amounted to 1,476,430 hectalitres in 1870-74 was reduced to 1,145,400 in 1901-5. At about the same time, similar effects occurred in the production of cotton, and more importantly, flax, when these commodities began to flood Europe from the United States and Russia. Also severe was the drop in the price of olive oil which decreased by 32 per cent between 1881 and 1896.[7]

An additional factor contributing to a depressed agricultural climate was the tariff war with France and the abrogation of the 1881 commercial treaty with that nation in 1888. A major effect of this protectionist stance by Rome, which was supported largely by Northern industrialists, was to "hit the South particularly, and hence ... to take capital away from southern agriculture and put it into the North and into industry."[8] France had been the main market for Southern agriculture and this new protectionist initiative by the liberal left under Crispi dealt a heavy blow to the production of olive oil, figs, and raw silk within the Rende area.[9] Here again, although the loss of French markets affected some peasant cultivators directly, the decline in olive and fig production affected others by reducing or eliminating altogether the part-time work they had performed for landlords.

Further, the onslaught of a pebrine epidemic just prior to Unification had a disastrous effect on silkworm cultivation, which had played an important part in the family economy of many peasants within the Rende area. Later, an additional strain was put on agriculture almost concurrent with the ill-fated break in commercial relations with France when phylloxera hit Cosenza in the 1880s, ruining many vineyards. Though wine production within the Rende area was geared mainly toward local consumption rather than export, for Cosenza as a whole the wine trade was of considerable importance. The province was the leading producer in Calabria and peasants who had relied on the grape harvests of the large vineyards of the Crati Valley to supplement their livelihood were adversely affected by the disruption of production.[10]

The confluence of population growth with economic contraction in the latter part of the nineteenth century resulted in a static, and even reduced level of living for the mass of people within Cosenza.[11] Taking the diet of the peasantry as a rough index of living conditions, there exists much similarly in government reports from 1811 through 1883. For most peasants, the diet was largely vegetarian, being composed of bread, home-made pasta, various vegetables (especially beans and potatoes), and some fruit (the prickly pear or *fico d'India* being commonly accessible). The class division between the peasantry and the *galantuomini* was reflected in the consumption of meat, which only the well-off could afford regularly.[12] Likewise, levels of living and social class differentiation were indicated by bread consumption. Toward the end of the century, as at the beginning, white bread was only widely available in some of the richer wheat-producing localities (such as the Rende area) and associated with the diet of the *galantuomo*. For most peasants the type of bread used varied from commune to commune and was dependent upon what crop was available. It was made of rye, barley, millet or even beans, and, invariably, it was hard and dry. Within the Rende area corn bread was commonly used in

the lower-lying communes, whereas in the more mountainous municipalities chesnut bread was substituted. Indeed, well into the twentieth
century both types were still widely consumed by the poor, or by the
peasants generally in times of economic hardship.[13]

In a similar manner, little change occurred in the housing conditions
of Cosenza's peasants through the nineteenth century. The 1811
inquiry described the peasant homes of the province as usually
composed of clay or slaked lime and consisting simply of one square
room. Houses were crowded, poorly ventilated and often shared with
poultry and other farm animals. They were heated by a single fireplace fuelled by either wood or charcoal and next to which peasants
placed their beds. Over the fireplace there was a spit for roasting.
Most peasants owned a few pots for cooking. For lighting, oil was used
though pinewood was substituted in some mountainous communes.
Seventy years later, though some improvement had occurred, the
Inchiesta agraria described essentially the same housing conditions:
overcrowded, uncomfortable homes, blackened by smoke and often
shared with domestic animals.

The clothing worn by peasants had also seen little change between
1811 and 1883. The *Inchiesta agraria* reported that much of it, especially daily articles, was still homemade of flax or, in the case of winter
clothing, of wool. Shoes were scarce and often wooden. Normally peasants wore pieces of crude oxen leather tied around their feet with
cord or linen.[14]

Another indication of the static nature of levels of living (i.e., actual
conditions rather than "standards") within Cosenza is given by the
state of health care. According to the 1811 survey, there were only
240 doctors within the province. The care of most afflictions underwent little if any improvement. In 1871 the total number of health-
care professionals in Cosenza – doctors, nurses, pharmacists and others
– numbered 810, administering to a provincial population of half a
million. Though local doctors were few and poorly paid, even more
acute was the provision of hospital care. Hospitals were rare, small
and poorly equipped. As late as 1902 there were only twenty hospitals
in the entire region of Calabria. Of the total staff employed in these
hospitals, fifty-two were administrators, four pharmacists, forty-six
nurses, thirty-seven religious order sisters, three chaplains and eighteen various other employees. The total number of doctors or surgeons
employed by the hospitals of Calabria numbered fifty-seven.[15] The
lack of hospital services within the region was so acute that many who
could afford it had to travel as far as Naples to receive adequate care.

The *Inchiesta agraria* of 1883 noted that the afflictions of the masses
– malaria and respiratory diseases, which, in themselves, reflected the
lack of public sanitation and poor housing conditions – went unat-
tended as they had in the early 1800s. Many peasants of Cosenza

continued to solve medical problems by administering folk medicines and therapies themselves or by invoking superstitious incantations or practices to which the local sorceress was often party. Even where medical attention was sought and received, the cost of pharmaceuticals was often beyond the means of poorer people and this stopped them from following through with treatment. Though Italian law imposed responsibility upon the commune to supply some care to the needy sick, few actually had any program of public assistance. Generally, as in the past, the task of administering to the health and other needs of the poor was left in the hands of the church.

The state of education was another index of the static nature of levels of living in nineteenth-century Cosenza. Though an attempt to remedy the almost universal illiteracy of the Neapolitan Kingdom through public education and a general abrogation of feudal institutions was made under Murat after 1808, these efforts came to naught with the Bourbon restoration of 1815. Education reverted to the hands of the clergy or private instructors and essentially remained the preserve of the rich.[16] After Unification, political expediency and patronage allied the new national rulers with the local elites and prevented vigorous state intervention in improving the social conditions of the South. Improvements in education were modest and as late as 1881 fully 85 per cent of the population of Cosenza district were illiterate.

One of the pre-conditions of socio-economic advancement in a society undergoing the transition from a traditional, peasant base to a capitalist one is the existence of an educated, entrepreneurial middle class. The neglect of education held back the emergence of a modern bourgeoisie. As Croce remarked, even after Unification, "in Naples there were only two classes 'les lettres et le peuple,' and ... a nonliterary bourgeoisie, engaged in business and trade, did not exist."[17] The high illiteracy rate of Cosenza was not only indicative of socio-economic conditions; the deficient state of education prevented the development of a modern capitalist class and means of production, which contributed to the perpetuation of unfavourable levels of living generally.

Though socio-economic conditions in Cosenza reflected population pressure which put a brake on what the system could deliver, this system was governed by men and the ultimate responsibility for the situation of the populace must lie with the elites who either actively or passively determined the shape of those conditions. While nineteenth-century levels of living could be seen as a "given" inherited from a pre-existing feudal society, nonetheless, whether these were improved or allowed to persist was determined by men.

In the nineteenth century, but especially after 1870, the static (or deteriorating) nature of levels of living within Cosenza can be explained by the confluence of population expansion and economic contraction.

It was in response to this state of affairs that out-migration from Cosenza occurred in the first instance.

SECONDARY CAUSES OF INITIAL EMIGRATION

The question of over-population was referred to by informants when speaking of population growth within the Rende area. For instance, one man from Rende *comune* told how in the late nineteenth century the number of families working in the local valley "could be counted on your hands," contrasting this to the situation in the early twentieth century when the number of neighbours had multiplied many times. More common, however, were complaints regarding the difficulty in obtaining land, often linked to the issue of *polverizzazione,* or sub-division of patrimonies. As one man from Marano Principato related, it was the fragmentation of peasant land that led to the migration of excess sons, himself included, from the *comune* to neighbouring, less mountainous municipalities.[18]

Certainly the prevalence of land fragmentation was closely related to population pressure. But *polverizzazione* was also the reflection of inadequacies in the new Italian state's agrarian policy which failed to provide the peasants with available land. To some extent it reflected uneconomic bilateral inheritance practices buttressed by law. Especially in the more mountainous *comuni* where good land was limited, peasant holdings often became too small to provide for a family's needs. The unequal nature of soil, topography and other agricultural conditions in these mountainous communes also increased the division of peasant holdings since the proprietor, in striving towards self-sufficiency, sought to put together a number of heterogeneously cultivated plots to form a viable whole. Such scattering of a peasant's holdings meant a loss of time and energy travelling from plot to plot; but more importantly, it made the necessary conversion to cash crops, which the peasant had to undergo in order to survive in the new economic order after 1861, difficult if not impossible. In the more mountainous western locales of the Rende area this contributed to the demise of the small peasant proprietor.[19]

Interwoven with this, the fact that Unification failed to fulfill the peasantry's expectations of a better life and, indeed, in many ways made it more onerous, further contributed to grievances and consequent migration. In 1860 Garibaldi was able to mobilize peasant support against the Bourbons by promising cheaper food for the poor – which he in fact instituted by eliminating the hated *macinato* or grist tax and by promising the distribution of land. After 1861 the division and sale of ecclesiastical, royal and communal domains to many seemed to augur well that Garibaldi's promise would be fulfilled. Initially a considerable number of peasants were able to acquire small plots that seemed to them like stepping stones to landed respectability. In the district of Cosenza, from the sale of communal land which had taken place in fifteen municipalities by 1880, 3,725 peasants had acquired propertied status. The problem was that the plots of these *quotisti* were too small to be viable, for these 3,725 peasants had to share among them 4,120 hectares. Rarely were the plots sold to peasants greater than an hectare.[20]

The precariousness of these small plots meant that at the first poor harvest many peasants were forced to sell out because they could not meet outstanding payments on their land or the high interest (often 10 per cent) on loans. Within the Rende area the biggest beneficiaries of these resales were the pre-Unification landed elite, though some middle-class speculators also benefited. Indeed, within the *comune* of Rende the comedy of distribution and resale hardly took place. There, the common lands of the municipality were appropriated without auction by the *gran signore,* Don Marco Magdalone. Rented to peasants, this alone netted the family more than 6,600 lire annually. Similarly, in 1861 much communal land within neighbouring Marano Marchesato was usurped by the Magdalone and other powerful families rather than being publicly sold.[21]

Within Cosenza little headway was made in strengthening the position of the middling peasantry; in fact, the concentration of land in the hands of the powerful few, such as the Campagna and Quintieri families, was actually augmented. For many peasants the state's land program, which was aimed at removing the remaining vestiges of feudalism, proved counter-productive since they lost the important rights they had hitherto held collectively with respect to the municipal commons *(usi civici).*[22]

As communal land came under the private ownership of landlords, the rights of grazing, gleaning, collecting firewood, and even limited sowing were lost and cut deep into the peasants' means of livelihood. As late as 1908, when Adolfo Rossi, a commissioner of emigration, conducted his informal study of Southern emigration, he was confronted in Cosenza by a demonstration of peasants, mostly women, who demanded the restoration of communal rights. One of these peasant women told the commissioner, "We want the return of the common lands that they took from us. I remember when I was young I used to go with my father to La Sila to collect wood and sow. Those lands were seized by the *signori* and we were left poorer than before."[23] Likewise, informants from the Rende area recalled the common rights of the past and, even after the First World War, many considered it their right to collect firewood and glean on former communal lands even though this brought them into conflict with local landlords.

The loss of common rights and fragmentation, alongside the increased concentration of land and the power of the *galantuomini,* contributed to the social distance and conflict between peasants and landlords after Unification. The new order brought with it changing contractual arrangements for the working of land which added fuel to the fire. As Nitti notes, up until Unification a dominant form of holding land was the emphyteusis: a rental arrangement which could be inherited and eventually end in ownership for the tenant. Because of this, it "was singularly useful to the labouring classes." After the introduction of the Civil Code of 1866, however, emphyteusis was progressively replaced by less stable short-term modes of holding land – especially the *colonia parziaria* and share-renting.[24] Surplus labour in the years before large-scale emigration allowed the landlords to set their own terms to these agricultural contracts, further embittering relations between them and the peasantry.

The 1905 work of Scalise argues that the material well-being of Calabria's agricultural population through the nineteenth century remained constant. In his words: "Before the coming of emigration, wages were not only at poverty level but also an insult to the dignity of the labourer. They varied from a minimum of 0.60 lire to a maximum of 1.10 lire [per day] at threshing and harvest times." Such were the wages of men. For women and children, the going rate was around 0.43 lire.[25]

Franchetti observed in his 1875 study of Calabria and other Southern regions that the supply of labour was much greater than the demand and hence the wages and working conditions of the peasantry were frozen at minimal levels to the benefit of the landlords. In Cosenza specifically, in the early 1880s the minimum wage was still around 0.50 lire per day including food, though the effects of emigration had already pushed the maximum level to almost 2 lire for harvest and threshing jobs in some areas.[26]

If, before the advent of emigration, agricultural wages remained static at best, it must be remembered that throughout the nineteenth century people had to deal with a steadily rising cost of living and, especially after 1861, rising taxation. In Cosenza in the 1880s taxes averaged 40 per cent of a man's income. Scarce capital that could have increased the productivity of peasant holdings or kept one solvent was drained off by national, provincial and municipal coffers.

Because of the fiscal burdens the new state had undertaken – military expenditures, railroad construction, and the like – the grist tax *(macinato)* which had caused numerous rebellions in the past was reinstated in 1868. This hit the peasantry particularly hard since their diet was composed to a large extent of bread. And that other necessity of the masses, salt, was also heavily taxed. A Calabrian paper commented on this regressive taxation in 1879: "In Italy the taxes on bread, salt and meat burden every inhabitant ..., of which more than half is for bread only; whereas in every other civilised country a similar tax does not exist ... [Such explains] ... the agitation of a society in which we have imposed heavy taxes on products of prime necessity, whereas objects of little necessity or luxury are spared."[27]

Through the 1870s the cost of renting land in Calabria had risen by almost 30 per cent over pre-Unification rents. Moreover, Cingari notes that local taxes – communal duties, road fees, and taxes on farm animals and land – rose 45 per cent in 1887-91 over those of the previous quinquennium.[28] On the whole, between the beginning and end of the century the cost of the necessities of life – bread and salt, for example – almost doubled.

For the majority of peasants the experiment and promise of Unification had run dry. Despite land reform, they remained propertyless and the *macinato* had returned along with a heavier burden of taxation than had existed under the Bourbons.[29]

It was in response to this increasingly intolerable state of affairs that emigration from Cosenza started. It was motivated by a combination of "push" factors, both of a primary structural and secondary nature, and essentially economic. Though other factors of a different nature, particularly social and "pull," may also have been operative, these were insignificant at this point and do not become salient until the period of migratory growth.

Contours of Emigration

THE INITIAL YEARS, 1876-81

Due to the large-scale emigration that emanated from Southern Italy between 1880 and the First World War the nation has commonly been viewed as one of the new world's most prodigious sources of immigrants. For some observers a fundamental motive lay in the character of the Southern peasants who reportedly displayed indifference or even disdain for the land. But this notion of a predisposition to emigrate has not always been widely held. Foerster notes how as late as the 1860s the popular opinion of Italians was the opposite of this stereotype save for a few colourful wanderers peddling either specialized goods or services (the image-makers from Lucca or the hotelkeepers from Lago d'Orta, for example). "As late as half a century ago," wrote Foerster in 1919, "men were led ... to regard the Italians as a people not given to emigrate – a people as attached to the soil, some one has said, as an oyster to its rock."[30]

At the same time, however, throughout the nineteenth century, internal migration within the peninsula was for some peasants a known quantity, so that a migratory tradition pre-dated and influenced the movement overseas. For Cosenza, prior to 1850 this seasonal movement was limited to a couple of thousand in any one year. The dislocation wrought by Unification, however, increased this number significantly so that in the 1860s the yearly ranks of migrants rose to over 10,000.[31]

Agricultural labourers and poorer peasants from the Rende area undertook seasonal sojourns to the La Sila mountains for woodworking and the spring sowing of rye, potatoes, or corn, as well as the summer harvest. On the other hand, they would descend into the Crotone plain for the autumn sowing and harvesting of grain. Women and children migrated to the olive orchards of the Rossano coastal plain where they were employed in harvesting and the production of oil. Gangs (or *compagnie*) of labourers from Cosenza organized every year to work in the sister province of Reggio where they specialized in spade and shovel work on the large grain plantations or pruning in the fruit orchards. Women and children often joined their menfolk on these excursions and were usually employed in hoeing or weeding. Other migrations from Cosenza, especially at harvest or threshing time, occurred to bordering regions. Then, too, there existed a regular, though much less numerous, intra-provincial migration of shepherds and cowherds. Such men would spend about half the year (June to November) in the mountains and the winter months in the coastal lowlands.[32] Though it is difficult to assess the influence such internal migration had on later overseas emigration, the important point is that overseas migration from Cosenza did not spring up full-blown at a particular juncture in time; rather it was preceded by an increasing incidence or "tradition" of local and regional migration.

In 1876 the Italian state commenced keeping an official account of its emigrants. These records were based on the issuance of the *nulla osta* (literally "no obstacle") or clearance certificate required of persons intending to emigrate.[33] Because of clandestine departures, official figures cannot be taken as complete, so it is reasonable to view them as a conservative measure. According to official statistics, emigration from Cosenza in 1876 numbered 774, this figure having been reached over a decade after the first few Calabrians emigrated to work on the Suez Canal.[34] In 1877 the number of overseas emigrants from Cosenza reached 1,000 for the first time and a year later this was doubled, a fifth of the emigrants in 1878 being drawn from the district of Cosenza. As can be seen from Table 5 (p. 258), by 1881 the outflow had doubled again to 4,022 and one-quarter of these were derived from Cosenza district. The increase in this emigration can be readily appreciated when it is noted that whereas in 1876 six people left Cosenza for every 10,000 inhabitants, by 1881 the ratio of emigrants had grown to 32 per 10,000.[35]

Internal migration had been composed mainly of agricultural labourers, but this overseas movement was primarily peasant-based. Roughly three-quarters of the emigrants from Cosenza were agriculturalists, about 85 per cent of these being peasants as opposed to agricultural labourers. Artisans, bricklayers, merchants, and other skilled people made up the remainder. In further contrast to prior migration, the flow overseas was very heavily composed of adult males. In these early years around 83 per cent of emigrants from Cosenza district were male, and, not surprisingly, only about 10 per cent of all emigrants were under the age of fifteen.[36]

During these years of initial emigration, Cosenza province formed nearly the sole source of emigrants from Calabria. Out of a total of 15,591 people leaving the region between 1876 and 1881, 14,184 were from Cosenza.[37] It is difficult to state conclusively why this was so. However, the basic fact that Cosenza was the most mountainous province of Calabria is suggestive. Forty-six per cent of its *comuni* were located over 500 metres above sea level compared to 33 per cent for Catanzaro and 16 per cent for Reggio.[38] Generally, the topography and climate of Cosenza made it much less conducive to the operation of latifundia compared to its sister provinces. Rather, in Cosenza small peasant holdings were relatively more common. Hence, it was more of a *contadino* society than Catanzaro and Reggio, where *braccianti* were much in evidence. This distinction was critical in the initial period of emigration for two reasons.

First, the cost required to emigrate could initially be borne only by those peasants with access to sufficient resources. The marketing of produce for cash, the sale of land or, more likely, its use as collateral on a loan, were all means of financing emigration that were closed to rural proletarians, whose lives truly were enmeshed in *miseria*.[39] Secondly, as pointed out by Arlacchi, emigration required social as well as economic resources much more likely to be found among *contadini* than *braccianti*. It required the aid of a wide circle of kin and *paesani* who could help with financing the voyage and assume the risks involved, care for one's dependants and property, and provide access to critical intermediaries. Such an extended network of primary relationships predominated in Cosentine peasant society, but was generally lacking among proletarians, especially in latifundia areas where kinship bonds beyond the nuclear family were weak. Related to this and notwithstanding their precarious position during the late nineteenth century, *contadini* were likely to view themselves within an entrepreneurial (albeit pre-industrial) framework, whereby emigration was seen as a strategy to protect or enhance one's status. Among the *braccianti*, on the other hand, people tended to see themselves in class terms and the amelioration of grievances was more likely to be seen in mass action.[40]

From the beginning overseas emigration from Cosenza was directed towards the Americas. In 1876, out of 774 emigrants, 416 went to Brazil, 240 to Argentina and 18 to the United States. The same was true in 1881: out of 4,022 emigrants, 1,231 were destined for Brazil,

965 for Argentina, and, significantly, 666 for the United States. Among the remainder, 286 emigrated to Algeria and 228 to France.[41]

The growth and direction of overseas emigration in the late 1870s reflected advances in cheaper and quicker ocean transportation, notably the replacement of sail by steam-powered vessels between 1865 and 1870. For the people of Cosenza and the South generally, by the 1870s overseas emigration via Naples cost less than continental travel beyond the Alps and rarely did the voyage take longer than two weeks. At the same period, both Brazil and Argentina were experiencing economic booms based on agricultural expansion and both their governments encouraged European immigration to meet the demand for labour.[42]

For the emigrants of the Rende area who were part of the initial emigration between 1876 and 1881, it was primarily Argentina and particularly Buenos Aires province that attracted them. While at first many of the *paesani* were part of the seasonal movement of *golondrinas* (or "swallows") that descended annually upon the wheat fields of Argentina during its "Golden Age" of agriculture, by the late 1880s urban and industrial work seems to have predominated (see Table 7, pp. 261-62).[43] Many were drawn to road and railway construction and to petty business as pedlars, merchants, and artisans. The subsequent decision of some to settle in Buenos Aires eventually gave rise to a substantial community. Even so, important changes in the direction of the migratory chain were taking place.[44]

GROWTH OF EMIGRATION, 1882-1903

Emigration from the province of Cosenza in 1882, which reached 8,453, was over double that of a year earlier. The outflow from Cosenza district itself rose even more sharply to 3,918 in 1882, almost quadrupling the volume of 1881. Through the two decades, 169,604 people emigrated from the province and 50,650 from the district. Between 1886 and 1890, an emigration rate of 185 emigrants per 10,000 population was reached for the province and 153 for the district, over five times the 1881 ratio in each case.

As in the initial stage of emigration, three-quarters of the emigrants from Cosenza province were agriculturalists, though the proportion of these who were peasants decreased somewhat to 80 per cent. Emigration during these years was still very much of a "birds of passage" type, since around 80 per cent of all emigrants were male and only 15 per cent were minors.[45]

During the first decade of this period, the number of people bound for the United States increased considerably, ranging in general between 1,500 and 3,000 a year and often surpassing the number emigrating to either Argentina or Brazil. After 1894, however, the United States stream was significantly below the South American currents, dwindling to a few hundred. In contrast, emigration toward Argentina in the second decade expanded to over 4,000 per year and that to Brazil was maintained at between 1,000 and 2,000.[46]

In the second decade an interesting pattern emerges. Both the Cosenza district and the Rende area show a downward trend in their emigration figures, whereas out-migration from the province as a whole remained essentially unchanged. While in the first decade emigrants from Cosenza district comprised 38 per cent of all provincial emigration, after 1894 they formed only 28 per cent. In the years from 1882 to 1893 a yearly average of 2,662 people emigrated from Cosenza district compared to 1,870 between 1894 and 1903. Similarly, whereas emigration from the Rende area averaged about 580 a year in the first dozen years, it decreased to aroung 360 a year in the next decade.[47] The correlation between the drop in provincial emigration to the United States with the drop in the outflows from Cosenza district and the Rende area, together with the fact that other district emigration rates and emigration to South America increased, point to the conclusion that emigration to the United States came much more from Cosenza district than the other three *circondari*.[48]

The decline in emigration to the United States after 1894 reflected a contraction of economic opportunities caused by the depression of the mid-nineties. It was not long, however, before a great expansion in American industry again beckoned emigrants to venture towards the northern republic as part of the mass exodus that marked the high point of Italian emigration.

MASS EMIGRATION, 1904 TO THE FIRST WORLD WAR

When reading contemporary accounts of emigration from Calabria at the beginning of the twentieth century, one is struck by the medical images used. Rossi, travelling through Cosenza in 1907, quoted witnesses referring to the increased emigration as a "contagious malady"; Taruffi, De Nobili and Lori referred to it as a "convulsion" or "fever"; and Scalise took the image even further calling it a "delirium," an abnormality in the collective psychology of Calabrians.[49] Despite these references to social pathology, it is obvious that this movement made a vivid impression on contemporaries and that they recognized the decade before the Great War as a period of mass emigration.

For Cosenza the era of mass emigration can be dated from 1904 when the provincial outflow reached over 14,000 (double the previous year's emigration) and the first time the yearly out-migration surpassed 10,000. As depicted in Table 5, throughout the decade after 1904 out-migration from Cosenza fluctuated between a low of 13,345 and a high of 22,103. During 1904-5 emigration from Cosenza rose to over 220 per 10,000 population, a ratio maintained throughout the period.[50]

During the period of mass emigration from Cosenza, agriculturalists still formed the backbone of the movement. Three-quarters were derived from the agricultural sector, and about 75 per cent of those were peasants. The 10 per cent rise in the proportion of farm labourers reflected, in part, the aid given by peasant emigrants to less fortunate kin and *paesani* of labourer status.[51] As such, this changed pattern was a reflection of the dissemination of the wealth created by emigration itself.

The mass period witnessed a noticeable shift away from a sojourn to a more settled type of emigration from Cosenza. From a level of around 83 per cent in the initial years of emigration, the male component dropped to 75 per cent between 1904 and 1913. This was in contrast to the proportion of male emigrants for Calabria as a whole, which was maintained at around 82 per cent for the period. Further, whereas the province saw an increase in the proportion of emigrant minors (those under fifteen years) from 10 per cent at the beginning of emigration to almost 20 per cent in the early twentieth century, the regional rate lagged behind Cosenza's by about 5 per cent.[52] This difference in the ratio of males and minors emigrating reflected the fact that emigration got under way earlier in Cosenza. Consequently, the establishment of migration chains and settlements from Cosenza was further developed, rendering emigration from the province, relative to the region as a whole, less of a sojourner type. At any rate, it can be concluded that, while emigration from Cosenza was still primarily temporary in nature, between the initial years and the advent of mass emigration the proportion of immigrants composing the movement, as opposed to sojourners, increased by about 10 per cent.

Between 1904 and the First World War major changes occurred in the destination of emigrants from Cosenza. Emigration to the Americas increased from about 80 per cent in 1884 to around 95 per cent in 1914. More importantly, the United States replaced South America as the main destination of emigrants. Of 21,799 emigrants bound for the Americas in 1905, 12,482 (57 per cent) were destined for the United States, 4,495 (21 per cent) for Argentina, and 4,211 (19 per cent) for Brazil.[53]

In the mass period, Cosenza district experienced the greatest increase in emigration of any *circondario* in Calabria. In the years 1903 to 1907 the district experienced a 343 per cent increase in emigration over the previous five years. This was far above the provincial and regional increases of 208 and 216 per cent respectively. In absolute terms, yearly emigration from the district ranged between approximately 6,000 and 9,000 during the 1904-7 period compared with an emigration of between 1,400 and 2,500 during the previous four years. It was with the commencement of mass emigration that Cosenza district regained the position it held prior to the American depression of 1893, contributing about one-third of the total outflow from the province.[54]

Emigration from Cosenza revived when the United States' economy experienced an expansionary thrust, showing its responsiveness to American conditions.[55] Growing dissatisfaction with Latin America after 1900 accentuated further the shift towards North America. The end of the pampas frontier, high land prices, rampant speculation, and gross exploitation on *fazendas* – all of which were criticized by Italian government officials – made the situation for Italians very difficult.[56] More importantly for Calabrian migrants, jobs in non-agricultural fields came to be seen as poorly paid in relation to the buoyant and increasingly well-publicized wages paid in American construction sites, mines and factories. A significant number of Rende area *paesani* had experienced life in Latin America and, finding it lacking, chose to remigrate to the United States.[57]

EMIGRATION, 1914-29

With the onset of the First World War emigration from Cosenza declined drastically. In 1914 overseas emigration from the province dropped by 10,000 over the previous year to 8,655 and in 1915, when Italy formally entered the war, it dropped even further to 2,710, this number dwindling to only a few hundred in 1917-18.[58] During the war years the proportion of males emigrating decreased from three-quarters before the war to almost half, and the proportion of minors increased from almost 20 per cent to about one-quarter of all emigrants. It is evident that families were joining their menfolk overseas who had decided to make a permanent commitment to the new world.

With the end of the war, total emigration from Cosenza province reached 6,088 in 1919. A year later, with the return of peacetime prosperity, emigration shot up to mass levels reaching almost 22,000 – much of this to the United States (see Table 5). After 1918 emigration from Cosenza assumed a demographic profile similar to that before the war. The proportion of males increased to just over 70 per cent and the proportion of minors correspondingly dropped to earlier levels. About 65 per cent of all emigrants were agriculturalists, almost three-quarters of them peasants.[59]

The year 1920 marked a brief return to prewar levels of immigration into the United States not only from Southern Italy, but from southeastern Europe generally. To the chagrin of restrictionists in the United States, who in 1917 had finally succeeded in having enacted a literacy bill providing for the exclusion of illiterates, 1920 also marked the first real trial of the legislation. Because of the simplicity of the test and the rise in European literacy rates, the measure proved less effective than anticipated. Consequently, restrictionist forces regrouped and, aided by a recession and favourable public opinion, in 1921 succeeded in passing the first quota law. This restricted immigration from Europe to 3 per cent of the number of foreign-born of each nationality in the United States as determined by the 1910 census, up to an annual total maximum of almost 355,000. The legislation had as its objective the reduction of heavy southeastern European immigration while leaving the flow from the more "desirable," but much less voluminous, sources of northwestern Europe undisturbed. For Italy, immigration into the United States, which had averaged over 204,000 a year during the decade of mass emigration, was reduced to a yearly quota of 42,000.[60]

But even this measure proved unsatisfactory since southeastern Europeans readily filled their national quotas whereas their northwestern counterparts left theirs underfilled. Hence, a second law was introduced in 1924 reducing European quotas to 2 per cent of the 1890 census figures of the foreign-born. Conveniently, the census date upon which the quotas were based preceded the high-tide of the "new" immigration which occurred after 1900, thus skewing the quotas in favour of the "old" established groups. This legislation had the effect of cutting the Italian quota to barely 4,000.

The effect of American restrictionist legislation upon Cosenza was clear. Total emigration from the province in 1921 was reduced by 65 per cent over the previous year. Henceforth, emigration from the province was never again to exceed 10,000 a year (see Table 5). The current to the United States itself was reduced to a mere 3,000 in 1921 and to a fraction of this after 1924.[61] At the same time, the quota caused many aspiring Rende area emigrants to turn their attention towards Canada. In any case, by 1929 the door to emigration was completely closed by Benito Mussolini, thus saving restrictionists any further worry about Italian immigration.

The Nature of Subsequent Emigration

LEVELS AND STANDARDS OF LIVING

Earlier it was argued that emigration from Cosenza in the first instance essentially resulted from the push of a static level of living. However, once emigration started to be woven into the life of villagers in the 1880s, the consequences of emigration became part and parcel of its causation. Henceforth causation became a matrix of push and pull factors, the latter gaining ground in proportion to the increasing diffusion of emigration until, with the advent of a mass movement in the early twentieth century, their influence became predominant. This process was reflected in the decreasing proportion of male emigration compared to the movement of women and children and corresponding decline in sojourning vis-à-vis immigration. Not until pull factors clearly outweighed push motivations were the Southern "birds of passage" sufficiently attracted by the new world actually to settle there.

It is clear that the nature of migratory pull became an increasingly important part of people's reality. Rising standards of living, derived primarily from experiences in America, outstripped the levels of living that the local society could deliver, the resulting discrepancy being resolved by emigration. I am employing the term "levels of living" here to mean the actual material conditions at a given time expressed in the goods, services, and economic opportunity provided by a society, whereas "standards of living" refer to a people's expectations or values regarding what the society ought to be able to provide in goods, services, and opportunity.[62]

For the people of the Rende area, it was emigration that effectively brought new standards of living enjoyed by the wider society to widespread consciousness, rendering these expectations part of daily life. Through movement overseas people came to believe in the possibility of attaining economic stability, improved housing, material goods, health and education. However, before examining this, we should briefly note the extent to which standards of living exceeding existing local levels were part of people's reality independent of emigration.

After Unification, the Rende area was incorporated into an industrializing society, a national market and a cash economy which activated new desires and standards that went beyond what could be attained locally. Northern travelling salesmen who peddled their wares throughout the rural South introduced the products and consumer values of urban, industrial society to peasant communities. Writing of their effect on Calabria, Taruffi, De Nobili and Lori observed: "It [emigration] was influenced originally by economic hardships, in turn, caused by political events (the change in government, the sudden passage from a protectionist regime to a liberal one) and by the destruction of cottage industries and the invasion of travelling salesmen from Northern Italy who flooded the market with their low priced products. This supply of low priced goods caused an increase in the demands of peasants, who formerly produced everything at home."[63]

Increasing linkage to the wider nation caused peasant demands to change and expectations to rise. Peasants were introduced to and came to desire leather shoes instead of the traditional hide coverings, factory-made clothing instead of homespun coarser clothes, sugar and honey instead of fig syrup. And through having before their eyes the example of *galantuomini* mirroring the bourgeois lifestyle of the North – ranging from gold pocket watches to spacious, modern homes – peasants became aware of the discrepancy between their actual material condition and of what could be if fate were on their side. More immediately, peasants were influenced by comparisons with neighbours always a notch better off than themselves. In a small community only a few examples of upward mobility – through marriage, education, patronage or migration – were needed to ignite aspirations.

Through pilgrimages to the monastry of San Francesco at Paola and excursions to the nearby provincial capital of Cosenza, villagers came into contact with relatively large urban centres. In these cities, as well as at the annual fair at Arcavacata, or the larger one at Spezzano where Northern merchants would set up stalls, peasants were exposed to clothes, household items, agricultural tools, hardware, and modest luxuries which they came to desire.

Furthermore, with the coming of conscription after Unification, an additional means by which people learned of the world beyond the local area was introduced. Young men were exposed to Italian city life and the products of expanding industry, and they often learned a skill which, though often rudimentary, could lead to occupations outside agriculture or stand them in good stead upon later emigration. Military service also showed peasants the heterogeneity of their own nation and of its diverse regions and people. This experience widened the horizons of men and contributed to the nexus between the peasant community and the modern nation.[64]

Though there existed within the Rende area a gap between standards and levels of living independent of emigration, there can be no doubt that through overseas migration the discrepancy between the two widened, thus spurring movement to the new world as men increasingly came to view emigration as *the* means by which their rising expectations could be met.

THE EFFECT OF *AMERICANI:* "THE MYTH"

After the departure of emigrants for the new world, one of the first means by which the expectations of villagers were raised was through the letters of the sojourners. Scalise, writing in 1905 of his native Calabria, gave a vivid account of the influence of letters. Maintaining that the "stimulus" to emigration "was more psychological in content than strictly economic," Scalise was one of the first writers to give clear expression to the thesis that it was the discrepancy between expectations and actual levels of living that was the motive force behind emigration:

> Meanwhile these bold emigrants would write, and along with their letters that described the Eldorado, they would send money. Their families, who had almost gone into mourning because of the sorrow of separation, began to comfort themselves and their *paesani* would run to hear the letters being read, which they then would repeat by memory to those who had not had the pleasure of listening to them. The news would circulate among the masses brutalized by harsh work and privation and often they would meet the incredible; the most minute particulars would ruminate in the young minds of the wretched to whom it seemed astonishing that there existed a country in which bread was made all of wheat, in which

meat was thrown away on the streets, and in which one could earn 15 lire per day. Now the poor young men had a true perception of their state; only now, since until that moment they believed and had to believe that everywhere life must be difficult and destitute for those who worked. From the comparison between the life they lived with that which was described they were forced to derive a view of contrasts and, from this, the first gleam of hope that shed light on the abyss in which they were damned. This produced the subjective sensation of misfortune along with the impression of grief. It was natural that finally all perceived the sensation of grievousness and necessarily the idea arose of leaving this or of alleviating it.[65]

This attitude, initially influenced by letters, was soon more directly the result of returned sojourners. The first thing that impressed people was their improved style of dress. Leaving the village as peasants, they now returned like *galantuomini*. Taruffi and his associates described one of the many returned Calabrians they met in 1908 as "dressed with town propriety, with patent leather shoes and sportive beret: he had all the appearance of an *americano*."[66] One man from Rende commune who witnessed the emigration of the early twentieth century explained how the *paesani*'s hopes were aroused: "Then, when they returned to Italy, people would talk. They would see them dressed better than those who stayed behind, understand. And they thought it would be easy to go and make some money in America." Such men would be swamped by crowds of young people with "animated faces" waiting to hear of the *americano*'s adventures, which many hoped to emulate. A woman from Rende captured the excitement of the return. "People used to jump at the mention of an *americano*," she said. "It was like Christ himself was coming home."[67]

Once home, returned emigrants spent many hours expanding on their stories of America and answering the myriad questions that awaited them from family and aspiring migrants. Invariably their reports were positive and enticing.[68] *Paesani* generally overlooked the many difficulties and hardships involved in the voyage, at the construction sites, or in the slum housing in which young men congregated. Notwithstanding the example of those who returned injured from working in construction, mines and factories, or with tuberculosis or syphilis, it is clear that the glitter of the dream outshone any of the warnings or reservations that may have troubled prospective emigrants. Each man was seeking to be a success story, show his mettle according to the precepts of the community and translate the economic struggle and social humiliation of generations into honour, independence and *civiltà*.

Of particular importance in spreading the success folklore of America was the exceptional emigrant who returned having amassed a handsome fortune and who sometimes was able to challenge the power of *galantuomini*. The mayor of San Fili in 1910 gave an example of such outstanding success within the Rende area, and also brought out the transition from push to pull factors that lay behind emigration:

> A few of the emigrants made a fortune of hundreds of thousands of lire; but all, in general, have improved their economic condition. One bankrupt family recovered, making in seven or eight years a fortune of about 200,000 lire. Returning here, the three sons bought a chestnut wood worth more than 100,000 lire and a mansion, along with other minor acquisitions.
>
> These examples constitute a major incitement to emigration. At first people left because of *miseria;* now even the small landowners leave to make their fortune.[69]

In another case a young man from Rende returned from a gold mining adventure with a substantial fortune with which he was able to establish a thriving tobacco farm employing several labourers.[70]

Emigration came to affect the very values of society so that, as the mayor of Cosenza remarked in 1910, it became a matter of shame or dishonour if a man did not attempt to improve his socio-economic status by emigrating to America.[71] People believed that at least modest success lay within the realm of possibility of every man. As a peasant from the *comune* of Cosenza stated in 1908: "The *contadini* are much better off in America. Whoever has a head on his shoulders makes money. Only the stupid or lazy ones return without savings." Or to put the matter in the form of a folk saying of the day, "Whoever the ocean will cross, he will buy a house." The American dream was a dream of success. While it embodied elements of social and even moral aspirations, at bottom its economic underpinning was clear to all. In the words of one *contadino:* "America is always America because there you can earn the money."[72]

THE SOCIO-ECONOMIC EFFECT OF EMIGRATION AND *AMERICANI*

What were the socio-economic effects resulting from the outflow of *paesani*? To answer this let us start where the *contadino* quoted above left off: what did it mean to "earn the money"? While it is impossible to know the exact amount of cash the average migrant accumulated while in America, a good indication of his success is provided by contemporary investigators during the decade of mass emigration. Although the amount saved or remitted would vary with the type of work done, the length of stay and personal habits, it can be estimated from the Cosenza evidence provided by Rossi that the average peasant returned with between 4,000 to 6,000 lire, in addition to the 1,000 to 2,000 lire a year he sent back to his family. This estimate was confirmed by the Calabrian testimony collected by Nitti, who added that the savings usually required four or five years work to accumulate.[73]

Deposits of cash by *americani* were primarily made with village postal banks, which were often staffed by friends, relatives or *compari* whom they trusted. The large savings banks located in the larger centres, on the other hand, were seen as instruments of the state and the preserve of the *galantuomini,* and hence virtually ignored. Likewise, on the American side, migrants preferred to entrust their savings with the neighbourhood immigrant banker (often a *paesano*) rather than with the impersonal officials of the Banca di Napoli.[74]

Scalise estimated that at least 80 per cent of the savings in postal banks were due to the deposits of emigrants. Hence, by following the volume of savings, a minimum estimate of the wealth created by emigration can be made (this is indeed minimal for most of the cash that entered the commune was spent). The impact of emigration on the disposable wealth of Cosenza province can be gauged by the fact that total deposits in postal banks rose from a scant 23,387 lire in 1876 to 6,876,409 lire in 1898, and to a surprising 16,832,770 lire in 1905 after the advent of mass emigration. Not unexpectedly, Cosenza, which had the earliest and most voluminous emigration, also had the highest amount of saving vis-à-vis her sister provinces.[75] Within the Rende area, the municipalities of heaviest emigration, Montalto Uffugo and Rende, experienced the greatest influx of emigrant wealth. In one fiscal year alone, 1905-6, the two *comuni* had an inflow into their postal savings banks of 151,358 and 110,191 lire respectively.[76]

Within the Rende area, what ultimately lay behind the emigrants' pursuit of cash was the desire to purchase a home and land, or at least to improve their tenured position. After 1900 the major destination was the United States, particularly Chicago and railroad work. One *paesano* made clear the central purpose of emigrants: "You see ... years ago, everybody tried to buy property in Italy. Everybody went to the United States. They did five, six, ten years and then bought some property .... Nobody stayed before. People mostly made a few bucks then go home; almost 80 per cent went back."[77]

Generally, the emigrant sought first to purchase a home and then land, as indicated in the following testimony: "My father went to America many times. They all did that. The first time he came back he bought a new home. The second time he bought some land. Then some more land and so on and so forth."[78] The reason for this priority was that a home was affordable and could be immediately taken advantage of while the sojourner continued to labour and save in the new world for land.

Often emigrants purchased the same home and land they had rented as tenants. Often, too, purchases were made from America through trusted kin. As one early emigrant's son recalled: "He bought the land before he returned to Italy. He bought the land from Chicago. He had his father buy it, you know .... He sent the money there and his father bought him the farm. Then he stayed another year or two, then he returned and ... got married."[79]

In contrast to the small plots traditionally held by peasants, it was not unusual for *americani* to purchase plots of four or more hectares. The *americano* referred to above, for example, after returning from Chicago and "work on the railroad trade" bought an olive grove of six hectares which became the envy of his neighbours, later augmenting this by acquiring two and a half hectares of wood and almost one of prime lowland for vegetables. But even for those peasants for whom emigration did not result in landownership, it usually made it possible for them to increase the amount of land they could afford to rent. One *paesano* who emigrated several times was able to keep up with the demands of a growing family by increasing the amount of land he rented as an *affittuario* and another was able to earn enough cash to allow him to rent over thirteen hectares as a *colono* from the Quientieri family, thus providing plots for his married children.[80]

Though the great aspiration of emigrants was to own property, there was a myriad more limited reasons for venturing overseas. These were often intimately linked with familial responsibilities and aspirations, reflecting the social values of the *comune,* the fulfillment of which, prior to the advent of emigration, often had to remain dormant.

We noted earlier how, as part of corporate families, young men were expected to support aged parents and help provide dowries for unmarried sisters. The words of one informant concerning his father's migration history in the early twentieth century illustrates the depth of these obligations:

> My father was in the States, eh. The only reason he went ... was for his mother and father .... He wanted, you know, to give them a nice home, you know, a place to stay, which they did stay [on] until my grandfather died .... People worked for their family then .... My father had three sisters and he married them all off himself because his father didn't have any money, eh .... Back home you had to have all the stuff, the dowry, eh. My father did them all for all three sisters. It was mostly my father that set them up, yea.[81]

Men also emigrated in order to be able to marry and provide for young wives. The birth of children and the responsibilities this entailed added to the familial motivations behind emigration. An old *affittuario* who sired eight children spoke of this: "I was two times in Chicago. One time was before I married. Another time was after I married .... The second time I went back in 1919. The family started to grow, you know. There was scarce money all the time. You work, work, work, and not have enough money. Not enough money .... You can't buy good shoes; you can't dress up the kids. So I go to the States. I go to America."[82]

The specific cause of any individual's emigration varied from voyage to voyage, marking various stages in a continuum of needs which often corresponded to a man's life cycle, as the responsibilities of being a son and brother gave way to responsibilities of being a husband, then a father, and then again a grown son supporting aged parents. To a significant extent, it was this multiplicity of family-linked obligations that accounted for the "birds of passage" nature of much of the emigration from the Rende area.

While the example of successful *americani* who were able to buy homes and land, as well as fulfill important social obligations, raised and reinforced the expectations of *paesani,* there were other standards that were diffused and widely adopted as a result of emigration.[83] Returned emigrants could afford better food, consumer goods and even some luxuries. Foerster, among others, commented on the increase of spending power in Southern Italy which he connected to the influence of emigration:

> What influence upon well-being have the savings of emigrants? ... An indeterminate part ... is surely applied to raising the standard of living. We know that shoes and stockings and other comforts of habiliment which once graced their wearers chiefly on holidays have arrived at daily use. We know that meat is a commoner dish than it was, that there is more wheat flour in bread, that the *paste alimentari* are more generally eaten, that sweets have lost in part their holiday connotations, that tobacco comforts more men than it did, and that sewing machines are in wider use. We know that the returned emigrants turn to such things and we infer that in varying degrees the stay-at-home population has also risen to them.[84]

Also *americani* came to express higher social standards of education. Demand for schooling was augmented by the example of mass education in North America witnessed by migrants, who now expected literacy on the part of their children. Further, the demands of migration itself – dealing with officials and letter-writing, for example – highlighted the practical need for education, a need made even more pressing by the 1917 literacy test of the United States. Taruffi and his associates, reporting on the effects of emigration on Calabria, specifically mentioned people's raised expectations in this regard:

> Emigration ... has unquestionably brought a new impulse towards literacy ... the emigratory movement has inaugurated the tendency to break open the snares which had gripped the function of the school in Calabria. A population of which 78-80% are illiterate, when they demand an evening or holiday school, when they protest against the administrators because the schoolroom of one class was so narrow that half the students had to sit on the floor like pigs on the main road of a village, such a population cannot

help but question the legitimacy of the authorities in charge of the school. Emigration has started to wake up this population, it has taken off the blinkers from the eyes of the poor slaves, it has placed them in a better position to put themselves on the road of all kinds of new contacts, it has generated a new tendency towards education.[85]

Exposure to America similarly influenced standards of health. For example, returned emigrants would no longer accept living under the same roof as their animals. Rossi commented on this, connecting the new health practices witnessed in a town near the Rende area with *civiltà:* "Several new and clean houses are rising in the better part of the *paese,* without swine, mules or poultry inside. And these have been built by returned emigrants from America so that the little *civiltà* that has until now penetrated this large *comune* is due exclusively to emigration." Similarly, *paesani* came to expect better medical care, the public supply of clean drinking water, and public lighting of the village.

Americani were able to enter into a new, less subservient relationship with *galantuomini* and their example spilled over to the population at large. Emigrants returned to the village with a new sense of strength and self-worth vis-à-vis their class superiors. One Cosenza witness interviewed by Rossi expressed the peasants' new consciousness succinctly. "Until now we were quiet," the informant said, "but from now on we will demand more: America has woken us up and made us open our eyes."[86]

This heightened consciousness on the part of returned emigrants as well as a labour shortage created by the out-movement changed the nature of the traditionally subservient relationship between peasant and landlord. It was with emigration that common folk began "to get brains" and assert themselves. "Mainly because of the new conditions created by emigration, in relation with landlords, peasants, at one time servile, now go about boldly," noted the Taruffi report. There can be no doubt that emigration led to a curtailment of the ill-treatment and contempt meted out to the peasant by the *baroni.* As Rossi wrote, paraphrasing a man in Cosenza, "at one time the landlords caned the *contadini,* but now emigration has put them in their place."[87]

Emigration brought a noteworthy change in the relationship between peasants and small to middling landowners. Not only did the condition of peasants and agricultural labourers employed by these landowners improve, but the increased wealth and status of the *americani* caused the gap between the two socio-economic strata to narrow. Indeed, many smaller landlords, recognizing the rising power and influence of returned emigrants, consented to the marriage of *americani* with their daughters. Though the small landlord was wealthier in land than the returned emigrants, a bad harvest could render him a debtor to a well-heeled *americano* turned local usurer. The convergence between peasant migrants and small landlords was such that it led Scalise to predict optimistically in 1905 that, "within a few years the relations between the two classes will certainly become more intimate so as to border on an almost complete unity." Furthermore, the Calabrian scholar noted that interaction with the new urban bourgeoisie also improved: "When, after many years in fortunate America, some young man returns preceded in the *paese* by his moneyed fame, the doors of the *impiegato* and professional open up quickly, like that of the landowner, to let him in."[88]

The new power and esteem given to *americani* by social classes which had formerly despised the peasant highlighted the reality of what can be called the "social capital" of migrants. Emigration came to be seen as paying dividends such as accessibility to formerly remote, powerful men, increased desirability as a marriage partner, and the liberal extension of credit (not only to the migrant himself but also to his kin).

In everyday life this social capital of migration was perhaps most apparent in the realm of courtship and marriage. *Paesani* told how some fathers would refuse to give their daughters' hands in marriage to young men unless they had been, or were willing to go, to America. Conversely, young suitors could often marry peasant women above their station and be given handsome dowries on the promise of emigrating. In such an arrangement, part of the dowry was often used to finance the voyage, and the marriage itself usually remained a civil and unconsummated affair until the spouse returned.[89]

Needless to say, the social wealth of migration was a further ingredient contributing to the perceived socio-economic discrepancy between peasants and *americani*, thus adding to the pressure felt by the former to join the migratory stream.[90]

Emigration led to an improvement in the terms of agricultural contracts within the Rende area. With respect to the *colonia parziaria* contract, the proportion of agricultural produce going to the *colono* increased significantly and new contract terms shifted responsibility to the landlord, rendering the agreement closer to the classical *mezzadria* system of Central Italy. In many instances the landlord was now obliged to provide the *colono* with seed, to offset part of the harvest costs, and generally to involve himself with the actual running of the enterprise. Similarly, lower rents were offered to the *affittuario* who paid a fixed yearly amount on his land, thus guaranteeing greater security.

In either case, however, these contractual arrangements did not meet the increasing demand of returned emigrants for the outright ownership of land. Most returning migrants were both willing and able to afford the rise in the price of prime small and medium-sized plots that resulted from the increased demand. Evidently, the former landless peasants turned *americani* had little faith in the new assurances of landlords and preferred to be their own masters.[91]

That the life of the peasant improved as a result of emigration is substantiated by the increase in agricultural wages. From the end of the eighteenth century until about 1880, when the effect of emigration started to be felt in Cosenza, there was virtually no change in wage rates, which ranged from 0.60 to 1.10 lire per day (including food) for men and around 0.43 lire per day for women and children. By significantly shrinking the supply of surplus labour and causing a net shortage, emigration quickly drove up agricultural wage rates. Through the 1880s they rose by about 20 per cent.[92] Within the Rende area agricultural wages for men in the first decade of the twentieth century more than doubled over 1880 levels to a range of between 1.50 and 3 lire a day. The daily rate for women and children rose to between 0.75 and 1.10 lire. Even so, in some of the mountainous *comuni* of Cosenza, irrespective of the financial inducements, the rate of out-migration was so high the landowners were faced with having their harvest go to waste.[93]

Though the cost of living also rose, after 1880 this was significantly less than the rise in wages, so that the peasant and agricultural labourer saw a substantial real increase in their incomes.[94] But in spite of this improvement, expectations were raised to such a height by emigration that they outshone the increased local levels of living. Consequently, the impulse to emigrate remained strong, a fact recognized by contemporary investigators:

> But, it is repeated from many quarters, today that wages have doubled, tripled – that in order to hire a *contadino* we pay 2.50 lire or 3 lire – and they still leave! Thus it is not economics that drives these masses to emigrate. Above all, it is not the wage rate alone that could retain the *contadino* on the land ... [but also] the setting [*ambiente*] in which he lives. Moreover, if at one time the economic question was the prime cause of this movement, today other factors intervene; the psychological element, the contagion, the action of agents, the ease of departure and of employment, through the part played by immigrant's relatives, etc. Also that which we call the *force of inertia* is important. It is an intense movement provoked by very potent factors, by many years of suffering. One cannot halt it by the offer of a salary that is always and by a great distance inferior to that of countries of immigration.[95]

To a large extent the mass emigration from the Rende area in the early twentieth century was the result of the feedback effect of migration itself. *Americani* returning to the commune acted to raise standards of living far above prevailing levels and the resulting discrepancy could only be narrowed by imitating the harbingers of the new standards. It is to the actual voyage that ensued that we next turn attention.

CHAPTER 3

The Process of Migration

Facilitators of Emigration

THE ROLE OF INTERMEDIARIES

In the emigration of *paesani,* the petit bourgeoisie came to mediate between the local society and the wider world. Though often subsumed under the epithet "agenti" by nationalists of the time, the local intermediaries were far from shady steamship agents inciting innocent peasants to emigrate. Indeed, those profiting from the "commerce of migration" were often part of the middle-class backbone of the local community. Notaries, merchants, teachers, pharmacists, postmen, and the like all came to rely to some degree on the emigration trade as ticket-sellers, letter-writers and readers, money-lenders, advisers, and contacts to important officials.[1]

In 1901 comprehensive emigration legislation was passed and a Commissariato di Emigrazione under the Ministry of Foreign Affairs was established to regulate the trade. At the local level, emigration committees *(comitati comunali)* were called for to advise emigrants and expedite their movement. In Cosenza, however, the Taruffi report found that although by 1907 fifty-two municipal committees had been formally established in the province, none was actually operative and most had never even been convened.[2] The authors observed that it was only through the use of intermediaries that the peasant emigrant was able to deal effectively with bureaucracy: "The Comitato is supposed to ... give information on the procedures required to obtain a passport and the other documents necessary to embark etc., etc. But who, instead, interests himself in all this? The *agenti.* It is the *agenti* who hastens the processing of all the papers necessary for the conscription clearance etc., etc. Otherwise entire years would pass by before attaining anything."[3]

Indeed, by complicating procedures, the 1901 legislation actually increased the number of intermediaries engaged in emigration. As the parliamentarian Nitti noted, "the *intermediarismo* that we wanted to suppress has grown ... we believed we were limiting the number of people that lived and live from emigration, but we have under a different form increased it."[4]

From the peasant's point of view, the local notable's dependence on reputation for business, his wish to maintain social status and respect within the *comune,* and mutual obligations between patron and client all imposed calculable limits on his behaviour. In contrast to the peasants' "more intimate and easy rapport ... with the *agenti,*" officials representing the wider society were viewed with suspicion since they had no vested interests in the community and "wouldn't even look in your face," as one *paesano* put it. Oral testimony underscored the necessity of using go-betweens in dealing with government functionaries:

> You have to know the right person. There's all these – like lawyers or teachers, doctors – all high-class people, they're all mixed up with police, the government, things like that. So if I'm a little person, if I know you, I ask if you know the guy that can help me. You have to go through the line till you find the right man .... Not just me – I can't fix it up – no way ... you have to give something under the table, and the man fix it up (or) nobody look after you, that's for sure .... A person has to know how to handle oneself, how to talk, to get a document or some paper work done or something ... that's the way it is.[5]

The fact that 79 per cent of Cosenza province's school-age population was unable to read in 1901 was obviously fundamental in the widespread use of intermediaries. Also common was the use of *agenti* to side-step regulations perceived by peasants as unjust obstacles to their freedom of movement and opportunity. For the peasant, the "rules of the game," since they were set by outsiders and were foreign to the local ethos, ought to be disregarded. Too much honesty when it ran against one's own sense of morality was perceived as irresponsible, not as virtuous.[6] One *paesana,* whose husband had been able to escape military service and thus emigrate through obtaining false documentation from the local doctor, compared such "favours" with the impersonal behaviour of professionals in the new world: "Don't think that back home doctors and lawyers were like here. Oh no! There such people helped you ... they did you favours. Over here, they're too honest for that!"[7]

Local intermediaries understood the peasants' values, assumptions and aspirations. To this extent the mediating *borghesia* and the peasantry were part of the same "moral community"; patron and client formed a symbiotic relationship cutting across class lines and forming a united front against the values and standards of the greater polity.

THE ROLE OF KIN AND *PAESANI*

Emigration for *paesani*, while full of promise, was fraught with anxieties. This was the anxiety of the illiterate, of one lacking the social comportment of *civiltà*. But it was also the anxiety of one who had all eyes turned upon his success, of having to prove himself a man. Because of past exploitation and because the stakes were high, trust did not flow easily; it was reserved for traditional and proven ways of doing things.

Within the Rende area the degree of trust one had in an individual was primarily determined by three considerations: Is he a kinsman? Is he "recognized," that is, part of the local community? What is his reputation? The closer a man was in blood, the more he was known within the local area, the more respected his reputation, then the greater the trust. One trusted first one's corporate (or nuclear) family, and then in sequence *familiari,* kindred, *paesani* of peasant status and, lastly, other local inhabitants (including the middling classes).[8] One only went to the next level when aid through the preferred level was not forthcoming. Hence, as kin and *paesani* came increasingly to be capable of performing services hitherto rendered by the mediating *borghesia,* by the turn of the century dealings with the latter became fewer.

One of the earliest and more obvious of the *agenti*'s functions to be challenged by *paesani* was the providing of steamship tickets. Even by 1908 most emigrants received prepaid tickets from their kinsmen in America. Others would purchase tickets for their *paesani* from steamship lines upon their return at Naples. Alternatively, many would make their purchases themselves from the carriers when they arrived at the southern port before embarking. As Rossi reported in the same year: "The [Cosenza] mayor says that there has never arisen an occasion to assemble [the Comitato Comunale] since the action of the carrier agents is almost useless. The major part of emigrants go to Naples and buy their tickets themselves."[9]

Americani became increasingly able to provide loans to their kin and *paesani,* thereby cutting into another service formerly provided by intermediaries. Within the Rende area this was an integral part of the informal organization of emigration which enabled impressive numbers to make the journey to North America. Loans were provided under informal conditions, often interest-free to close relatives and at low rates to others.[10] In some cases, returned emigrants emerged as substantial money-lenders in their own right, entering into open competition with *agenti* and forming part of the "small idle bourgeoisie of ex-*americani*," to quote Nitti. Where an aspiring emigrant's circle of kin and *paesani* was not able to finance his journey and an impersonal loan became necessary, they often aided the man by acting as guarantors. In such cases, the influx of new money from *americani* often had the beneficial ripple effect of lowering interest rates.[11]

Increasingly, worldly-wise kin and *paesani* could provide aspiring emigrants with the advice formerly asked of intermediaries. *Americani* were able to advise as to what steamship lines and ships were best, which officials were most lenient, where to stay in Naples, how to avoid hustlers and similar matters. Such knowledge, orally transmitted, played an important role in preparing *paesani* for the crucial experience of migration. It was not the written word emanating from steamship and colonization companies, but the spoken word of local *americani* that held sway with people and contributed to their mass emigration.

Lastly, not all peasants were illiterate. In the Rende area there arose common folk who provided the literacy formerly the monopoly of the *borghesia*. Although such men were not usually able to supplant the more involved functions of intermediaries (as in the case of translating and filling out legal documents), they were popularly employed as letter readers and writers. One man related how his father, an early *americano*, was used by *paesani* in such a capacity: "My father left for New York around 1885-86 to work on the railroads. He came back after three years and made his land like a garden .... He was one of the first in Rende who could read, so all the relatives of the emigrants would come to him to have their letters read and write back. So I always heard lots of news from America, from all over the States."[12] When the literate peasant was an *americano*, his help was especially sought since he could expand on the information contained in the emigrants' letters. Not surprisingly, these men were highly respected and popular. They were often considered the informal leaders of their communities and their "good name" was shared by kindred.

Agenti charged their clients a fixed price for their services. Payment was usually in cash, but sometimes wheat, wine, or some other staple was accepted. They were also regarded with respect and presented with gifts at Christmas, Easter, and other important holidays. For similar services provided by kin and *paesani*, however, no formal payment was made. Respect was usually sufficient to reciprocate the help given, though repayment could also be made through useful favours, such as helping to build a new house. Reciprocation was flexible and the form it took depended on the degree of aid, one's ability to pay and, most importantly, kinship. The closer the tie of kinship (or friendship) between *paesani*, the less was expected in return for the service.

Aside from providing services formerly the domain of intermediaries, *paesani* aided emigration in less obvious, though no less important, ways. The traditional system of rights and obligations between kin was made use of in the migration process and, indeed, the exigencies of emigration itself had a feedback effect expanding and strengthening these ties.[13] One of the most important forms of aid within this context was the support given by kin to the married emigrant's family in his absence. For example, one man told how his *colono* father, who himself had worked in the United States early in the century, supported a poorer sibling's family upon the latter's emigration:

> What my father did for his brother's family! Boy, my father growed his family .... Because he was in America, eh; *Zio* (uncle) was here. He left when his kids were still small. They had four or five kids and my father looked after *Zia* and the kids. You know, they were living at Rende and they didn't have nothing, no food, nothing. *Zio* didn't have any money at that time, eh. My father even paid his trip ... so they used to be on our farm all day, every day .... *Zia* had four, five kids and my father was like a stepfather.[14]

The emigrant's closest male relatives also took responsibility for protecting the honour of the emigrant's wife and daughters, and the emigrant's female kin provided domestic help and emotional support. The emigrant was even assured that in dire straits – should he become disabled or lose his life – kindred would act as a sort of insurance against his family's destitution. Orphaned children would be supported by *familiari*, though formally adopted by a better-off brother or sister of the emigrant.

In turn, once relatives or friends had gained a toehold in the new world, they were called upon to help in the emigration of young men. In addition to forwarding steamship tickets and money, relatives in North America were expected to help the emigrant get through bureaucratic hurdles and aid him in finding accommodation and employment.

Women played an important role in emigration, which corresponded with their position in the cycle of family formation. As unmarried sisters, they stimulated emigration in the common case where their brothers, as part of familial obligations travelled overseas to help put together the dowry required of young brides. As young women open to courtship, they had a decided influence in changing the consistency and upgrading the quality of the local marriage market. They did this by adding emigration to the list of desirable attributes in a husband. Young women perceived *americani* as men with a future and preferred them over local suitors.

As wives and mothers, women participated in the decisions surrounding emigration. Many wives encouraged emigration, though some were against it. The newly married young wife especially, was likely to see the emigration of her spouse as a potential threat to marital stability. Local norms which winked at, or even lauded, a man's promiscuity – since such was regarded as a sign of masculinity – gave such women precious little consolation. One young wife, for example, was against her husband's emigrating in the 1880s for she believed that slavery still existed in the United States and that her husband might be tempted to take a woman as a personal chattel. A close relative recalled: "He was young when he went to Chicago. His wife, bless her soul, she was a beautiful woman, and she was very jealous that he would take up with a black woman ... you figure he was twenty-four to twenty-five when he went there."[15] In comparison, another young woman discouraged her husband from emigrating to Buenos Aires, where one of his aunts had settled, and favoured instead the United States, for it was popularly believed that Argentinian women were even more of a threat to fidelity than American women.[16] And, in fact, in the Italian *boca* colony of Buenos Aires there was a well-known red light district that catered to the many Italian sailors and transients who passed through the harbour area.

Commonly, however, wives encouraged the emigration of their spouses, for they believed that only through such separation could they achieve a better life. This was so especially later in the marriage when the burden of a growing family started to be felt. As a mother, the woman's first duty was now to her children, and any reservations about her husband were put aside. Also, since the husband was now a father, often women felt more assured that added familial ties would lessen the possibility of moral lapses and would help maintain the marriage.

Sometimes, however, the encouragement of wives was to no avail. One woman, the mother of nine children, who wanted her husband to emigrate to the United States, remained embittered after restrictionism because of the lost opportunity. Her husband, as a *fattore*, was relatively well off and his family never lacked the necessities of life. Nevertheless, the woman never forgave him that there was never enough cash to improve the home or dress her children nicely. And she resented the fact that socially inferior families whose males had emigrated were able to improve their condition while her own remained stagnant.[17]

With the widespread out-movement of men at the turn of the century, emigration came to affect the very values and daily proceedings of society. It became a matter of honour for a young man to attempt to improve his lot by emigrating to America. As a Cosenza mayor testified: "The emigration is spontaneous and the action of subagents has not affected anyone. Everybody desires to go to America; in fact, they are *ashamed* if they haven't been there."[18] In many ways it could be said that a "culture of emigration" permeated the Rende area. Wherever *paesani* congregated – at carnival, at the local Arcavacata fair, at *feste,* or more routinely at church or in the village square – news of emigration was exchanged and useful contacts were made. Rites of passage among the kindred acted as a similar forum, where loans were promised, steamship schedules discussed, and young men planned leaving together after the next harvest. At marriage, the wedding date itself was often set to coincide with a man's departure. And the selection of one's *compare* was now sometimes made with a view to gaining preferred access to a prominent *americano* who could facilitate one's going overseas.

Children born after 1900 were raised with a consciousness shaped by the culture of emigration. They heard constant talk about emigration and they witnessed their closest male relatives – fathers and uncles – going and coming between home and some wondrous *paradiso* named America. One informant from Rende commune recalled growing up in such an environment:

> Zio Luigi, Zio Tono, Zio Nibile, Papa, Rosso that lived in Arcavacata, Santu and Francesco too: it was always five or so of those guys getting together and talking. You know, they all lived in the area. They used to get together and talk about beautiful America once a week or maybe more .... Everybody that goes by or talk to my father, and I was there, they were always talking about America. I hear mostly of Chicago, because that's where they'd been .... They told different stories: like it was easy to get money, the different jobs they had, that it was beautiful.[19]

For a young boy living in such a milieu, the concept of becoming a man became inexorably linked to the wish of "going to America." As Nitti reported in 1910 regarding the aspirations of young Cosentini, "Already it is said that among the humble classes one is born with the idea of going to America. Questioning any young boy about what he intended to do, the Commission ... heard it repeated: 'When I grow up, I will go to America.'"[20] Perhaps it was in this sense of being socialized into a culture of emigration that the role of kin and *paesani* exerted its most primal and powerful influence on the migratory movement.

The Migration

PROCEDURES IN THE VILLAGE

The first necessary procedure in emigrating to the new world was to obtain a passport, which after the legislation of 1901 often became a complex and unnerving affair. The initial step involved obtaining a birth certificate from the *municipio* (town hall), for which *paesani* had to present themselves to the authorities. The secretary of the municipality consulted the town registry and, after verifying the applicant's place and date of birth, would issue a birth certificate signed by himself and the mayor. Next the birth certificate had to be forwarded to the local police headquarters, along with an application for a *nulla osta* (literally "no obstacle") giving the applicant clearance to receive a passport.[21] The police headquarters (or *questura*) was located in the provincial capital of Cosenza. Since it was a short distance from the Rende area, most people reported to it personally. Here a man's criminal and military records were checked and, if in order, he would receive the *nulla osta* and consequent passport. Despite the various steps involved, if the peasant received efficient help dealing with government bureaucracy, if all went well with his records, and if his business could be taken care of personally rather than by mail, it was possible to receive one's passport in about a week.[22]

For those who were part of the country's military and reserve system, the process of obtaining a passport was more involved. Young men eighteen years of age or over who were registered for conscription had to receive authorization from the local recruitment office, also situated in the provincial capital. While normally a passport was valid for three years, for this class of emigrant it was valid only until the young man's name was scheduled to be drawn for service. As well, discharged soldiers under twenty-eight years of age had to receive clearance from local military authorities or the mayor.[23]

Although in theory the potential emigrant could only buy his steamship ticket after his passport had been issued from government-licensed agents,[24] tickets were readily available from local intermediaries, often acting as sub-agents for licensed brokers. Prepaids sent by relatives or *paesani* also by-passed the stipulation.

Besides obtaining one's passport and passage ticket, a number of other arrangements had to be made. Designating responsibility for the care of dependants and property, deciding what belongings to bring, and perhaps having a mass said for a safe journey all had to be arranged. Most important was the organization of small groups of kin and *paesani* who would go to the new world together. Almost all these groups ranged from three to a half dozen men, usually under thirty, either single or with young families. These groups were formed to render mutual aid along the way and foster a sense of security in the face of the unknown; they were usually led by a veteran.[25]

Once these preliminaries were taken care of, *paesani* were ready to start on their journey. The first leg involved travelling to Paola on the coast where people would connect with the railroad leading north to Naples. The distance from the Rende area to Paola was covered by the variety of means. Poorer peasants simply walked the fifteen or so miles carrying their modest baggage with them. "They went to America not with suitcases," recalled one informant of these sojourners, "no, the things they had were all packed in a small hide sack, strung over their shoulders."[26] Others would hire a mule and attendant to cover the rugged terrain to the coast. Wealthier peasants, or those intending to settle in North America who had heavy luggage, for about two-and-a-half lire could take the coach service that ran daily between Cosenza and Paola.[27]

After 1911, with the construction of a spur line to Paola, villagers had the option of travelling the mountainous distance by cog railroad.[28] However, the fact that railroad stations were located in the valley, where the railroad ran parallel to the main carriage road, rather than through the hillside towns (except for San Fili), was of small comfort to many peasants within the Rende area. As one man pointed out: "I took the train from Rende to go to Naples. But the train didn't pass near the *paese*. Over there, in the old country, it wasn't like here where the railway passes through the village, you see. Here the railroad is in the city. Over there, some little towns are on top of the hill. Some is about twelve miles far from the railroad. And then you got to walk, that's all."[29]

After arriving in Paola *paesani* boarded the train to Naples. Because of the frequent stops at the many coastal towns along the way, Naples took about nine hours to reach. Emigrants travelled the 176 miles third class in uncomfortable wooden seats for which they paid about twelve lire. The route northbound was long and tiresome, yet spectacular in its scenery.[30]

THE DEPARTURE

For many emigrants, arrival at Naples was their first experience of city life. After decades of post-Unification stagnation, the surge in Southern emigration at the turn of the century shook Naples out of its torpor.[31] In 1900 it was the first in third-class passenger traffic and a year later it handled almost all of the 208,874 departures from the Deep South and the majority of the 34,806 emigrants from Central Italy (as compared to 34,496 departures from the North which were processed through Genoa). By 1910, years of general economic expansion and the emigration boom had again made Naples Italy's chief port. By the First World War, forty-eight international lines serviced Naples and passenger service between it and New York was provided weekly or fortnightly by North German Lloyd, Hamburg-American, White Star Line, Cunard, Italian Royal Mail Line, Navigazione General Italiana, as well as others.[32]

Thus, as the emigrants arrived from the Rende area by train at the Stazione Centrale, they found themselves in the centre of a bustling city of over half a million people. At this juncture *paesani* whose knowledge (with the exception of local travel and perhaps a military stint) had been limited to Cosenza, merged with the common experience of hundreds of thousands of Southerners. As they filed out of the railway station, within a short walking distance were numerous *pensioni* (lodging-houses) and only minutes away lay the main port area containing the offices of steamship companies, a telegraph office, and the large customs house. In this downtown area were also to be found the bankers, money changers, consular officers, doctors, pharmacists, post office officials, and others the emigrant might have need of.[33]

Arriving *paesani* were beset by a plethora of pedlars and hustlers who relied on the emigrant trade for their livelihood.[34] While their activity belied the pre-industrial roots and abject poverty of the city's masses, for the Rende area emigrants the most lasting impression was that they were being taken advantage of. *Paesani* agreed with the derisive characterization of Naples given it by an American journalist as a "city of thieves." "That's how they live there," said one emigrant, by "swindling."[35]

For some *peasani* their first experience with Neapolitan petty crime occurred even before they stepped out of the train station: luggage or trunks had "disappeared." Greenhorns were warned by veterans to be wary of porters volunteering help with baggage. For others, their initiation to city deceptions came when they were beset by runners for the numerous *pensioni* and hotels crowding the area adjacent to the Station. As one man recalled, "Those from Calabria, they all went to Naples .... When you arrived at Naples, you go to the – what you call it? – hotel. Everybody, you know, these people, they tell you, 'Go to this hotel,' 'Go Hotel so-and-so!,' 'Hotel so-and-so!'"[36] While some emigrants succumbed to the wiles of the runners and ended up being over-charged, most followed the advice of veterans and sought out tested lodging-houses, those that had been recommended as being "the cheapest place possible."

Though emigrants knew from others' experiences that they "had to watch out," some were unable to escape the many pitfalls awaiting them. One *paesano* told of how a group of hucksters had been able to prey upon a party of seven men who emigrated at the turn of the century, notwithstanding the fact that they were accompanied by a veteran:

> They were people raised in the country. They had never seen anything. Imagine, not reading, nothing .... It was in 1901. Well, there was one man by the name of Giuseppe that had been a short time in Argentina, and he thought he knew how to do more than the others because he knew how to sign his name, and the others were illiterate. Well, in Naples he played the "master of ceremonies" since he said he knew more than the others.
>
> "Well," he said, "let's go visit the Galleria di Umberto Primo," at Naples. You know the Neapolitans, they've always been swindlers. Well, they (a Neapolitan gang) saw these people at the entrance there and a man approached them and said, "So, you've entered in here. You've got to pay!"
>
> "But they say there's no charge."

"No, no, you pay! Who told you there was no charge? Ten lire. Ten lire or you can't leave from here!"

Poor men. They looked at each other. There were seven of them. The swindlers made seventy lire. In 1901, with seventy lire, by God, you could have bought a *tomolata* of land! Instead they [the gang] fooled them. It wasn't true. You didn't have to pay anything. They didn't know it. This shows you the poor people – they were men who had never travelled, they had never seen anything.[37]

Though the line here between outright extortion by a street gang and being naively hoodwinked is vague (probably the reality lay in a combination of the two), it is clear that the time spent in Naples, even innocuous sightseeing, was full of hazards from which not even the presence of a veteran could guarantee protection.

After the *paesano* had survived the trials of keeping track of his baggage, finding a hotel, and evading the many hustlers milling about the Neapolitan streets, he had to go through the formal procedures necessary for embarkation. This involved essentially five steps, which (except for vaccination) took place within the Capitaneria, or harbour compound, encompassing the customs house, fumigation station, medical centre, police station, and similar offices. The first step involved having hold baggage inspected by American consular agents and Italian health authorities, after which it was received and receipted for by the steamship company's agents.[38] Next, emigrants and their portable luggage were piled into small steamers which took them to the fumigating station, half a mile across the harbour, on the breakwater. Here again both the Italian and American governments were represented in the disinfection of effects, both issuing certificates attesting to their clearance. Third, just outside the compound, emigrants proceeded to be vaccinated for smallpox. They then entered the final phase of the process held within the customs house (the main building of the Capitaneria). Here the emigrants underwent a strict medical examination carried out by American and Italian doctors. This procedure and the suspense surrounding it was described by Brandenburg, who in 1904 accompanied a group of emigrants on its way to America as part of an investigation of the immigration question: "We were examined; our eyelids were turned up for trachoma; our heads rubbed over for favus; any defective-looking parts of the body touched for hidden disease; and every now and then a man, woman or child would be told to stand aside for further examination, and a wail would go up from the group to which that one belonged. It was as if a touch of death had come among them."[39]

For the great majority, however, no complications arose and they could proceed to the final passport check before boarding ship. One *paesano* spoke of the inspection at Naples and this last procedure before setting sail: "You have to wait one, two days sometimes in Naples, you know, before the ship go. Over there you got what you call the *visita* (medical and customs examination) by the *consolati* [consular officers] .... You know, you need the *visita* for emigration .... Then they check if you got the right papers .... They say 'Line up! Line up!' and you go in the office and they search the papers to see if you're all right or not all right."[40]

Along all five steps, hustlers and sometimes corrupt officials were available who promised to "fix" matters for a fee. Gangs worked the fumigation station selling false certificates to those who wanted to escape the procedure; others sold documents which would allegedly exempt emigrants from the dreaded smallpox vaccination, or promise treatment for blinding trachoma; and false passports could be bought for the asking.[41] While such avenues for petty fraud were available, few *paesani* made use of them, for the peasant emigrant's fear of "getting into trouble" and being barred from America ensured that proper procedures were followed. Usually it was only the desperate emigrant who was diseased or escaping conscription who sought the services of hustlers.[42]

The *paesani*'s experience in Naples had repercussions that influenced later stages of the migration process. First of all, their experience in Naples helped to prepare them for the new world city that lay just weeks away. Coming from a setting in which the population of the provincial capital numbered about 24,000 in 1911 to Naples, a city of over 600,000, the Rende area emigrants had to overcome their initial disorientation as they endeavoured to adapt to new standards of size, space, and pace of life. Being forced to deal with "practical" affairs such as finding lodging, eating at a restaurant, or dealing directly with strangers – which were all matters that loomed large in the minds of peasant emigrants – foreshadowed similar situations in New York, Chicago, and Toronto, and contributed to the *paesani*'s ability to cope with these.

Secondly, the *paesani*'s exposure to Neapolitan swindlers taught them to beware of similar types that awaited them as they disembarked at New York or got off the train at Chicago or other cities. Whether or not the new world city had quite the proliferation of hucksters and petty criminals relying on the emigrant's naïveté that Naples did, people were more successful in keeping their pockets from being emptied in America. Further, the exposure to Naples' underside reinforced the *paesani*'s tendency to distrust outsiders and to rely on themselves. If one could be swindled by men who spoke one's own language (albeit a different dialect), would the risk of being cheated by those who spoke a language altogether different not be greater? Hence, in the new world emigrants were reluctant to separate from their *paesani*.[43]

Thirdly, while emigrants were anxious about the officials at Naples, it was the inspection at Ellis Island that worried them most. Inasmuch as the embarkation procedure involving health and passport checks and the necessity of confronting bureaucrats acted as a prelude to the new world inspection – and softened the anxiety surrounding it – this, too, stood the *paesani* in good stead.

THE VOYAGE

In the early part of the century, ships plying the Atlantic between Naples and New York ranged from the 30,000-ton vessels of Cunard and Hamburg-America lines which were built after 1900 with comfortable third-class accommodation and total passenger capacity of over 2,500, to the small ships of Lloyd Sabaudo and Adria dating back to the 1880s with tonnages of 5,000 to 10,000 and a total passenger capacity of some 1,500, mostly steerage.[44] *Paesani* made the crossing in ships ranging from what the Commissariato di Emigrazione classified as the "superior class" *Giulio Cesare* of the Navigazione Generale Italiana, to the third category *Belvedere* of the Cosulich line.[45]

Conditions on the voyage, then, varied greatly, though with their increased exposure to ocean travel, emigrants from the Rende area became aware of the reputation of individual ships and were able to plan their choices more knowledgeably. Though the cost of the voyage varied with the quality of the ship, the season of travel, the amount of baggage and the type of booking, generally the emigrants' passage cost around $40 to $50. The voyage usually took about two weeks, and the great majority of *paesani* emigrated in steerage.[46]

Oral testimony regarding "old type" steerage corresponded closely to the written reports of American observers who made the journey and viewed this class of travel as crowded, unsanitary and an affront to both body and spirit. The stench of foul air, the crowded quarters and the constant wail of women and children were conditions that former peasants and middle-class humanitarians alike found oppressive.[47]

One *paesano* who emigrated from Naples in 1904 and then again in 1913 provided valuable testimony contrasting his first voyage on a White Star ship of 1880s vintage with his second on a much improved vessel of the same line. Steerage conditions on the 1904 voyage were characterized as "dirty like a pig-pen." Almost one thousand passengers were thrown together below the main deck with little light or ventilation and scant provision for personal hygiene. Washrooms were located above deck and water for personal use or washing utensils was scarce. Within the galley, passengers were allocated to compartments, each consisting of about six portable double-tiered bunks arranged in blocks. Beds were constructed of iron framework, and burlap-covered bags of straw or grass served as a mattress. There were no pillows or sheets; only one blanket was allocated per emigrant. As the old-timer recalled: "Say this is the room. You have beds like one on top of the

Postcard view of town of Rende from Via Giudeca, 1917.

Street scene in Rende, peasant woman carrying firewood.

Returned *americano* and wife, Rende, ca. 1919.

Typical work party of *familiari* during grain harvest, Rende.

Rende family in front of fig-drying shed during winter, 1940s.

Saw mill in Rende area: an example of rural industry.

Home built by *americano*, Rende, early twentieth century (now abandoned).

Italian railroad construction workers, early twentieth century. *Courtesy:* University of Illinois at Chicago, The Library Manuscript Collection (Italians in Chicago Project).

Young Italians in bar, early twentieth century. *Courtesy:* University of Illinois at Chicago, The Library Manuscript Collection (Italians in Chicago Project).

Above: Storino and Furgiuele brothers: settlers and sojourners, Chicago, post-World War One.

Left: Re-united Rende area family, Chicago, pre-World War One.

Above: Rende area immigrants gardening, southwestern Wisconsin, 1930s.

Left: Rende area immigrants, Miller Street, Near West Side, Chicago, 1930s.

Paesani wedding party, southwestern Wisconsin, 1911.

Paesani funeral at Our Lady of Pompei Church, Near West Side, Chicago, 1924.

Edward Street in St. John's Ward, Toronto, 1918, *Courtesy:* National Archives of Canada.

Italian road workers, Yonge Street and St. Clair Avenue, Toronto, 1916. *Courtesy:* Multicultural History Society of Ontario.

Advertisement in the 1935 Italian city directory for Francesco Tomaiuolo's steamship agency, private bank and general store. The establishment was located in the heart of the College Street Little Italy.

Passport photo of Rende sojourner, 1920s.

Postwar Rende labourers sponsored by Toronto relatives laying telephone cable under Don River, Toronto.

Postwar Rende *familiari* in Brockton district, Toronto.

other. You sleep over here, another up there, another over there. You put some bag, bag like a sack, over the frame. [You] sleep with one blanket, no sheets .... And you slept like that."

Men and women occupied opposite ends of the galley: "The women were all in one place, the men in another ... the people that had family – a daughter, wife – we were separated. You know, in the sleep-time the women got to sleep separate. Then at lunch-time, in the daytime, stay all together. Even if you have a wife, the wife has to sleep over there, and you, you sleep in another place."[48]

For their meals, emigrants received a fork, spoon, cup, and dish. Passengers were instructed to arrange themselves into groups of six with a head man who would be issued a two-gallon pan and a gallon bucket with which to fetch the ration for his group. For the *paesani*, these groups were usually composed of the small group that had started from the Rende area. At meal time food was served out by stewards from huge tanks and announced by the ringing of a bell:

> Oh, don't mention the food. Always pasta: plain pasta, pasta in soup. Sometimes they cooked a chicken – roast chicken – but first, they'd make soup of it. At lunch time, you know, somebody come with the bell. "Ding! Ding!" You line up and go to the kitchen.
>
> The boat company, they gave us something like a tin dish with a handle. Every six men get this tin dish – not clay – a tin dish. And one man go get the soup. And you got a little spoon and a cup .... Every bunch, about six people, you divide it every six people, you see .... And after, yourself, you got to wash the dishes.[49]

Dinners consisted of pasta, soup, bread, vegetables, and the occasional tough meat, and breakfast was coffee and sometimes hard biscuits. Though passengers with money could surreptitiously buy extra and more varied food from the cooks and stewards, it was more common for *paesani*, having been forewarned of what to expect, to have brought their own preserved meats, cheese, and fruit.

In contrast to the experience depicting conditions on the old type of steerage, the same informant spoke enthusiastically about his second voyage in 1913. Here he described what had emerged as standard third-class fare. The second vessel, which also accommodated about one thousand common passengers, was described as modern, clean, and comfortable. It had lavatories within close range, enclosed berths affording privacy, and comfortable beds. The cabins had enough space for baggage, hooks for clothing, were supplied with towels, and had an electric alarm nearby to summon stewards if needed. The relative privacy allowed people to change clothing before retiring. Families could now be kept together rather than segregated.

The eating arrangements were also greatly improved. The food was more plentiful, varied, and served in dining rooms, and utensils were now washed by stewards: "Oh yeah, after the ship was better. You could go to eat at the table. You ate a few at a time. At lunch time, you know, you found the table ready. They change the food once in a while. Once rice, another time *pastasciutta* [with sauce], pasta in soup .... It was pretty good."[50]

A few emigrants experienced sea-sickness on the voyage. For them, the aid they received from *paesani* was vital, as the following indicates:

> It took seventeen days to get here from Naples. Like Cristoforo Colombo. That's a long way. I was almost dead when I got here. I got sea-sick. I only went to the table one or two times. I couldn't eat or I got worse. I had to stay in bed .... I had a friend, a *paesano*, that used to bring me an apple or orange a day, and a little dry bread. That's all. The friend of mine was from the "Stazione di Rende." He was a really nice guy. Every half hour he used to come over and check on me. He was the guy who saved me. I was dead if it wasn't for him.[51]

Throughout the voyage, *paesani* groups under a veteran were schooled on what to say at Ellis Island, what to expect of the job market, and even some broken English. As the ship approached shore, emigrants became increasingly anxious about the imminent inspection by American authorities, especially the critical questions they would be asked by the contract labour inspector.[52] Veterans urged emigrants to contravene this confounding law, which, against all logic, made it a crime to be assured of a job. As Brandenburg noted, peasant emigrants expressed incredulity that this would be so, since obviously, having a job waiting, they would be seen to be self-sustaining and responsible.[53]

Around Nantucket, preparations for landing were set in motion. On the voyage the passengers' health had been regularly monitored and now a final check was conducted by the ship's doctors. The crew set about scrubbing the deck, washrooms, and galley in readiness for the health inspection upon landing. Nearing New York, great excitement was felt among the passengers as they jostled to get the best view of the skyline and wash up for the landing. Men shaved and put on their suits; women put on their finery and dressed up their children. Soon after such preparations, *paesani* would make their first contact with American officials in the new world.

ARRIVAL IN THE NEW WORLD

As the emigrant ship entered the harbour entrance between Brooklyn and Staten Island, steerage passengers were assembled by the crew for quarantine inspection. Medical personnel from the Public Health Service boarded the vessel and checked for the sick. Those with non-contagious illnesses were sent to a hospital on Ellis Island, and those with contagious ones were taken aboard the quarantine boat to hospital on Hoffman Island or to isolation at the lazar-house on nearby Swinburn Island.[54] At the end of convalesce, the emigrant would either be free to undergo the regular inspection or be deported. Emigrants from the Rende area recalled the quarantine check and reported that not a few passengers were removed at this juncture.

Once quarantine approval had been given, the ship proceeded into the harbour and docked at one of a row of piers along the Hudson River. At dockside, steerage passengers then boarded a ferryboat for Ellis Island where they would undergo medical examination and be asked the list of critical questions they had rehearsed.

At the island they were met by an interpreter who helped them along to the red brick building where they were ushered into one of a dozen rows. There they underwent their first inspection as a doctor observed them as they paused briefly and filed by. The doctor looked for any obvious signs of disease or defects, such as rashes or lameness, and any who should be given a more detailed examination.[55] An informant recalled a *paesano* who had been singled out and deported at this stage, paraphrasing his bitterness: "'But what turds!' Michele would say. 'Why didn't you [officials] turn me back at Naples? At Naples you examined me too! No, at New York a higher *visita* deported me.' You see, the official said he was too short and had no business going to America ... he was like a dwarf."[56]

For the great majority of *paesani* without obvious defects, following the crowd of newcomers forward led them to more medical checks, where they were examined for contagious diseases such as tuberculosis, leprosy, trachoma, or favus. More rejections occurred: "Filettu didn't have any hair on his head. He had a disease [favus] when he was a young man. They [inspectors] noticed this. They said, 'You have a sickness, a bald head,' and deported him .... It's like scabies. It attacks the roots of hair, right inside, and then leaves like a crust. It's here too. I've seen it .... Oh, how the doctors can recognize it right away!"[57]

When the emigrants were through with their medical checks,[58] they proceeded to the gate of the immigration inspector, where they were asked a series of questions. Though these were seemingly simple, there were twenty-nine of them and many were asked to reveal inconsistencies in the emigrants' responses and to screen those contravening the 1885 contract labour law. The questions were in quick succession, asked beginning: "What work do you do?" "Do you have a job waiting for you?" "Who paid for your passage here?" "Is anyone meeting you?" "Where are you going?" "Can you read and write?" "Have you ever been in prison?" "How much money do you have?" "Show it to me now." "Where did you get it?"[59] A *paesano* referred to this: "It wasn't one inspection you had to pass at Naples. You had to pass another one in New York, at the *batteria* as they called it .... This was a more important *visita*. After you arrived there you had to tell them what you were going to do, your name, the address you were going to, lots of things like that .... This shows you that to go to America it was pretty complicated."[60]

While medical inspections were a source of concern, for peasant emigrants ill versed in the demeanour of bureaucracy, largely illiterate, and usually having some promise of work, the interview at the gate posed the greater threat. Though the overall proportion of deportations among immigrants was rarely more than a few per cent and though there is no reason to believe that those from Cosenza had a higher rate of rejection than average, the occasional cases that were rejected evoked the ire of *paesani:* "Over there, how many people they turned back from New York itself! Poor people. People dying of hunger. They didn't have any money, then back they had to go .... They turned you back without making you pay; at the expense of the [steamship] company. But what you already paid, you lost."[61]

After undergoing questioning by the immigration inspector, emigrants proceeded to claim their baggage, visit the post office, exchange money, and queue in the railroad room where tickets to every part of the country were sold by a dozen agents. A few took the ferry to New York where they would look up *paesani* and perhaps lodge briefly before setting off for other destinations. Most Rende area emigrants, however, took the ferry to the railroad terminal on the Jersey shore to board a train for Chicago.

CHAPTER 4

The Sojourn Phase of Migration

The Sojourn Nature of Migration

THE CHICAGO *PADRONI:*

> In those days – especially some of those guys – what they need
> to do was come over here, work in the summer and go back in
> the winter. Some guys did that every year, quite a few did it. One
> guy came across eleven times. It's true. He worked here in Toronto
> on construction. Before World War I. He came over here, worked
> in the summer, then in the wintertime, if he had stayed over here,
> there was no unemployment insurance at that time, and he had
> nothing to do. So he goes home, maybe buy a piece of land, and
> work; and then come back over here in the springtime. Eleven
> times.[1]

This early villager's contact with the new world was both atypical and
eminently typical.[2] The majority of emigrants from the Rende area
did not make annual seasonal voyages back and forth across the Atlantic; they were more likely to live out the winter in a North American
city. Nor did many embark upon almost a dozen migrations; four
were about average. Nor did most head for Toronto; the majority
were destined for Chicago. In one significant respect, however, the
paesano epitomizes the villagers' experience: he was a sojourner. As
Canada's Superintendent of Immigration observed coolly in 1910:
"They [Italians] are usually looking for work as railway navvies and
are to a great extent birds of passage and have no desire to make
Canada their permanent home."[3]

My intention here is to examine this sojourn experience of *paesani*
both because of its pervasiveness and because it formed the basis of

later settlement. Essentially, what will be examined is the world of work which, after all, was what brought the emigrant across the Atlantic in the first place. In particular, the interrelated issues of the *paesani*'s relationship with *padroni*, their experience on the railroads, and their concomitant camp life will be explored. Boarding was also an important part of the sojourner's life, and that will be examined in the next chapter.

The change from being a sojourner to being an immigrant was not primarily determined by any objectively defined historical event as, for example, the First World War changed a mass of men overnight from civilians to soldiers. Rather, the sojourn-to-immigrant transition was an imperceptible process; foremost, it was an individual process of change of consciousness. When it occurred depended essentially on personal factors: when one first emigrated, one's level of success (in the old world as well as the new), one's stage in the life cycle, and the like. Nonetheless, for *paesani* it was during the decade of mass emigration prior to the First World War that the sojourn experience was most widespread.

In the early part of the century, Chicago was indisputably the mecca for Rende area emigrants. Other destinations, such as New York, Pittsburgh, Buffalo, Denver, and Toronto also existed. But except for New York, the prime port of debarkation, these played a relatively minor role and only became emigration destinations as men followed the construction or maintenance of transportation systems, utilities, and other public projects throughout North America. After the American restrictionist legislation of 1921, Toronto was to emerge as the most significant of these lesser centres, and its infusion of *paesani* in the twenties came to embody the characteristics of modern-day "immigration." This immigrant phase will be examined in the last part of the study, but, in anticipation of this, the Canadian experience, where applicable, will be incorporated in the present discussion.

The *paesani* who were drawn to Chicago were part of a general wave of Southerners who converged on the city after 1880 and within this group immigrants from Cosenza province formed a major part.[4] It is not surprising that Chicago was a magnet for Southerners, as it was for a great many of immigrants, or for that matter for many native-born from the farms and small towns of rural America. By 1880 Chicago, barely fifty years old and with a population of over half a million, had already emerged as the greatest inland city in the United States. It was the nation's major grain, lumber, and meat-packing centre, the metropolis of a vast and rich hinterland. The founding in Chicago of firms such as McCormick Farm machinery works and the Pullman Car Company, as well as several large retail mail-order companies such as Montgomery Ward, established the city as a manufacturing and commercial giant second only to New York. Textiles, brewing, and distilling were also industries of major importance. By 1910, thanks to its proximity to Mesabi iron ore and nearby plentiful coal, Chicago became the nation's leading steel-maker. And it surpassed New York as America's leading printing and publishing centre.[5]

Within all this activity, of course, the construction industry boomed. Factories, houses, streets, sewers, trolley lines and similar necessities all had to be built by human brawn, as swamp and prairie gave way to industry and urbanism. As late as 1892, for example, of 2,900 miles of city streets, only 900 were paved and almost all the sidewalks were still made of wood. The city set itself the task of paving its sidewalks and of constructing an impressive system of urban transportation based around its trolley lines and elevated railways. By the First World War the surface lines alone took up one thousand miles of track and there were over fifty miles of tunnels under downtown streets. Obviously the potential for employment was great.[6] As one scholar has put it: "The legend grew that if a man couldn't 'make it' in Chicago, he couldn't make it anywhere."[7]

But even more important for the early sojourners than the work to be found in Chicago was the fact that, being strategically located between the Great Lakes and the Mississippi River valley at the tip of Lake Michigan, Chicago was the nation's transportation hub. Beginning at mid-century, a long series of railway ventures – the Chicago and North Western, the Chicago, Rock Island and Pacific, the Chicago, Burlington and Quincy, and the like – linked the city to its hinterland, so that by 1880 fifteen thousand miles of railroad connected it to the Upper Mississippi valley and northwest regions alone. Chicago was also connected to both coasts, making it the hub of the great transcontinentals.[8]

Just as the city had emerged as the major distribution centre of natural resources and manufactures, so it would also become the major clearing house for common labourers bound for the continent's numerous infrastructure projects. And the human agent in this distribution task was the *padrone:*

> Bosses directed Italian immigrant labourers to all parts of the United States and even into Canada to build railroads and work at other construction jobs. Chicago became an important padrone stronghold, partly because of the city's position as a railroad centre and partly because of its geographical location. Railroad and other construction jobs tended to be seasonal, and Chicago served as a clearing house for seasonal workers of the entire country as well as the Middle West.[9]

While *padroni* directed migrants to construction jobs across the continent, testimony from Rende area immigrants revealed that for them the matter of destination was quite subtle. For the majority, the choice of Chicago was made neither because of the city's vibrant economy nor because the migrant had potentially helpful kin there: the choice was primarily determined by the presence in Chicago of *paesani* go-betweens servicing the Rende area who could assure a man of a job. It is relevant here to consider briefly the MacDonalds' concept of chain migration, or movement "by means of primary social relationship with previous migrants." What arose among *paesani* prior to the war was similar to what the MacDonalds postulated as the earliest type of chain formation: the migration of young male workers through *padroni*.[10]

The men who emerged as *padroni* were part of the early Rende area migration that made its way to the United States in the late nineteenth century. Establishing themselves as informal intermediaries helping others to find employment, it was through these men that Chicago had emerged by 1890 as the major destination of *paesani* bound for North America.

At the turn of the century there were at least three important Rende area *padroni* operating out of Chicago. Luigi Spizzirri from San Vincenzo la Costa, Francesco Principe from Montalto, and Giuliano Sicilia from Marano Principato were all well known as men of considerable power who could supply *paesani* with work, who had influential connections, who "could get things done."[11] These *padroni* came from economically hard-pressed villages with an early tradition of emigration. Yet in the era of mass emigration, they acted not only as intermediaries for sojourners from their own *comuni*, but for the Rende area as a whole. The socio-economic linkages that bound the Rende area into a cohesive unit – intermarriage and kinship, common *feste* and markets – were used by villagers to make contact with the *padroni*. The names and deeds of the Chicago *padroni* were widely known and were part of the day-to-day communication between *paesani*.

In Toronto the situation was quite different. There, no *paesani* emerged as professional labour agents whose reputations were known and trusted within the Rende area. As a consequence, the *padroni* who were consulted were only local in their job placements. As a small centre, Toronto was simply not strategic enough to develop into a major clearing house as did Chicago, with full-time professional *padroni* concentrating on servicing Rende area clients. Even the villagers who worked on Ontario railways often remained in the orbit of *padroni* south of the border. These labourers would come up from the United States and upon completing their sojourn would usually return south, sometimes using Toronto as a winter stay, to do business with the same go-betweens. There, they would seek other jobs or buy passage tickets back to the village.[12]

In Chicago the Rende area *padroni* who ran their businesses on the basis of *paesano* networks and reputation were essentially middling brokers with links to North American employers (mainly railroads), and larger *padroni* who acted as major suppliers to capitalists. For *paesani,* the "padrone" was the broker with whom they had immediate contact, not the large-scale agent who remained behind the scenes. Hence, although for the Chicago *paesani* the *padrone* system essentially functioned within the parameters of a Rende area social space, from the vantage point of the *padroni* themselves, their services linked up to regional and national systems of labour delivery.

Traditionally the *padrone* has been viewed as a dishonest compatriot who imported workers, sold their labour, and otherwise acted to exploit the ignorance of newcomers.[13] This view, however, had little relevance to the experience of the Rende area immigrants. For them, *padroni* were part of the social landscape of the immigrant community; they were not, as had been the case with their *gran signori,* singled out as exploiters. Often the term was simply used to refer to the status of a proprietor: of a business, lodging house, or some other establishment.

Rende area go-betweens were frequently referred to by the new world neologism, "bossi." This term was primarily used in the context of work to denote a man who had the power to deliver jobs or to hire. Hence, a railroad gang foreman or a factory supervisor could be a *bosso.* And further, the unknown factory owners or the impersonal company itself could also be referred to as *bossi.* That villagers often employed the English derivative "bosso" rather than *padrone* in their speech is instructive. For while native North Americans spoke of the foreign nature of the labour agent's practice, the migrants themselves modified an English word to express what they perceived as a primarily new world experience.[14]

While migrants went to see the Rende area *padroni* primarily to find work, the *padroni* had roles aside from this, such as travel agents, contractors and lodging-house owners. For the sojourner this often involved services that linked him to the village of which psychically he was still part: the writing of letters, the forwarding of money, the supplying of steamship tickets. Increasingly, however, as immigration unfolded, other men who were spoken of mainly as saloon-owners, grocers, public employees, and the like also came to supply many of the services of the original *padroni.* This did not mean a diminution in the power and influence of the older *bossi,* for with a growing *paesano* base in Chicago, the old timers increasingly took on the role of political power-brokers.[15]

The widespread anxiety surrounding migration also influenced the sojourn experience. The very way in which the *paesani* thought of themselves as sojourners had a subjective telescoping effect on geography, softening the unsettling impact of great distances and unfamiliar surroundings. More consciously, the use of *padroni* who were knowledgeable of the North American environment and would assure the migrant in the dialect and familiar ways of the commune that his central purposes would be fulfilled was a means by which the insecurity of the peasant migrant could be allayed.[16]

To a large extent, the part played by *padroni* was the North American counterpart of the intermediary role of *agenti* across the Atlantic. While labour agents and similar go-betweens were of peasant background and lacked the *civiltà* of the old world lawyer, teacher, or functionary, they likewise acted as intermediaries, smoothing the jagged edges between largely illiterate peasant communes and the wider industrial world.

FACTORS PROMOTING MIGRANT INFRASTRUCTURE WORK

For *paesani,* migration was a temporary affair from which they hoped to earn as much cash as possible as quickly as possible. This placed a number of well-defined parameters on the type of employment towards which an emigrant would gravitate. The work had to be immediately available and easily acquired, it must pay relatively well, it must not require any facility in English or degree of literacy or any particular skill or long-term commitment, and it was essential that it could be engaged in by groups of *paesani* for reasons of security, emotional support, and economy. Work on an expanding North American infrastructure fitted these criteria.

Construction work, while labour-intensive, was also seasonal, of short duration, and highly sensitive to economic fluctuations. Hence, it needed large pools of highly mobile, unskilled labourers. It required a flexible system of employment that could easily assemble and disband large groups of labourers in keeping with the sector's variable demands.[17]

Bringing the concerns of the peasant migrant and the needs of North American employers together was the labour agent, who performed two valuable tasks. First, since he was often a *paesano,* the *padrone* was able to employ informal communication links through kin and friendship networks to bring word of job openings quickly to ready workers, thus assuring employers of their supply of men when they needed it. Secondly, the *padrone,* in making possible the recruitment of kin and *paesano* groups, which facilitated mutual support and camaraderie, assured a relatively high degree of morale and efficiency on the work site for the employer.[18]

Further, the socio-economic background of *paesani* inclined them toward construction work. Pick and shovel work on railroads, sewers, gas-lines and such all had similarities with the peasants' reliance on hoe-work in the intensive farming of the Rende area. As one man said: "The Polish went to the factories, the Russians went to the factories, but not Italians.... They liked to go work outside.... Oh, I was good with a shovel. The work came easy to me. It didn't bother me."[19]

Similarly, the practice of forming agricultural work parties of kin and *paesani* at harvest and other labour-intensive times, and the formation of agricultural labour gangs which migrated within Cosenza and beyond, were both useful social models for the railroad and other construction work *paesani* undertook in North America. The fact that many Rende area peasants had experienced part-time employment on local roads, public works, and railroads provided even more direct job exposure which prepared them for, and channelled them toward, similar work in the new world.

While infrastructure work fitted in well with the *paesani*'s intent to remain only temporarily in the new world, there also existed important local values which contributed to the sojourning phase. These values helped justify their years away from home, and contributed to the perception of sojourning as socially admirable. One such value was what Morel has termed the "peasant ideology of hard work [which] is based on the principle that the individual can only be judged by the work he performs, by his personal efforts to overcome every obstacle."[20]

Time and again Rende area immigrants spoke of hard work as virtuous. It was also a reflection of physical prowess, and therefore manliness. Hence, as a barometer of both a man's moral and physical state, it was a major criterion for assigning social standing among *paesani* and an important ingredient in gaining respect. Within the framework of a culture of emigration, a stint in the new world and its concrete rewards – ultimately land and homes – were signs not only of success and respect, but also of one's capacity for hard work. One man described an early emigrant who was highly esteemed:

> In his youth, Francesco was strong as an ox. He was respected, and generous to his neighbours. He went to Chicago to work on the track before the War, then bought one of the best fields in Rende with a stream going through it. He worked hard and made it fruitful.... When he used to cut his wheat with a scythe he did it so fast and neat that people far off could hear it whisk through the air as it came down on the wheat.... No one in Rende could match his work.[21]

Related to, and a justification of, hard work was the value, or perhaps more appropriately, the "cult," of sacrifice. The married male, by virtue of his role as the family's head and provider, was expected to sacrifice personal ambitions and comforts for the benefit of his family. Likewise, the other family members, especially male sons, were expected to sacrifice individual inclinations for the status and wealth of the whole family. It was the willingness to sacrifice for the benefit of others that transformed the deprivations of migrant life into virtues. Along with low levels of living, this peasant cult allowed the sojourner to live with the minimum of comforts in the new world in order to maximize savings and expedite his return home.[22]

It was within this spirit of hard work and sacrifice, then, that one Montalto immigrant who eventually settled in Toronto referred to his early years in North America: "You can say this for sure, America was a land of *sacrificio*. You had to work hard in those days. You don't make money without working. You need to work, like I did and hundreds and hundreds of Italians. I was alone for many years. I cooked and washed for myself, too. Because at that time I didn't have my wife. She was back home.... You had to work, it was a *sacrificio*."[23]

Another value that favoured sojourning was that of female seclusion, and the concomitant chastity of women. If a husband provided for his wife and children through hard work, a wife reciprocated by remaining faithful. With *paesani* remaining away from homes, wives, and daughters for years at a time, the peasant restrictions on female sexuality assured them that their absence from home would not lead to dishonour. It assured them that their families would remain intact, for, indeed, the sojourn itself would have little meaning without the assumption that there would be an honourable family to return to. And, since hard work and virility were associated with each other, to the extent that the decision to emigrate implied the capacity for the former, the sojourn experience was a means of bolstering one's sexual honour, not a threat to it. It was the knowledge that the sexual honour of their womenfolk would be protected that made sojourning psychologically possible for the male.[24]

On the part of the male, the traditional association of sexual prowess (and aggressiveness) with maleness gave tacit approval to sexual exploits, should he be so inclined.[25] This too softened the sojourner's separation, for it meant he could take advantage of the availability of prostitutes or enter into liaisons with other women without losing his honour or membership in the community of *paesani*. Should he take up permanently with another woman and compromise his responsibility to his family, however, he would meet with censure.

The Railroad Experience

TRACK WORK AND CAMP LIFE

While sojourners took on jobs that varied considerably, it was railroad work that represented their experience *par excellence*. As Foerster wrote in 1919:

> What is characteristic in the labour of Italian men in North
> America is nowhere so apparent as on the railways. Both relatively
> and absolutely, the South Italians, as construction and repair

workmen, have there achieved a foremost position.... The circum-scribed studies of the Immigration Commission of 1907 found the Italians to be 15 per cent of the workmen examined in steam railroad transportation and 44 per cent of persons engaged in construction work.... The Italians have succeeded the Irish as the predominant unskilled railway labourers of the country.[26]

And Egisto Rossi, a commissioner of the Italian emigration service, reported in 1902 much the same thing about Canada:

I say without hesitation that generally the conditions which make them [Italians] manual labourers in Canada, are not notably different from those that make them so in the United States. These so-called pick and shovel men...are made the most use of for railway work, mining, sewer work, and for other building ventures.... In Canada the major part of these workers are absorbed by two principal railroad companies, that is, the Canadian Pacific...and the Grand Trunk.[27]

From the North American, as well as the European, end of the migration process, conditions were conducive to railroad employment. Though the peak in new railroad mileage was reached in the 1890s, capital continued to be invested to improve the national network.

The wave of new line construction was followed by progressive improvement of existing railroads, especially in the United States where many of the original roads were lightly built. A tremendous effort was put into extensions and betterments, sometimes to accommodate the growing traffic, sometimes to reap the benefits of advancing technology. Over widening stretches of the railroad system single track roads were converted to double track, sidings added, grades reduced, curves eliminated, automatic signals installed, iron rails replaced by steel rails, light rails by heavy rails, wooden bridges by bridges of steel or concrete, and a hundred other improvements in road and equipment made.[28]

All this activity meant that, in fact, the high point in railroad expend-itures occurred in the first decade of the twentieth century.[29] The years of heaviest railroad investment coincided with the era of mass emigration from the Rende area and the Italian South generally. It is understandable, then, that prior to the war, almost all *paesani* at one time or another were engaged in some aspect of railroad work. "They'd all been to Chicago...they all work on the track," as one *paesano* put it.[30] To cite but a few examples, one emigrant from Marano Marches-ato who made many voyages over a period of seventeen years worked on railroad projects throughout the Midwest; another from Rende made several short sojourns of one of two years working widely on railroads from the east coast to the Mississippi; a third from the same *comune* who first emigrated around 1885 went farther west yet, being sent from Chicago to a road in Colorado; a fourth from Montalto worked in the eastern states and then followed the demand across the border into Canada; a fifth who emigrated in 1910 and worked locally in the Chicago area was able to capitalize on his experience as a *fattore* on one of the Rende area estates, and, breaking from the ranks, emerged as a foreman of a gang of *paesani* and other Southerners.[31]

The majority of *paesani* worked on the repair or improvement of track rather than the construction of new roads. Such work often involved short-term jobs which meant a high degree of transiency and the turnover was high. One *paesano,* for example, who emigrated around 1904, within four years had worked for almost a dozen lines, including the Pennsylvania, Chicago and North Western, Wabash, Indiana Harbour, Baltimore and Ohio, Nickel Plate, Pere Marquette, Chicago and Western Indiana, Chicago and Milwaukee, and the Chicago Great Western.[32]

For men who worked on the track a major component of their sojourn was life in the camp. While migrants used labour brokers in Chicago to find employment, once they arrived at the work site they often came into contact with a different type of *padrone,* the commissary. One of the better descriptions of the commissary's role was given by Roberts in 1913:

> He is the intermediary between the contractor and the men, he is responsible for the men being there, and it is he who keeps up the supply of labourers. His services are compensated by monopolistic concessions. He collects the rent for the bunks, he has full control of the supplies of food and luxuries, nothing can come into the camp save through him, he knows the men and can converse with them, his store is the rendezvous for the men in the camp, and, there, all matters of importance are discussed and settled.[33]

In comparison to this rather objective description, the commissary, as an extension of an ubiquitous "padrone system," was generally described in the same Manichean manner as the labour agent. The potential for exploitation by the camp boss was seen to rest on his control of accommodation and food. Many observers pictured the accommodation, in box-cars, as filthy, stifling and with scant protection against the elements. The *padrone* was also accused of unfairly profiting from the rental of the cars which the company often supplied free to him.[34]

The characteristic response of *paesani* to camp life was to accept conditions in a spirit of "roughing it," a note echoed by the president of the Canadian Pacific Railway when he wrote, "men who seek employment on railway construction are, as a rule, a class accustomed to roughing it. They know when they go to the work that they must put up with the most primitive kind of camp accommodation."[35] Living out of box-cars for a season or so was not all that different from life in the bachelor flats of Chicago's Near West Side or Toronto's immigrant shacks in the Ward.

Moreover, the discrepancy between being housed in railroad cars and their overcrowded peasant homes at the turn of the century was not so great as to discourage work on the track, or for shelter to emerge as a major complaint.

The converted box-cars held about a dozen men, often divided into two or more smaller groups of *paesani*. The cars contained a small coal stove around which makeshift, wooden bunk beds were placed. One former track worker recollected:

> North Western sent me out. But they only sent you out if you wanted to go. During the summer they formed these "gangs," you know, so I went to Michigan....
> The work was the same [as in Chicago] except for the fact that there they had a "room" to live in. I slept in the box cars. But that was more economical....
> Usually there was a cot where I slept and a stove to cook on. The company, you know, the railway, provided these things.... It wasn't great, but we were young.[36]

Track work and camp life were viewed by *paesani* as freely chosen and as "more economical." Indeed, it was reported by one railroad superintendent that in camps where they had the option of better accommodation, Southern Italians persisted in living in the converted cars in order to maximize their savings, whereas other nationalities complained that even bunk-houses were unsatisfactory.[37]

At most of the camps accommodation cost only about one dollar per month, and *paesani* related that on some sites no fee at all was levied. Though conditions were rough, labourers paid much less than they did for a bed in a dilapidated room in the city, which cost at the minimum three dollars a month to rent.[38]

Contemporary accounts would lead one to believe that money saved on housing costs in the camps was more than offset by the commissary's gouging of workers through his control of the sale of food provisions and other necessities. The *Ninth Special Report of the Commissioner of Labor*, surveying Chicago's Italians in 1897, calculated that the markup on food at the camps over Chicago prices was over 59 per cent. Even assuming that such a figure was representative of the majority of the camps, it remains debatable whether the difference in prices was seen to be as "exorbitant" by the sojourners as they were by native observers.[39]

For many *paesani*, the most expensive camp food, meat, did not seem excessively priced by Rende area standards. Around 1908 labourers who worked for an average of two dollars a day received

more than three-and-a-half times the *maximum* daily wage they could
hope to earn in Cosenza (the equivalent of about 50 cents). Even if
the commissary charged double for meat over Chicago prices, this
merely made its cost equivalent to village prices.[40] For the migrant,
the cost of meat at the railroad camps remained relatively stable, while
his wages had increased greatly. Hence perceptions of what constituted exploitation, especially in the sojourn stage of the migration
process when men were psychically still part of the *paese,* were bound
to appear differently to the migrant and to the native, middle-class
observer.

The report of the Commissioner of Labor also accused the camp
padrone of selling inferior goods. The migrant, for his part, was charged
with maintaining a poor diet and deliberately underfeeding himself
to increase his savings. Lacking the nutritional minimum for health,
he was characterized as susceptible to disease and ineffective at work.[41]
There is little doubt, however, that though the migrant may have eaten
poorly by North American standards, he fed much better than he had
in the village. An Italian government study of camp conditions in
1908, while noting deficiencies, had to acknowledge that "the feeding
of the Italian manual laborer is more abundant, varied, and rich in
the United States than in our native land. The immigrant, generally
speaking, is not used to consuming in Italy the foods he acquires daily
at the commissary."[42]

There is also considerable evidence that sojourners helped to create
and sustain the commissary system. As was pointed out in a 1914
Italian consular report from Ontario, the Southerner wanted his own
familiar food: "The most happy worker is the railway labourer who
eats what he wants, who in the labour camp unites with compatriot
friends to cook according to the custom of his own *paese.*"[43]

The Southerners' desire to prepare their own food was made possible by the *padrone* commissary. While this preference reflected their
sojourn frame of mind and their determination to resist new world
ways, it also stemmed from the sound calculation that they could eat
more cheaply buying and cooking their own food than dining in the
railroad boarding trains as other nationalities did. This was recognized
both by Iorizzo in his revisionist account of the *padrone* system at the
turn of the century and by Bradwin's eye-witness study of conditions
in Canada prior to 1914. Iorizzo estimated that the Italian buying and
cooking his own food could live for as little as $6.90 per month, repre-
senting "a savings of $11.10 on the cost of absolutely essential items
to non-Italians," and Bradwin calculated a corresponding monthly
cost of less than $10, much of the difference over Iorizzo's figure being
accounted for by inflation. On a monthly basis, Iorizzo estimated the
Italian's salary at $35, of which $25 or more was saved, compared to
other nationalities who reported saving around $20. "The difference

saved by the Italian," he concluded, "was due generally to his utilization of the padrone's services." And Bradwin similarly calculated that, working overtime, "the Italian navvy counted it a poor month that he did not clear from $40 to $45."[44]

Moreover, the contention that labourers spent significantly more on food in the camp than in the city is itself open to question. The degree of control held by the camp boss varied according to company policy, the degree of isolation, the season and local geography, as well as the personalities involved. Some *paesani*, for example, reported that camp life, rather than tying them to a system of exploitation, provided definite advantages. It gave workmen access to wild greens and game which could be introduced into their diet, thus cutting down on the quantity of food they would have bought had they remained in the city. According to one early migrant, "they'd go hunt like a wild chicken [quail] in the woods and get fresh fish from the river. And they'd make their own pasta [dough] with lots of water to dilute it. So they had few expenses and had little to do [i.e., entertainment], so saved a lot of money."[45]

While being in the woods could encourage efforts at self-reliance, *paesani* were usually within reach of urban centres. Being involved in secondary construction close to towns and villages gave *paesani* an advantage over earlier navvies, since they were not dependent on the commissary for necessities to the degree isolated camp workers would have been. Hence, one track worker recalled:

> We used to go out in groups of four or five to buy our food. We ate well.... If there wasn't a store where we were, there would be one within a few miles. It wasn't a barren desert. There were little villages. They were small, but there were some.... There just wasn't any [Italian food] in those stores of the little villages. So we ate meat instead, veal and steak. At that time steak was only 25¢ a pound. We ate well.[46]

EXPLOITATION

Roberts observed of the camp *padroni*, "most...are not dishonest. They have their prices, their rates, and adhere to them."[47] The commissary, like the labour broker, immigrant banker and other *padroni*, was essentially seen by migrants as a necessary go-between. Another type of *padrone*, on the other hand, was often viewed with a hostility usually reserved for the peasant's landlord in the old world. This was the gang foreman.

In comparison to *padrone* intermediaries who were commonly *paesani* or Southerners, gang foremen were often of English-speaking "old" immigrant background. Bradwin noted that railway workers in Canada were divided into "whites" and "foreigners." Of the former, which included the native-born, Americans, British, and Scandinavians, he wrote that "To the white-man falls most of the positions which connote a stripe of some kind, officials in one capacity or another – walking bosses, accountants, inspectors, the various camp foremen."[48]

In the United States, the Irish in particular were conspicuous as foremen, a role dating from when they, instead of the Southern Italians, formed the backbone of North America's pick-and-shovel brigades during the mid-nineteenth century.[49] Indeed, the Irish were so predominant at the beginning of the century that Gino C. Speranza, corresponding secretary of the New York-based Society for the Protection of Italian Immigrants, saw the abuses perpetrated at the camp sites and the labour difficulties employers had with Italians as being due to the application of a sort of "Irish system" of surveillance. Employing the racial categories of his time, he wrote that this supervision was "fundamentally wrong because the Italian is essentially different from the Irish ... the cursing, the threats, and the blows of the foremen and bosses who cannot understand his nature will never get the best work from him." He recommended "developing and encouraging a class of Italian foremen as a distinct species from the purely American, or Irish boss, or middleman." Somewhat naively, Speranza felt that "Italian middlemen that know the idiosyncrasies and characteristics of this class of laborers will result in good all round."[50]

Paesani, too, drew a distinction between good and bad bosses, and the latter were more likely to be native-born North Americans or English-speaking rather than other Italians. While migrants sometimes had bosses who treated them decently, more often they found themselves under camp foremen who were hard-driving and frequently brutal. A *paesano* who worked on the track for several years prior to the First World War spoke of his treatment under a "crazy" boss, making reference in passing to what Roberts called America's "hurry-up habit": "If you had some good boss, all right. If you had some crazy boss – if I worked with a crazy boss – I quit, that's all! What are you going to do? At that time, they beat you, too. The bosses beat you. They kicked you. 'Quick!' 'Come on!' 'Hurry up, hurry up!' Just like a horse, eh.... Like slaves, that's all."[51]

The slave and beast-of-burden metaphors were popularly used by *paesani* to describe their life at the hands of driving foremen, just as in the old world they had been employed to characterize their status as agricultural labourers sweating for the landlord. Migrants frequently placed the image in a distinctly American context: as one remarked succinctly, "we were treated as the blacks were."[52]

Interestingly, common labourers were referred to by their superiors in the same way. The *paesani*'s use of the same images marked the peasant migrants' psychic appropriation of their exploiters' categories of themselves as brutish men. Hence, while the majority of sojourners were able to fulfill their objectives of making money and returning to the commune as successful *americani,* they had to pay a price. For some, that price was injury or disease suffered on the job. That was measurable and easily identifiable. For most, however, the price was psychological and took the form of an assault on their self-respect, of a descent into that very brutishness they had experienced as peasant labourers and had emigrated to escape from.[53] To maintain hope of honour in the village, they had to forsake its reality in the new world. The frustration suffered at the camp site was an important ingredient that led many sojourners to look favourably upon the world of the factory and seek employment there upon subsequent migration.

But the image of slavery was just that: images, not fact. For all the physical and verbal abuse suffered by many at the work site, men did have an escape. At least in the early twentieth century, *paesani* were neither as isolated nor as helpless in the face of maltreatment as the image implies. Migrants came to a buoyant economy, where the demand for labourers generally outstripped the supply. There were always other jobs and other bosses, and *paesani* had the option of quitting their employment and moving on. Contrary to the impression given by sensationalist stories of the day (replete with armed guards and Gatling guns),[54] there was little employers could do about the loss of their men. Towns and villages were usually not far from camp sites and *paesani* had little difficulty simply picking up and making their way to the nearest railroad station: "I always went to Chicago: I tried a lot of kind of work. Eh, there was lots of companies over there! About forty-two little railroad companies in Chicago. Lots and lots of jobs.... I changed jobs all the time. Oh, how many padroni I changed in the States! If I worked with a bad bosso, I find another padrone, another gang."[55]

A second, though much less frequent, reaction against mistreatment by the boss was one of primitive rebellion, usually involving acts of isolated violence. We discussed earlier the fact that brigandage and violent individual outbursts within the Rende area were an expression of protest against the landlords' abuse of power. This past had an influence on the response of some *paesani* to ill-treatment at the hands of gang bosses.[56] In the most extreme example, one man took revenge on his foreman by murdering him. A *paesano* related:

Fiorio went to work on the railroads in Chicago around the First War. Italians had the worst jobs. They couldn't speak English or anything.... Fiorio was about nineteen, he was savage though, that guy.... His boss said he didn't know how to use a pick; that Italians were stupid and dirty. Well, Fiorio knew some English and understood, so he asked his boss to show him how to use a pick. The boss was stupid and bent over to show him, and Fiorio hit him from behind with his pick and killed him. Then he fled to Italy.

He was from "Sette de Mai" [Rende]. He stayed "underground" there for a long time since the *carabinieri* knew of the murder in the United States.[57]

The *paesani* thought of violence on the part of the labourer with the same ambivalence as they did old world brigandage. Since the rebel had shown a "savage" nature he was feared and could not be trusted; at the same time, since his rebellion was a response to an unjust situation suffered by many *paesani*, he was frequently vicariously identified with and circumspectly respected.

While incidents of physical violence by Southerners were isolated incidents, enough occurred to provide newspapers and nativists with easy ammunition to add to the "journalistic idea that Italians are both frightfully ignorant and instinctively criminal," as Speranza put it.[58] Such violence by "primitive rebels" also added to the newer postwar stereotype of the Italian as a political anarchist or violent radical, though as far as the experience of *paesani* is concerned, the migrant's reaction to exploitation was essentially individualistic and unorganized, not fertile ground for either serious radicalism or unionism.[59]

Paesani were not passive victims at the hands of omnipotent *padroni* as much of the literature maintains. Sojourners showed little resentment of living conditions in the camps, and no doubt the knowledge that they would only temporarily be employed on track work contributed to this. Moreover, the relative isolation of the camps and consequent lack of diversions such as theatres and saloons, as well as women, while it made life harsher, encouraged even more frugality in the lives of people already accustomed to making sacrifices.

The central fact was that real wages in North America were far above any that could be imagined in the old world. The widespread manner in which *paesani* participated in track work and their utilization of *padroni* in itself argues that they generally found these contributed to rather than detracted from their purposes. It was their success in finding work, after all, that enabled many peasant migrants to purchase homes and land back in the *comune* and fulfill important familial obligations. As men with a purpose, they had an active input in shaping the nature of their new world experience.[60]

CHAPTER 5

The City Experience

Work in the City

THE SOJOURN-IMMIGRANT NEXUS

Paesani from the Rende area, whether they formed part of the majority of sojourners or the minority of immigrants, had a life in the new world city, and at this point their experience in the main colony of Chicago will be of prime concern, although Toronto will also be dealt with where relevant. In discussing the experience of *paesani* from their own perspective, their testimony has been organized in the way it was presented – that is, thematically, rather than on strictly chronological or geographical lines. While the concept of a socio-economic Rende area network had a definite territorial basis in the old world, with the advent of emigration this reality became more a matter of *mentalità* than place. In the testimony of villagers, their prime concern was their day-to-day life among other *paesani* and their confrontation with daily necessities. Here, therefore, we will attempt to understand the structure behind the experience they described.

Throughout the early twentieth century, an increasing number of *paesani* made the transition from sojourner to immigrant. Two main factors led many to settle in the new world. First, there was the perception of discrepancy between levels and standards of living. The process of socio-economic incorporation into the wider world of the nation was not only inimical to the Rende area peasant economy that strove for familial self-sufficiency, but this incorporation, in addition to the sojourner's experience of North America, reinforced expectations and standards of living that were continually higher than those that the local society could deliver. The levels of living of the *comune*, while they could improve, could not match those of the industrial city which *paesani* strove to emulate. Because of this discrepancy, even very successful and comfortable *americani* could experience dissatisfaction with the village and chose to settle in the new world.

Secondly, the well-being of the peasant emigrant was continually being challenged by economic pressures. For most, migration, at least initially, proved successful in that it allowed men to fulfill family obligations and often to buy homes and land. Maintenance of these gains, however, proved often to be difficult, if not impossible.

The economic pressures which the industrializing Italian nation put on the local peasant economy, though temporarily held at bay by the gain afforded through emigration, could not be overcome. While many *paesani* continued to believe that their striving towards stable, landed status within the village could be fulfilled, others thought differently. For these, the conclusion was reached that though they might re-emigrate in order to bolster a newly found, but faltering, level of living, ultimately their future lay in the new world. As indicated by a prewar questionnaire sent to 116 Calabrian communes, *americani* who had become landowners often found that the return on capital invested in land proved inadequate to cover expenses; and for those who had not become property owners, their savings were soon exhausted. Also, the addition of new members to a family, a poor crop, or the unexpected succession of a new, more exacting landlord were all enough to offset gains made through the initial migration.[1]

With the First World War, moreover, the economic pressure increased. Italian state expenditures, heavily drained by the war, multiplied alarmingly from 2,501 million lire in 1913-14 to 30,857 million lire in 1918-19. By the end of 1920, the accompanying inflation had decreased the buying power of the lire to one-fifth of its 1914 value. Further, in an attempt to offset the heavy national debt, taxes in the postwar period were substantially increased.[2] This, along with demobilization and a rate of population increase of 12.4 per thousand – the highest in Italy's history – aggravated the demographic problem that had burdened the country since the latter part of the nineteenth century.[3] In comparison to the prewar decade, then, conditions after 1917 appeared bleak to most peasants.

The effects of the war were clearly visible within the Rende area. Inflation, especially among the *affittuari* segment of the peasantry who relied on rented land for their livelihood and were less self-sufficient than the landed peasants, was acutely felt. As a former *affittuario* from Montalto who had served at the Alpine front related: "After World War I, it was terrible.... All the soldiers that returned from the war had nothing. The government gave us a small payment (bonus) of 1,000 lire, but you couldn't buy anything with it. My father and brother were here [Toronto]. They called me and gave me some money as a 'present' to go to Canada. So I made my application [for a passport] at the *paese* and left."[4]

On the new world side of the migration process, too, there were important factors which helped transform sojourners into immigrants. To start with, the high wages, relative to the *comune*, acted as a sort of double-edged sword; while they allowed men to fulfill aspirations in the old world, they also encouraged others to start a new life in the new. As the nucleus of settlers grew, this in turn encouraged additional immigration, since people came to have an increasing number of relatives and friends who could help them adapt to the city should they choose to stay. Just as growing emigration from the village and the effect of *americani* spurred men to emigrate, so, too, the example presented by Rende area settlers acted to encourage others to remain in the new world.[5]

Secondly, the effects of the First World War promoted the transition to immigrant status. While a few *paesani* who found themselves in North America at the outbreak of hostilities returned to enlist in the Italian army, most elected to remain. Although many of the latter returned to the Rende area in the postwar years with substantial savings, for others the war had acted as a sort of benevolent "trap" enticing them to settle. As more stable, better-paying jobs became available to the *paesani*, they had more at stake in remaining in North America. And, not insignificantly, Southerners experienced the most receptive response on the part of the native-born in over three decades, which lessened somewhat social tensions between them.

Further, in acting as a benign trap, the war facilitated greater exposure to the host society than would otherwise have been the case. *Paesani* were exposed to new world patriotic fervour and not a few were involved in the war effort as industrial workers. Hence, by the time shipping lanes were once again open after the war, a considerable number of migrants found their new position in North America too advantageous to abandon.[6]

While such were the forces that converted sojourners to immigrants, the reality of the transition for any one person was much more complex. The change that occurred within a migrant was heavily influenced by individual factors; it was often gradual, imperceptible, or oscillating; and frequently it was seen as the result of circumstance, rather than explicit choice. While the complexity and psychological dynamics of the transition to immigrant status are difficult to document, some of the issues involved will emerge in the discussion of major aspects of the *paesani*'s life in the city.

TYPES OF URBAN WORK

Although railroading had met the objectives of sojourners, many *paesani*, after experiencing the track, attempted to gain work in the city. Ill-treatment at the hands of hard-driving gang foremen, the generally higher wages of urban jobs, the desire for more steady employment, the attraction of a growing colony and the ambivalence many felt vis-à-vis sojourning and the consequent desire to test out "immigrant" life – all these were factors that led men to seek work in the city. Some discussion of this work history is essential for, as Vecoli observed, "employment is virtually synonymous with the Italian immigrant experience."[7]

In the city, essentially three types of employment were available to *paesani:* outdoor labour, civic employment and factory work. Regarding outside work, although railroading was the major pursuit of sojourners, their work experience was often much wider than this. Many migrants who had worked on the track combined this with outdoor jobs in or around Chicago at some point or another in their sojourning history.[8] One migrant, for example, upon his second voyage, combined railroading with hauling coal at the Chicago Cooper Gas Company; a second track worker was able to use the building skills he had acquired in the *comune* to work in the Windy City as a concrete finisher in sidewalk and building construction; a third spaced his jaunts on various lines so as to work in between on construction at the union depot and as a coach cleaner for the Pullman Company. Other *paesani* were employed in similar fields, including sewer work, expansion of the city's streetcar and elevated systems, road construction, warehousing and, of course, maintenance on the numerous miles of railroads within Chicago. Moreover, in an attempt to maintain some continuity of employment, when laid off during the winter small groups of *paesani* would hire themselves out as snow shovellers.[9]

In the minor colony of Toronto, villagers who had heeded the call of *paesani* already resident there were employed in similar work, or found jobs fortuitously in transit either to or from railroad work. Just as the building boom in Chicago had been precipitated by the great fire of 1871, so a conflagration which destroyed downtown Toronto in 1904 stimulated that city's construction industry. New building codes in both instances led to the replacement of wooden buildings and walkways with brick and cement, work in which Southerners generally excelled.[10] Speaking of this early Toronto, an informant from Montalto reported how Rende area migrants contributed to the city's pick-and-shovel brigade: "They [*paesani*] were almost all *contadini*. They did construction work here, *fondamenti* [literally, "laying foundations"]. They did the worst jobs, every dirty work. They took whatever they could get; all kinds of work as long as they made some money. They had to work; in those days there was no help from city hall, you know."[11]

Most *paesani* expressed strong dissatisfaction with this "dirty work." Men spoke of the danger of excavations in the unstable alluvial soils of both Chicago and Toronto, of back injuries, of infected blisters, and long hours. A common complaint, especially among young men who had had little experience with winter jobs, was voiced over the illness, injury, and frost-bite that often accompanied work in severe temperatures. As a former railway yard worker who lost two fingers and was laid up for three months related:

> I start to work on the job January 2. It was terrible cold, my dear friend. It was awful cold. What happen to me? I thought I froze both my hands, I really did. When the quitting time come, I clean up, wash my hand, but it was hurt so bad. It was terrible....
> This cousin of mine was there, he had been there longer than me... [and] decide to take me to the doctor. When the doctor looked over my hands, he said, "Jeez, my dear son, your hands are frozen." He says, "What happened to you? Why didn't you have good gloves?"
> But, I didn't have no experience like this other guys. This other guys – bunch of coloured guys, you know – they work a little bit and then take off and warm up a little bit; they had different gloves.[12]

Others who worked in building construction, and especially hod-carriers, in tones echoing the oppression of construction workers by the "Job" in DiDonato's 1937 novel, *Christ in Concrete*, lamented the sheer physical toll exacted by their work.[13] One Toronto hod-carrier recalled hauling bricks up three stories along shaky scaffolding, with a wooden T-shaped apparatus on his back: starting with eighteen, then twenty, twenty-five, then thirty bricks. "They used to call it the cross; the cross that Christ bore," he said.[14] Not surprisingly, it was common for such *paesani* to refer to themselves as having been worked like "oxen" or "slaves." Further, construction workers complained how native city dwellers would look upon them with an air of superiority and how they were often referred to as dirty ditch-diggers or shiftless dagos.

Nonetheless, not all city pick-and-shovel work was referred to so harshly. Lighter jobs, such as setting up telephone lines, laying gas mains, and urban transit maintenance were often sought after. Some *paesani* who remained in the construction field were able to rise within it, learning a trade, becoming foremen, and, in a few cases, starting their own small businesses. As a result, for many migrants engaging in city outdoor work was a first step towards putting down roots in the new world. Life on the track was lived with other sojourners, whereas in city infrastructure and related work *paesani* came in contact with immigrants who presented an example of settled life in the city.[15]

Many construction jobs in Chicago overlapped with the second category of work: civic employment. Because of the city's pervasive patronage system, work with firms providing public utilities (such as transit companies) which relied on franchises from city hall, was often available only to a man who could ally himself with a local political boss. In return for a job, the ward boss would ensure the worker's vote to the local political machine at election time, sometimes after obtaining the man's hasty naturalization.[16] Obviously sojourners were in a less powerful situation to engage in such political alignments than immigrants, and hence were most conspicuous in jobs outside the city's spoils system.

While patronage-linked construction work involving public utilities was not easy to obtain, those jobs directly linked to city hall such as street sweeper, garbage collector, park labourer, municipal maintenance man and the like were even more difficult to come by. These were reserved for politically reliable settlers who had made a long-term commitment to America. For those who could obtain it, civic employment was more secure, less arduous and often better paying than city infrastructure work.[17] City hall jobs were less susceptible to lay-offs and rushed schedules than comparable low-skill work in the private sector, and hence were among the most sought after by *paesani*. As one woman related, her father, returning from Chicago in the early part of the twentieth century, often repeated to folks in Rende that "garbagemen have the best jobs in America."[18] She was somewhat puzzled by this statement until she herself emigrated and saw the relative comfort of such workers. In contrast to the Chicago situation, in Toronto jobs with city hall were not a factor in the employment record of early *paesani*.

Almost as desirable as working for city hall was factory work, which had the advantage of being shielded from inclement weather and, in many instances, was considered "cleaner" than outdoor work. While in the case of civic employment, villagers in Chicago had to contend with what had become known as "the principle of Tammany Hall," factory work at first was generally closed to sojourners and immigrants alike, not out of political considerations, but because of ethnic rivalry and discrimination.[19] Here *paesani* did not have the leverage to open up employment opportunities as they had by the use of their vote in the case of city patronage jobs.

The difficulty in obtaining factory work is vividly illustrated in the following testimony:

> Don't think we worked in the factories or anything. Naw, always these joe-jobs, like laying sewers, work on the railroads. We always did these joe jobs. Even at the end — just before the war — it was just the same. They used to tell us we couldn't go work in the factories; that we didn't know anything. For example, there were those who didn't understand [English] or how to read so they didn't want us to work. Others went to the factories, but the bosses didn't want us.[20]

More specifically, *paesani* blamed blockage at the factory gate on the monopolization of work there by Germans and "the English," the latter referring to both native North Americans and immigrants from the British Isles. One immigrant recalled of Chicago:

> On the railway they were mostly all Italian. But in the other places, no. They were all Germans and English.... In those days you couldn't get [better jobs] if you weren't English or German....
> The Italians were discriminated against like the blacks. Could they go where they wanted at first? No.... They said Italians weren't civilized enough to live in an advanced society. They thought *they* were civilized, ha, ha. [This wasn't said] to your face, but they wouldn't give you the job, though.[21]

In Toronto discrimination in factory work was also known. As one informant said, "They always had the excuse you don't speak English, so they gave you the worst jobs."[22] At the same time, there were relatively few good jobs in industry for the *paesani* to take advantage of, the standard of measurement here being the economic situation in Chicago. As one *paesano* remarked: "In Chicago there were a lot of jobs. But at that time there were few factory jobs in Toronto. All we could do were these small construction jobs around the city. But these weren't many either and didn't last long."[23]

Despite such perceptions, some *paesani* obtained particular lower-rung positions – for example, as janitors – while others made inroads into low-skill, labour-intensive industries such as meat packing, baked goods, and clothing.

While the First World War caused great expansion in industry and created labour shortages which provided employment for immigrants, *paesani* pointed to another, less obvious, factor that acted to their advantage. German-Americans formed one of Chicago's major ethnic groups, so with America's entry into the war in 1916 anti-German sentiment swept the city. The Bismarck School, for example, was forced to change its name to Frederick Funston, the Kaiserhof Hotel became the Atlantic, and the Goethe monument was put into storage for safety. Within this climate, *paesani* maintained that with the war many Germans now lost their jobs or had work closed to them, especially in the armaments and related fields. And, indeed, as an historian of Chicago's Germans has noted, "employers in vital war industries began to scrutinize their payrolls with an eye to extirpating potential subversions."[24] As Germans lost favour, the position of *paesani* and Southerners generally rose, and they often filled good jobs left vacant by their former rivals.

It would seem, then, that the ethnic factor, as well as the general economic climate, influenced employment patterns. There is no doubt that the jobs taken by *paesani* in the years during and following the war underwent significant improvement over those prior to it. Aside from jobs in packing houses, textiles, tanneries, bakeries, and confectionary factories, it now became relatively common for *paesani* to hold positions in the city's foundries, machine shops, appliance factories, and similar concerns paying relatively high wages and often offering good possibilities of on-the-job training and mobility.

It is interesting to note that the war years led some Rende area villagers to leave Chicago to join *paesani* who had established themselves in a number of industrial towns along the lower Lake Michigan shore. Of these, Kenosha, Wisconsin, had a particularly strong pull on *paesani* seeking good factory jobs. There, Chicago villagers joined relatives and friends within the small satellite colony of *paesani,* which traced its origins to the turn of the century.

By the end of the nineteenth century Kenosha was already an important Midwestern manufacturing centre. Wartime expansion, of course, gave great impetus to its local economy, especially its motorcar, tools, metals, and textile industries.[25] Within this, a substantial number of the *paesani* migrated from the Windy City to work in the foundry owned by the Chicago Brass Company. As early as 1900 the company was one of Kenosha's five largest employers with 240 workers. After 1914 the firm underwent great expansion manufacturing war materials and changed its name to the American Brass Company.[26] One *paesano* experienced the transition from railroad to construction to factory work:

> The last time I went to Chicago, I worked on the railroad for a couple of years. Then with the gas company for a couple of years putting gas pipes in the ditch. You know, digging ditches – not too deep – about three to four feet. Then, after that I was working for years with American Brass. Inside in the factory. American Brass, that's what they called it. We made this brass metal, silver, copper, bronze, any kind of metal, you know.... They keep me to work in the factory making war materials. At Kenosha, Wisconsin. It's pretty close to Chicago – one hour by train.[27]

Significant Rende area concentrations were also to be found in the town's Nash Motors plant, Allen and Sons Tannery, and the Simmons Manufacturing Company. Such examples of *paesani* job concentrations leads us to a discussion of the dynamics underlying their formation.

AUSPICES OF EMPLOYMENT

While villagers had often attained employment through professional brokers, as kin and friends emerged as senior workers, foremen, and supervisors they came to act as informal recruiters of *paesani* in their own right. Indeed, for many immigrants, the *padrone* became almost an alien figure. As one Chicago settler from Castrolibero put it:

There were also agencies [to find work], but we – at least the Calabrese – we took one another. If we were working and a *paesano* came to us we would go to the boss and ask if he needed someone. This is what we Calabrese would do. I don't know about the others....

I've never been to one, but there were agencies. You would go there and pay $3 and they would send you to where there was work. Of our *paesani,* no one used the agency. We would help each other. Whoever was working would help a cousin or *paesano* to find work.[28]

In one of the more pronounced cases of such aid, a *paesano* who emigrated to Chicago in 1901 and rose to be sub-foreman in a large utilities firm laying and repairing gas lines, for over twenty years consistently delivered jobs to a series of brothers, nephews, cousins and friends from the Rende area. Villagers held the "uncle" in high regard and perceived work with "his" firm as desirable.[29]

Construction work was sometimes found with *paesani* who, especially after the war, rose to be small contractors in the areas of residential construction, sewer work, and road-building and paving. In Toronto during the twenties, for example, at least four Rende area contractors originating from the northern communes of Castiglione, Montalto, and San Vincenzo were in operation. Often such *paesani* were small businessmen operating with little capital who could seldom afford the wages offered by large concerns and utilities. While villagers realized the precarious position of their small *paesani* employers, it did little to soften the bitterness regarding the low wages, long hours, and harsh working conditions which characterized their employ. Moreover, as *paesani* they often felt entitled to better treatment or more benefits than if they had been working for an impersonal employer.

Small contractors employed anywhere from a handful to a dozen or more men, depending on the company's size and seasonal as well as cyclical fluctuations. Villagers could make use of such *paesani* employers as a first step up the urban occupational ladder, and then transfer to more desirable work at the earliest opportunity. Because of the high turnover, many more villagers had at least some experience working with known contractors than the employing potential of their small firms would suggest. There were few *paesani* contractors relative to the number of villagers willing to take on such work. Hence, despite their hardships, people were grateful for the work these men provided. For many others the contractors were important not as employers, but as go-betweens who could refer *paesani* to contacts and potential jobs within the wider construction industry.

As the *paesano* colony grew, those seeking outdoor work had a greater number of kin and friends they could call upon who could help link them with those in a position to hire. As in the old world, the migrant's preference regarding whom to deal with followed the gradations in trust that ranged from close family members to kindred to friends to *paesani*. In securing any one job, a number of individuals could be called into play, ranging from a man's uncle, who referred him to a cousin, who in turn "recommended" him to a Rende area foreman at the job.

As had been the case with village *agenti* who profited from the commerce of migration, in the new world it was not only the labour agent proper who could benefit financially from those searching for work. Foremen, supervisors, and worker-recruiters were all in a position to demand some payoff for delivering jobs. Where primary bonds of kinship or friendship prohibited a cash exchange, employment favours were often repaid with "presents" and, certainly, social esteem. Often both formal paid auspices for finding work and informal non-paid auspices could intersect. In such cases while cash accrued to the "boss," also the cousin, uncle, or other *paesano* who linked villagers to a job "as a favour" gained significantly. Such a *paesano* go-between could gain much stature and a good reputation within the Rende area community and emerge as a patron to many, thus building a base of influence.[30]

In the case of factory work the use of professional go-betweens of various hues and the transfer of money was minimal. In contrast to their experience with outdoor city work, *paesani* now made use of connections with kinsmen and friends more extensively and effectively.

In contrast to civic employment, political patronage in obtaining factory work did not enter the picture in Chicago. And such jobs did not move from site to site, contractors and sub-contractors did not come and go, employment was not short term and sporadic: in short, professional go-betweens who kept on top of an employment situation continually in flux were no longer necessary. Equally important, the villagers who entered the factory were largely immigrants rather than sojourners, as had been the case on the track or on urban construction jobs.[31] Like the work itself, factory employees in both Chicago and Toronto were relatively stable. They were more knowledgeable of the society about them. Hence, they could be approached by job-hunters from the Rende area for information and references regarding factory work more readily than outdoor workers who were often only transiently on the work site.

There is little doubt that employers viewed the informal recruitment of kin and friends by senior workers favourably and often encouraged ethnic concentrations as a means to labour tranquillity.[32] Not only did inter-ethnic fragmentation and rivalry at the shop militate against workers' solidarity, but also — as had been earlier realized by railroad employers – at the intra-ethnic level, the camaraderie among foreign workers linked through primary relationships imbued the group with social satisfactions which acted to divert attention from potential labour grievances.

It cannot be said that *paesani* showed much awareness of this. Their concerns were more immediate: the finding of a factory job, the comfort of working ·alongside known men, the pursuit of security. In this context, an exceptional link to factory employment for the *paesani* was provided by Fred G. Salerno, who after the war emerged as "one of Chicago's most successful Italian executives."[33] Born in San Fili in 1877, Salerno arrived in the city when he was a boy, and at the age of twelve started his career in the baked goods industry as a greaser of pans with the Kennedy Biscuit Works. Over the years he worked his way up, emerging by the late twenties as vice-president and general manager of the Sawyer Biscuit Company, vice-president of United Biscuit and director of the West Side National Bank. Shortly afterwards he formed his own large firm, the Salerno-Megower Biscuit Company.[34]

Salerno seems to have been instrumental in recruiting a concentration of villagers in the baked goods industry. Moreover, men who later rose to influential positions as senior workers or foremen in turn brought their own circles of kin and friends into the workplace. Work in the baking industry (and the handling and food generally), though not highly paid, was looked upon favourably by *paesani* since it was not overly exhausting and was relatively "clean." Few villagers who gained employment in the food industry – and this was to be repeated later in Toronto – left it.[35]

It can be concluded, therefore, that although the interaction between formal and informal agents varied, three general patterns emerged. First, in the case of sojourners seeking quick work on the railroads and similar projects, Rende area *padroni* played a major role and informal contacts with kin and friends were of minor importance. Secondly, when both sojourners and immigrants sought outdoor city work, the roles played by paid gate-keepers on the one hand, and kin, friends, and informal labour recruiters on the other, were generally of equal importance. Thirdly, in the case of factory work, informal contacts were used the most and paid auspices of employment became relatively insignificant.

Moreover, the auspices of employment changed as the migration process unfolded. This was especially important where the sojourn motivation gave way to the immigrant's need for long-term, stable employment. While professional go-betweens could effectively link the migrant with seasonal labour needs, the immigrant's search for employment and his commitment to the new world, preferably with some modicum of social standing, was best served by using wider, informal contacts among kin and *paesani*. It was primarily through kinship connections that villagers were able to experience a variety of jobs and move both laterally and sometimes vertically along the occupational pyramid in the course of settling in the city.

THE INFLUENCE OF BACKGROUND ON EMPLOYMENT AND OCCUPATIONAL MOBILITY

In the city, old world networks between kin and *paesani* were used by villagers to gain positions in factory work and, to a lesser extent, in outside employment. While these networks led to concentrations of Rende area migrants in particular companies and industries, there were other elements of background which influenced the direction of employment.

Villagers often attributed their prevalence at Chicago Brass, Falbo Cheese, the Pullman works, Canada Packers, and other firms not merely to the fact that a kinsman acted as a link to employment, but also to the reputation of the kindred as a whole. It was maintained that when the first representatives of a kindred group had been able to establish a "good name" for hard, reliable work, this reputation served to pave the way for subsequent kinsmen and friends. Hence, for example, one *paesano* who worked alongside numerous relatives in a Chicago bakery during the twenties explained his family's concentration there not so much by the fact that his uncle was a sub-foreman in the plant, but by the fact that as an early employee he had proven himself to be "a good, honest worker...one of the top workers." It was his uncle's good example that served to benefit later arrivals, not kin connections *per se*.[36] It would seem that for many Rende area migrants the role of one's reputation and the value of hard work upon which it was based remained as important in the new world as it had in the *paese*.

Also, while kin and *paesano* auspices of employment resulted in what has been termed "chain occupations," it is significant that the niches generally reflected the past economic experience of *paesani*.

It has already been mentioned how the migrant's background in intensive agriculture and part-time employment on railroad construction and public works within the Rende area prepared him for work on the track and the varied construction projects of the new world. Similarly, as former peasants experienced in the growing of life's staples and processing of their own food, the *paesani* could enter the food industries without having to master much new skill or breaking with the past. As men who made their own bread and pasta, the peasant migrants certainly knew of baking, as likewise they did of slaughtering and dairying. This past experience in preparing food was not only of the household kind practised for their own consumption; in many cases, it had also involved working for the various local grist mills, abattoirs, dairies, and bakeries within the Rende area.

Furthermore, other less agriculturally based village industries contributed to the *paesani*'s predisposition to cluster in particular lines of factory work in North America. It is unlikely that it was mere serendipity that the small industries to be found within the Rende area — the metal works, textile mills, confectionery factories, tanneries, and even to some extent, the saw mills — were all reflected in the industrial pursuits of *paesani* in the new world. There was a substantial amount of similarity between many work processes in the Rende area and those entered into in the city.[37]

Moreover, it is important not to confound industrial processes with mechanization, the latter being a late component of the former. Within the Rende area, as hired labourers many peasants had experienced significant aspects of the industrialization process, aside from mechanized work. In particular, the regularized work day, wage salaries, authority relations, and the massing together of workers under one roof (as well as the massing together into agricultural work parties) — all important aspects of industrialism — were experienced by many *paesani* prior to their emigration. Though distinct, the Rende area existed in relation to the wider industrializing society around it; it embodied, albeit in embryonic form, industrial patterns *paesani* encountered on a mass level in North America.

Many villagers, as they progressed from railroad work to employment on the city's projects and thence to work for city hall or in factories, underwent considerable occupational mobility. Though usually all jobs remained unskilled or semi-skilled, the progression was a definite improvement, as temporary jobs in isolated work camps gave way to more secure, better paying and often less arduous jobs in Chicago or Toronto.

While this movement was possible through a generally buoyant economy, equally important was the subjective factor of *mentalità*. The majority of *paesani* entered the new world as sojourners, and while wartime prosperity may have placed them in lucrative jobs which encouraged them to stay, often their improved positions were merely a way of accelerating the future fulfillment of aspirations in the village. Mobility as a conscious career plan — the perception of outdoor construction work as merely a stop-gap to more secure, long-term employment in North America — could only come when the sojourner's frame of mind had become an immigrant one. In such instances movement up the occupational ladder was not merely an accident of favourable economies, but a matter of choice. As one Toronto informant expressed it: "Everybody worked outside for a while.... As soon as you come from the old country — out! At the same time you look for a better job, eh? And after a while you make yourself up a bit. You meet people and you go inside."[38] The conscious choice to improve oneself marked the transition from the temporary reaping of cash in North America to the permanent investment there of time and effort, the transition from aspirations which had the village as their object to those which had as their goal a fresh life in a new land.

As common labourers, whether working "outside" or "inside," few Rende area immigrants moved beyond the unskilled category. Yet it would be misleading to conclude that they experienced no mobility. For once gross occupational categories are replaced by the nuances of *mentalità,* the definition of what constitutes mobility undergoes a radical shift. Rather than relying on the application of purely external criteria for measuring social movement, the occupational definitions, values, expectations, and perceptions of the villagers themselves must also be considered. For the majority of Rende area immigrants, as they moved from being track men and construction workers to street sweepers and low-skilled factory workers, their perception, and therefore their reality, was that they did undergo considerable mobility.

Although commonly the movement was from an unskilled to semi-skilled position, the degree of this experienced mobility cannot be measured using conventional categories of occupational skill. Indeed, as Laurie, Hershberg, and Alter have pointed out, the very distinction that is generally made between skilled and unskilled occupations is in itself open to serious questions because of the wide variety of jobs within each category and because of the uniqueness and complexity of any particular occupation when it is examined from shop to shop or at various junctures in time.[39]

At any rate, most *paesani* measured mobility in terms of whether a job was unstable or relatively steady, whether it was exposed to a harsh climate or inside, whether it involved backbreaking labour or a less demanding effort, whether it paid at the lowest of wages or something above that, whether it involved commuting or was within walking distance, whether it was hazardous or reasonably safe, and whether it involved working with other ethnic groups or alongside *paesani.* Lastly, it was certainly measured against what had been known in the village. These factors were weighed by an immigrant when considering the merits between any two unskilled or semi-skilled jobs and the purpose as one moved from job to job was to win the best combination possible. For many *paesani* their conditions of work did improve; in their own terms, they had undergone occupational mobility.[40]

For a small minority of immigrants, their occupational improvement was especially noteworthy. While much of the factory work and civic employment was viewed favourably, more preferable still was attainment of small business proprietorship (sometimes involving a craft), this being a reflection of the peasant's unceasing search for familial self-sufficiency and security. While relatively few succeeded, many who made a commitment to fulfilling their aspirations in the new world strove to establish themselves as greengrocers, butchers, storeowners, saloon keepers, restaurateurs, barbers, shoemakers, tailors, bakers, Italian food processers, and the like. Though modest, such positions represented the urban fulfillment of the small-property aspirations of many former peasants; and they approached, much more than other occupations open to *paesani*, the attainment of *civiltà*. They were as far as the peasant immigrant could go towards achieving "white collar" status; and indeed, one visible characteristic that in the village had distinguished men of *civiltà* from mere *bestia,* from common labouring men, was the privilege of being able to wear a white shirt at work rather than soiled clothes.

This was the dream many attempted to fulfill, but relatively few succeeded. Along the way many things impeded success: the lack of capital, illiteracy, lack of confidence, competition, feuds with potential or actual partners, or ineptitude.

Another factor that stopped *paesani* from entering the world of small business was the calculation made by many that they could make more money working for others than on their own. Of course, if one was fortunate enough to have a wife who could mind the shop while one was away at work and, just as important, if one was open enough to allow such a wife to share the economic responsibility, then the immigrant could experiment with business while remaining otherwise employed.

In a particularly good illustration of how some *paesani* climbed the occupational ladder and the kaleidoscope of jobs this often entailed, one *paesana* told how her husband, a former peasant from Montalto, starting as a camp worker, after much effort finally established himself as a barber in Toronto's Little Italy:

> My husband was here from before the War. He had his own business and was okay. But he suffered at first when he had to go to the North to work.... Then he came to Toronto and worked digging sewers. But that was only from April to November so he worked in a hotel before I came too. Then – it was during the War – he went to relatives in Niagara Falls [and learned] how to work as a barber.
>
> After the War, he worked on streetcars. When I arrived here he was a ticket-man on streetcars.... A little at a time he built up his wealth. Then he bought the barbershop near home around Dundas and Bellwoods, where we stayed a long time.[41]

In both Chicago and Toronto some *paesani* had an artisanal skill, in particular barbering, and to a lesser extent shoemaking and tailoring, which they used to gain mobility and propriety. Some of these had come from peasant families and had been apprenticed as young men to local *maestri*, others were of *artigiani* origin. Once these skilled immigrants had established themselves in the new world, they were able to train aspiring kin and friends in their trade, thus transplanting more or less intact the apprenticeship system which had traditionally been a mobility route in the village. Those *paesani* who acquired grocery stores, butcher shops, or restaurants were also well placed to supply a similar channel for modest mobility.[42]

In several cases – for example, food stores – *paesani* who were employed by Rende area proprietors or other Southerners entered the small business field not as apprenticed young men but as permanent employees. Such work in the small shops, while not well paying, was well thought of and represented a vicarious playing out of the proprietorship many men were too timid or unable to attain themselves. Then, too, such places of work often put the employee at ease within the familiar setting of *paesani* and harked back to village ways where employers were personally known and employment was a direct relationship between people.[43]

In sum, for most *paesani*, movement from outdoor to factory work constituted an improvement in their work situation and for a minority this was extended into the world of small business. Whether to a lesser or greater degree, villagers generally experienced some form of occupational mobility. That this mobility often went undetected by native observers did not lessen its reality for *paesani*.

Residence in the City

THE VIEW FROM NATIVE NORTH AMERICA

As Rende area migrants entered Chicago or Toronto in the early part of the century, they proceeded to immigrant receiving areas, low-priced and conveniently located, a short distance from major railroad terminals – Dearborn Station in Chicago and Union Station in Toronto. In Chicago the original colony adjacent to the station had been displaced by commercial development, and much of it had migrated westward across the south branch of the Chicago River to the Nineteenth Ward, or what was more popularly known as the Near West Side. In Toronto the major residential and commercial centre for the city's Italians was located north of Union Station in St. John's Ward, or more simply, "The Ward"[44] (see Map 3 on page 169).

The majority of *paesani* found housing in the modest dwellings that had been originally designed for single families and predominated in both immigrant areas. In neither case was the tenement significant, at least not in the sense of the classic multi-storied "dumbbell" common in New York. The dwellings were more likely to be old wooden homes, small working-class "cottages" and sheds, housing two or more families and often tucked away in lanes to the rear of the main thoroughfares.

West of Halstead, however, in the newer "Little Italy," fairly substantial two- and three-storey homes were common.[45] Similarly, in Toronto the Bureau of Municipal Research concluded as late as 1918 that "there are no tenements in the 'Ward' in the real meaning of the word. Families are, for the most part, housed in small buildings."[46] Perhaps more so than in Chicago, the Ward, relative to its size, at least prior to the war, still contained a great number of small frame and rough-cast "cottages" reminiscent of the early immigrant shantytowns in Chicago before the fire of 1871.

The opinion of native observers regarding the immigrant areas was strikingly similar. The neighbourhood was usually spoken of as a "slum" – defined by the United States Commissioner of Labor investigating Chicago and other major cities as an area of "dirty back streets, especially such streets as are inhabited by a squalid and criminal population; they are low and dangerous neighborhoods."[47] The *padrone* and slum stereotypes were sometimes directly linked. In either case both were depicted as foreign malignancies within the social fabric. Similarly, in Toronto the medical officer of health, Dr. Charles Hastings, in his 1911 report, *Recent Investigation of Slum Conditions in Toronto*, documented the many hazards to health – cesspools, windowless rooms, filthy lanes, and the like – posed by the Ward's decrepit housing; and while written in a moderate and objective manner, the report strengthened the association between the "slum" and "immigrants."[48]

Contemporaneous descriptions of the "foreign quarter" in both Chicago and Toronto were often difficult to tell apart. Hull House's Agnes Holbrook, for example, wrote:

> Little idea can be given of the filthy and rotten tenements, the dingy courts and tumble-down sheds, the foul stables and dilapidated outhouses, the broken sewer-pipes, the piles of garbage fairly alive with diseased odors, and of the numbers of children filling every nook, working and playing in every room....
>
> Fruit-stands help to fill up the sordid streets, and ice-cream carts drive a thriving trade. One hears little English spoken, and the faces and manners met with are very foreign.[49]

And the *Canadian Magazine* just prior to the war was also compelled to mention Toronto's ubiquitous, "innumerable tumbledown shacks standing, in a state of slatternly decay, on both sides of the street." Then the author, Margaret Bell, speaking more particularly of the Ward's Italian section, continued with what she called her "cosmopolitan" sense: "The odours of garlic and spaghetti come from the kitchens in the Italian district. And lazy-looking workmen lie sprawling on the doorsteps. The gang from down the street come lurching home, with their pickaxes. Urchins are everywhere, under your feet, peering saucily into your face.... If it were not for all the filth all around!"[50]

In short, the immigrant – and specifically the Italian – quarter was usually associated, in the minds of middle-class observers and reformers with dirt, disease, overcrowding, ignorance, and often immorality and vice.

For perceptive observers like Robert Foerster, the Italians' poor housing conditions were somewhat "the inevitable result of low wages," and "somewhat they follow from the desire to save." Moreover, many reformers realized that "the Italian quarter is filthy because it is neglected by the City," and because of speculation by "money-grasping property-owners."[51] Most natives, however, like Chicago's chief buildings inspector in the late nineteenth century, or Toronto's public health officer in the early twentieth, subscribed to the social darwinist thought of the day and believed that the problems they perceived in the immigrant areas stemmed from the inherent deficiencies of the foreigners themselves.[52]

For *paesani*, it can be said that the low levels of living in their home village – whether in the sphere of housing, health, or nutrition – softened the harshness of life in the new world immigrant quarter. At the same time, while people in the Rende area had often lived in crowded housing, many were country dwellers, not inhabitants of hill-top villages. Especially for the former who found themselves in the sprawling, congested, working-class neighbourhoods of Chicago (and to a lesser extent Toronto) adjacent to factories and their spillover of industrial wastes, the North American city was a new, and not particularly pleasant, experience. The often-heard comment contrasting the "pure air" of the Rende area with the smoke and filth of the city was both a cliché and a matter of fact. More importantly, although levels of living were low, standards were not, and hence acceptance of residence conditions must be seen in light of future aspirations as well as past experience.

This helps one to understand why, from the perspective of the *paesani*, what was most salient about their residence in the city was not the same as what appeared important in the minds of the native social workers, government officials and reformers about them. Rather than the overcrowding, poverty and the rest, what was uppermost in the minds of villagers — both immigrants and sojourners – was that the present was a temporary condition which would allow them to fulfill obligations and aspirations dear to them. Present arrangements were but a stepping stone to a better future.

That the dark portrait painted of the immigrant slum by many contemporaries perhaps missed some such element of the residents' reality was sometimes hinted at by the native observers themselves. A

1915 Chicago housing survey of an Italian neighbourhood near the Near West Side, while reporting that the majority "in the district are enduring physical discomfort of one kind or another, and in addition, in most instances are existing under conditions endangering health and morals," at the same time was forced to observe of the neighbourhood's boarders:

> Several of these men, generally Italian, club together and rent an apartment or a whole house and keep bachelor quarters. About eighty per cent of these men are unemployed, but they do not appear to be depressed over the fact. They live very cheaply and seem extremely light-hearted. In general these bachelor quarters are quite clean, and in good order. The chief objection to their mode of life from a sanitary standpoint, is the excessive crowding in which they indulge.[53]

For many villagers the reason they did "not appear to be depressed" at being unemployed was because they were sojourners, not permanent settlers, and the quality and pattern of their residence in the city must be viewed in this context. The majority of *paesani*, who knew they would soon be returning to the village, found their stay in the city was generally favourable, or at least acceptable. Desirous of maximizing his savings, the bird of passage did his utmost to reduce housing costs. Within this context, it was the boarding system, both for the majority of sojourner/lodgers and the minority of immigrant/landlords, that played a central role in Little Italy and gave rise to many of the social grievances – overcrowding, unsanitary conditions and immorality – charged against them.[54]

THE BOARDING SYSTEM

Though boarders were usually sojourners who either worked in the city or used it as a base from which to find seasonal work, others were immigrants who also lived frugally with a minimum of comforts. The purpose of the immigrant's Spartan ways, of his "sacrifice" and saving, was not to return to the village and purchase land, but to allow him to finance the immigration and reunification of his family and ultimately the provision of a home. Just as the temporary migrant would not attempt to return to the Rende area until he had amassed sufficient money to allow him to make some significant investment in the village or contribution to the family's upkeep and status, so the immigrant would not send for his family until he could provide them with at least some minimally acceptable accommodation – often a modest flat.[55]

While the boarding system practised by Italians was an essentially transitory arrangement, it followed certain distinct patterns which often varied from other ethnic groups. The small groups of villagers that departed from the Rende area often remained at least partially intact, and hence members of these parties (*compagni,* which could number up to half a dozen or more men) then boarded together in the city. As one immigrant recalled, "Well, they were three guys, three brothers: Salvatore, Nibile, and Michele. They all went at the same time in 1910 – and they were all living and working together in Chicago. They were all in one room on Miller Street."[56]

Within the boarding arrangement of *paesani,* laundry and cooking patterns varied widely. Where men stayed with non-Italians or in boarding situations without women, they invariably took care of their own needs, often cooking in their rooms on small stoves. Where boarding was with other Italians, and women were present, some arrangement for laundry service was made, though cooking was frequently omitted. The service provided to one *paesano* who was a barber, for example, consisted simply of the *padrona* having ready one laundered shirt every week, the barber and his fellow boarders doing the rest of their laundry as well as supplying and preparing their own food.[57]

Much preferred by villagers were arrangements with other Rende area residents, particularly kin. Here, men were supplied with accommodation or services which would usually have cost considerably more outside the circle of *paesani.* Cooking was most likely to be included in the boarding arrangement, and a familiar and supportive environment could be found.[58] The preference for living with kin or friends among Southerners was evidenced as early as 1897 by the United States Commissioner of Labor's report on Chicago's Italians, which indicated that the majority of boarding arrangements investigated had a kin connection. The report's investigator surveyed representative Italian "slum" districts throughout the city and canvassed 1,348 families. Of these, an overwhelming 93.8 per cent were classified as private or "normal" families, "in which all or most of its members are related by ties of blood." Although the report did not specify what proportion of these "families" contained boarders, it can be estimated from tabulations in which all the households were listed with their occupants that almost 40 per cent of Southern Italian households did so.[59]

For the villagers from the Rende area, the fact that most were sojourners and not immigrants meant that there was a great demand for *paesano* accommodation. This was an important reason behind the congestion of the Italian districts noted by contemporaries, and which the early social worker, I.W. Howerth, called "the worst feature of Italian immigration."[60] For the *paesani* the boarding shortage meant that the help of kin and friendship was employed to sort out living arrangements. Kin and *paesani* with homes were expected to offer accommodation and boarding services to migrants in accordance with a priority system based on the closeness of the relationship. In the case of kin, priority corresponded to the levels of kinship outlined earlier with respect to trust and the auspices of work: *familiari*, relatives to second cousin, and lastly, remaining kindred to fourth cousin. In the case of *paesani*, priority was by and large a matter of the degree of friendship between individuals. Hence, while laundry service was commonly provided in boarding arrangements, where the *padrona* had a number of boarders to care for, cooking was usually reserved for kindred. In the case of close kin (or *familiari*) the boarder might even take his meals along with the landlord's family and buy food in bulk with them, thus contributing to saving.[61]

Though some native observers pointed to the danger of immoral behaviour presented by the boarding-house, this was more a flight of fantasy than fact. Indeed, the fact that immigrant homeowners saw boarding as a means by which their wives could add to the family income without compromising their honour illustrates the strength of old world social and moral checks placed on illicit affairs. It was not uncommon that the *padrona*, especially if she was an older woman and close kin, was viewed by young migrants as a mother figure and hence treated with the appropriate respect. Further, in several instances young men (especially if they were immigrants) established romances with the daughters of their landlords and eventually married them. What few moral infractions may have occurred were more probable where villagers boarded with non-*paesani* (or occasionally non-Italians), that is to say, outside the moral community formed by Rende area men and women.[62]

While kinship was the key to sorting out living arrangements among *paesani*, boarding also involved an important commercial aspect. From the point of view of the *paesano* landlord, the collecting of rent was usually seen as an aid in meeting necessary household expenses rather than as "business." As one Toronto *paesano* recalled: "Many Italians that I know had relatives with them as boarders, and in this way they helped with the expenses and were able to *tirare avanti* [get ahead].... I was a boarder for a time myself."[63]

The amount the landlord could profit depended upon the degree of kinship and friendship. Generally, the closer the relationship, the more stringent were the limits on what the landlord could charge. What compensated for this and made it acceptable was the important benefit that accrued to the landlord's social standing in the community and the fact that renting to *paesani* provided him with the socio-psychological assurance that the reputation of his wife and daughters would be protected.

Further, while boarding involved a cash exchange, it is important to note that in times of need, such as unemployment, injury, or upon first arriving in the city, *paesani* landlords often aided kinsmen by reducing their rent or forgoing it all together. Where aid was exchanged there was sometimes the expectation that it would one day be repaid in some form, often by a gift or service rather than cash. Where the aid was between *familiari,* the expectation usually remained implicit; otherwise it was often made more explicit in verbal agreement.

It should be noted that uncles (and also brothers) were commonly turned to for accommodation as well as employment. This reflected a pattern that frequently repeated itself in the course of emigration. That is to say, the married emigrant often relied on his brothers in the village to safeguard the honour of his wife and daughters left behind, and generally to help provide for his family. Hence when it happened that the village brother had children of his own who desired to emigrate, they set out for their uncle's house, for now the *americano* brother was expected to repay familial aid rendered in the past by his village sibling. This was one way in which the village system of rights and obligations binding people to one another transcended distance.[64]

In further reference to the old world, for many *paesani* the boarding arrangement was similar to living conditions in the village. Within the Rende area it had been quite common to find one or more families living in crowded quarters along with several unmarried adult siblings. With the advent of emigration, the migration process itself contributed to this village pattern in as much as the family of the sojourner was housed by his brothers, parents, or other close kin. Lastly, an additional feature of background that influenced *paesani* refers back to the fact that relationships between kin in the Rende area were not only social, but also intrinsically economic. The boarding relationship offers us an important example of the nexus between the *paesani*'s social obligations and economic reality that was worked out in the new world.

CONTOURS OF THE RENDE AREA COLONY

Until 1921 Chicago was the major destination of Rende area villagers, and generally their movement corresponded to the MacDonalds' concept of chain migration. With the advent of the war, as an increasing number of villagers made the transition from sojourn to immigrant status, both the *padrone*-related migration and the movement of working males gave way to the MacDonalds' third and last type of chain, delayed family migration.[65]

As emigration expanded after 1904, Chicago's Rende area element grew from modest beginnings to several thousand by the time of restrictionism. Within the Near West Side the *paesani* comprised an important component of the Italian-born population, which numbered about 15,200 in 1920. Toronto, on the other hand, until the First World War was home to an estimated 500 villagers.[66]

To some extent, the difference between the major and minor colonies reflected the relative size of both the general and Italian populations of the two cities. That is, whereas Chicago in 1900 already had

1,698,575 inhabitants, and the Italian element totalled 26,046, in Toronto, a city of 208,040, they numbered 1,098. By 1920 Chicago had expanded to over 2,701,705 and its Italian component to 124,284. Similarly, Toronto's population underwent an increase to over half a million, and the number of Italians reached almost 9,000. The immigrant populations here are drawn from census estimates regarding people of Italian origin and omit the large number of short-term residents in the colonies. Egisto Rossi, for example, reported in 1902 in the *Bollettino dell'emigrazione* that, though Toronto had a population of 1,000 Italian settlers, the total with sojourners numbered around 4,000.[67]

In Chicago after the war a well-defined colony of villagers emerged in the Near West Side consisting of both sojourners and settlers. Focused around Miller Street, which was almost solidly inhabited by *paesani* – such as the Furgiueles at 827, the Mauros at 828, the Stilos at 837 and the Storinos at 874 – the Rende area colony was located almost in the centre of the Nineteenth Ward.[68] Speaking of this, one villager recalled:

> I lived [boarded] at 827 Miller Street. It was near Halsted – between Polk and Taylor. In the "West Side," they called it. I lived across from Giovanni Stillo. Luigi and Sam Storino were just next door. Oh, there were so many *paesani* on Miller! Lots from Rende and San Fili. Every night a gang of us used to get together and play cards at Luigi's house.... There were so many factories around there. And dirty – lots of dirt along the streets and smoke too [from the factories]. But that's why everybody went; there were so many jobs there.[69]

Radiating outward from Miller, which ran north-south, the colony encompassed segments of such streets as Vernon Park, Sholto, Aberdeen, Morgan, Polk, Taylor, and Harrison streets. The last three were important avenues intersecting Miller and synonymous since the late nineteenth century with Chicago's major Little Italy. Also Halsted Street, which was the community's major longitudinal artery at the turn of the century, lay just two blocks east of Miller. As Schiavo observed in 1928, "From Clark and Polk [opposite Dearborn Station] the Italians kept on moving west...along Harrison, Polk and Taylor," so that by "about 1900 the centre of the west side 'Little Italy' was Halsted and Taylor."[70] And, speaking of the postwar settlement, Nelli observed that "the most solidly Italian block on the Near West Side – and in the entire city – was that bounded by Vernon Park Place on the north, Polk Street on the south, and Sholto and Aberdeen on the east and west," that is to say, this concentration was virtually across the street from the Miller Street *paesani,* and indeed villagers formed part of its density. *Paesani,* then, formed an integral part of the Near

West Side's community of Southern Italians, which was drawn especially from the two Calabrian provinces of Cosenza and Reggio, the provinces of Aquila, Campobasso and Caserta, and Western Sicily.[71]

For the majority of *paesani* who were workers, the Miller Street colony, aside from being part of the social and economic world of Little Italy, was within walking distance of the industrial complex of factories, warehouses, railroad yards, as well as retail stores, which before the end of the nineteenth century had started to concentrate in the old Near West Side immigrant area just across the river. While the incursion had involved readjustment for many residents of the area, it did have the effect of moving the population into the more substantial housing west of Halsted while creating numerous local jobs. Also, for those *paesani* who were employed outside the vicinity and could not walk to work, the Miller Street colony was within easy reach of the Blue Island, Halsted, Taylor, and Harrison trolley lines leading to the various construction sites, railroad yards, and factories where they worked. Where possible people went to their work in known groups.[72]

Many villagers who lived in the Near West Side formed part of the community's commercial life, delivering the multitude of goods and services demanded by *paesani* as well as other Southerners. The observations of the Near West Side's Little Italy made as early as the mid-nineties by the Southerner, Mastro-Valerio, who acted as Hull House's liaison with the area's Italians, captured the essential self-sufficiency of the community:

> The Italian colony consists of professional men — newspaper-men, bankers, publicans, employment agents, lawyers, interpreters, midwives, musicians, artisans, laborers, sweaters' victims, grocers, bakers, butchers, barbers, merchants, etc., all of which are necessary one to another and cannot bear separation without disorganization. It is a town within a town, a stream, a rivulet in the sea, of such intense force of cohesion that it cannot be broken, as the mighty ocean cannot break to Gulf Stream.[73]

For villagers, at least after the First World War, the size of the Rende area colony was large enough that many "Little Italy" businesses such as groceries, shoe repairs, and tailor shops, were often contained within the *paesani* grouping itself. Though villagers did business with other Southerners, it was considered preferable to patronize a *paesano*, an increasing number of whom entered small commercial life as the Rende area concentration grew.

In Chicago and increasingly in Toronto, villagers formed an identifiable colony of *paesani: padroni* from the Rende area were used by migrants from its various communes; *paesano* contractors and other employers hired men from the Rende area; and immigrants who set up as merchants, artisans and tradesmen were able to call on *paesano* connections on which to build their businesses. Rende area networks were transplanted with migration and activated in the new world. In the major colony a further integrating role was played in the 1920s by a few of the kindred's younger, educated members as they emerged as notaries, bureaucrats, city officials, and the like, drawing requests for information, aid and favours from a wide spectrum of the Rende area colony.[74]

In Chicago one way in which identification with the Rende area could be detected was in the development of mutual benefit societies. In the early twentieth century over one hundred small societies were established by Italians in the Windy City, the general purpose and operation of which was described by Schiavo:

> Societies of that type had two main purposes, or rather, were divided in two bodies. One would take care of the mutual benefit end of the organization, the other would attend to the annual celebration in honor of the Patron Saint.... Usually a member would pay from 50¢ to $1 a month, according to the amount of benefit he would draw in case of sickness.
> The death benefit was levied from among the members each time that a death occurred....
> Functions other than those of mutual benefit and pleasure clubs these organizations never had. No lofty aims such as those professed by the Order Sons of Italy and the Dante Alighieri for the whole country, or the Italo-American National Union, of late, have ever been their own. Their associations were strictly the product of the poorer classes and to a certain extent a reproduction of the *società di mutuo soccorso* existing among the middle class of Italy.[75]

As indicated here, mutual aid societies had their roots in the old world, though there is no reason to believe that the example of "middle-class" institutions had to be drawn from. While not large in membership, town workers in the South – mainly artisans – as well as some rural workers and peasants, had their own societies which could act as models for similar associations in the new world. Within the Rende area, the villagers of Cerisano, for example, had established a mutual aid society as early as 1878, four years before townsmen in the provincial capital of Cosenza.[76]

In Chicago a number of such associations were founded by the migrants from the Rende area. The first of these was established by 1890 as one of the city's first mutual benefit societies and seems to have been a vehicle by which an early Rende area *padrone,* Luigi Spizzirri, attempted to win influence over *paesani,* as well as over other Southerners. The society, the Bersaglieri [infantry] di Savoia, as well as including the *padrone* as president, had a kinsman as treasurer and probably a *paesano* as secretary.[77] The society's name here is significant and notwithstanding the Piedmontese connotation, should not be assumed to reflect pan-Italic aspirations. Like similar organizations in Cosenza – for example, the Umberto Primo society of Paola, or the Principe di Napoli society of San Lucido – it reflected strong monarchistic loyalties which, as mentioned earlier, were traditionally used by common folk as a lever against local landlords. In any case, in order to widen his influence outside the society, Spizzirri apparently made use of a second organization, the more broadly based Società Cristoforo Colombo, which held its meetings at 208 La Salle Street opposite Dearborn Station in the city's original Italian district.[78] Later, another widely based, regional association, the Circolo Calabrese, attracted members from the Rende area. While the Circolo originally received support from villagers because of its many social functions, its activities were disrupted once fascism became an issue and its generally pro-Mussolini leadership discredited.[79]

In Toronto, Cosenza immigrants were involved in two mutual aid societies, the Vittorio Emanuele III founded in 1902 and the Circolo Operai dell' Ontario founded in 1902. As well, successful *paesani* were members of the Italian National Club, established in 1907 just west of the Ward.[80]

With the growth of Rende area immigration to Chicago through the early twentieth century, clubs which were more exclusively based on the support of *paesani* and freer from the influence of the old *padroni* emerged. The San Raffaele club, for example, was established by immigrants from the *comune* of Castrolibero and named after its patron saint. Another club, the Società di San Francesco di Paula was established by *paesani* around 1911 in the satellite colony of Grand Crossing near the large Pullman establishment, where many villagers worked. The society was organized to oversee the *feste* procession of this important saint of Rende immigrants, which was held at San Francesco da Paola Church. (Indicative of the inter-ethnic rivalry that could flare up within the Catholic Church, however, the society was forced to disband when this popular procession was banned by the local Irish priest.)[81]

A more influential group was the Società Rende–San Fili. As reflected in its very name, the clientele of the society was drawn from the Rende area, not from the South more generally. The presence of such societies argues that, at least for the period under study, no linear relationship can be made between the age of the colony and fellow-feeling. Rather than an increasing sense of Italian nationalism or *italianità* being fostered with the passage of time thus tending to break down local loyalties, the growth of the Rende area settlement seems to have fostered and strengthened local solidarity.

Tellingly, the Rende–San Fili society was named after two communes that were among the largest in the colony. Moreover, being pivotally located in the centre of the Rende area, through which the major transportation route leading from the provincial capital to the coast passed, Rende and San Fili had both been well known by *paesani* from other municipalities. At any rate, as well as offering its members insurance against misfortune, the society was involved in organizing various social and religious events, drawing participants from throughout the colony. The most important of these events were the popular religious *feste,* such as that of Our Lady of Mount Carmel, which, as noted earlier, within the Rende area had been a specialty of Marano Marchesato and had attracted celebrants from throughout the vicinity. Such feasts, as well as banquets, dances, and the like were an important social means by which the people of the Rende area were drawn together in the new world city.[82]

In Chicago *paesani* formed part of a Southern concentration which was located alongside various nationalities. In the Near West Side significant numbers of earlier settled Germans and Irish, later Jews, Poles, Bohemians, and Blacks from the South, as well as numerous other groups, all lived nearby the *paesani.*[83] Moreover, villagers lived nearby one of the main institutions of resocialization about them — the settlement house. Hull House, the pioneering and widely renowned social settlement founded in 1889 by the sagacious Jane Addams and Ellen G. Starr, was located at 335 Halsted Street, only a few blocks from the Miller Street colony.[84] Yet the villagers had little to do with other ethnic groups and, except for its imposing physical presence, the settlement house remaining largely irrelevant to them.

The concerns of the majority of migrants focused around the obtaining of employment and accommodation, which, as already illustrated, was accomplished through kin and village contacts. Goods and services, friendship and sociability were likewise largely provided by *paesani.* In the evenings after work and dinner, groups of villagers would assemble in the main *paesano* households to play *scopa* and talk over matters regarding their migration and aspirations for the future. Information was traded regarding job possibilities, and the strength of the economy was discussed, as was the price of land in the village, immigration regulations, the marriage potential of young women, and the reputation of individuals and families. Commitments were made or reaffirmed, favours were exchanged.[85]

There was an essential social self-sufficiency about the villagers which gave rise to a rich social life beyond institutional structures — a significant aspect of the Rende area colony which will be highlighted in our final chapter.

CHAPTER 6

The Diversion of Chain Migration

Government Policy and *Paesani*

THE COMING OF AMERICAN RESTRICTIONISM

While an increasing number of migrants made the transition from birds of passage to immigrants in the decades after 1880, the mentality of many *paesani* remained largely that of sojourners and oriented towards the village. Often, even on the part of those who considered themselves settlers, the possibility that they might return to the village remained open. The event that changed this state of affairs was the American quota law of 1921. With the passage of this restrictionist legislation a basic transformation occurred in the outlook of villagers. Those who found themselves in North America or those fortunate enough to be able to leave the Rende area after 1921 realized that the era of easy emigration had come to an end. People no longer had the luxury of living between two worlds, of criss-crossing the ocean numerous times in order to fulfill long-term goals. They were now forced to make a solid choice: for the village, or for the new world. Villagers realized that restrictionism made the option of returning to the Rende area extremely risky. In short, the quota law of 1921 had a major impact on the outlook of *paesani*, transforming them from sojourners to immigrants.

American restrictionism, however, did not enter upon the stage of history or the lives of villagers all at once, full blown. Early signs that the new immigration would be radically curtailed had been many. The villagers themselves, especially after the advent of mass emigration, had long been aware that they were neither welcome nor liked by the older settled population. In the words of one immigrant, "The English couldn't stand us,"[1] a sentiment that Howerth, for one, linked in his Chicago observations to the Southerners' resistance to assimilation. "Of our immigrants the most refractory are undoubtedly the Italians," he said. "This fact with certain other characteristics makes them in the eyes of many the worst of all our immigrants."[2] Such an attitude had been one ingredient contributing to the insecurity villagers felt regarding their acceptance in the new world.

Italian observers of the South, too, felt uneasy about the movement and expressed on numerous occasions doubts that the United States would tolerate its continued flow. As early as 1896, for example, Nitti expressed concern over the restrictionist changes being made by politicians such as Senator William E. Chandler and intellectuals such as Richmond Mayo-Smith. Nitti regretted that the characteristics of Italian migrants – foremost, their low standard of living and willingness to work for wages lower than American norms – would increase popular pressure for restrictionist action, unless the emigrant flow was upgraded. Himself not immune to using gross racialist categories, Nitti saw the Southerner as almost inherently in conflict with the North European ethos of America:

> In the labour market we must fight today in the States with races that are stronger or better organized. Three powerful groups...*Britons,* the Scandinavians and the Germans, are in the nature of things, against us. Stronger, more resistent, better nourished, and better dressed, above all they desire to live well – they are not content with low salaries and humble occupations. Anglo-Saxons, Celts and Scandinavians represent ethnic and linguistic groups that have a strong affinity to one another and naturally little sympathy for the life and customs of people from the South...The habits of their [Southerners'] homeland – of privation and filthy – do not cease, even if well paid...they remain always below those of other workers. And it is also noted how, as if to stir up their adversaries, there is added the antipathy of the powerful Irish, who believe, rightly or wrongly, that our immigrants are enemies of the Church and the Pope. Thus can one have a clear idea why our emigration to the United States appears to Americans as "undesirable." Already there are calls from every quarter for restrictive measures and outbursts of popular wrath, more or less deplorable, in addition to sinister lynchings.[3]

A decade later both Nitti and Taruffi and his associates focused attention on the literacy question. These *meridionalisti* proposed that, in order to end the "shame" Italy's peasant migrants were bringing upon the nation, especially in the United States, Italian legislation be introduced to limit emigration to those who were literate; and to counter charges of entertaining illiberal tendencies, they proposed a vigorous state commitment to education which would work towards eradicating the problem and ensure that freedom of movement would not be out of reach for potential emigrants.[4] Taruffi and his co-investigators, in their 1908 Calabrian study, also argued that raising the nation's educational level would contribute to its prosperity, which, in turn, would act as a natural "corrective" to emigration. Their call for improving the quality of emigration was, of course, influenced by American events. The investigators were aware of the long-standing agitation in the United States for a literacy test and the sentiment of the Immigration Restriction League established by Boston brahmins in 1894. They were also aware of the narrow defeat by presidential veto of the literacy bill supported by Senators Henry Cabot Lodge (who had a close connection with the League) and Chandler in 1897 only months after rising Italian immigration had given impetus to the cause. And they were aware of another attempt (also supported by Lodge) at restrictionism on the basis of literacy in 1903 and of a third during 1906-7.

Further, the *meridionalisti* were aware of union opposition to immigration (especially of illiterates) and that business support was conditional on there being an industrial demand for unskilled labour:

> In speaking of education in Calabria from a demographic point of view, we have raised again how in the United States the illiteracy of the immigrants is seen with suspicion and hostility; an illiteracy with which our *contadini* of the South *(Mezzogiorno)* distinguish themselves in a special way. Thus there remains always suspended over the heads of the great mass of illiterate immigrants from Italy, the threat of seeing their debarkation on the opposite shore of the Ocean come to an end...The Americans regard Italian...emigrants...almost as if they were white negroes, useful only to furnish cheap labour for the coarsest work; but in the other respects they consider them almost a calamity for their nation.[5]

While Taruffi and his associates correctly anticipated the literacy test enacted by the United States in 1917 – directed specifically at stemming Southern and Eastern European immigration – they were in error as to its potential efficacy. In particular, with respect to the Rende area, in comparison to the late nineteenth century when the illiteracy rate was over 80 per cent, by 1911 it had dropped to 66 per cent, and even lower to 55 per cent if males alone are considered. Further, in 1911 Rome implemented the single most important measure called for by *meridionalisti* regarding illiteracy. The Daneo-Credaro Law nationalized communal schools after Camillo Corradini's 1909 report documenting their ineptitude, and the petty politics that often interfered with local education had made illiteracy an issue in national politics. This centralization of education gave much needed bite to the compulsory school attendance legislation of 1877 and 1904, so that by the time European immigration resumed after the First World

War, the generation that benefited from the new measures, as potential emigrants, had little difficulty with the literacy test, which consisted of reading a simple passage in one's own language. Hence, by 1920 emigration from Cosenza had increased to its prewar levels.[6]

Emigrants were well aware of legislation concerning them and they were advised by veterans how to respond to the inquiries of government inspectors. And they knew of the constant rumours about restrictionism. In this connection, writing in 1904, Broughton Brandenburg noted that there was less than strict correlation between economic conditions in the United States and immigration rates. Between 1901 and 1903, for example, though the United States actually saw a slight decrease in its average daily wage, the immigrant flow almost doubled. Perceptively, the journalist observed in his travels through Southern Italy that, aside from economic determinants, speculation about restrictionism (and the literacy test in particular) had spurred many men to emigrate lest the potential legislation bar their entry.[7]

In any case, while the 1917 law was a blow for many villagers, because of their increased education the majority of *paesani* remained optimistic. For them, emigration was still open; until 1921 they remained birds of passage: "There was free immigration at that time, you know. Everybody go over there. I was two times in the States, but then no more. Yeah, it continued from 1904....It was free, free immigration. They come from all over Europe, you know: Polish, Hungarian, Czechoslovakian, Russian, French, Rumanian. Yeah...Italians, there were many; lots and lots....Then it closed. United States closed up immigration around 1920-21. Nobody can go. Just some relations, that's all."[8]

After the 1917 literacy test most villagers tended to assume that their cross-Atlantic freedom of movement would suffer no further setbacks. For *paesani* who for over three decades had had restrictionism "suspended over their heads" and had learned to live with the fact, the sudden rise of nativist fever in 1920-21 and the consequent quota legislation caught them unawares. As one woman related, her brother-in-law had made two voyages to Chicago prior to the war, and believed himself safe because of his literacy: "When Francesco wanted to go, he waited because a law came out saying that those who knew how to read could go to America; those that didn't had to stay in Italy. He dropped everything and rushed off quickly to make his papers. Then he said, 'I'll stay another year or so and then go. I can read.' But he stayed too long and then neither those that could read nor those that couldn't could go."[9]

Another informant spoke of how his father and other *americani* had chided themselves for their easy "birds of passage" assumptions and decision to make their life in the village.

The last time he wanted to go to Chicago was when the Fascists were getting into power, around 1922...but they stopped him at the port. Most of them were regretting they had come back. They thought America was good compared to the life they were doing. Yeah, they were talking about those old days, there back in Chicago, and regretting they didn't stay. Even my father used to ask why didn't he make citizenship papers, which he could have gotten for a few dollars. They would have given it to him in those days, you know. If he had gotten those papers, even if he came back to Italy, he was always eligible to go back to America; and he used to regret why he didn't do that. You know, because those days, life [i.e., emigration] was so easy. They never thought about the future, eh...I used to see this all the time.[10]

It becomes clear that American restrictionism undermined the sojourn premises of villagers and converted their "birds of passage" *mentalità* to an immigrant one. For a great many already in North America, restrictionism, like the war, acted as a powerful trap keeping them there. At the same time, it led *paesani* in Italy to seek an alternate new world destination in which to fulfill some of their basic aspirations. For many within the Rende area (and the South generally) this alternative was found in Canada, and in particular Toronto. As the American playwright and novelist Israel Zangwill, who prior to the war had coined the term "melting pot" to describe the social reality of the United States, observed in 1924: "On the Statue of Liberty they have an invitation to the 'huddled masses yearning to be free.' That ideal has now been abandoned but I am glad to see that Canada is taking in people who have been refused by the United States."[11]

Within the history of Italian emigration as a whole the diversion northward was of minor proportions. Given the preponderate size and pull of the United States and the fact that the American quota, up until 1924, still allowed 42,000 Italian immigrants per year, and thereafter 4,000, as well as the entry under a separate non-quota classification of the wives and minor children of those who had become citizens, the flow to the States still heavily outweighed that to Canada. Between 1921 and 1930 the number of Italian labourers bound for Canada numbered 6,518 or one-thirteenth the number destined for the Republic. But since the total population of the United States was 105,711,000 in 1920 and that of Canada 8,788,000, the proportions are about the same. Nonetheless, the diversion northward was very real, for the Italian stream to Canada after 1921 relative to the United States flow more than doubled over that of the prior decade and a half. Not surprisingly, this was reflected in the foreign-born statistics of the two nations; in 1920, whereas the United States held 70 aliens per 1,000 population to Canada's 56, by 1930 the proportions were roughly reversed with the United States containing only 51 foreigners to Canada's 62.[12]

But this macrocosmic profile, while it reflects the Rende area diversion towards Canada, obscures its concrete reality. For the Italian quota in any year after 1921 was so overfull with eligible immigrants from throughout the peninsula that precious few *paesani* succeeded in entering the Republic under it. And while a significant number of dependants of Chicago immigrants did leave, the fact that only the wives and *minor* children of United States *citizens* (rather than residents) could qualify for non-quota status limited the extent to which villagers in Chicago were able to effect reunification with their families.[13] Hence, aside from close dependants, after 1921 for many *paesani* emigration to "America" meant going to Canada. It is interesting to note that by 1930 there were an estimated 2,000 Calabrese in Toronto out of an Italian origin population of 15,623. At almost 13 per cent of the Italian element, the Calabrese comprised about the same proportion as in Chicago, where it can be estimated they numbered 26,000 out of an Italian population of 200,000.[14]

In any event, diversion north of the forty-ninth parallel did not mean that emigration to Canada was achieved by all who sought it, for the door to that particular region of the British Empire was only partially open. Numerically, the reported 500 or so *paesani* who emigrated to Canada in the twenties was probably no greater than the movement – primarily of dependants – towards the United States.[15] But the significance here does not lie in strength of numbers, it lies in the shift on the part of villagers towards a committed *mentalità* of immigration superseding the prior sojourn or wavering immigrant frame of mind of pre-restrictionist emigrants. Further, the twenties movement illustrates the resilience of peasant emigrants in making the first major change in the direction and organization of their chain migration in response to modern, bureaucratic, state controls on their movement and purpose.

DIVERSION OF IMMIGRATION TO CANADA

An important factor which made the rerouting of Rende area immigrants to Toronto easier was that the Canadian alternative had been a known quantity to many before 1921. Prior to the quota law, there had long been villagers who, because they were ineligible to enter the United States, had migrated to Canada instead, often using it as a back door to the United States. What allowed *paesani* to do this was the consistent lag in the strictness of Canadian regulations vis-à-vis their American counterparts. When the United States passed the contract labour law in 1885, Canada followed suit with similar legislation a decade later but rendered the law almost a dead letter by making its enforcement subject to individual action before the courts rather than a government responsibility. Likewise, the enforcement of regulations against various "loathsome and contagious" diseases was tighter in the

United States than in Canada.[16] Indeed, in the passage of Canada's immigration law of 1902, Canadian regulations aimed at ensuring the "quality" of immigrants seem to have been drawn up as much in response to American pressure as out of concern over domestic union or nativist protestations. Migrants who were intending to use Canada as a back door to the Republic because they could not meet American regulations were not inclined to declare this to Canadian officials so that they could be directed to American authorities. Understandably, the United States attempted to secure parity in legislation and its enforcement in order to stem the movement of what it considered "undesirables" from the north.[17] Further, as an implicit admission that they did not have full confidence in the Dominion's ability, or willingness, to enforce stricter controls, the Americans increased surveillance along the border shortly after promulgation of the 1902 Canadian legislation. The results, however, were negligible. A year after the Canadian legislation took effect, the United States special immigrant inspector reported from New York that "we cannot escape the conclusion that a large number of undesirable emigrants succeed in reaching our shores in spite of the vigorous enforcement of our immigrant laws at the Atlantic seaports as well as the Canadian border."[18]

At any rate, as the social scientist W.G. Smith pointed out in 1920, official statistics leave little doubt as to the relative laxity of Canadian immigration procedures in the early part of the century:

> ...prior to 1910, when the new Canadian Immigration Law laid down more stringent regulations than hitherto prevailed, a number of "misfits" would enter Canada. While the number of rejections was considerable the ratio of rejections to immigrants was not at all equal to that of the United States. Taking the year 1908 as typical, there were admitted to Canada 262,469 immigrants, and 1,002 were rejected, a proportion of one to 262. In the United States for the same year there were 782,820 admitted, but 10,907 rejected, or one to seventy-two. This evidently indicates that, after due allowances are made, the medical and other requirements for immigrants into Canada were either much less rigid, or less energetically enforced, or both, than those of the United States....
>
> In [1908]...Canada's hand was eight times as lenient as that of the United States toward northern and western Europe, for the ratio is 1:876 compared with 1:106; and almost twice as lenient toward other European immigrants.[19]

It is not surprising, then, as Brandenburg discovered in his 1904 voyage from Naples to New York, that Southern Italian emigrants afflicted with trachoma, favus, or other disbarring diseases, or who were otherwise uncertain about being accepted at New York, attempted to ship to Halifax or Montreal where they stood a greater chance of being let through.[20] Such emigrants, travelling through French or

British ports, were also assured of more lenient treatment there than at Naples, where inspection was more severe.

After the introduction of stricter American legislation in 1917, much the same situation prevailed. In 1919 Canada once again followed American initiative and introduced new regulations calling for its own literacy test. The legislation carried the important rider that the test "shall not apply to such persons or classes of persons as may from time to time be approved by the Minister." Thus, as Smith pointed out, "the real worth of the prohibitory clause is minimized considerably."[21] In the early twenties, as in the past, when specific groups of Italian labourers were required by railway, mining, and other interests, regulations could be relaxed.

Rende area villagers were aware that entry into the Dominion was generally easier than into the United States and those who needed to used Canada in order to "go contraband" to the Republic. There they sought out relatives and friends in Chicago who could help the *paesano* obtain work. The important point is, however, that prior to the diversion, *paesani* had already been exposed to the Canadian route. The experience of those villagers who found it necessary to emigrate to Canada prior to 1921 was known throughout the Rende area. This was enough to make emigration to Canada a logical ambition of *paesani* once the door to the United States had closed for them.

Another major element that contributed to the diversion to Canada was the fact that the Dominion contained a small colony of *paesani* stretching back to the late nineteenth century. In following railroad work across the United States *paesani* not infrequently were led northward across the border into Canada since Canadian railways, in particular the Canadian Pacific and Grand Trunk, looked upon Italian navvies with favour and actively sought their recruitment. Prior to the First World War, Canada essentially pursued an open door policy towards Italian immigration, particularly the entry of railway labourers.[22] Despite the frequent opposition of top civil servants responsible for immigration, who strongly favoured the entry of agriculturalists, the economic arguments of business interests who lobbied for access to malleable, cheap labour generally held sway with Canada's politicians. With respect to Italians, the effects of this reached a peak in 1913 when 30,699 left their homeland bound for the Dominion.[23]

Within this relatively hospitable climate for the common labourer, migrants from the Rende area were part of the large-scale continental drift northward into Canada from the United States. One informant from Montalto, for example, told how his father settled in Toronto after being employed on Ontario railways after working in both South America and the United States:

> Papa came here before 1900. He was a number of years in South America at Buenos Aires, then to Pennsylvania where he

worked in a coal mine for a time. My father went around the world, then he came here and worked in the North for three to four years. He worked for 25¢ an hour. With the railway – the Grand Trunk and CPR in the North – on the track, building stations.

They were worked hard by the bosses, then. There were no unions or anything. It was cold in those days, too – the snow started in October....Then he decided to leave. It was too cold and far. He'd suffered enough.[24]

Similarly, in another case, three Rende area brothers entered Ontario via Buffalo around 1901 after working out of Chicago on railroads "all over the states," and they also settled in Toronto upon completing work with the province's major railways. And in a third case another *paesano,* crossing the Michigan border, ended up working on the track in the Sudbury area before settling there.[25]

While in a few instances villagers emigrated directly from Italy to *paesani* in Toronto, the general pattern was to enter Canada via the United States, most commonly at Buffalo or Detroit. As Harney has noted, "Two-thirds of the Italians entering Canada at the turn of the century were ticketed through New York or other ports, while count-less other migrants worked their way into Canada along the railroad rights-of-way."[26] Of the villagers who entered Ontario to find work, many came to Toronto – to look up *paesani,* as a stop-over, or as a winter residence. Some villagers decided to settle there, either directly or eventually after further wanderings in the United States or a return voyage home.

In Toronto, among the earliest Rende area settlers were fruit trad-ers from the communes of San Vincenzo La Costa (especially the village of San Sisto), Montalto Uffugo, and Cerisano, who in the 1880s opened shops in the city core. At the turn of the century, a move uptown by a number of the early settlers to what became the College-Grace streets Little Italy naturally attracted *paesani* who looked to their hometown shopkeepers to link them with jobs and provide them with accom-modation. Storeowners Salvatore Turano and Raffaele Bartello from San Sisto, Vincenzo Muto, a tailor from Cerisano, Carmine Spizzirri, also from San Sisto, and Pasquale Molinaro, a motorman for the Toronto Transit Commission, all provided housing and other services for their *paesani.* The most important and earliest of these local *paesani* was Sal Turano whose grocery and boarding-house/agency on Mans-field Avenue supplied the various needs of Rende area labourers seek-ing jobs at street railway construction, the macadimization of dirt roads, or laying of sewers. It is relevant to note that in Chicago the most important of the Rende area *paesani,* Luigi Spizzirri, was also from San Sisto. There can be little doubt that cooperation occurred between the Chicago and Toronto intermediaries in facilitating immigration and referring *paesani* to job opportunities on either side of the border.[27]

A related factor that made the transition easier has to do with the concept of a Rende area network. Prior to the war many, perhaps a majority, of Rende area settlers in Toronto were drawn from the two northern communes of Montalto and San Vincenzo. Informants from the two *comuni* and others recognized this. As one early settler remarked: "The major part [of *paesani*] were from the same villages: from Montalto, San Sisto, Vaccarizzo, Parantoro – all those little villages near Cosenza....They all knew each other before, and were mostly *contadini*."[28]

Vaccarizzo and Parantoro were the two largest villages that made up the commune of Montalto, along with the municipal capital of the same name; and San Sisto village was located just south of the municipality within the commune of San Vincenzo. What is significant here is that after the war, and particularly after 1921, the Toronto settlement's population base was expanded to include an increasing number of immigrants from throughout the Rende area. The inhabitants of the local area relied on kin and *paesano* contacts existing with the small, and largely southern Montalto–San Sisto colony in Toronto to effect a northward change in the direction of the chain. In this response to restrictions imposed by the United States, villagers illustrated the resilience of old world ways. For *paesani*, it was the reality of a social space encompassing the Rende area and the interconnecting network of villages and families which made the northward movement possible.

How the deflection of emigration from the Rende area and the workings of a local area network was manifested concretely at the level of the individual migrant can be illustrated by tracing individuals belonging to one specific chain, or, more accurately, chain segment linked by kinship. The story here starts with the movement into Toronto of two brothers from the Chiappetta family of San Vincenzo at the turn of the century. Like other peasant emigrants from the Rende area, the brothers had earlier disembarked at New York and worked on railroad projects throughout the eastern and mid-western states. On one of their work stints they followed railroading northward through Buffalo into Ontario. Making their way to Toronto, they eventually settled in the midst of the small colony composed heavily of migrants from their own commune and Montalto. Shortly afterwards the two men were joined by a third brother.

The nine communes of the Rende area were effectively linked by intermarriage between the various families, and the Chiappettas were no exception; their kinship ties stretched southward to Marano Marchesato. There they had a sister who had married into the Ruffalo family. In the early part of the century, the brothers sponsored one of their Marano nephews, thus planting in Toronto a contact which other potential emigrants from the commune could activate when needed. Further, this Marano immigrant was related through marriage to the Consentino family of Rende. Specifically, the Marano man's sister had married into this Rende family, and it is noteworthy that when the couple decided to emigrate, the role of "sponsor" fell on the nearest kindred able to provide aid: that is to say, on the sister's Toronto brother (Ruffalo), not on her uncles (Chiappetta). In any case, with the entry of this Rende immigrant to Toronto, others from the same commune who had had Chicago as their destination were able after restrictionism to alter their plans and divert their energies towards Toronto.[29]

Hence, in this instance, it becomes clear that after the war what might appear on the surface as a "village" migration to Toronto from Rende commune was in actual fact an intervillage movement by which the communes' emigrants were linked through kin and friends to the outflow from Marano, and behind this to the more primary San Vincenzo stream. This pattern of intervillage linkages, giving concrete meaning to the concept of a Rende area social space, was repeated in several other chain segments. Similar interpersonal linkages, for example, connected Rende immigrants to Castiglione and San Fili. The phenomenon was a common occurrence, not an exception, and indeed, in light of earlier discussion, this interplay between villages comes as little surprise.

The last factor facilitating diversion to Canada relates to characteristics of kinship among *paesani*. However, before delving into this, some discussion of Canadian immigration policy will be necessary, for it was with respect to this policy that certain characteristics of kinship were brought into stark relief.

CANADIAN IMMIGRATION POLICY VERSUS *PAESANI*

While immigration to Canada was possible for some *paesani*, entry was not achieved by all who sought it. After 1920 economic slowdown contributed to a tightening of Canadian immigration policy. But this stricter course was also instituted in response to American pressure after the passage of the U.S. quota law. Referring to the heightened interest in Canada shown by Italians, the secretary of the Department of Immigration and Colonization, F.C. Blair, wrote to his Canadian agent in Harrisburg, Pennsylvania: "There has been a great deal of activity recently in the way of inquiries about Italians coming to Canada. A few months ago we had a visit from the Royal Italian Emigration Commissioner from Rome, who...[was] anxious to make an arrangement for the removal from Italy to Canada of a large number of Italians for whom undoubtedly some outlet is required."[30]

Canada, however, was only willing to serve as a minor outlet. After 1921 stricter application of existing legislation was sought. Enforcement of the money requirement stipulating that immigrants were to have at least $25 plus a ticket to their destination, application of the continuous journey clause requiring them to enter Canada on through tickets from their country of citizenship, as well as stricter health and literacy inspections were all means by which the flow of newcomers could be limited. Most significantly, after 1921 the Department of Immigration enforced an "occupation test" by which continental emigrants were generally able to enter Canada only if they were farmers, agricultural labourers, or domestic servants. Of these, immigrants claiming to be farm labourers were by far the most numerous.[31]

This policy in favour of agriculturalists in the 1920s was a reflection of the traditional bias of immigration officials concerned with fulfilling Canada's agricultural potential on which its economy still heavily rested; but it was also a response to specific forces of the decade. Besides the economic slowdown that beset North America in the first years of the decade and decreased the demand for industrial labour, there were particular ingredients within the Canadian economy that lent themselves to the emphasis on agricultural labour in immigration policy. Despite the fall in the price of wheat in the early twenties, Canadian agriculture as a whole remained relatively buoyant. Particularly in Ontario and Quebec, where farming had become intensive and tied to large urban markets, and where valuable cash crops, especially tobacco and fruit, were important, the sector was well sheltered from the international fluctuations that were a problem for much of Canada's staples-oriented export market. Also, throughout the twenties, the movement of the rural population to the cities, which had begun two decades earlier in response to an growing industrialism, continued unabated. In Ontario, while the importance of agriculture vis-à-vis other economic sectors declined, as did the number of farmers, the amount of productive acreage did not. Agriculture became increasingly consolidated and intensified. This, in addition to the decline in the rural birth rate, created a net demand for labour. Politicians and immigration policy were sensitive to this, and indeed, through the decade the number of farm labourers in Ontario increased.[32]

Moreover, immigration policy reflected concern over organized labour, which, as in the United States, was vocally opposed to newcomers and placed sustained pressure on politicians to restrict the inflow of potential competitors. After 1917 Canadian officials, like their American counterparts, were acutely aware of the radical ferment in Europe and anxious to prevent its expansion into Canada.[33] Prompted to action by the recession of 1920, policy-makers, by favouring the entry of "farm labourers," avoided the wrath of unionists, and could also claim to be protecting the social order from the threat of radical urban workers from Europe's agitated cities. Further, the fact that most farm labourers sooner or later found their way to the city was not altogether looked upon with disfavour by some urban politicians, since they generally drifted to low-paying, unskilled jobs in construction, manufacturing, and service industries. These were jobs employers had difficulty filling, and they actively lobbied government to supply them with labour.[34] Any protests from labour could conveniently be deflected on the part of politicians, by claiming that whatever influence immigrant workers had in the marketplace occurred in spite of government efforts, not because of them.

Lastly, while government policy may not have been explicitly influenced by the protests of Canadian nativists, it certainly dovetailed with their aspirations. As in the United States, Canadian politicians, clergymen, social workers, and the like lamented the decline of traditional rural life and warned against the growing social evils of the city.[35] Urban problems were often seen as synonymous with the "foreign" problem, an equation which sometimes entered into the thinking of immigration officials. So, here, too, the Canadian government's preference for "farm labourers" seemed to coincide with the concerns of Canadian public opinion and intellectuals disturbed by the rapidly changing nature of their society.

Within this general framework the Canadian government allowed common labourers to enter the country as the need arose to fill specific needs, particularly in the mining, metals, and pulp and paper industries. Blair stated the matter succinctly in a letter to the White Star–Dominion steamship line: "If any concern in Canada finds it impossible to secure labour here, we will consider the application [for general labourers]. You will see that this means that instead of such labour seeking a job in Canada, some employer in Canada must seek the labour."[36] In Toronto, employers such as the Christie Henderson Lime and Stone Company succeeded in using this escape clause to obtain several Italian immigrants. But such company sponsorship was problematic and only a few *paesani* gained entry through it.[37]

Fortunately for some villagers, family members of newcomers in Canada were excluded from the "occupation test." Unlike the American case, Canadian rules as to who counted as "family" were more encompassing. Not only wives and minor children could join the immigrant abroad, but also unmarried adult offspring, unmarried siblings, parents, and fiancées – provided the sponsor could guarantee their support if required. Moreover, the immigrant did not have to be a citizen to sponsor relatives as in the United States, but merely legally resident in Canada.[38] However, while those with close relatives in Canada could gain entrance, since the admissible categories did not include married children or siblings, only a limited chain effect was possible. And, since the existing colony was small and many immigrants had already sent for their close kin prior to 1921, the number of villagers who could emigrate under kinship auspices was not large. The sanction to sponsor close kin and be united with one's family by and large merely served to solidify decisions made before 1921 to settle in the new world; it did not allow for the potential settlement of new families left in the village. What did allow for this, what provided the bulk of the Rende area's movement to Canada, was the immigration of villagers through the farm labourer channel. Hence it was this regulation that had to be dealt with if even some of the many *paesani* left stranded in the village by American legislation were to succeed in reaching the new world. The informal strategy that was evolved by villagers to deal with this major administrative hurdle, what can be termed the "farm labour system," relied heavily on the nature of kin and *paesani* relations among Rende area villagers.

In the emigration from the Rende area during the twenties, it became necessary for the villagers to have a kinsman or *paesano* in the new land who could sponsor him. While villagers had made use of Rende area contacts prior to 1921, it was only now, with the advent of modern bureaucratic controls, that it became a necessary precondition. It was in this respect that the small pre-restrictionist colony in Toronto took on a significance much beyond its size. It was only for those Italians (in great measure Southerners) who had such a bridgehead that emigration still remained a possibility.[39]

Because of the structure of interpersonal networks within the Rende area, because individuals and families were widely known through reputation, and because every successful new immigrant himself or herself became a potential contact for other villagers, this precondition of sponsorship was not as serious an impediment to emigration as the small size of the pre-1921 colony in Toronto would lead one to believe. Hence, many villagers who desired to emigrate could establish some sort of contact with *paesani* in Canada who would be willing to help them.

The characteristic of elasticity of village kinship ties therefore became of prime importance at this historical juncture, allowing a substantial number of Rende area emigrants to change their destination from Chicago to Toronto. The important aspect of kinship elasticity here relates to the fact that, though one was born into a kin group and behaviour in this group was prescribed, there was a significant degree of personal choice in determining whom to affiliate with and the exact form the prescribed behaviour would take.[40] The four progressively less binding kin groupings – ranging from immediate family, to *familiari*, to relatives up to second cousin, to distant kin – were far from rigid and in actual fact one could "acquire," through close association, a closer level of kinship than genealogically ascribed, and hence participate in the rights and obligations concomitant with this *de facto* relationship. Such a state of affairs could even become formalized through *comparaggio* involved in the celebration of baptism, confirmation, or marriage.

Prior to 1921 the villagers who preferred to emigrate to Chicago had their closest kin there. Rights and obligations were both deepest and widest there and the individual could be assured of receiving maximum aid and support. After restrictionism, however, many *paesani* looked to more distant kin in Toronto for a linkage with the new world. The elasticity of kinship meant that the prospective immigrant could establish contact with kinsmen in Canada with whom he had little to do and whom sometimes he did not personally know. Once contact was made and relationships hitherto lying dormant were made manifest, a new cycle of reciprocal rights and obligations was set in motion. A similar dynamic was at work between villagers in the playing-out of connections of friendship.[41] This elasticity was an important mechanism allowing for the Rende area chain, in meandering fashion, to change its course of destination and future development. Further, it allowed for the evolution of constellations, or "circles," of kin and friends of different composition from those in the old world and indispensable to the social and economic welfare and community life of the peasant immigrants.

In short, *paesani* contacts in the new world were a necessity for the Canadian diversion to take place, and the elasticity of kinship contributed significantly to the ability of distant kin in the village to call upon the aid of new world settlers who were indispensable for their immigration. But exactly why was it that the prerogatives of a functioning kinship relationship had to be resurrected where hitherto they had lain dormant? What purpose did this serve? To answer this, it must be noted that government restrictions not only made new world *paesani* contacts indispensable, these barriers also made reliance on new world intermediaries more of a necessity than ever before. Access to *paesani* in North America became a precondition for emigration because it was necessary to have trusted contacts who could deal with the various professional go-betweens required by the workings of the farm labour system. And because this imposed upon the new world *paesano* heavy responsibilities and effort, it called for the activating of substantial rights and obligations.

The emigration of *paesani* to Canada was not easily accomplished and, for most, several administrative hurdles had to be surmounted. In this endeavour, peasant villagers often found themselves pitted against the bureaucratic apparatus of the state. Or, as expressed by the MacDonalds, the "latent functions of informal networks" came up against "the manifest functions of bureaucracy". the former, of course, aiming towards entrée into a land of plenty and the latter towards restricting and checking a movement deemed undesirable or, at least, second-rate. In this confrontation those very elements of background which were "judged relics of another age" – kinship, particularistic friendship and also patronage – proved to be the means by which villagers succeeded in surmounting modern bureaucratic barriers.[42]

The Farm Labour System

THE WORKING OF THE SYSTEM

For the Rende area villager who had made up his mind to emigrate to Canada, the first step was to establish contact with a Toronto kinsman or friend expressing his wishes. As one informant reflected: "I want to go to America again. I have a friend over here [Toronto] – a cousin, a little relation, see. He had married a cousin of mine, this Cosentino.... He had come before me and he had an uncle over here.... I write, "Please can I come to Canada?" So he made my way; he make my papers. But I gotta pay some money."[43]

Once communication with a *paesano* was established and he agreed to act as a sponsor, the contact then proceeded "to make the papers." This consisted of applying to the Department of Immigration and Colonization to have the potential immigrant enter as a farm labourer, and having an affidavit drawn up documenting that a particular farmer was willing to hire the villager.[44] While affidavits were not formally required by immigration regulations, the trade that quickly grew up in their issuance resulted from the villagers' recognition of Canadian immigration policy which favoured "farm labourers" and required that "some employer in Canada must seek the labour." Also, after application for sponsorship had been approved, the Italian government, in order to protect its citizens against possible detention or deportation, required that the application be visaed by its emigration officials in Canada before it would allow the exit of the nominee. Since this endorsement was easier to obtain if accompanied by assurance of employment and maintenance guarantees, affidavits also served as an effective response to the growing paternalism in emigration affairs by the Fascist regime.[45]

In the handling of documents it was natural for the sponsor to seek out intermediaries to expedite the process. Steamship and travel agents, immigrant bankers, notaries and lawyers were all solicited to mediate with government functionaries and to have the all-important papers filled correctly. Usually go-betweens put the *paesano* in touch with an available farmer who would attest to needing the labour of the aspiring immigrant, though sometimes the Toronto contact would take it upon himself to solicit the support of an Italian farmer near the city. In any case, as one informant described the purpose of these affidavits, or farm labour contracts:

> See, before for coming over here, you got to make application from a farmer, just for working on a farm – or the lumber – not for the city. If some farmer need some labour, you know, they make the papers for immigration. They say, "I need the people," for example, from Italy, from Russia. And Immigration they make the papers. You supposed to go work for one year, and after the farm, you can be free. I was working for a farmer too![46]

As the number of potential immigrants outstripped the supply of farm employers, a growing number of farmers were recruited to sign affidavits who in actual fact had no employment to offer. Such men naturally required some monetary incentive for their endorsement as did also those farmers who, learning of the payoffs, actually did need labourers. Hence, in addition to the cost of the affidavit provided by go-betweens, which was between $25 to $75, villagers were faced with paying off farm sponsors and often immigration officials.[47] All this amounted to costs of $200 or more required to grease the various palms involved in the farm labour system as the following testimony indicates:

> Then, you see, there came out – what do you call it? – the "black market." They made the papers, the farmer made them. Some lawyers, some immigration officers, they make these papers. They [*paesani*] say, "I got a friend from the Old Country in this country" and they make the papers. The papers were signed by Immigration; they eat too, you understand ... you paid $300 and had your papers made for you. Then it would be split between everybody; Immigration, the lawyer and – what do you call it here? – travel agency! where they make tickets for passage, for everything.[48]

This farm labour system was not restricted to the *paesani* in Toronto, but was widely practised by Italian immigrants generally. The system prompted a letter to immigration officials in Montreal from the Reverend R. De Pierro, pastor of the city's Italian Presbyterian Church and Rossland Mission:

> I feel it as a duty of my conscience to inform you, with a request that you bring this to the notice of the Immigration authorities at Ottawa, that there seems to be a widespread idea to have immigrants from Italy under false pretenses. This is what I mean: Italians living in Canada, seeking admission for their relatives from Italy, have made almost a customary [*sic*] to ask one of the few Italian farmers who have farms in the outskirts of Montreal, and have him sign an affidavit promising employment on their farm, although it is clearly understood that the coming immigrant will never go to work there. The affidavit is done with the evident intention to evade the Canadian law, which is unfair to this Dominion. I don't want to venture any too abrupt statement, but I believe that many of the applications of Italian would-be immigrants now under consideration of the Immigration Department, as well as several of those that will forth come, stating that these people are to be employed by farmers nearby Montreal, are made along the line spoken of, and should be dealt accordingly.[49]

The pastor was not telling immigration officials anything they did not already know, but there was little they could do about the matter. The affidavits were not legally binding nor were they required by immigration regulations. They were merely written statements of intent: assurances expediently used by intermediaries to increase the chances that applications for their clients would be seen to correspond with government policy and be dealt with favourably. For their part, the potential immigrants, as former peasants, could properly claim to be considered under one of the favoured occupational categories – "farm labourers" – in their applications. Further, any action the immigration bureaucrats wanted to take against the farm labour system was sure to be opposed by politicians. The federal government was responsive to the cheap labour needs of bona fide farmers (whose own sons were packing for the cities) as well as the labour needs of mining, pulp and paper, and construction interests.[50] In this connection, not a few Liberal politicians, who were part of the government of the day and whose party traditionally cultivated the "ethnic" vote, were sensitive not to antagonize this base of support. As was lamented by the secretary of the Department of Immigration and Colonization, referring to the farm labour system: "One of the most unfortunate features of this business is the use made of these intermediaries of Members of Parliament and other public officials and influential men on the one hand and of Canadian farmers on the other...were it not for the approaches by public men, who are not aware of the ramifications of this cursed system, it would be comparatively easy to stop it."[51]

Aside from the non-binding nature of the labour agreement, another consideration in the villagers' use of the farm labour system and readiness to abandon their placement and proceed to the city stemmed from the immigration regulations themselves. That is to say, the nexus of Canadian and Italian regulations made it desirable for the immigrant to have a sponsor who could guarantee his maintenance if need be, and once the immigrant left the farm he invariably made his way to his guarantor who proceeded to take responsibility for him. As one informant related: "Cicco came with the contract to work on the farm. But he came home after only a few days. He come home from the farm to Toronto; he went to the house of my uncle. Zio took responsibility for him. He had called him. Then he stayed in Toronto. Nobody liked to work on the farm, see. The money was too low."[52]

Because of the guarantee of kin support, Canadian immigration officials could not claim that the newcomer who had left farm labour and was searching for work in the city had become a public charge which, like similar charges, could be laid up to three years after the immigrant's arrival.[53] Hence, the immigrant had little to fear in the way of possible penalties. In this sense it was the immigration policies themselves which made it easy to disregard their intent. For while bureaucrats aimed at ensuring that intended agricultural workers served out their time on the farm, their regulations encouraged the promise of kin support for the newcomer and hence emboldened him to abandon the farm for the city.

Following the severe American quota regulations of 1924, some tightening up of the farm labour system was attempted in the same year in Canada with the introduction of "permits of entry." These form letters, issued by the Department of Immigration and Colonization, were intended to replace the use of affidavits and to control "misrepresentation" by having the farm labourers' agreement initiate with immigration officials. But the peasants' distrust of the institutions of the wider society and its functionaries was not easy to break, and Toronto immigrants continued their patronage of the traditional go-betweens. In fact, local immigration officials freely dispensed the permits to the usual intermediaries, frequently involving some kickback; the latter then proceeded to have the forms filled out as in the past.[54] Like the affidavits, the letters of permit were informal agreements, not legal documents. Legally, there was nothing to stop immigrants who entered the country under the farm labour system from joining *paesani* in Toronto after their arrival if they found that the farm labour promised did not exist or that working conditions were intolerable, or if they simply decided to ignore the agreement and proceed to city jobs.

The farm labour system, despite the efforts of Canadian immigration officials to control it, proved an effective means by which villagers were able to gain entry into Canada. When the system finally came to an end, it was not the Canadian government that wielded the axe, but the Fascist regime in Italy which, commencing in the summer of 1927, reversed its prior policy of promoting an open door on emigration. The Italian consul general, Dr. E. Bonardelli, like his immigrant compatriots, was caught unawares by Italy's new restrictionism and graphically communicated to Canadian authorities the shift in policy decided upon by the Fascist regime. In an official memorandum, Blair, now assistant deputy minister of the department, recorded:

> Dr. Bonardelli explained that he had made many and various proposals to his Government during the past few months for the adoption of a system which will allow a freer movement of Italians than under the scheme as now ordered by the Italian authorities. He said that he had come to the Department originally to get an open door and now he was in the position of coming to the Department to have the door closed and that this he understood to be the policy of his Government.[55]

The effect of closing the door was promptly felt by villagers. The first Fascist restrictions, introduced in the fall of 1927, limited the exit of relatives up to the third degree of kinship. This effectively blocked non-related *paesani* and distant kin (essentially cousins) from taking advantage of the farm labour system, since the Italian government did not recognize their sponsorship by contacts in Canada. Unless one fell under an eligible category of kinship, the only means of gaining an exit permit to Canada was to register with Italian manpower authorities and have one's name placed on a central waiting list which was processed as the need for labourers by Canadian employers arose.[56] Since Rome looked with disfavour upon the out-migration of agricultural workers, which it now saw as indispensable both for its domestic "battle for grain" and plans for overseas colonization, emigration through the impersonal auspices of the state provided small hope indeed for villagers, and Italian *contadini* generally.[57]

Nonetheless, since the categories of kin subsumed under the eligible list was extensive, some movement of relatives was still possible. Toronto villagers could still sponsor wives, unmarried children, parents, siblings, uncles and aunts, grandparents and mothers- or fathers-in-law.[58] As before, those relatives that were part of a sponsor's immediate family gained entry into Canada by virtue of being close kin, and the more distant relatives had to be sponsored under the usual farm labour auspices.

Unfortunately for villagers, this state of affairs did not last long. Months after the original restrictions were introduced, the list of those relatives eligible to leave Italy was steadily cut to narrower proportions. The first categories to be eliminated were the parental in-laws, uncles and aunts, and unmarried brothers. By the beginning of 1929 – obviously for manpower and military reasons – sons over the age of twenty-one and unmarried sisters with parents or siblings in Italy were also prohibited from emigrating. While Fascist regulations allowed immigrants who travelled to Italy to take back with them two relatives within the third degree of kinship upon their return to Canada, the economic plight of the Great Depression nullified any potential this had for villagers.[59]

At any rate, it can be seen that the introduction of Italian emigration restrictions effectively destroyed the farm labour system by which *paesani* had continued to move to North America through the twenties. In the words of an informant: "The Italian government stopped all permits [for farm labour]. Immigration was taking hundred of dollars. The Italian government found out and said, 'Stop!'... It was the Italian government that wouldn't let them [*paesani*] go, or else they would have continued to leave."[60] After 1929, to all intents and purposes, only members of an immigrant's immediate family were allowed to emigrate from Italy. This, of course, brought to an end the first era of chain migration that had spanned half a century. Additional restrictions introduced in the spring of 1930, which stipulated that immigrants who had left Italy after 1928 through kin sponsorship could not themselves call relatives, merely provided the nails to be driven into the coffin of chain migration.[61]

The farm labour system, as it developed in the 1920s, involved a definite and structured commerce of migration. The money that changed hands in this commerce brought together the immigrant, his *paesano* contact in Toronto, various go-betweens, farmers, and often local immigration officials. The cost to the potential immigrant to gain entry into Canada was often around $300. This was a considerable sum to pay for the people of the Rende area. Their widespread readiness to do so was a strong manifestation of their commitment to, and aspirations for, permanent settlement. A man operating from a sojourn frame of mind would not be willing to spend hundreds of dollars to gain access into the new world and incur debts in the process when his net savings from a stint at hard labour would often amount to little more than his costs. Further, the activity most suited to the sojourner – railroad work – after 1921 was virtually closed to *paesani*. Instead, the villager was faced with the possibility of doing a year's work on some isolated Canadian farm where he could expect the lowest of wages. While such a period of wasted earning power was often acceptable to the immigrant with long-term objectives in Canada, it was not to the would-be sojourner who desired to build up his savings in the shortest possible time.

Hence, not only did American restrictionism contribute powerfully to the transition to an immigrant *mentalità*, but concurrently, the contours of Canadian regulations also actively militated against the movement of sojourners, while they did relatively little to discourage the committed settler.

IMMIGRATION AND KIN COHESION

It was usual among villagers for kinsmen to offer support, both economic and emotional, to the aspiring migrant. He was lent money or forwarded passage tickets, his wife and children were taken care of, and *americani* offered worldly-wise advice and guidance. The cost of up to $300 involved in immigrating and the necessity of dealing with various go-betweens made the provision of loans and the informal mediating of relatives and friends indispensable. And, of course, now the new world sponsor often had to be prepared to guarantee the maintenance of the potential immigrant. In many instances immigration to Canada required the coordination of a greater number of kindred and *paesani* than had previously been the case and often forced villagers closer together in the effort to make the Atlantic crossing possible for any one individual.[62]

Within this aid network, the Chicago kin played a significant role. The farm labour system often led to a triangular flow which connected the Rende area, Toronto, and Chicago. In one case, for example, a villager made contact with his Toronto cousin who proceeded to deal with the necessary go-betweens; borrowed $300 from a Chicago brother to finance the greasing of palms; and was given another $50 to cover part of the cost of the voyage by a well-off brother in the village, who further consented to watch over his wife and children until they could join him in the new world. In a second instance, the aspiring emigrant borrowed several hundred dollars to cover the necessary costs from his father in the village (who himself had been a sojourner); a cousin in Toronto acted as trusted contact; and, further, a brother in Chicago was able to use his connections with *paesani* in Toronto to help the emigrant find construction work. In a third case, the emigrant was able to entrust his large family to the care of his well-to-do sister and brother-in-law in the Rende area and relied on his Chicago brother both to finance his immigration and to make the necessary bureaucratic arrangements in Toronto.[63]

Assisting immigrants bound for Canada by kinsmen in the United States was not unique to the villagers from the Rende area. When in 1923, for example, over three hundred Italian labourers were detained at Ellis Island en route to Canada by its immigration officials (ostensibly because of fraudulent documents, but more substantively to place political pressure on the Fascist regime to reinstate an open door on British lines competing for the emigration trade),[64] Gaspare M. Cusumano, manager of the Society for Italian Immigrants of New York, assured the Canadian minister of immigration of the aid relatives in the United States were ready to give the labourers:

> There is very little possibility that these men may become public charges in Canada as they have relatives and friends in this country who are ready and willing to furnish a guarantee to the Canadian Government to the effect that the men will be provided and cared for if they are allowed to come to Canada. The Immigrants themselves have asked me to state that they are ready to furnish a cash bond of at least one hundred dollars. The Society for Italian Immigrants will arrange to have the men accompanied to the border.[65]

Similarly, of the same immigrants, Italian Aid Society officials in Toronto assured immigration officials that since most of the detainees had relatives in Canada they would be taken care of by the Italian community and not pose a potential drain on social services. While it is difficult to gauge the effect of such assurances, a great many of the immigrants were subsequently allowed to proceed to Canada.[66]

In another illustration of kin linkages cutting across the North American boundary, Mabel Sutherland, director of Nicholas County Welfare Work, West Virginia, wrote to the Canadian Bureau of Colonization in 1927 that the Italians in her area "have to send a large part of their earnings to support their sons and brothers who are living

in Italy. Of course it makes a great hardship on the ones living here."
To alleviate the burden of support placed on the immigrants, who
were prevented by the quota law from calling their kin, Sutherland
somewhat naively requested that Canada take in the relatives of the
Nicholas County workers whose movement the immigrants were willing to assist. Further, she assured the Canadian authorities that if
accepted the Italian immigrants would remain in Canada and "not
cross over to the United States."[67]

While kinsmen in the United States were willing to help those aspiring to emigrate to Canada, as Sutherland inadvertently revealed, the
ultimate destination of immigrants was not always what they claimed
it to be. Sometimes the trek to Canada was merely a prelude to entry
into the United States. As stated earlier, traditionally some villagers
considered Canada, because of its less demanding immigration regulations, a convenient back door to the Republic. Obviously the flow
to Chicago – the villagers' preferred destination – would have continued had it been possible, or as one Toronto *paesana* expressed it, "Of
course, we would have gone to the States if we could. There we had
all our *parenti* (relatives)."[68]

While this was the wish, few of the post-restrictionist Toronto immigrants actually attempted to cross the border. Of those who did, low
wages and ill-treatment as farm labourers were in some instances
contributing factors. More important was the fact that in proceeding
to Chicago, immigrants calculated that, since kin relationships were
more numerous and closer in the Windy City, their chances of obtaining well-paying, desirable work was greater there. One informant who
had "gone contraband" related: "My [close] relations were all in
Chicago....My brother came up here one day to see me. He told me
about all the good jobs in Chicago. I was working on small construction
jobs at the time, so I decided to go there."[69]

The informant went on to relate how his construction foreman in
Toronto put him in touch with a "mafia" man who upon the payment
of $300 had him smuggled into the United States through Buffalo.
Upon reaching Chicago, the man's uncle helped him to find a good
paying job working as a labourer on the city's gas mains. Shortly afterwards, another relative was able to find work for him with the Wonder
Bread Company. He added that he always used his legal name and
was never checked by American immigration authorities.

Such instances, however, were the exception. Notwithstanding the
concern expressed by Canadian immigration officials that Italian
immigrants were using Canada as a back door to the United States –
while conveniently ignoring the much greater exodus of native Canadians moving south – the reports of informants indicated that relatively few *paesani* sought to leave.[70] In light of the ready contacts and
avenues for entering the United States known to villagers, of the general

perception that this contraband trade was efficient and well organized, and of the powerful pull of the Chicago colony, the question that arises is not why those who left did so, but rather why more villagers did not take advantage of the contraband route. While the cost involved in resettling in the United States was substantial, this was not a major barrier. Money to cover the expense, like the cost involved in emigrating from the village, could usually be borrowed from settled kin and friends if it was truly needed.

More centrally, there were two major reasons for their reluctance to seek entry into the United States. The post-restrictionist *paesani*, as immigrants, had made a long-term commitment to settlement in the new world. They certainly did not want to be deported. It took only a couple of examples of thwarted attempts to cross the border and resultant prosecution to convince the majority of *paesani* not to risk the same folly. The following testimony is indicative of this caution: "At that time you couldn't go to Chicago. If you came to Canada, you couldn't go to the United States....But there was a black market. There was no right way, only wrong way to go....It cost $300 on the black market. They would take you to the frontier where there was no guards. But if they found you, oh! They would shoot at you if they saw you! They wouldn't let you pass. If they caught you, they would send you to Italy, oh yeah!"[71]

More importantly, the very centrality of kinship which lay behind the villagers' preference for Chicago motivated them to remain in Toronto. As immigrants, men now ventured to the new world to pave the way for their families to join them. The Toronto immigrants realized that even if they succeeded in joining siblings or uncles in Chicago, they would not be able to sponsor their wives and children left in the village from the United States. Since the 1906 American naturalization law brought citizenship under federal control, ending the era when certificates could be easily acquired through the individual states, the *paesano* who ventured to the United States as an illegal immigrant was prevented from obtaining citizenship, and hence, being joined by his family.[72] Because of this, even where the decision to cross into the United States had been successfully carried out, in a number of instances villagers returned to Toronto to be able to send for their families to join them. And where this occurred, the "black market" had again to be resorted to, causing not only another substantial outlay of money, but also another round of anxiety and uncertainty. As expressed by an informant: "They [American immigration authorities] have a list of all the immigrants. My name was not there and I couldn't bring my family [wife and son]. They would check and see my name wasn't there if I tried to call them. Then I'd be in lots of trouble, you know....So I paid $300 to get out of Canada, then I paid again going in."[73]

Such facts impressed themselves upon the post-quota *paesani*, militated against the lure of Chicago, and hence encouraged the growth and solidification of the Toronto colony.

THE FARM LABOUR EXPERIENCE

After 1920, more than at any other time in the past, the new world experience was shaped by government policy. After following the farm labour system through its many steps and arriving in Canada, *paesani* divided into two main categories. Many villagers made some effort to fulfill the terms of contract under which they had emigrated. Others arrived either knowing that their agreement was merely a formality or they decided on the strength of previous examples to ignore it and proceed directly into the urban labour force. In any case, only a minority worked a full year at farm labour as both the affidavits and farm permits had stipulated. A complex amalgam of *paesano* networks, aspirations, and the relative decline of agriculture within the Canadian economy itself all combined irrevocably to direct villagers to the city. This predilection towards urban work was critically recognized by immigration mandarins. As Blair, the acting deputy minister of immigration, wrote at mid-decade: "Canada has for many years had some immigration from Italy. When the occupational test came into effect some three or four years ago, a class of Italians who up to that time had been coming in as general labourers, fruit vendors, bootblacks, etc., and going to our cities, were suddenly changed to farm labourers, but their destination was the same and it was not long before we found that their occupation had changed only in name."[74]

The success of the farm labour system brought increasing criticism of Italian immigration. Especially with the failure of the permits plan to check the movement after 1924, some officials within the Department of Immigration and Colonization showed an increasing frustration as the matter came to be viewed along neat Manichean lines. Within this framework the immigrant, his sponsors, and various intermediaries were cast as villains; government bureaucrats who were fighting a rearguard campaign viewed themselves as safeguarding the integrity of their department, and perhaps also the nation's moral and racial fibre. The acting deputy minister, for one, viewed the immigration of Italians under the farm labour category as almost entirely fraudulent:

> [We] decided to investigate applications submitted to us by Italians, almost all of whom were living in our cities. We found that a regular business had been established for buying and selling so-called Permits to come into Canada and foreign agents, some of whom were Italians, but most of whom were Jewish people, were engaged in the enterprise. We have investigated hundreds of these in various parts of Canada and I am safe in saying that 95% of

the cases investigated were bogus. What we most frequently found was (a) that some employer's name had been signed to a bogus contract or that some person in Canada had been influenced by a payment of money or otherwise, to sign a bogus labour contract, and (b) that the immigrant had no intention of following farm work in Canada and that the labour contract was put up simply with the intention of getting a Permit.[75]

While there is some truth in this statement and the common bogus use of the farm labour system cannot be denied, what is disturbing and false here is the exaggeration or distortion of certain aspects. First, although steamship agents and similar intermediaries undoubtedly did a brisk trade handling the department's form letters, these, as recognized by other officials, were neither usually "foreign agents" nor "mostly Jewish," but go-betweens — both formal and informal — indigenous to the immigrant community. The experience of Toronto *paesani* made no reference to travel agents, notaries and the like outside Little Italy being used to arrange for the immigration of kin and friends under the farm labour system, though other Southerners may have done so. In this connection, Sidlofsky remarked on the new-found importance after 1921 of local go-betweens in Toronto's Italian colony:

> The preference shown agricultural workers [after 1921] influenced the status of segments within the local population. Since immigrant arrangements could be made with those able to employ farm labour, more attention was paid the food-store owners, who had their own market-gardens or know the small farmers in the suburban areas....
> The travel agents also assumed major roles. Their functions as remittance men declined as the pre-War settlers brought their families...[but] Their basic transportation function increased in importance.... Their established intermediary role had given the agents access to all segments of the community including those who wanted to bring immigrants, as well as those who had begun to save or invest in land upon reducing their remittances to Italy.... The ties of national identification made it almost mandatory that those able to assist in immigration through providing farm jobs would do so.[76]

Ironically, while some top immigration bureaucrats complained of "foreign agents," the department itself was party to the official use made of Canada's largest and most powerful *padroni*. The Montreal labour bureaus run by Cordasco, Rossi and Salviati, who recruited and distributed several hundred men at a time, were used openly not only by private employers but also Canadian government departments concerned with regulating labour demand and supply.[77]

Secondly, although many farm labour applications involved misleading statements, to claim that practically all were fraudulent, as did the acting deputy minister, was a different matter, contradicted by the basic fact that the information on the contract forms was checked by the department's own field officials. That is to say, unless one posits the view that these officials were totally inept – or the Italian immigrants exceptionally cunning – it is difficult to fathom how fully "95% of the cases" put before them, and which allegedly contained falsehoods, escaped their notice. Indeed, at least one of the department's three division commissioners, Thomas Gelley, based in Winnipeg, expressed views diametrically opposed to Blair's disparaging claims. Writing to W.J. Egan, the deputy minister of immigration in 1926, Gelley noted:

> I am certain that the settlement arrangements covering these [farm] permits were satisfactory and that the interested parties [farmers] here were bona fide in their intention....
> The Italians are good workers and many of the farmers who have seen them at this work are well satisfied with their services and this is the reason they are making application for them.
> ...the percentage of Italians actually at farm work who came forward this year is larger than any other nationality, either from preferred or non-preferred countries, with the exception of Mennonites.[78]

The commissioner was here speaking from his experience on the prairies, but it should not be thought that his observations lacked support in Ontario, even though the pull of industry there was much greater. Farmers in the central province were generally in favour of an open immigration policy. Though obviously as agricultural employers they had their own vested interests in this, the letter of a Windsor area tobacco farmer to that city's newspaper in 1925 illustrates that in the experience of many farmers, Italians proved to be desirable workers:

> Last year a number of Italian men were admitted to this country for farm work. Some of them were sent down here in the tobacco district, and proved so satisfactory as labourers, that more were applied for this Spring.... Would it be possible to secure your good offices in recommending these applications. The influx of these men WILL NOT affect the local labour situation and as these men are guaranteed work and will mean so much to the development of the tobacco growing industry, it does not seem good business to hold up bona fide applications. From my experience with them, they are a desirable type – quickly learn our methods, language, etc., and are honest, thrifty and industrious. They do work in tobacco farming that you can scarcely hire native citizens to do.[79]

Luckily for Canadian farmers and for many villagers, the more liberal view of politicians held sway over the bureaucrats who, until the last, were never quite given the "free hand" they desired to put an end to the "cursed system."

Thirdly, though it is difficult to deal with the question of intent, the view of mandarins that the Italian "immigrant had no intention of following farm work in Canada," and that almost to a man the "labour contract was put up simply with the intention of getting a Permit," can also be called into question. The social worker Gaspare M. Cusumano, for example, perceived the situation quite differently. Although he too saw the farm labour system as conforming to a Manichean scheme with immigrants wearing white and agents and farmers wearing black, nonetheless his testimony provides a valuable counterpoint to the accusations made by ranking immigration officials:

> As Manager of the Society for Italian Immigrants of New York, stationed at Ellis Island, I come into immediate contact with all Italian Immigrants who are detained at the U.S. Immigration Station. This naturally has given me the best opportunity to obtain first hand facts and information as to the reasons for the detention of the Immigrants. Particularly as to the Canadian bound Italian Immigrants I find that the men came from Italy in good faith; spent their own money to pay passage and expenses and on arrival they are detained because either the farm and fruit gathering seasons are over, or that the steamship agents and farmers deceived them. I find that the men are not to blame for this unfortunate situation but, on the other hand the blame should be placed upon the farmers who signed the affidavits in blank when in reality they do not need them or upon the unscrupulous agents who have farmers sign affidavits in good faith and then sent for the men in Italy with no intention to supply the needs of the farmers.[80]

With regard to the question of farm labour, the accounts of Rende area informants reveal a much more complex picture than that presented by top immigration officials, or, in contrast, by satisfied employers and immigrant aid workers.

For the majority of villagers for whom the farm labour agreement was something more than an empty formality, the decision of whether to report for farm duty was not a simple matter. While on the one hand as immigrants who sought to make a permanent investment in the new world they were anxious to avoid the disfavour of Canadian authorities, on the other hand as devoted family men who were committed to bringing over their immediate relatives and providing for their support, they could ill afford precious time at low-paying farm employment. Since greater security was felt to lie in the former route – in reporting for farm labour – many proceeded with this. But here a number of situations could arise which acted to encourage, if not force, the immigrant's movement to the city.

As indicated by Cusumano, in some cases where the immigrant sought to report for farm labour, he found that there was no work for him to do and sometimes no farmer. As one informant related:

"They [*paesani*] would come over here. But there was no work, no farm. The farmer just put it down....they made the papers. The papers were all right, you see. They were done by Immigration; but there was no work. They were made for a farmer – but this farmer, you never know the farmer."[81] In a second example, one *paesano*, speaking of his own experience, told how he had entered into a labour agreement with an Italo-Canadian farmer on Toronto's outskirts. Reporting to him upon his arrival he discovered that the employer was really a part-time truck farmer with no work for him. Naturally he then proceeded to try to find a job in the city.[82] It is evident that in such cases immigrants were unaware that their sponsoring farmers – often small general producers – while taking advantage of payoffs, actually had no real capacity to supply employment.

In other instances, the immigrant was engaged by farmers who required seasonal but not full-time labour. One villager was placed on a northern farm and his employer told him after merely three weeks that he no longer needed his labour and hence recommended a second farmer he could work for. Reporting there, the immigrant stayed on for another two and a half months until winter, when he was given the task of harvesting logs from the woodlot. Though he was treated well, was allowed to operate the farmer's tractor and other farm machinery, and enjoyed the family's company, he was underemployed and asked the farmer if he could leave, to which his employer had no objection. The man's decision was based on the simple calculation that he could earn in a week working in Toronto what he earned monthly employed on the farm.[83]

Some villagers were also faced with harsh living conditions and illtreatment which spurred them to act upon their preference for the city. One elderly woman told how two kinsmen who had emigrated and been hired together were made to sleep outside the farmer's house in a shack, given poor and insufficient food, and generally treated as "slaves." In a manner reminiscent of the underground railroad of the mid-nineteenth century, the informant told how the men abandoned their employer, and, after making their way to the Toronto colony, "fled" to close relatives in Chicago: "They came with the farmer [labour contract] to work on the farm. But they were treated so badly! They had to sleep outside the house – like in a barn – and were not even given a plateful to eat [at supper]. They couldn't take it any more, so they ran away – on foot. They fled to the States. For Chicago they didn't make any papers, so they had to go contraband – to their brothers in Chicago."[84]

Such conditions might have been tolerated prior to the First World War by sojourners on railroad gangs whose morale was kept up by the knowledge that they would soon be returning to the village, by relatively high wages, and by the camaraderie of fellow *paesani*. But they were not tolerated by post-restrictionist immigrants whose levels of living in the village had improved, who as farm labourers worked for the very minimum of wages, and who were usually isolated from their fellows. Indeed, observers of the native Canadian exodus from the countryside recognized even in the boom years before the war that living and working conditions for farm labourers were inadequate and would have to be substantially improved if farmers wanted to retain their help. The Reverend John MacDougall of Spencerville, Ontario, for example, propounding the social gospel, wrote in 1913: "The problem of the farm laborer is an unsolved one in Canada as yet, nor will it be solved until greater efficiency is demanded, higher wages paid, and a home for the farm laborer and his household provided...what modern industry has discovered modern agriculture must learn, namely, that the best paid and cared for labor is the most profitable."[85]

In a similar vein Dr. George C. Creelman, president of the Ontario Agricultural College in Guelph, lamented over the working conditions of farm labourers. Speaking of "rural problems" before the Canadian Club of Toronto just prior to the war, he made the following remarks, which, moreover, reflected some of the thinking behind official immigration policy:

> A third problem is the securing of better and more permanent hired help. A great many men could put up a cottage and let it on terms to make that hired man a human being. We forget that the hired man is the farmer of to-morrow.... On the farm you need to keep a man busy all the year around, to give him a house, so his children can attend school and get a chance to become bright, young, intelligent Canadian citizens.... We need all the farm help we can get, and perhaps we could do with fewer so-called mechanics – Jacks of all trades.[86]

It was recognized, then, that the problem of maintaining labour on the farm could not be solved until conditions and opportunities were upgraded to at least approach those offered by industry, a precondition that was, of course, to prove structurally impossible.

Like their native counterparts, many *paesani* initially intended to make do with the farm labour route, albeit temporarily as a means to later city employment. However, like Canadian agricultural labourers – not to mention sons of the farmers themselves – they too were often forced to abort their intentions by underemployment, low wages, and unacceptable living conditions. The abandonment of farm labour by Rende area immigrants before their work stint was up was not very different from the wider, rural Canadian discontent, which, somewhat surprisingly, immigration officials, perturbed by the workings of the farm labour system, not once admitted to. To the complaint that conditions which the Italian farm labourer faced were often exploitative, officials could merely remark that "They are at liberty to return to Italy if they wish to do so."[87]

Aside from this, however, there remained the experience of a minority of villagers who did serve out their first year on the farm. Among these, one former peasant immigrant who expressed the view that "everything come from the land" and that the "farmer was the most important" member of society, deplored the fact that "everybody wanted to go to the city." The *paesano* remained, in accordance with his contract, with the general farmer who had sponsored him until he was given his "release papers." Likewise working to the end of his one-year stint was another immigrant who was employed by a mushroom farmer west of Toronto. In a third example, another villager who worked for a relatively well-to-do Italo-Canadian truck farmer on the city's outskirts also fulfilled his terms.[88]

In any case, immigrants who reported for farm labour could either find themselves on farms near the city or hundreds of miles from it. Hence, villagers stayed on the farm for various lengths of time and also found themselves in a variety of different locations. As a *paesano* expressed it: "It was this way at that time. At that time you could only come to Canada as a farm labourer. Some were sent far, far away — to the West even — way to hell out there. But mostly, we worked close to Toronto. Some guys stayed a year; others after two or three months, they finished."[89]

Through the twenties the first employers that were approached to act as sponsors were the Italian truck farmers in the vicinity of Toronto. The farm labour system brought new status to those Italians in and around Toronto — mainly small farmers and grocers — who were able to facilitate immigration, and evidently it intensified national identification as every possible employer was canvassed for his support. Once these contacts were exhausted, however, farmers outside of the Toronto vicinity were approached by intermediaries (sometimes with the aid of the government employment service) in order to gain sponsors for potential labourers. By 1924 the farm labour system spreading outward from Toronto had encompassed the general agricultural, dairy, and tobacco areas of western Ontario as well as the fruit belt between Hamilton and Niagara Falls.[90] Both western Ontario and the Niagara peninsula were prosperous, labour-intensive districts which employed a number of villagers as the Toronto vicinity became saturated with labourers.

It is clear from these examples that the farm labour experience of the villagers cannot be easily characterized in the derogatory manner leading immigration officials used when referring to Italian immigrants, and Southerners in particular. It is noteworthy here that the testimony of *paesani* when pieced together proved an effective vehicle by which the complexity of their experience could be approached and appreciated. More so than the written record on the matter, informants presented an array of experiences which goes beyond easy stereotypes. They freely admitted that while immigrants often came with the intention of ignoring their labour agreements, many others were willing to make an effort to fulfill them. While the farm labour experience touched the great majority of the post-1921 *paesani*, there was considerable heterogeneity as to its specific content from individual to individual. What was common, however, was the villagers' commitment to moulding a new life in the new world. Whether a day, a month, or a year after their arrival, this new life involved the city, not the country.

CHAPTER 7

Settler Patterns in Toronto

Settlement in the City

THE COLLEGE STREET SETTLEMENT

The immigrants from the Rende area who arrived in Toronto after restrictionism found an Italian community that had grown in population from almost 4,900 in 1911 to over 9,000 in 1921. The near doubling of Toronto's Italian population in that decade represented a greater rate of increase than that for Toronto's population as a whole, which grew from 376,500 to well over half a million. Forming almost 2 per cent of Toronto's population in 1921, Italians approached the representation they had in Chicago of over 3 per cent in 1910; and by the time of the 1931 census, they had expanded to 15,600.[1]

By 1921 the Ward no longer contained Toronto's major Italian concentration, nor did it still function as the major commercial and reception area for newcomers. Its decline was primarily the result of development projects which had started as early as 1911 with the construction of an expanded general hospital in the vicinity of the Central Neighbourhood House, this alone causing the razing of two hundred homes.[2] Further commercial development in subsequent years accentuated the decline of the Ward as an Italian immigrant area.

As had been the case in Chicago, Toronto's Italians did not form a single unified colony. Indeed, residential mobility and diversity among the city's Italians stretched back into the 1880s when they numbered less than five hundred. With growing immigration and occupational improvement through the early twentieth century, the numbers involved in residential diversity increased considerably.[3]

In the 1920s there were four Italian concentrations corresponding roughly to regional and, to a lesser extent, occupational demarcations.

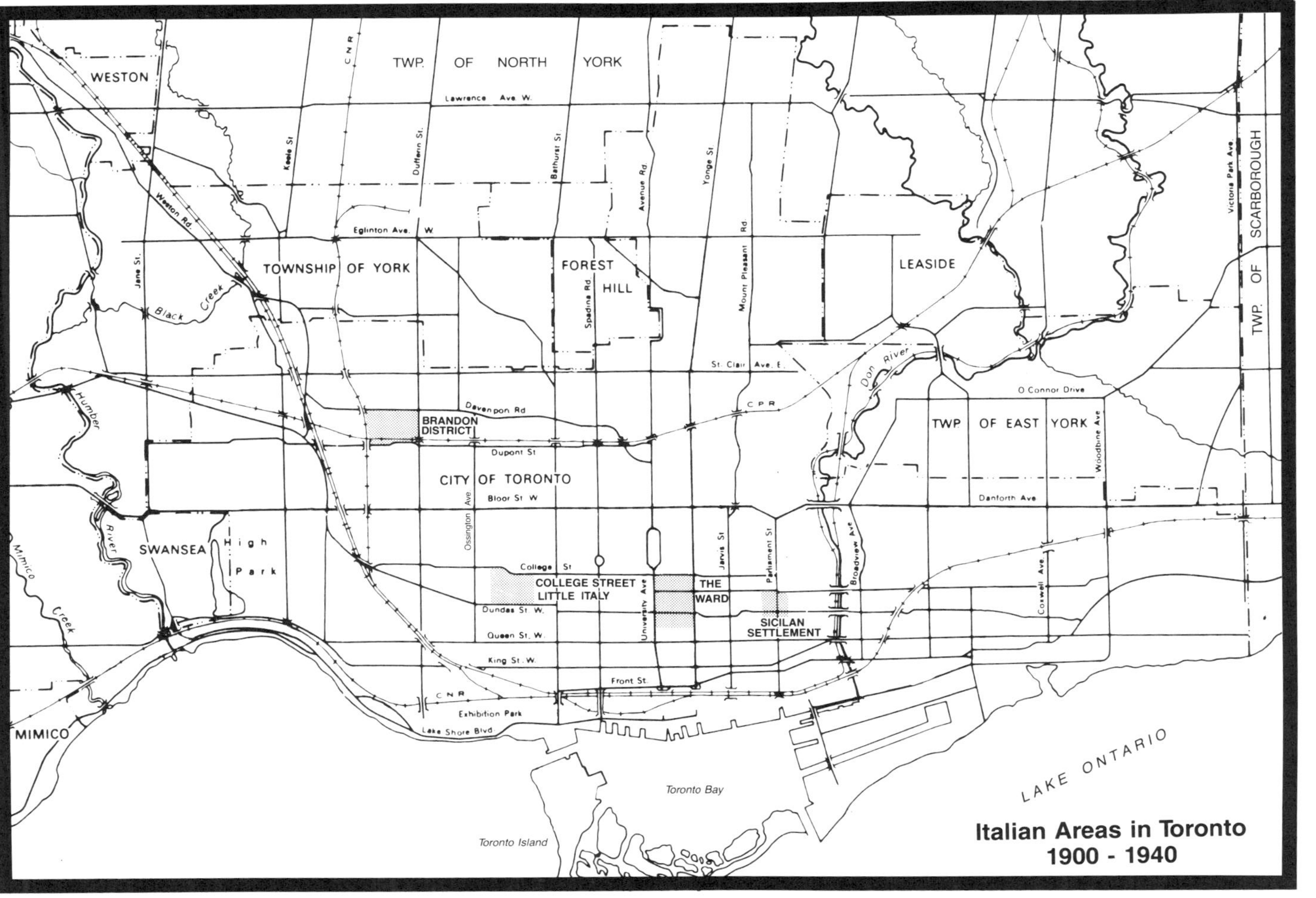
WESTON
TWP. OF NORTH YORK
C N R
Lawrence Ave. W.
Keele St
Dufferin St.
Bathurst St.
Avenue Rd.
Yonge St.
Mount Pleasant Rd.
Victoria Park Ave
TWP. OF SCARBOROUGH
Jane St.
Weston Rd.
Eglinton Ave. W.
TOWNSHIP OF YORK
FOREST HILL
Spadina Rd
LEASIDE
Black Creek
St. Clair Ave. E.
Don River
CPR
O'Connor Drive
TWP. OF EAST YORK
Woodbine Ave
Davenport Rd
BRANDON DISTRICT
Dupont St
CITY OF TORONTO
Bloor St W
Danforth Ave
Humber River
Ossington Ave
Jarvis St
Parliament St
Broadview Ave
Coxwell Ave
SWANSEA
High Park
College St
COLLEGE STREET LITTLE ITALY
University Ave
THE WARD
Mimico Creek
Dundas St. W.
SICILAN SETTLEMENT
Queen St. W.
King St. W.
Front St
C N R
Exhibition Park
Lake Shore Blvd
MIMICO
Toronto Bay
LAKE ONTARIO
Toronto Island
Italian Areas in Toronto
1900 - 1940

In the Ward, immigrants from Puglia (Monteleone and Modugno di Bari) still lived around Walton Street, with heavy representation in the boot-blacking and barbering trades. To the southeast, Sicilians from the eastern part of the island (Pachino) lived in the Queen Street East and Sackville Avenue area and were prominent in the fruit trade. To the northwest, at Dufferin Street just south of Davenport, and focused around Brandon Avenue, were to be found a cluster of skilled and unskilled construction workers from central Friuli and the Chieti area of Abruzzi. Finally, between the Ward and the Brandon district in the increasingly important College and Grace area, immigrants from Puglia, Molise, Basilicata and, most predominantly, Cosenza lived, a large number of the *cosentini* being involved in road and street railway construction.[4]

Although this represented the general contours of Italian settlement, it goes without saying that not all Italians lived within these residential concentrations; many western Sicilians, for example, were market farmers in the city's outskirts in West Hill. Furthermore, within the Italian districts, there was considerable mixing and virtually all regional groups were represented in Toronto.

While each concentration developed its own commercial and institutional framework, it was the College Street colony, which was also the largest, that in the 1920s emerged as Toronto's major Little Italy, the main immigrant reception and commercial centre.[5] A government report on Toronto's Italians documented both the increasing dispersal of the immigrants and the demographic shift from the Ward to the College settlement:

> In 1901, 65% of all Italians in the Toronto area resided in the central part of the City [St. John's Ward] while 15% lived in the West End. In 1911 about 42% lived in the centre of the city and 21% in the West End. By 1921 a large proportion were in the West End (27.6%), while only 23.6% still lived downtown. Thus there was a centrifugal population shift from the centre of the city towards the outer regions, especially the West End.[6]

The West End, or College Street, Little Italy, was bounded by Manning Avenue on the east, Crawford Street on the west, College on the north, and Dundas Street on the south. Indicative of the demographic transition from the Ward to College settlement was the establishment in the latter in 1914 of the city's second Italian parish, St. Agnes, at Dundas and Grace, just to the west of the Ward's Our Lady of Mount Carmel located on St. Patrick Street. Similarly, around the same time a new Protestant, but non-proselytizing, social settlement, St. Christopher House, was founded at Dundas and Bathurst; the Methodist mission on Elm Street in the centre of the Ward established a branch in the College settlement; a new Italian Pentecostal congregation, also stemming from the older centre, was set up; and new mutual benefit societies and clubs were founded. Most significantly for villagers, the Ward's characteristic migrant institutions – its boarding-houses and hotels, travel agencies, immigrant banks, and employment bureaus – were increasingly being established in the College settlement, alongside the usual array of grocery stores, barber shops, tailor shops, and so on.[7] The Venezia Hotel at College and Clinton streets played an important role, not only as a boarding-house, but also as the headquarters of Francesco Tomaiuolo, one of the city's most influential *padroni,* who was primarily a private banker and steamship agent.

In any event, by 1921 the majority of *paesani* were to be found in the College Street Little Italy. Though some villagers remained in the Ward through the twenties, when Rende area immigrants arrived in the city in the post-restrictionist decade, they invariably made their way to the College colony, bypassing the old centre altogether.

Fed on the one hand by old settlers deflected from the Ward and on the other by new immigrants arriving from the old world, by the end of the twenties a distinct Rende area colony had emerged within the College Street Little Italy. It tended to cluster around the homes and boarding-houses of *paesano* pioneers, many of whom hailed from the village of San Sisto. The earliest of these centres was the grocery store of Salvatore Turano, established in the 1890s, on Mansfield Avenue. Earlier, Turano had been a fruiterer on Queen Street West and at the turn of the century Mansfield Avenue became the focal point for other San Sisto fruit traders. On the same short street another early immigrant, Raffaele Bartello, also owned a grocery store which, like Turano's, doubled as a boarding-house. The premises of the latter had the additional function of serving as a labour bureau for *paesani* seeking local construction jobs.

Around 1910 Vincenzo Muto from Cerisano moved his tailor shop from the Ward to College and Grace streets, just a few blocks from Mansfield, and some of his employees lived above the shop. In the 1920s the home of Carmine Spizzirri, again on Mansfield, also came to be used by *paesani* as a boarding-house. Just two blocks away on Grace Avenue the home of Pasquale Molinaro, a motorman for the Toronto Transit Commission, came to have particular significance for *paesani.* Molinaro could point the way to potential jobs and, as part-time correspondent for the *Progresso Italo-Americano* of New York, was a man of some influence.[8]

Such early immigrants and their homes were important to *paesani* while they were still sojourners or in the initial stage of settlement. When villagers could afford houses of their own, these of course became the addresses of preference for their kin and friends. Through the early twentieth century the Rende area settlement, while focused on

Mansfield, radiated outward to nearby streets. By the 1930s the Rende area immigrants constituted a well-defined, substantial neighbourhood within the more general Little Italy. *Paesani* were concentrated along the north-south arteries of Bellwoods, Clinton, and Manning, and the short intersecting streets of Treford and Gore. Among the dozen or so large Rende area families that lived in the vicinity were the Alfano, Chiappetta, Costabile, Greco, Leone, Lucchetta, Miceli, Molinaro, Manaco, Paolucci, Sannuto and Spizzirri.[9]

The living quarters of *paesani* in the College colony were generally better than those of the Ward since many of the structures were substantial two- and three-storey brick houses, but in the southern end of the settlement around Dundas and Bellwoods older rows of small, one-storey, rough-cast cottages were to be found. These offered scant improvement over conditions in the older centre. As one immigrant recalled: "I first lived at Dundas and Manning. It was all shacks there. The small [row] houses were all the same. Somebody repair the house, but it was still all shacks.... I remember some cellars too. They were like pig-sty, dirty. But they was cleaned up by us."[10] However, such homes were in the minority. As a rule, the more substantial houses acquired by villagers in the College settlement influenced post-restrictionist immigrants to settle there since they were much more likely to find available accommodation among kindred – often the newcomer's sponsor – than in the declining, congested Ward colony.

Another advantage offered by the College settlement was related to the *paesani*'s work. For many, especially in their first year or so in the city, the district was a recruitment centre for Toronto's pick-and-shovel crews offering jobs at road-building, the laying of streetcar lines, paving sidewalks, and the like. For men and women who worked in the nearby garment district or in laundries, bedding factories, and other low-skill jobs, their workplace was often within walking distance or easily accessible by the Dundas, College, Bathurst or Spadina streetcars. Of course, for *paesani* shopkeepers such as the grocers from San Sisto, or *artigiani* such as the tailors from Cerisano, the College Street colony provided an abundance of clients.[11]

All in all, residential concentration of Rende area immigrants in the College district contributed to the "critical mass" required to render old world local loyalties operative in the new. In Toronto, as in Chicago, work parties of *paesani* were formed for the renovation of homes and the making of wine and *salsiccia* and *soppressata* in the autumn. People preferred to frequent the groceries, tailor shops, or shoe repairs of *paesani,* and they congregated in mutual aid societies such as the Circolo Operai dell' Ontario. Moreover, the evidence for Toronto suggests a further indicator of Rende area ties – that is, endogamy.

In a study examining the marriage patterns of Italian immigrants in Toronto, it was found that while marriage within "home town" groups may not have been particularly significant, marriage in the local area cluster was often impressive. Of forty-three immigrants from communes in the Rende area, while 35 per cent married immigrants from their respective home towns, fully 61 per cent married within the Rende area group. A similar pattern existed for immigrants from the Susa area in Piedmont and for those from central Friuli as well as others.[12] In any event, it can be stated that in the new world, as in the old, Rende area endogamy among *paesani* was an enduring index of the reality of a local social space. Along with rites of passage celebrations and numerous other interactions, such endogamy tended to extend the *paesani's* sense of social space beyond the immigrant generation and neighbourhood base.

The College Street Little Italy which emerged during the twenties, with a population of over 2,500 Italians, was far from a rigid and homogeneous entity. First, while people from Cosenza, especially those from the Rende area, formed the most numerous identifiable concentration, other Southerners were also in evidence. To the north of the Mansfield centre were located an important group from the Pisticci area in Basilicata, alongside *paesani* on Manning lived immigrants from Modugno di Bari (Puglia), and clustered around Claremont were other Italians from Sora (Lazio).[13] Moreover, even on the streets with the heaviest concentration of Italians, they rarely formed more than 60 per cent of the immediate neighbourhood. Also important in Little Italy were Anglo-Canadians, Jews, and Slavs. Nonetheless, the Southern Italian *ambiente* was unmistakable in the area and villagers had little to do with the other nationalities.[14] Although *paesani* interacted closely with one another, contact with other Italians was necessary and socially unavoidable. Hence, informants spoke not only of the primary coherence between *paesani,* but also of social cohesiveness within the more general Southern Italian community. Fluctuating between both levels of cohesion, one immigrant from Montalto related of Little Italy in the twenties: "It was more united when I came. There was respect for people and *paesani* visited each other. At *feste,* we [Italians] all got together. We didn't try to outdo each other, try to see who can do something different.... That's because there were fewer Italians then."[15]

Paesani viewed the College colony as existing detached from the world of "the English," as the Canadian-born and British immigrants were called. Referring to this as well as the community's cohesiveness, another twenties' immigrant said: "In those days people [immigrants] stuck together more. We entertained ourselves; made money. People worked and were happy – we weren't greedy.... And we minded our own business in America. We didn't bother with the English."[16] Many villagers viewed both themselves and the Southern settlement as existing in a state of tension, if not antagonism, with the host society. Though *paesani* still referred to discrimination as resulting from their lack of English, foreign ways, or unskilled employment position, and of being called derisive names as had the earlier migrants, for the settled immigrant discrimination was now often seen to spring from a quite different motivation: jealousy on the part of the natives because of the villagers' material success:

> The English couldn't stand us because they saw that the Italian worked. Working he bought a home and they'd put seven to eight boarders there. And within a few years they had already paid their homes. They were jealous. I know that Italians are hard workers. They are honest people. Everyone tries to improve their home. As a matter of fact the mayor got complaints saying, "Look at these Italians here in America. They work even on Sunday. They work – they make a racket in the morning. I want to sleep." But we were improving Toronto, isn't that so?[17]

Such evidence suggests that though chain residence patterns in the new world were an outgrowth of chain migration based on kin and village linkages, the coherence and persistence of the latter were not unrelated to the hostile attitudes of the host society. While the spatial and social detachment of *paesani* reflected their past separation from the wider polity in Italy, the view of the immigrant colony as a "protective" response to native antagonism, while it has justifiably been criticized as inadequate, cannot be entirely discounted.[18] The great majority of *paesani* did experience at least some hostility, insults, and slurs. It is not difficult to see that for most of them this would reinforce their old world propensity to rely on each other and minimize contact with the host society.

RESIDENTIAL DISPERSION

In the College colony of Toronto, fellow feeling, accessibility to work, and the provision of diverse goods and services provided the *paesani* with an optimum setting during the twenties. In order to determine the degree of concentration of the city's *paesani* within the College settlement, an effort was made to trace the villagers. Information was gathered from interviews, from an 1880 list of municipal electors in the Rende area, and from recent lists of *paesani* contributors to a Rende area religious charity. These all yielded an extensive catalogue of surnames that were then traced residentially in the Toronto Italian directory for 1935.[19] By the 1930s, out of a *paesani* population of about one thousand immigrants, it can be estimated that over 40 per cent were located in the College area.

The remaining villagers were not dispersed throughout the city at random, however. First, the Ward, with about 14 per cent of *paesani*,

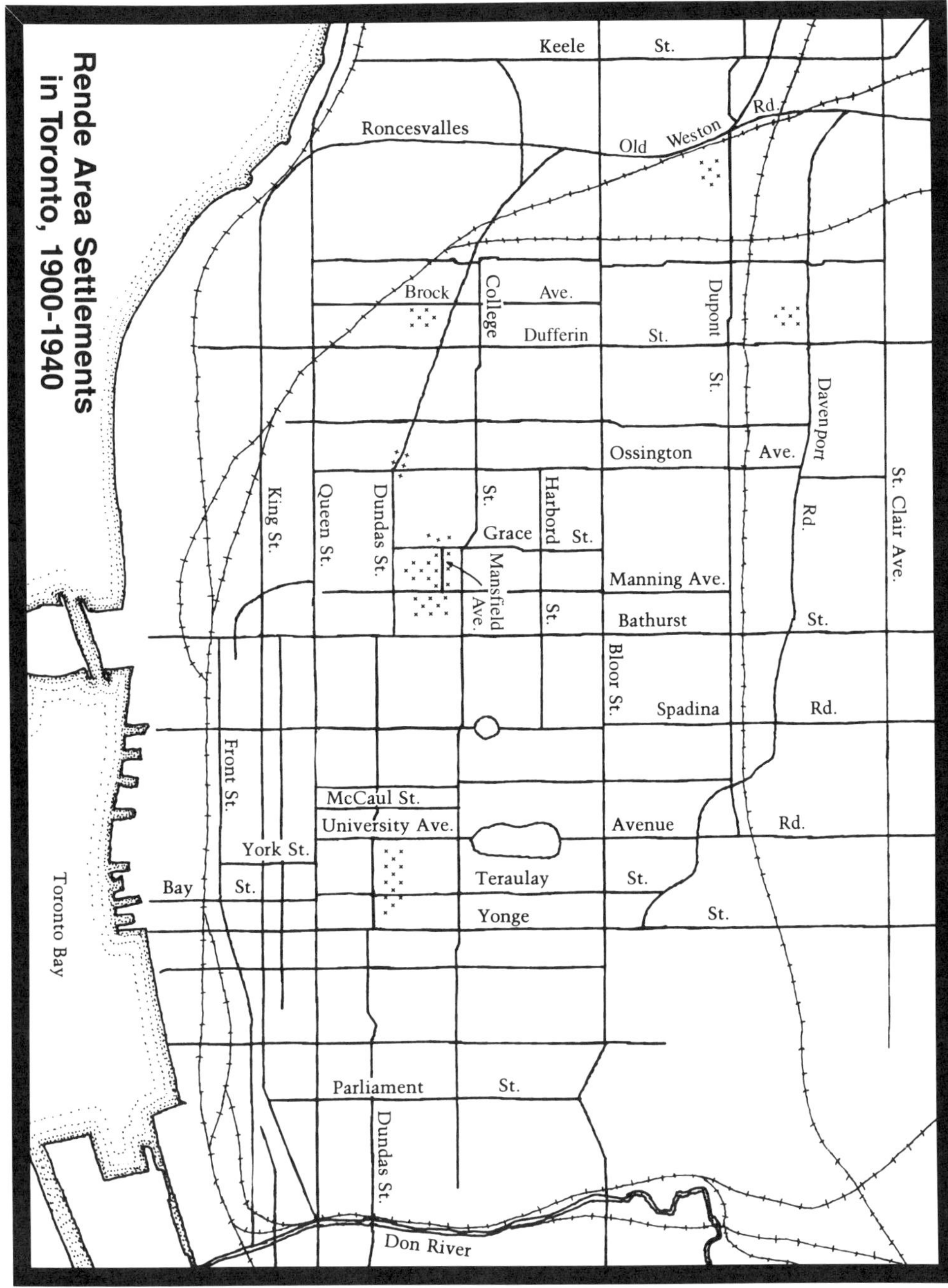

Rende Area Settlements
in Toronto, 1900-1940
Keele
St.
Roncesvalles
Old Weston Rd.
Brock
College
Ave.
Dufferin
St.
Dupont St.
Davenport
St. Clair Ave.
Ossington
Ave.
Rd.
Harbord
St.
Grace
St.
Queen St.
Dundas St.
King St.
Mansfield Ave.
Manning Ave.
Bathurst
St.
Bloor St.
Spadina
Rd.
Front St.
McCaul St.
University Ave.
Avenue
Rd.
York St.
Teraulay
St.
Bay
St.
Yonge
St.
Toronto Bay
Parliament
St.
Dundas St.
Don River

contained the largest cluster outside the College centre and was composed essentially of prewar immigrants. Second, to the west of the main colony, in the working-class Brockton district of the city (around Dundas and Sheridan) an exclusively *paesani* cluster containing roughly 5 per cent of the immigrants was starting to emerge. Third, between the College settlement and the Brockton cluster, another small concentration comprising about 7 per cent of the *paesani* had formed around Dundas and Ossington, almost contiguous to the main colony. To the northwest of the College colony, in the Brandon area, a fourth grouping, comprising about 6 per cent, contained many skilled construction workers and small contractors of Rende area immigrants. Adjacent to this, around Dupont and Old Weston Road, in the heavily industrial "Junction" area an extensive neighbourhood of *paesani*, also containing around 6 per cent, could be discerned.[20] Of the remaining villagers, almost 13 per cent were dispersed residentially, though most were located either between or near the main colony or the minor concentrations. Others within this category formed small pockets of upwardly mobile individuals located in lower middle-class districts of the city or York Township. Lastly, about 9 per cent were to be found along the city's major thoroughfares in various small shops and businesses. Interestingly, half of these were situated on the heavily commercial streets of Bloor or Yonge or nearby arteries.

What is reflected here – the tendency for immigrants to disperse after an initial period of settlement in the central receiving area – has been viewed by many scholars as an indication of greater assimilation into the wider society.[21] While no doubt the minority status of Rende area immigrants outside the College colony meant greater integration with other Italians, it is far from evident that greater assimilation took place vis-à-vis native Canadians. The *paesani* concentration that emerged in the Brandon district and the nearby Junction neighbourhood cannot be said to be a movement by villagers towards greater assimilation into the host society. Here *paesani* had access to neighbourhood immigrant stores and services which, while not as extensive as the central colony's, provided for basic needs. The presence at Dufferin and Davenport of a third Italian parish (established in 1915), St. Mary of the Angels, also gave them a community church. While villagers in these areas moved towards greater interaction with other Italians, contact with "the English" remained slight.

On the surface, the Brockton and Dundas/Ossington concentrations, which together contained sixty or so *paesani*, would be more in tune with the equation between residential dispersion and assimilation. Both clusters were primarily the result of villagers who wanted to own their own home following lower real estate prices outward from the crowded central colony. While the influence of employment factors here were not as evident as in the Brandon and Junction areas, where the pull of the construction industry on the one hand and of factories on the other influenced settlement, the fact that *paesani* in the Brockton and Dundas/Ossington neighbourhoods could easily commute to work by streetcar (or in some cases walk) contributed to the villagers' decision to settle there. In any case, both the Brockton and Dundas/Ossington clusters remained socially if not spatially part of the central colony. In fact, the latter, being near the College settlement, could almost be considered territorially part of it. The Brockton concentration was within easy reach of the College colony by streetcar (or about forty-five minutes by foot) to which *paesani* returned regularly for their shopping, services provided by barbers, immigrant bankers and other intermediaries, and for visiting and recreation. Moreover, the central colony's St. Agnes Church at Dundas and Grace streets was attended weekly by the devout, the occasion often being combined with a Sunday stroll. In contrast, the heavily Irish St. Helen's Church, conveniently located at Dundas and St. Clarens streets only a few blocks to the east of the Brockton concentration, was regarded as the "English" (actually it was heavily Irish) parish and spurned.[22]

In sum, while a considerable number of *paesani* had moved out of the central College colony by the mid-thirties, it cannot be said that this denoted greater assimilation into the host society. Several of the villagers listed in the Italian directory and city directories as fruit-market owners, grocers, tailors, and barbers spread through Toronto did not live at their shops, but commuted from residences in the central colony. Where an important level of participation in the wider society did occur was in the few cases of *paesani* who, having received at least some education in Toronto, underwent significant mobility from working-class jobs to petty white-collar positions (office clerks, food salesmen, shippers and such) and combined their achievement with moves to lower middle-class neighbourhoods. Numerically, however, these individuals were not significant.[23]

The chain settlement of villagers as well as their chain migration essentially occurred within the parameters of a Rende area social space transplanted from the old world. Within such a local area dynamic, however, the experience of *paesani* revealed an additional reality. With settlement and family reunification through the twenties, there emerged a unit of interaction which knitted villagers together at a more primary level than the Rende area association. As pointed out earlier, between the nuclear family and the kindred as a whole there had existed in the old world an intermediate level of kinship. This was the *familiari* or "family circle," composed of several neighbouring households, primarily of relatives up to the degree of cousin, but frequently also including close friends. The *familiari* interacted closely as a cohesive socio-economic group whose members perceived themselves, by virtue of their association, as distinct from other kin. As immigration unfolded and the new world settlement grew, in some instances previously separated *familiari* groupings were reunited or, more frequently, new ones sprang up.

The formation of the new family circles was accomplished by the playing out of traditional characteristics of the *paesani*'s kinship structure: its elasticity with respect to closeness and concomitant rights and obligations, *comparaggio* or ritual kinship, and the multi-stranded nature of kinship and interpersonal relationships generally. While the economic function of the *familiari* lost a good deal of its rationale in North America, the grouping's social function survived and even prospered after the Atlantic crossing.[24] Where sufficient members of a kindred had immigrated for a family circle to be reactivated, information gathered from city directories as well as oral testimony indicated that the group members frequently attempted to live in the same neighbourhood or street. This process could be readily observed in the College Street colony, especially along Bellwoods, Manning and Clinton, where pockets of *familiari* arose. Members of the Chiappetta, Lucchetta, and Cocomile kindred, for example, formed one early and influential *familiari*. Visiting was frequent and informal among the group, and rights and obligations were extensive. As in the village, the family circle often numbered between one and two dozen adults.[25]

Significantly, it was this *familiari* principle which also lay behind the small concentrations in the Brockton, Brandon, and Junction areas, each numbering several dozen *paesani*. With the resumption of immigration after the Second World War, the Brockton area was to emerge as the major settlement of Rende area immigrants, both because of the pivotal intermediary role played by its early residents and because of its strategic location. Interesting, too, was the Brandon cluster, which was primarily drawn from *paesani* with an occupational status higher than the mass of villagers. What we have here are indications of a process that was to unfold increasingly over subsequent decades: the emergence of new world *familiari* groupings – corresponding to distinct residential concentrations – not only on the basis of kinship and personal preference, but also social class. In any case, for *paesani* who were to be found outside the main settlement after the closing of immigration, one cannot assume that they moved towards greater assimilation. When considered in light of the *familiari* principle, the various clusters can be seen to have incorporated a flexible unifying element which, being more encompassing than the nuclear family, was better equipped to meet many of the *paesani*'s social needs.[26] Indeed, the *familiari* principle probably put a damper on the extent to which villagers became integrated with other Italians, even in the Brandon and Junction concentrations, as well as in the central colony.

Furthermore, while the Rende area villagers did not all live within the same section of the city, there were several social occasions transplanted from the old world when they came together. Aside from the *feste* which united villagers as a whole, foremost among these occasions were the rites of passage. At these times large numbers of kin and friends gathered together, the rights and obligations between *paesani* were reaffirmed, and the solidarity of the group reinforced. At these occasions (except, of course, for funerals) the institution of *comparaggio* cemented informal but close ties made in the new world into formal ones. Moreover, kindred and friends were bound together by the exchange of goods and services. As in the Rende area, in Toronto there was constant exchange between *paesani* of complementary aid and services (in rebuilding a house, for example); of "samples" of domestically made products such as preserved meats, pickled vegetables, and wine; and of visiting and gifts. Even for *paesani* who lived at a distance, rapid urban transportation and the telephone reduced to a minimum the effect of space on such interaction. In short, it was participation in an evolving network of rights and obligations transplanted from the old world that lent coherence to the city's Rende area immigrants in the years prior to the Second World War.[27]

FAMILY REUNIFICATION AND HOME OWNERSHIP

Thus far we have spoken of immigrant settlement in terms of the *paesani* as a whole or the wider kindred. Here we wish to narrow our focus to the level of individual families. Quite naturally the first priority of the immigrant was to bring over to the new world his immediate relatives: wives and children, or fiancées, or parents and siblings. For the majority of *paesani* this reunification could only come after certain prerequisites had been taken care of. Debts incurred on the voyage had to be paid off, a relatively stable job had to be found, and savings had to be accumulated to provide sponsored newcomers with some minimum standard of living conditions and security. Often married men refused to call for their families until they could provide at least a decent flat, some furniture and basic household utensils. Not surprisingly, it could be half a dozen years or more before immigrants were reunited with their families.[28]

However, such lengthy periods of separation resulted also from the realization that the purchasing power of the dollar in Southern Italy was over three times as great as in North America. Hence it made compelling economic sense for an immigrant to support his dependants in the village at home as long as need be, rather than bring them over prematurely to a precarious standard of living in the new world. Then, too, the cult of sacrifice and the security of knowing that dependants would be taken care of by trusted kinsmen rendered separation socially acceptable and made reunification a less urgent matter than it might otherwise have been.

Moreover, in many instances, as a sort of compromise between their desire to be reunited with their families and economic considerations, immigrants would stagger the sponsorship of relatives. Whereas the immigrant's wife and young children would join him after a time, older children would often be left in the village under the care of grandparents or uncles until the immigrant family could afford to incorporate the additional members into the new world household.[29]

Many *paesani,* of course, found spouses from within the Toronto Little Italy. Indeed, a majority of marriages were between Rende area immigrants, and they were often "fixed" – that is, introductions were made and courtships sustained through the intervention of trusted kin and *paesani.*

For the Rende area immigrant, the arrival of family, or his marriage in the new world, often was the occasion when he moved from boarding-house conditions to living in a "home," although this was rarely more than a one-bedroom flat. One informant, for example, who sponsored his wife and children six years after his arrival in Toronto, related: "I didn't call my wife earlier because I didn't have a home for her. I stayed in a small flat at first. When she came we moved in a nice flat at Bellwoods near College, where my brother lived. We stayed there until we found a house for ourselves. In those days houses were affordable and we bought one with six rooms.... But you had to work hard for it."[30]

The immigrant's most widespread aspiration was to own his own home; and while not all *paesani* thought that houses were particularly "affordable," definite progress in home ownership could be detected through the early part of the century. Indeed, often *paesani* took no more than five years to acquire their own homes after the arrival of their families.[31] The above informant, for example, was able to afford his own home (albeit a modest six-room structure) within a year of being joined by his family. In a second instance, an immigrant from Rende commune in the 1920s first boarded with his sponsor – who was an early Montalto settler – on Manning Avenue and waited eight years before sending for his wife and children. At this point he took a flat with another Montalto kinsman on Bellwoods Avenue. Yet, even with the economic depression of the 1930s, he was able to move from there to his own house in the Brockton area in about four years. And a third villager, who had lived in Toronto as a single man, after eight years returned to the Rende area to find a bride and marry. Having accumulated substantial savings in the interval, he was able to afford a home around Bellwoods and Dundas after less than a year of living with his new spouse among *paesani.*[32] For *paesani,* then, work, family reunification and home ownership were inexorably tied to one another.

As one Toronto immigrant put it, "You know how we are. For the family, we are all. No other people is like us.... We don't know any other way besides work and the house."[33]

To a considerable degree, it was the boarding system, both before and after marriage, which made it possible for *paesani* to satisfy certain aspirations. For the Rende area immigrants it was to a large extent through the boarding system – both as an economic form and an embodiment of village values – as practised among kin and *paesani* that enabled them to buy their own homes. The provision of room and board at minimal expense, joint food purchases, the granting of services on credit or as favours in emergencies, the cult of sacrifice which transformed life in crowded rooms into an honourable act, as well as the emotional support provided by kin and *paesani* – these were the main constituents of the system which provided lone males with a socially sanctioned interval of "self-exploitation," allowing them to cut living costs to a minimum so as to accumulate substantial savings for investment in family formation.

A somewhat similar situation obtained when the immigrant family lived as a tenant in the flats of *paesani* or kin, quite frequently brothers or sisters. The Rende area family, while boarding, lived extremely frugally with a minimum of furniture, appliances and other household goods. Though the sojourner's cult of sacrifice gave way to some material comfort, the immigrant family postponed the purchase of many household items until after its own home was acquired. Often a good deal of the family's effects, especially kitchenware and linen, was provided by the immigrant's wife and represented her dowry and wedding presents, so that little had to be spent on new purchases. *Paesani* at this stage made do with a small kitchen and bedroom, quite frequently sharing washrooms, laundry facilities, front porches, and occasionally living rooms with their landlords.[34]

Though the boarding immigrant family lived in conditions below what was considered as proper for a respectable family, it was readily assumed that money was being saved for eventual home ownership. Consequently, unlike the village where poor families that fell below accepted levels of living were often mocked or pitied, the boarding family was often regarded with respect on the basis of its future status. This, too, had its influence: this social attitude made it possible for the immigrant family to forgo consumption of goods which might temporarily raise its status but jeopardize its aspirations. Supported in this deprivation and poverty by the social consensus of *paesani,* the boarding family could remain oblivious to the condemnation and condescension of the wider society while quietly building for a better future.

Every *paesano* strove to set up his family in its own household, with the exception, of course, of retired elderly parents who would be supported by their children. While in some cases homes were bought jointly by pairs of siblings, or by parents and a married son or daughter, such purchases seem to have been primarily the result of financial necessity. At times, however, it was a chosen preference, reflecting a past in which extended households were frequently found. Indeed, in living arrangements where nuclear families could be separately accommodated, as in homes with separate entrances, for example, this situation was more akin to living "near" one another rather than living "with" one another. In any case, for the great majority of *paesani*, once they had their own homes, they now took in boarders in their own right, thus acquiring an important financial source to meet mortgage payments and other household expenses.[35]

Although family reunification and home ownership can be viewed as the putting down of roots in the new world and a break with the old, it is not difficult to see how both goals marked the fulfillment of traditional village aspirations, thus representing continuity with the past. After all, the *raison d'être* behind the sojourner's emigration had been to allow him the means by which his precarious peasant existence could be stabilized in a developing capitalist economy. *Paesani* thought that through landed status and concomitant self-sufficiency one could gain security against proletarianization, as well as the social respectability that was synonymous with peasant proprietorship. But further, the effort of villagers to be masters of their own home and land marked a significant attempt to add economic reality to the family unit as a corporate group. The family served both social and economic functions and emigration was a means by which the material foundations of its corporate nature could be strengthened in the face of disintegrative market pressures. More specifically, what the *paesani* aimed to realize was the ideal of *sistemazione* – the setting up of offspring as independent adults. This was the prime rationale behind the corporateness of the village family, the members of which on a *de facto* level owned property in common. Obviously *sistemazione* was tightly bound up with the father's role as provider for his family and it was through emigration that *paesani* attempted as far as possible to meet their obligation of setting up the next generation.

In the Rende area, however, opportunities for this were both limited and transitory, so that for many *paesani* home ownership in the new world city became the means by which it was hoped that old world goals could be met, albeit imperfectly.[36] Home ownership served as a sort of surrogate peasant farm for the immigrant which could fulfill the major purposes of owning land: security against unemployment and want, social respectability, a focus for family cohesion and, lastly, a property that could be bequeathed to offspring. Moreover, in those cases where *paesani* embarked upon small entrepreneurship and the home doubled as the family business (as in the case of grocery stores especially), or in the few instances where *paesani* became small truck farmers at the city's edge, then economic self-sufficiency was added to the list of objectives it was hoped home ownership would provide.

It is interesting to note that the attainment of home ownership relates to another aspect of the *paesani*'s experience discussed earlier: their perception of upward mobility. As villagers moved from unstable outdoor construction jobs to more secure indoor factory work, home ownership, whether spoken of as an aspiration or an achievement, reinforced the *paesani*'s conviction of improved social status in individualistic or traditionalist terms, and further contributed towards conservative tendencies.

Acquisition of a home was inseparable from the *paesani*'s view of family and the concept of adulthood. Insofar as villagers thought in terms of "mobility," it can be said that the focus of their aspirations for improvement was not occupation, education or even income as such, but ownership of a home. To a considerable extent it was through the supportive ties between *paesani* and kin that were activated in the new world – especially in boarding arrangements – that such ownership was made possible, just as prior to this stage of the migration process such ties determined the shape and destination of the villagers' emigration, their world of work and, with American restrictionism, their surmounting of bureaucratic barriers to their freedom of movement.[37]

Women and Family

WOMEN'S WORK

With family reunification and settlement in North America, the role of women in the immigration process became pivotal. The contribution of women to the family economy became especially important where home ownership put heavy monetary demands on the family, and the home itself increased domestic work. While a minority of women contributed to the family's income by working in the factory, the majority worked within the home. Their contribution was generally less clear-cut but significant nonetheless.

Families which had converted their homes to boarding-houses left it up to the women to oversee the running of this enterprise. Not only were women responsible for the cleaning, laundry and often cooking involved in the boarding arrangement, but often also for the collection of rents and keeping of accounts. As an outgrowth of her role as the family's shopper she exercised substantial power over the familial budget and allocation of money to meet domestic needs. While formally the family's income was under the husband's authority, in actual fact it was often the wife who decided on its allocation: how much to spend on food, the children's clothing, and other necessities; what home repairs were needed; what new appliance or piece of furniture should be bought. Though such decisions, especially those involving substantial costs, commonly had to have the consent of the husband, this was often a matter of "rubber stamping" decisions the wife had already made rather than a subject for real debate. This role as the administrator of the family purse was common to most wives, but it took on a particular importance when women were also responsible for day-to-day business transactions.[38]

The economic contributions of women who combined domestic responsibilities with work at home was also illustrated in those instances where *paesani* established small businesses such as grocery stores, shoe stores, or tailor shops. In the case of grocery or fruit stores that were at the family home, the wife often ran the small shop, sometimes with help from her children, while the husband worked elsewhere in the city. In the case of the *paesani* who were shoemakers and repairers, or those who were tailors, their wives often worked alongside them. Thus, for example, the wife of one *paesano* who ran a tailor establishment on College Street helped with the simpler tasks or attended to clients while he worked in the rear of the shop. And a second immigrant who worked as both a shoemaker and repairer combined this with selling shoes, and his wife acted as a saleswoman in the retail part of the premises. In addition to this, men who acquired suitable skills at the factory (for example, uphostering) often freelanced in their spare time, being helped at their home operations by their wives.[39]

Much more common among *paesani* was the taking in of homework. As has been widely noted, in various cities where Southern Italians concentrated and a textile industry employing a putting-out system existed, homework centring around the garment trade was both widespread and preferred among Italian women.[40] In Toronto *paesani* women worked for local clothing firms at simple tasks which formed a small subdivision of the manufacturing process. These subdivided jobs were labour-intensive, repetitive and usually required little skill beyond nimble fingers. One of the more common forms of such work involved the cutting by scissors of lace patterns, decorative designs and decals from large machine-made sheets, after which the various trimmings would be sewn at the factory to blouses, dresses, undergarments, children's clothes, hats and the like. *Paesani* were paid on the basis of piece-work, as had been the norm for both agricultural and industrial labour within the Rende area. While villagers had been proficient at sewing, as well as knitting and the spinning of flax and cotton in the old world, the sewing machine had been essentially unknown and hence in Toronto few did jobs which required it.

In addition to many women working as home finishers for the

garment trades, some villagers engaged in a type of homework not mentioned in the literature of similar colonies. This involved working for a local Toronto food-processing plant specializing in the pickling of vegetables. For example, the firm would deliver bushels of onions to *paesani* women who would peel and wash them, after which they would be picked up to be processed and jarred at the factory. Payment at this task was by the bushel.[41]

Such unskilled homework tasks were simple enough that, as in the Rende area, children helped with the mother's work. The jobs were monotonous, time-consuming, and demanded a quick pace to be remunerative. In order to ward off boredom, lift morale, and maintain productivity, women often worked in pairs or in small groups, reflecting the *paesani*'s old world past whereby tasks were often performed in groups of kin and close neighbours rather than by the nuclear family alone.

Though less often, many immigrant women took factory jobs. Like other Southerners in other North American cities, female villagers in Toronto – especially young unmarried women – in the early twentieth century entered the city's textile industry as low-skilled employees performing small and repetitive parts of the garment-making process as cutters, pressers, finishers, and the like. Few *paesani* were sewing machine operatives, and those who were typically learned how to use the machines in Toronto. Employed by such firms as the William H. Leishman Company and Tip Top Tailors, women, whether they lived in the College Street Little Italy, the Ward, or the western end of Toronto, were within convenient travelling distance by streetcar to their workplace in the city centre.[42]

It is interesting to note that if the woman was proficient enough at the use of the sewing machine to manufacture an entire article of clothing she had the option of working as a freelance seamstress *(sarta)* in her own home, taking on a role that constituted the female counterpart of the tailor. Being a seamstress within the Rende area was one of the very few stable occupations women could enter. It was probably the highest level of working skill reached by *paesani*. Significantly in Toronto this integrated and relatively high skill was attained within the confines of the home, not the factory.[43]

While it is important to recognize the value of the paid labour of female villagers, it is equally important to acknowledge the substantial contribution made by women to the family economy through unpaid work at home.[44] The contribution of Rende area women to the family economy was manifested in numerous ways. Aside from the "housewifely" or conventional work which was common to most women whether native or foreign-born, certain "pre-industrial" domestic work was specific to *paesani* (and, no doubt, other immigrants from similar backgrounds) and embodied within it clear continuities with a peasant past.

In performing many of the conventional household tasks, even through the twenties, villagers had few of the benefits of the household technological revolution that was transforming the lives of the middle class.[45] Almost all *paesani* homes in Toronto contained coal stoves for cooking; most did not have central heating so that water for washing had to be hauled and heated; and while the majority of dwellings were electrified, few immigrants could afford the necessary appliances. All but a few families did without gas stoves, hot running water, washing machines, refrigerators and even the electric iron. In many ways housework was not much less arduous than it had been in the Rende area. As one woman from Montalto related, speaking of her laundry and shopping tasks: "We had a house on Dovercourt. It was hard then. I had five children and relatives living with us. It was hard washing. I had to heat the water in large basins on the charcoal stove. I had to wash everything by hand. There were no refrigerators then either. We only had an icebox, so I had to buy food every day."[46]

Working in the home, because there was no evident wage attached to it, could be taken lightly by males. But it did not take too much reflection on his boarding past for the *paesano* to realize that such services as cooking and laundry (not to mention sex for those who had frequented prostitutes), when obtained outside the immediate family, could take on a definite market value, which was now being provided by his wife in exchange for his "support." Whether he recognized it or not, the "product" of the housewife's labour was the husband himself, not to mention their children.

More evident than this was the manner in which "pre-industrial" domestic work contributed to the family economy.[47] Primarily, as befitted their peasant background, such domestic labour among *paesani* in the new world revolved around the production of food. Along with their husbands, women tended their gardens in which familiar vegetables of the Rende area – tomatoes, beans, lettuce, peppers, and such – as well as herbs, and sometimes fruit trees, were grown. Even those with tiny plots (some scarcely covering a dozen square feet), by making use of every inch of available soil, were able to meet most of their fresh vegetable needs for much of the summer and sometimes beyond. While this provided for traditional tastes, people recognized the importance of gardens for the family budget.

In addition to gardening, every autumn *paesani* women had responsibility for supplying the family with traditional preserves that would see it through the year. Chief of these tasks was the making of the tomate purée used in so much of Southern cooking. This involved boiling the produce into a pulp in large cauldrons, after which it was passed through a sieve, bottled and then boiled again to pasteurize the preserve. Eggplants and peppers were likewise preserved, as were pears and peaches. Moreover, Toronto women worked alongside their husbands in the annual production of preserved meats (sausage, salami, ham, bacon) and wine. Women alone, however, were responsible for making blood pudding, jellied pork hocks, and the like. As in the Rende area, such tasks were often undertaken not by the nuclear family, but by small work groups of *familiari.* Joint purchases of meat and vegetables were made by families (thus reducing costs) who would help each other with the work, and then divide the product.[48] It may be added here that the preparation of traditional dishes, aside from economic considerations, in itself played a socially cohesive role by acting as a focus for the family and *paesani,* both at daily meals and at festive occasions. The extent to which Southern Italian fare was almost chauvinistically looked upon as superior to native food, thus acting to draw together male and female, young and old, should not be overlooked.[49]

Moreover, the meats and vegetables needed for preserving could be bought from small Italian farmers on the outskirts of the city. *Paesani* part-time farmers were especially patronized by Rende area immigrants. It was common for families to travel to nearby farms to pick bushels of tomatoes for the year's stock of purée which required more produce than their gardens could supply. In buying direct from the farmer, villagers were able to save substantially over retail prices in the city.[50] In addition to this activity, *paesani* women would search the nearby parks, fields, and railroad rights-of-way gathering wild greens such as chicory, orach and dandelion. Hunting for mushrooms, which often involved treks beyond the city, was undertaken with their husbands. Gleaning, of course, was a direct outgrowth of the *paesani*'s reliance within the Rende area on communal property to augment not only their food supply but also their supply of fuel, and for those fortunate enough to own livestock, grazing land.[51]

For Rende area women in Toronto, an additional contribution to the family economy was made through their manner of shopping. *Paesani* wives, unlike many middle-class women, spent a great deal of time and effort each day going from store to store minutely comparing prices, searching out "specials," and bargaining over the "just price." Where possible, they sought to buy directly from the small bakeries, dairies, and other producers in their neighbourhood, thus saving over retail prices. Moreover, women shopped in a similar manner for clothing and household goods, the more practised shoppers finding their way to local warehouses and manufacturers.

Further, *paesani* women, as in the Rende area, made as much of the family's clothing as possible. Socks, sweaters, and even underwear were knitted, simple garments such as aprons or baby smocks were hand-sewn, and tablecloths, handkerchiefs, and bed sheets were embroidered. In this last task especially, a woman's purpose was to add to the stock of her daughter's dowry rather than to supply her own family. Embroidered linen was something of a luxury to be given as a present, not a necessity for one's own consumption. Such efforts too, of course, contributed to the family's savings.[52]

The pre-industrial labour of *paesani* women – especially that involved in the growing, collection and preparation of the family's food supply – cut the household's expenses to the minimum possible. For the woman to replace various producers and middle-men in supplying the family's necessities required much time and energy, and some husbands recognized this. At least a few realized that if a wife worked outside the home, the extra money she earned (especially after taxes) would be at least partially offset by the fact that she would have less time to spend on money-saving tasks domestically.

Like Southern women, children also contributed to building up the family's resources. Frequently they were expected to add to the family economy, not so much to ward off dire poverty as to help it meet its objectives, above all, attaining home ownership. In Toronto young children, particularly girls, in a similar manner as in the Rende area, helped their parents with work done in the home or in the family shop, not to mention their constant attending to many domestic chores. Very often boys as young as ten added to the family income by working after school and on weekends in grocery stores, shining shoes, helping deliver bread, and the like. In summer, adolescent boys worked in nearby factories and on construction projects. Commonly, the young villagers acquired their part-time jobs through their fathers or other relatives and worked alongside them or under their supervision at the work site. For many boys, such jobs became permanent upon leaving school or, more accurately, starting points for their adult careers. As men, these young *paesani* emerged as skilled factory workers or tradesmen, or more significantly as white-collar employees: shippers, salesmen, office clerks, and the like.[53]

In the years following the First World War, villagers came to appreciate increasingly the advantages of education. Rising literacy rates within the Rende area itself, stiffer immigration regulations, and a growing appreciation of the complexities of urban, industrial life made villagers aware of the need for education, at least in its functional sense. The children of *paesani* often completed elementary school before entering the labour force. For many children who immigrated to Canada as older boys and girls, however, the experience of being placed in grades behind their Canadian peers often made schooling a painful and humiliating test of endurance from which they were only too anxious to escape at the earliest opportunity.

For the few that proceeded to the secondary level, education was seen as an investment which should contribute to the family's material and social status, not a vehicle for individual fulfillment. A son was expected to reciprocate the sacrifice parents had made for him by adding to the good standing of the family. Hence, although he might be encouraged to pursue technical or commercial training, he was not supported in liberal or artistic interests which, because of their less concrete nature, were difficult for the parents to comprehend.[54]

A daughter was much more likely to be discouraged from pursuing secondary education because her future was thought of in terms of wife and mother. The girl's good reputation and later success as wife and mother added to the family's good name, whereas female career-ism was distrusted. Nonetheless, immigrant daughters did enter the labour market. While daughters who had been raised in Italy were not averse to working in the garment and other female-dominated industries, those who had grown up in Toronto aspired to better positions within the commercial sector. A common occupation was that of sales clerk, and the T. Eaton Company, for example, hired several *paesani* women in this capacity. But in any case, work outside the home was done within the acceptable context of contributing to the young woman's family wealth or her trousseau, in anticipation of marriage and the fulfillment of her traditional roles.

It was expected that both sons and daughters should turn over part of their salaries to their parents. The portion in the new world was smaller than village standards and greater for females. But even young men kept little for personal use beyond that required for necessities such as transportation and clothing, and the odd entertainment. Children thus contributed directly to the family economy, and they were expected to do so until they married and established households of their own.[55]

THE QUESTION OF FAMILY COHESION

For *paesani,* work and home ownership were synonymous with their attempt to maintain the family's corporate cohesiveness in the new world. Many students of immigration, however, have not seen this attempt as having much hope of success. By linking familial forms with economic development, several scholars have concluded that the immigrant, pre-industrial family would undergo a period of disintegration in the face of its new industrial reality and be changed in the process into a "modern" form characterized by the narrow base of its kinship ties more or less limited to the nuclear family, individualism of its members, and differentiation of its functions.[56]

This view has not gone unchallenged. In an influential work on the employment patterns of Southern Italians in the United States, it was effectively demonstrated that the family did not simply respond as a "dependent variable" in the face of industrialism. Rather than seeing the family's values and relationships as disintegrating in the new world economy, the investigator was struck by its resilience and maintained that "south Italian values played an important part in determining family work patterns." The earlier view was turned on its head by a demonstration of how women's work remained consonant with old world values and hence contributed to the family's stability.[57]

However, the traditional view of the disintegration of the immigrant family assumes that employment in the factory separated the husband's work from its old world location at his home, that is, the peasant farm. In taking the man's work away from the family plot, the factory caused differentiation of the pre-industrial social and economic linkage that had obtained in the old world, thus fragmenting familial solidarity.

Within the Rende area, while to live and work at one's home was an aspiration of *paesani,* it was only rarely achieved. And while the Rende area contained cottage industries around the production of textiles, these were worked by peasant women and did not involve whole families. In short, the Rende area comprised a peasant society, not a "proto-industrial" one, in which rural domestic industry based on the family unit (and combined with merchant capital) had over-taken agriculture in importance.[58]

Though the peasant family in the Rende area formed one coop-erative unit, unlike the proto-industrial family the type and locus of production differed among its members. *Affittuari* and landless agri-cultural labourers often lived in town and commuted to their work in the countryside while their wives and children frequently worked for other landlords or in the small mills and factories of the Rende area. While the better-off *coloni* and landed peasants could at times work alongside their families on their land, the small size of their plots commonly forced men to hire themselves out as agricultural labourers for part of the year, or to work in small local industries. The wives would frequently take on part-time work weaving wool, spinning cotton, or cultivating silk at home. Thus within the Rende area, though the family strove to act as a unit of both production and consumption, it was common for men and women, as well as parents and children, to work separately.[59]

It is clear, therefore, that the "differentiated division of labour" was known to *paesani* long before they were introduced to the factory system of the new world; indeed, factory work was often part of the villagers' past. Hence, work differentiation could hardly have been the disin-tegrative influence it has been suggested. Indeed, the act of immi-gration and the eventual reunion of families in the new world, rather than diluting familial cohesion, strengthened it. Many people inter-acted much more closely with their families once they settled in Toronto or Chicago than they had when home was still in the Rende area.

The traditional view of the immigrant family placed great importance for its assumed disintegration on the fact that the wife became more dependent and subordinate to the husband, since in the new world she was "deprived of the usual chores of the garden, the needle, and the loom."[60] Some social scientists, however, while they essentially concur with this view, placed the cause of this disintegration not on the woman's increased dependence on her husband but in her greater independence. According to this perspective, the advent of women's work in the city removed women from their traditional roles within the family, thus undermining male authority and familial stability.[61]

For *paesani* in Toronto, however, neither view is correct. For most, continuity with the past was solid enough that women experienced neither a radical augmentation nor a diminution of their traditional position within the family. Rather, continuity with their former reality in the Rende area contributed to both the stability and cohesion of the family, even though it was transplanted into a world of different values. The work of *paesani* women presented little threat to old world familial values and relationships. Though living within an advanced economy, villagers, like other Southern women, sought occupations on the fringes of the industrial structure similar to the type of work they had done in their homeland.[62]

The preference of villagers in Toronto for work that could be done at home over factory employment is in keeping with the findings of various observers who noted the greater prevalence of homework among Southern Italians than any other immigrant group. There are a number of reasons for this which are applicable not only to *paesani* but also to Southerners generally: homework recalled their old world experience at domestic industry through which they had contributed to the family economy, often with the help of children at their side; it allowed a woman to integrate income-producing work with domestic responsibilities – especially her role as mother – by which she was primarily defined; lastly, because homework was unstable, seasonal, and low paying, the earning power of the woman did not approach that of her husband's, so that the latter's role as provider and chief authority (and hence the family's traditional coherence) was not threatened.[63]

One element seems to have been paramount in accounting for the prevalence of homework: the pervasive concern over female honour. This concern underlay the importance of other factors, since sexual honour was essential for a woman's proper performance of her domestic responsibilities as mother and wife, and it was also essential for her husband to be recognized as the family's chief authority and provider.

In speaking of female honour it is not sufficient to simply refer to "jealous Italian men" and the "Mediterranean attitude" of the immigrants. The concept of female sexual honour was more complex and more concretely linked to everyday reality than much of the literature on Southern Italian immigrants suggests.[64] It was the relationship between female honour and the family as a corporate economic unit which at root explains the pattern of women's work.

This relationship was both direct and indirect. It was direct because property was conceived by *paesani* as a familial trust to be bequeathed to offspring; and because property was the material vehicle through which the family's corporate unity could be given continuity through time, villagers were anxious to guarantee the legitimacy of their progeny or, to phrase it another way, the legitimacy of their hard work and "sacrifice." The value of female honour was grounded in the system of small family property which men strove to acquire and maintain. Why should a man work so hard for his family, why should he seek to bequeath property and security to his offspring, if there was any doubt that his children were his own? And it was imperative that his children be his own, for in a small community of peasants, socio-economic relations, in the absence of an external, "rationalizing" centre, must of necessity be founded on ascriptive and kinship lines rather than on attributive and universalistic ones.[65]

There was also an indirect relationship, in that a family's good standing among *paesani* was determined not only by its economic wealth but also by its social capital. Corporate wealth without corporate honour, manifested through the female, was empty. A woman's "betrayal" was thought to disgrace not only her family of marriage and family of birth, but also her unborn children. Through "tainting" her children she cast aspersions on the whole socio-economic edifice of familial wealth as a collective entity with continuity through time. Hence, within the Rende area, while the local landholding elite had been feared and given formal respect, in a family where the sexual behaviour of a female was considered lax the woman was branded disreputable and the whole family was privately ridiculed, no matter what its wealth and power.[66]

Female honour as a prime form of social capital was closely guarded by male kin as well as by women themselves. A family's prestige rested on this and, conversely, on the degree to which the male was able to fulfill his role as provider. Hard work and "sacrifice" legitimized the male, sexual honour legitimized the female; and as husband and wife the failure of one meant the failure of both.[67]

A man's striving for socio-economic status in the new world made little sense if this was to be spoiled by his wife's, or daughter's, shame. Homework, while allowing for the woman's input into the family economy, provided an avenue by which a man's prestige could be ensured. This was so not only because of the greater security homework provided for female honour, but also because a man who could afford to keep his wife at home was generally regarded as a better provider than one who could not, and therefore prestige was doubly received. Even more so was this true if a man could afford to support his wife at home and, like the village bourgeoisie, not have her do any paid work at all. In any case, since homework was poorly paid, this renunciation of additional income was consciously made in order to ensure that what wealth *was* accumulated remained honourable. It was this nexus between female sexual honour and family economy, then, that fundamentally determined the prevalence of homework.[68]

Even those women who worked in Toronto's garment factories operated within definite parameters that were meant to safeguard female honour. Women travelled to and from work in groups of *paesani,* they worked alongside other villagers, and sometimes at the same establishment as a male relative. Hence, though they worked outside the home, under such conditions the reputation of women was constantly under the public eye of villagers. Even in the case of daughters who escaped the factory and worked as salesgirls, employment was often in pairs or small groups, so that a public account of the woman's hours outside the home could be given. Such patterns of work reflected the woman's own attempt to protect her reputation, as well as the insistence of husbands and fathers that the jobs taken allowed the supervision of kin or trusted friends, and hence not place females outside the moral community of *paesani.* Further, as was true in the case of men who worked in small gangs of *paesani* both on the railroad camps and in the city, the grouping together of women at work resulted from the general advantages to be gained from the *paesano* connection itself as expressed chiefly through kin-linked employment and the meeting of the villagers' desire for mutual aid, protection and sociability.[69]

Though the primary roles of man as provider and woman as the repository of family honour obviously placed limits on the freedom of action of both sexes, there was no doubt on the part of either where power within the family lay. Because a woman's behaviour was always under surveillance and because the limits on her freedom involved, much more than the man's, the private sphere of life, women felt the constraints of their community, both within the Rende area and the new world, more acutely than men. While *paesani* women from early childhood had accepted the precepts of female honour sufficiently to deter overt transgression, the constant pressure to suppress sexual or even sensual expression, the frequent checks and even harassment on the part of fathers, husbands, brothers and uncles, was often resented.[70]

Paesani women expressed their rebellion against the pervasive demands of female honour in several ways. Some women admitted how, had their husbands approved, they would have chosen to contribute to the family economy through factory work rather than homework – especially in the interval before the birth of children or after their infancy – both because factory work was better paid and sometimes more readily available, and because it was seen as less monotonous and stifling. As daughters, some women complained of how their fathers' concern for their honour, in conjunction with the emphasis on their future roles as wives and mothers, prevented them from completing even the elementary grades in school, thus restricting their potential to obtain non-factory jobs. Other women complained of the strict surveillance of men which often led to false and bitter accusations regarding their honour.[71]

Often dissatisfaction on the part of women was expressed, whether overtly or implicitly, among themselves. Within female work or social circles, *paesani* frequently ridiculed the physical or character quirks of their husbands; their unkempt attire, tempers, and penny-pinching. They told mocking stories of excessive chaperonage when they were young, of women pressured to marry old *americani* by their parents for economic convenience or, more seriously, of being abused by their husbands. In the company of other women, or in later life after menopause bestowed on them greater sexual freedom, wives were not above telling bawdy jokes or hurling insults at their husbands, thus giving vent to frustrations. In cases where marriages had failed, women lamented the loss of their virginity and youth in exchange for lives of unhappiness and acrimony. In their rebelliousness, women took pleasure at the ways in which male dominance was subverted: through the pennies saved and pocketed without their husband's knowledge, through the little luxuries purchased without the correct price being told, and through the very act of speaking of their lot with other women.[72]

To acknowledge strife within the Rende area immigrant family is not to say that it underwent disintegration, but rather to point out that it was not an idyll. The family functioned as a corporate group, but conflict too existed. Cooperation did not mean egalitarianism. Power was heavily skewed along sexual lines in the man's favour, leading to dissatisfaction on the part of women. This conflict, however, did not result, as various scholars would have it, from a differentiation of the family's traditional functions along sexual lines, nor from the exposure of immigrant women to "liberating" industrial work. Rather, among villagers, conflict arose from the very ingredient that was vital for the family's stability: female honour, embedded in male authority. Hence, for the Rende area immigrants, family discord was not primarily a product of the new world, but a continuation of the sexual politics of the old.

For the *paesani* immigrants, work, home ownership, family cohesion, and *sistemazione* of offspring were all interwoven. Women contributed actively to this constellation, most concretely to the world of work which materially underlay the other aspects. Home ownership was arguably the most important single aspiration of villagers; and women, through patterns of work consonant with traditional social values, contributed significantly to the setting up of immigrant homes. Their balancing of economy and traditional values enabled women to contribute to the cohesiveness of the corporate family and the honourable *sistemazione* of children.

It can be stated by way of summary that within the Rende area, the peasant's reality of socio-economic insecurity had given rise to aspirations of providing a locus for the family as a self-sufficient corporate group. Similar aspirations in North America motivated the remarkable expenditure of the immigrants' energy towards home ownership. Such property ownership, in turn, required family cooperation and cohesiveness, since the pooling of the individual members' resources was usually indispensable for accumulation of the social and economic capital necessary for the maintaining of a home. For its part, this striving of family members towards a common goal reinforced the very cohesiveness necessary for the attainment of the goal. The end result was that by playing out traditional roles in the settlement of their families, common-folk *paesani,* in their own way, helped lay the foundation for an emerging Italian ethnic community in the new land.

Conclusion

In presenting a case study of the migration process, I have attempted to keep the *paesani*'s experience, mental frame, and social response at the centre of the account, though it was also my intent to compare this specific response with the written record of both contemporary observers and current scholars in an effort to link the history of particular individuals with the wider social history of which they were a part. Because the main purpose was to present a view of migration from inside the process itself and not to test a particular hypothesis, it is not easy to summarize in one or two sentences the major findings of the study. If pressed, however, I believe it would be fair to say that its main result has been to demonstrate that the experience of peasant emigrants manifested significant social and psychological continuity in the face of economic, political, and cultural discontinuity emanating from the larger society. At various junctures through the late nineteenth and early twentieth centuries, on both sides of the Atlantic, *paesani* came up against the dictates of modern industrialism and the nation-state. Yet rather than succumb to centripetal pressures destructive of local community life (at least through the half-century examined) *paesani* were able to maintain traditional social forms and values. Indeed, migration, in both its sojourn and settler forms, can be seen as an attempt to maintain continuity with village patterns, rather than as an abrogation of them. The villagers, though they were directly and profoundly influenced by big events and forces around them, still had considerable latitude for self-preserving manoeuvrability. *Paesani,* as ordinary people, still had some power over their own lives; they were not simply the playthings of history and they could, to a considerable extent, protect what was near and dear to them against upheaval.

APPENDIX

Method and Sources

The decision to produce a volume on Southern Italian immigration to North America was related to a long-standing desire to synthesize a dual interest in history on the one hand and the social sciences on the other. Exploration of works on immigration convinced me that investigation of the phenomenon was important in its own right, since international migrations touched the lives of vast masses of various peoples after the nineteenth century. But I was also convinced that such a study could be an elegant point of entry into several pivotal issues concerning the nature of contemporary society; these, too, having their immediate antecedents in the nineteenth century. While the migration of a group of Southern Italians is my focus, in a sense I am dealing with what is in many ways the central fact of recent centuries – the rise and spread of industrialization, which on all fronts has affected the way the masses lead their lives, the way they work, think, socialize, and even reproduce.

This was my general academic interest in immigration. But behind this interest lay an attraction that was more personal. My parents had been post-Second World War immigrants to Toronto, my grandfather had voyaged several times in the early part of the century to Chicago to work on America's railroads, as had my great-grandfathers in the late nineteenth century. The majority of my kin had been part of the great waves of Italian migration that gravitated towards the United States in the early twentieth century and towards Canada after 1945. Growing up in Toronto in the midst of the latter movement, I was socialized from a very early age into a culture of emigration, the roots of which stretched back to the nineteenth century. All this, not surprisingly, made for a sense of personal exploration in my research.

This aspect of my academic interest, along with a growing conviction that the study of Southern Italians generally was on too large a scale to examine the *experience* of immigration, propelled me to consider the possibility of researching the story of the very "group" I had been born into, this originally being rather loosely conceived of as "kindred." Though I received encouragement, I had doubts about mixing family with business, as it were; I wondered if my research might not be regarded as filiopietistic, parochial, or even opportunistic. Whether this has turned out to be so, however, is for others to answer. I also wondered whether probing into the lives of kin and acquaintances might not jeopardize my rapport with them. Against that was the fact that the endeavour would provide the immigrants with an opportunity to tell their own story rather than have it written without them. It would offer them a chance to "set the record straight" in the face of an outside world that often regarded their presence as insignificant.

Recognizing that studying one's own close ethnic group could lead to distortion, I was concerned to distance myself from my background in order to gain some measure of scholarly detachment. In essence, the distancing I had to master was twofold: it involved an emotional disengagement from an inherited past that was organically linked to the community I intended to study, and the more conventional ideological disengagement from the values and assumptions of the larger society of which I was a part.

Nevertheless, I concluded that there were significant advantages to be gained from the strategy which outweighed potential drawbacks. First of all, any detailed investigation of common people requires an "imaginative leap" into the community of interest. Anthropologists have long realized that there is no substitute for becoming part of the particular group one wishes to understand. Since I had spent a portion of my life (especially until late adolescence) in the immigrant community I intended to study, since I had acquired its interpretation of reality, I was already "inside" the group. I had little doubt that my membership in the community would make my "imaginative leap" into its ways as a researcher easier, and probably more empathic, than would have been the case for an "outsider."[1]

Furthermore, one of the prime advantages of studying a society in small scale is that it allows the researcher to draw upon personal interviews with its members in the process of reaching a point of analysis. Moreover, in my own case, my familiarity with the community's norms, its folk knowledge, its aspirations, would give me a sense of plausible hypotheses worth pursuing, of how to pose questions, and of when to clarify testimony. Here, the relationship of trust, which so many investigators of Southern Italian peasants or peasant immigrants had reported as difficult to establish, was already operative. Another advantage was my familiarity with the local dialect and idioms of my specific community. By using my knowledge of the immigrants' local dialect, I hoped to be able to tap the "colour" of personal lives.

The final advantage in examining the small community of immigrants I was familiar with lay in the fact that this would aid me in solving a central problem of social history: the question of scale. As Goubert has pointed out, studying a nation's stock of great men is humanly possible; studying its common folk as a collectivity, however, is not, and requires a strict delimiting of scale: "It is not too difficult to study thirty French intendants or twenty ambassadors; trying to study the hundreds of thousands of townsmen and millions of countrymen in all aspects of their lives presents insuperable difficulties .... Lacking any adequate sampling techniques, and given the state of the archives, historians tried to limit their difficulties by restricting their gaze to a particular region."[2]

Focusing on a specific network of villagers in the new world provided me with a "particular region" from which to begin my account of the immigrant experience. More specifically, although originally I had conceived of the immigrants' place of origin as being the commune of Rende in the southern province of Cosenza, early research pointed to a larger unit of common interaction, which, having Rende as its approximate centre, encompassed other communes within a radius of roughly ten kilometres. From this local area immigrants recognized each other (either personally or through reputation) as kin or friends bound by substantial rights and obligations. Collectively within the immigrant colony they commonly referred to each other as *paesani,* a term which, while it can be translated as "fellow-villagers" or as "country-folk," within the context of the present study is most accurately, though awkwardly, designated to mean "fellow Rende-area country-folk."

It was the peasant immigrants from the Rende area who became the subject of study for over a decade, commencing in 1974. Field work and the conducting of interviews was an integral part of my research. More than two years were spent as a sort of "participant-observer" with Toronto *paesani* in order to render my personal knowledge of their immigrant experience less impressionistic and more objective. Field work was also extended to Cosenza and the midwestern United States. Throughout this endeavour my aim was to put into practice the dictum of George Ewart Evans that social historians conducting field work ought to tap "the history that is visible in the community itself."[3]

Attending weddings, baptisms, *feste,* work parties, and other functions, I became more appreciative of the social interaction and patterns among *paesani.* This, along with the observation of family life, helped me understand the nature and purpose of kinship ties in the community. Moreover, on both sides of the Atlantic it was possible to observe a pervasive system of rights and obligations harking back to traditional peasant ways: the mutual visiting of kin and neighbours, exchanges of goods and services, and family politics – all of which had implications for understanding the immigrant experience – could be readily witnessed and appreciated. In Toronto surveying the early *paesani* neighbourhood of College Street provided an immediate sense of what housing, enterprise, and community life must have been like in the early twentieth century. In the Rende area, it was important to gain first-hand knowledge of the physical geography, the cultivation of fields by peasants, the social relations between the various strata of society and other aspects of the *paesani*'s background which impinged on their emigration.

Obviously, it cannot be said that observed patterns among *paesani* had been preserved immutably over the decades so as to represent a mirror image of past social or economic relations, and my field observations could not be used unaltered as a data source for an account of the *paesani* set in an earlier time. Nonetheless, I do believe that the perceived patterns reflect close approximations of past life, especially since, as noted above, "social change lags behind economic change, and change in attitudes lags behind social change." Hence, while information drawn from my position as a participant-observer does not enter directly into the account, combined with earlier-based testimony and written sources, it did act to inform my description and analysis of the *paesani*'s social activity. This material acted as a sort of backdrop, and additional check, to the evidence explicitly considered.

The consultation of informants as a source of primary data was indispensable in order to fulfill the major purpose of the study – to present an account of the immigration experience from the perspective of the *paesani* involved. Since many of the peasant immigrants were illiterate, letters or memoirs could not easily meet this purpose, nor could conventional written sources, especially on the North American side. My interest was in writing a case history of migration "from below," and most North American sources viewed Southern Italian migrants as a homogeneous mass and their perspective was distinctly that of the native middle class. In addition, although I was interested in the *paesani*'s experience as a matter of historical fact that could be compared with relevant written records and scholarly works, I was just as interested in the informants' oral testimony as a means to uncovering their subjective reality or "interior history." As several investigators have pointed out, it is especially in this latter sense that oral testimony provides its most important and almost irreplaceable function in the study of immigrant groups.[4]

Material was gathered from over 120 *paesani*, sixty of whom were interviewed intensively in lengthy talks which ranged from a single sitting to half a dozen or so over several days.[5] The starting point of these talks was my own kin and familiar acquaintances, discussions with whom quickly fanned out to other less well-known, or even unknown, *paesani*. Half of these individuals interviewed were recorded on tape; the remainder were recorded through written accounts usually drawn up from notes taken during the conversations.

Aside from these primary informants, the remaining immigrants were consulted less intensively and for a shorter period. Information here was often obtained in the course of impromptu conversations, and was recorded in written rather than taped form. These talks formed a valuable supplement to the more central interviews and were employed as a source of expansion or as a check on them.

The informants interviewed had either been part of the great migration of *paesani* in the early part of the twentieth century, or they were the close kin of the immigrants – wives, children, brothers, and sisters – who had witnessed the movement. I attempted to tape record the interviews but I found that some informants felt uncomfortable or objected to the use of a tape recorder. So it was not used in such cases so that the conversation could flow as freely as possible. More frequently, these non-taped interviews, especially the impromptu talks, took place in a social setting – a wedding, dinner, or outdoor gathering, for example – where tape recording would have been inappropriate or even offensive.

Throughout the collection of testimony, the interview format was open-ended. Although leading questions regarding the main themes of the migration process were asked – for example, Rende area conditions, work, and settlement – no set schedule of items to be answered was presented to the informants. There were several specific reasons for this decision. As various researchers have discovered, peasants, working-class people, and immigrants all respond better to open-ended than to structured interviews. The presentation of a set schedule of questions is met with distrust, regarded as prying into one's personal life, and often the interaction is seen as an attempt to do "business" within the bounds of the private sphere of life which is reserved for sociability. As the social anthropologist Andrei Simic discovered in his study of migration in Serbia, "peasant urbanities," to use his phrase, "do not, on the whole, respond well to a formal interviewing situation, and regard the activity as an opportunity for socializing rather than as a productive effort .... Allowing the conversation to develop in a natural way, and at the pleasure of the respondents, proved to be the most workable technique."[6]

Even as a member of the *paesani* group I was investigating I had to observe the cultural expectations of my informants. On one occasion, for example, when my questioning became too probing and detailed, one respondent asked what other motives I had besides the desire "to hear the story of their immigration." Did the study have something to do with the government, would the responses remain confidential, why did I choose him, and the like. An effort had to be made, then, not to pose questions which would be seen as too obtrusive for propriety.

Related to this, the open interview very often quite spontaneously answers the questions an investigator may have in mind, hence serving to generate the desired information without risking the unproductive effect of casting the investigator as a prying "outsider," as the structured interview is wont to do. In this regard, the wisdom of "Doc," who acted as guide and counsel to the young sociologist William Foote Whyte in his classic study of working-class Italian Americans is instructive. Whyte, who was a participant-observer between 1937 and 1940 in Boston's West End, related what was probably his most important lesson:

> The next day Doc explained the lesson of the previous evening, "Go easy on that 'who,' 'why,' 'when,' 'where,' stuff, Bill. You ask those questions, and people will clam up on you. If people accept you, you can just hang around, and you'll learn the answers in the long run without even having to ask the questions."
> I found that this was true. As I sat and listened, I learned the answers to questions that I would not even have had the sense to ask if I had been getting my information solely on an interviewing basis.[7]

In my own case I found that a great many questions I was interested in asking proved unnecessary. Given sufficient time in a free-flowing discourse, informants would address these concerns of their own accord, since usually these involved logical, though more specific, subjects that emerged naturally from the general prompting questions originally asked.

Aside from the above consideration, in light of the prime purpose of my study, it made perfect sense to allow the individual informants the freedom to express what for them were the most salient aspects of their migration. Not every topic making up this experience operated at the same psychological level for people, and the best results, it seemed to me, would be attained through letting *paesani* speak as much as possible of those issues that were of personal importance to them. Hence, while some informants chose to stress, for example, the home conditions that propelled them to emigrate from the Rende area, for others the world of work in North America was uppermost in their memory, while for still others the attempt to circumvent government restrictions in order to emigrate was important. In this fashion, when the interviews were processed, a rather complete account of the migration experience emerged. Though this account did not come equally from all informants interviewed, since some were more articulate than others, the piecing together of information into themes and sub-themes produced a fairly coherent and authentic narrative.

Be that as it may, it must be noted that the purpose of the interviews was not to elicit the history of individual immigrants as individuals, but to gain a sense from their lives of the "social" history – that is, of the communal experience – of the people of the Rende area. As laid down by Bronislaw Malinowski, one of the founders of social anthropology: "We are not interested in what A or B may feel *qua* individuals, in the accidental course of their own personal experiences – we are interested only in what they feel and think *qua* members of a given community."[8]

The testimony of informants given here has been presented to reflect as well as possible such a communal experience. With respect to the specific statements of individuals, their selection was made after checking the internal logic of the testimony and comparing the statements with the content and the sense of other informants' pronouncements. Often the conversation of *paesani* meandered and people spoke in hybrid *italiese* rather than English or Italian. Hence, where necessary, passages have been edited to facilitate understanding on the part of the reader. In any case, this oral evidence is meant to be representative of common patterns among *paesani* generally, rather than a reflection of a particular individual's experience. With respect to the general narrative assertions made of *paesani*, these are likewise representative of common experiences, but are derived from a consensus of reports from several informants, rather than from any one individual's testimony.

In part because of this diagnostic rationale of the evidence presented, in part because much of the material was collected in the course of impromptu conversations rather than formerly agreed-to interviews, but chiefly in order to respect the privacy of the people involved, I have followed standard social science practice and preserved the anonymity of informants. Moreover, since I was originally interested in following the migration experience into the post-Second World War period, considerable material for the 1940s and 1950s was collected. Some of this evidence, inasmuch as its reality would have remained constant since the earlier part of the century – accounts of the various parishes in the Rende area or the importance of kinship in the migration process, for example, and certainly accounts of folk life or folk lore which extended back for centuries – has been utilized in the present study, but only after the validity of such material over time was compared against testimony concerning the earlier years and against the written record.

The collection of oral testimony and field work was conducted along with the consultation of written sources of both a secondary and primary nature. The testimony of informants and field observations were continually compared to the historical and social scientific literatures regarding Southern Italian peasants and immigrants in order to develop an analytical framework within which to place my subject. Moreover, printed sources as a whole, from both sides of the Atlantic, served the valuable purpose of aiding my effort to link the particular history of *paesani* to the more encompassing general history of which they were a part, and throughout the text I have tried to make this linkage clear. Government records and reports, contemporary studies and observations, monographs, directories, censuses, and like sources were all used to throw light on the experiences of *paesani*.[9]

Written sources were particularly important at certain junctures in the argument where slight recourse could be had to the *paesani*'s testimony. In particular this was true in discussing the causation of emigration in the old world and the contours of post-First World War immigration policy in the new. While *paesani* could very well speak of the immediate personal reasons for their emigration, they could not, of course, provide the quantification of statisticians or the economic analysis of scholars found in various monographs and government sources, through which I have attempted to determine the structural causes behind their leaving. And while villagers certainly were aware of the government policies which impeded their movement to the new world, they could not know of the intricate machinations of officials and politicians whose perceptions and policy decisions, especially after the Great War, played such a crucial role in their lives. Particularly in documenting the increasing importance Canadian policy came to play for *paesani* in the 1920s, the dearth of existing studies made archival research at this point necessary.

In short, the written sources used along with the testimony of *paesani* are diverse and meet various purposes. They range from Italian government sources and early studies of Calabria by *meridionalisti* which were employed to build a general profile of the social and economic background of *paesani*, to contemporary sociological and anthropological literature which throw light on the question of immigrant resocialization in the new world city. This book then, is a synthesis: a case study of the migration experience drawing on oral testimony and field observation on the one hand, and the written record, both primary and secondary, historical and social-scientific, on the other.

Notes

INTRODUCTION

1. For an excellent summary of the historiography in the field of immigration history, see Rudolph J. Vecoli, "European Americans: From Immigrants to Ethnic," *International Migration Review* 6, no. 4 (Winter 1972): 403-7, 418-29. An update is presented in Rudolph J. Vecoli, "Return to the Melting Pot: Ethnicity in the United States in the Eighties," *Siirtolaisuus – Migration* 3 (1984): 117-27.
2. The classic statement on Italian immigrant continuity is given in Rudolph J. Vecoli, "Contadini in Chicago: a Critique of the Uprooted," *Journal of American History* 51 (Dec. 1964): 404-17; a significant assimilationist study is that of Humbert S. Nelli, *The Italians in Chicago, 1880-1930: A Study in Ethnic Mobility* (New York 1970).
3. The term "migration" is employed herein to denote a general movement of people encompassing both the elements of emigration and immigration, and often as being composed of both sojourner and immigrant components. Depending on the context, however, it may at times be used simply as synonymous with a sojourner movement. The term "migrant," on the other hand – in distinction to migration as a process – is usually employed to refer only to sojourners.
4. Joan W. Scott and Louise A. Tilly, "Woman's Work and the Family in Nineteenth-Century Europe," *Comparative Studies in Society and History* 25 (Jan. 1975): 42.
5. I am using the Italian term *mentalità* in the same manner that the *Annales* school has employed the concept of *mentalité* to highlight the fact that the peasant immigrants themselves employed the former word to refer to their way of thinking in distinction to that of the wider society, and often in distinction to other small-scale communities about them. In any case, the definition employed here is derived from Frank E. Manuel, "The Use and Abuse of Psychology in History," in *Historical Studies Today*, ed. Felix Gilbert and Stephen R. Graubarb (New York 1972), p. 217.
6. Pierre Goubert, "Local History," in *Historical Studies Today*, ed. Gilbert and Graubard, p. 300.
7. John S. MacDonald and Leatrice D. MacDonald, "Chain Migration, Ethnic Neighbourhood Formation, and Social Networks," *Milbank Memorial Fund Quarterly* 42 (1964): 82-97.
8. I refer to the concept of "ethos" in its sociological sense to imply "the sum of the characteristic usages, ideas, standards, and codes by which a group is differentiated and individualized in character from other groups." See William G. Sumner, *Folkways* (Boston 1907), p. 36.

CHAPTER 1: THE SOCIO-ECONOMIC BACKGROUND

1. Italy, Ministero di Agricoltura, Industria e Commercio, Direzione Generale della Statistica, *Censimento della popolazione del Regno d'Italia al 31 dicembre 1881*, vol. 1, parte 1: *Popolazione dei comuni e dei mandamenti* (Rome 1883), pp. 120-23; ibid., *Circoscrizioni ecclesiastiche in relazione con circoscrizioni amministrative secondo il censimento del 31 dicembre 1881* (Rome 1885), p. 180, ibid., *Circoscrizioni giudiziarie in relazione con le circoscrizioni amministrative secondo il censimento del 31 dicembre 1881* (Rome 1886), pp. 83, 263.

2. Rende was the seat of the local district magistrate's court and the electoral centre in times of provincial elections when each *mandamento* sent representatives as councillors to the provincial capital at Cosenza. For a good account of local government in Italy – that is, the responsibilities of communes and provinces and their electoral systems – see Luigi Villari, *Italian Life in Town and Country* (New York 1902), pp. 217-25.

3. An excellent detailed map of Cosenza province prepared by the U.S. Army, *Army Map Service, M[ap] 593* (Washington, D.C., 1943) and made available by Professor Robert F. Harney of the University of Toronto made the geographic comprehension of the Rende area much easier and acted as a valuable supplement to informants' accounts.

4. Emrys Jones, *Towns and Cities* (Oxford 1966), p. 3.

5. Giovanni So., (taped interview), 29 May 1976.

6. Statements of a general type, representing a synthesis of information, usually derived from several informants, will be acknowledged collectively as "Interviews." References to specific individuals and the date of interviews will be used for consequential statements or specific quotations. In the latter case, it will be indicated whether the citation was taken from tapes (T) or notes (N).

7. Luigi Conforti, *Risposta all'opuscolo "Una provincia fuori legge: con documenti"* (Cosenza 1881), pp. 19-23.

8. Interviews.

9. Conforti, *Risposta,* pp. 63-65.

10. Interviews.

11. Gerardo Giraldi, *Le chiese di Rende: Itinerario storico-artistico* (Cosenza 1985); Touring Club Italiano, *Basilicata e Calabria,* 3rd ed. (Milan 1965), pp. 407-8. Note that while Michaelmas falls on September 29, May 8 is the date of the apparition of St. Michael the Archangel to San Francesco da Paola, the chief saint of Cosenza, and San Gennaro. Ida S., 16 September 1976; Ernesto S., 16 September 1976.

12. Interviews.

13. D. Taruffi, L. De Nobili, C. Lori, *La questione agraria e l'emigrazione in Calabria* (Florence 1908), pp. 137-38.

14. Gaspare C., 2 November 1976; Ida S., 16 September 1976; Giovanni Ca., 23 September 1976.

15. Eugenio S., 17 April 1976; Ernesto S., 16 September 1976.

16. Mauro Francesco Minervino, *L'Ultima Cremagliera: La ferrovia Paola-Cosenza 1915-1987: Ricerche, immagini e testi originali* (Cosenza 1988); Ilario Principe, *La Calabria* (Florence 1968), pp. 144-45; Vincenzo Co., 27 June 1976.

17. Interviews. See, for example, J.A. Pitt-Rivers, *The People of the Sierra* (Chicago 1961), pp. 160ff.; and M.A. Heppenstall, "Reputation, Criticism and Information in an Austrian Village," in *Gifts and Poison: The Politics of Reputation,* ed. F.G. Bailey (Oxford 1971), pp. 153ff.

18. I refer to the idea of a "moral community" of *paesani* in the manner outlined by Bailey, "to emphasize the continuous judgement of right and wrong which characterized interactions within the community." Furthermore, as noted by the author: "Standards of honesty, respect and consideration in so far as they are moral imperatives are diminished as the status of the person at the other end of the relationship becomes more marginal." Interestingly, in a parallel to my idea of a Rende area, Bailey draws the boundary of the moral community of the Indian peasants he studied, not at the village, but at the inter-village local area interconnected through kinship and caste fellow-feeling. (F.G. Bailey, "The Peasant View of the Bad Life," in *Peasant and Peasant Society,* ed. Teodor Shanin [Harmondsworth, England 1971], pp. 302-3).

19. The English writer and painter, Arthur John Strutt, for example, travelling through Calabria in the late nineteenth century, documented the distinctive dress and flavour of various villages. See Luigi Parpagliolo, "La Calabria negli scrittori straniere," *Almanacco Calabrese* 1, no. 1 (1950): 94, 101-2.

20. Rosario P., 29 May 1974; Trentina C., 21 January 1978; Gaspare C., 21 January 1978.

21. It is evident that my account of the cohesiveness of the Rende area differs from that literature on Southern Italy which focuses on *campanilismo,* or "village mindedness," as marking the boundary of peasant interaction and loyalties. Moss and Cappannari, for example, in their study of a contemporary Southern Italian village in Molise, present a picture of extreme *campanilismo* in which the inhabitants of the village were divided along parish lines between "Lower" and "Upper" town residents. According to the authors, the two sectors of the village lived in virtual isolation of each other, rarely intermarrying, forever in bitter conflict, and even speaking with "dialect differences." Though somewhat less extreme in their concept of *campanilismo,* other students of Southern Italy and its emigration have concurred with this perspective, describing the experiences and world view of southerners as "confined within the shadow cast by [the] town campanile," to borrow a phrase from Vecoli. Though it would be premature to state that the concept of *campanilismo* is false, the evidence herein suggests that it has certainly been overdrawn.

    My findings are similar to those more recently reported by Alain Morel in France. In his study of the "social space" of a Picardy village from the eighteenth to the twentieth century the author found that contacts through family, migration, religious fêtes, and other socio-economic spheres bound together a group of villages within a radius of fifteen to twenty kilometres. His study supports the contention that the world of the peasant did not end with the village but was concretely tied to a much wider entity given life through multi-faceted contacts.

    Such a position is in line with the conceptualization of peasant society as a "part-society." According to this view, a peasant community exists, and is defined, in relation to the larger society of which it is a part, while at the same time manifesting itself as a unique local entity. This linkage is all-encompassing and occurs on the political, economic, cultural and social levels. Such a view, linking the national (or regional) plane with the peasant's local reality, I believe to be a necessary corrective to the picture drawn by many in which Southern Italy is seen as composed essentially of traditional villages dominated by *campanilismo.*

Such considerations aside, it could be simply argued that my conclusions and the work of authors like Moss and Cappannari differ because different areas of Southern Italy were studied. Though this may be so, the discrepancy is more likely due to the fact that social scientists have tended to interview villagers in Italy for whom an account of their insularity may have been salient at the moment, whereas my account was generally derived from immigrants, that is, former villagers, whose description of local life was influenced by the migration process. Migration frequently made manifest exiting, but often latent, socio-economic linkages outside one's village or *comune*. Also the fact that informants' kinship networks were traced helped highlight extensive local area contacts between villagers that went unnoticed by others. Then, too, it could well be the case that while *campanilismo* was held by Southern Italian peasants as an ideology, the actuality of their day-to-day experience was very different. At least as expressed by the immigrant informants, their daily reality in their place of origin exhibited a much more complex, richer, and wider world than the official ideology attributed to them. See Leonard W. Moss and Stephen C. Cappannari, "Estate and Class in a Southern Italian Hill Village," *American Anthropologist* 64, no. 2 (1962): 287-300; Rudolph J. Vecoli, "Contadini in Chicago: A Critique of the Uprooted," *Journal of American History* 51 (Dec. 1964): 406; Alain Morel, "L'Espace social d'un village picard," *Études Rurales* 45, no. 73 (1972): 62-80; Stanley H. Brandes, *Migration, Kinship and Community: Tradition and Transition in a Spanish Village* (New York 1975), pp. 1-5; Andrei Simíc, *The Peasant Urbanites: A Study of Rural-Urban Mobility in Serbia* (New York 1973), pp. 10-21.

22. Taruffi et al., *Questione agraria*, pp. 168-69.
23. Interviews; Raffaele Ciasca, "Le trasformazioni agrarie in Calabria dopo l'unità," *Archivio storico per la Calabria e la Lucania*, anno 25, fascicolo 1-11, vol. 25 (Rome 1956), p. 85.
24. The agricultural zones outlined here are derived from Taruffi et al., *Questione agraria*, pp. 168-69, and are roughly equivalent to two major gradient zones utilized by Dickinson. Below 750 metres in the "hilly" or "plains" terrain, slopes of 40% or less predominated, making the land cultivatable. Above 750 metres in the "mountainous" terrain, slopes were greater than 40%, relegating the land to forest and pasturage. Robert E. Dickinson, *The Population Problem of Southern Italy: An Essay in Social Geography* (Syracuse 1955), p. 33.
25. Interviews.
26. Italy, Ministero di Agricoltura, Industria e Commercio, Direzione Generale della Statistica e del Lavoro, Ufficio del Censimento, *Censimento della popolazione del Regno d'Italia al 10 giugno 1911*, vol. 1: *Popolazione presente, popolazione temporaneamente assente, popolazione residente* (Rome 1913), pp. 180-83 (calculation mine).
27. Ibid., pp. 180, 570 (calculation mine). Luigi Izzo, *La popolazione calabrese nel secolo XIX: Demografia e economia* (Naples 1965), pp. 95-98.
28. Moss and Cappannari, "Estate and Class," pp. 289-90.
29. Taruffi et al., *Questione agraria*, pp. 187-88.
30. *Censimento 1911*, 1: 180-83 (calculation mine).
31. *Censimento 1881*, 1: 120-23; *Censimento 1911*, 1: 180-83.
32. Interviews; Domenico Demarco, *La Calabria: Economia e società* (Naples 1966), p. 81.
33. *Censimento 1881*, 1: 120-23; *Censimento 1911*, 1: 178-83 (calculation mine).

34. Izzo, *Popolazione calabrese,* pp. 95-97. Between 1871 and 1901 the population of Cosenza living in the countryside rose from 17% to 24% and that of Calabria from 11.2 to 17.3%. By 1901 the proportion of people living in the countryside in Cosenza was starting to approach the national average of 28%.

35. Demarco, *La Calabria,* p. 77; Denis Mack Smith, *Italy: A Modern History,* rev. ed. (Ann Arbor 1959), p. 239.

36. Mack Smith, *Italy,* pp. 42, 258-59, 282-83.

37. Izzo, *Popolazione calabrese,* p. 98.

38. Ibid. Aside from emigration, Giorgetti states that the organization of the first agricultural leagues and consequent strikes played a role in the improvement of conditions in the South. Giorgio Giorgetti, *Contadini e proprietari nell'Italia moderna* (Turin 1974), p. 230.

39. Izzo, *Popolazione calabrese,* pp. 123, 130-37.

40. F.G. Bailey, "Changing Communities," in *Gifts and Poison,* ed. Bailey, pp. 29-30; Teodor Shanin, ed., introd., *Peasants and Peasant Society,* pp. 14-15. Also see Gideon Sjoberg, "Folk and 'Feudal' Societies," *American Journal of Sociology* 58 (1952): 231-39.

41. Taruffi et al., *Questione agraria,* p. 93; Izzo, *Popolazione calabrese,* pp. 331, 364.

42. Francesco Nitti, *Scritti sulla questione meridionale,* vol. 1: *Saggi sulla storia del mezzogiorno, emigrazione e lavoro* (Bari 1958), pp. 265-66; Sydel Silverman, *Three Bells of Civilization: The Life of an Italian Hill Town* (New York 1975), ch. 3.

43. Both the census and some immigrants interviewed also used the term *contadino* to apply to the *affittuario* rather than to peasants as a whole. Alternatively, some turn-of-the-century census records used *contadino* inclusively to refer to regularly employed farm labourers as well as peasants. To avoid confusion, I shall employ this rather abused term to refer only to peasants as defined above.

44. Izzo, *Popolazione calabrese,* pp. 130-36. Specifically, the proportion of landed peasants in Cosenza rose from 9% (10,632) in 1871 to 18% (30,061) in 1901. Similarly, the proportion of *mezzadri* rose from 7% (7,915) to 16% (26,941).

45. Ibid., p. 137; Taruffi et al., *Questione agraria,* pp. 114-15.

46. Alberto S., 14 March 1976; Salvatore S., 18 April 1977.

47. Santo St., (T), 16 November 1975.

48. Taruffi et al., *Questione agraria,* pp. 194, 762-69; interviews.

49. Alberto S., (T), 14 March 1976.

50. Conforti, *Risposta,* p. 67; interviews.

51. Taruffi et al., *Questione agraria,* pp. 313-14, 364; Giovanni So., 29 May 1976; Alberto S., 14 March 1976.

52. Interviews. Also see Carlo M. Cipolla, "Four Centuries of Italian Demographic Development," in *Population in History: Essays in Historical Demography,* ed. D.V. Glass and D.E.C. Eversley (London 1965), p. 578.

53. One *tomolo* = 64.5 litres; 1 *tomolata* = 40 acres (approximately half a hectare). Both the *tomolo* and *tomolata* were part of the system of measurements introduced to the Kingdom of Two Sicilies by Ferdinand I of Aragon. They were formally abolished in 1841 with the introduction of the metric system, but continued as the *de facto* standards of measurement among the peasantry well into the twentieth century. The pre-metric measurements often differed from province to province. Hence, though the equivalents given here are correct for Cosenza, they are not accurate for the South as a whole. See Izzo, *Popolazione calabrese,* p. 9.

54. Santo St., 16 November 1975; Rosario P., 29 May 1974; Alfredo Ce., 25 September 1976; Adamo S., 13 June 1976. Also see Giuseppe Scalise, *L'emigrazione dalla Calabria: Saggio di economia sociale* (Naples 1905), pp. 49-50.
55. Taruffi, *Questione agraria,* pp. 364, 318-19; interviews.
56. "The original historical form in which capital appears at first sporadically or *locally, side by side* with the old modes of production, but gradually bursting them asunder, make up *manufacture* in the proper sense of the word (not yet the factory). This arises where there is mass-production for export ... manufacture does not initially capture the so-called *urban crafts,* but the *rural subsidiaray occupations,* spinning and weaving, the sort of work which least requires craft skill, technical training ... manufacture first establishes itself not in the cities but in the countryside, in villages lacking guilds, etc. The rural subsidiary occupations contain the broad basis of manufactures, whereas a high degree of progress in production is required in order to carry on the urban crafts as factory industries. Such branches of production as glassworks, metal factories, sawmills, etc., which from the start demand a greater concentration of labour-power, utilise more natural power, and demand both mass-production and a concentration of the means of production, etc.: these also lend themselves to manufacture. Similarly paper-mills, etc." Karl Marx, *Pre-Capitalist Economic Formations,* ed. and introd. Eric J. Hobsbawm, trans. Jack Cohen (New York 1965), p. 116.
57. Izzo, *Popolazione calabrese,* pp. 9, 46-47.
58. Gaetano Cingari, *Storia della Calabria dall'Unità a Oggi* (Bari 1982), p. 8. Scholarship emphazing the early economic potential of the South is in contrast to the work of "deterministic" *meriodionalisti,* post-Unification writers on the Southern Question, who saw the root cause of the South's poverty and "backwardness" in the region's geographical and "historical" disadvantage, primarily its lack of natural resources. See Giustino Fortunato, *Il mezzogiorno e lo stato italiano,* vol. 2: *Discorsi politici, 1890–1910* (Bari 1911), pp. 312-15, 326. A *libbra* is another pre-metric form of measurement used in Naples to calculate weight. One *libbra* (akin to the English pound) was equal to 12 *once* (ounces).
59. In this connection, Emilio Sereni has argued that all the major sections of Italy entered Unification with roughly the same proportion of workers involved in industry and transportation. By 1921, however, the policy of the central state which strengthened Northern industry at the expense of the South had disrupted this equilibrium, which was later exacerbated even more by fascism. Hence, whereas 27% of the population of the South was involved in industry and transportation in 1881 compared to 29% in the North, by 1921 the proportions were 26% and 34.6% respectively (and by 1936 32.7% and 46.4%). Emilio Sereni, *La questione agraria nella rinascita nazionale italiana* (Turin 1975), pp. 49-56.
60. Izzo, *Popolazione calabrese,* pp. 50-51. For the importance of silk for Calabria, see also Domenico de Giorgio, *Figure e momenti del risorgimento in Calabria* (Messina 1971), pp. 76 77.
61. Izzo, *Popolazione calabrese,* pp. 47, 137-46. For Calabria as a whole, whereas women outnumbered men almost three to one in the rural industrial sector in 1881, by 1901 the ratio had decreased to less than two to one.
62. Ibid., pp. 47-48, 51, 60, 137.
63. Taruffi et al., *Questione agraria,* p. 662. Also see Ciasca, "Transformazioni agrarie in Calabria," p. 92. In the late nineteenth century Calabria as a whole had the worst communications in Italy. The region had barely

41 metres of road per square kilometre compared to 100 metres for the South generally and 500 metres per square kilometre for the North.

64. Demarco, *La Calabria,* pp. 95-96, interviews.

65. Eugenio S., 17 April 1976; Adamo S., 13 June 1976; Giovanni So., 29 May 1976.

66. Izzo, *Popolazione calabrese,* pp. 183-84.

67. Eugenio S., (T), 17 April 1976.

68. Izzo, *Popolazione calabrese,* pp. 137-44; interviews.

69. Interviews; Demarco, *La Calabria,* p. 96; Taruffi et al., *Questione agraria,* pp. 551, 554. For the province as a whole between 1896 and 1902, an annual average of 59,597 hectolibres of olive oil was produced. Production was promoted by the establishment of a school for the study of the olive industry in the capital in the early twentieth century.

70. Eugenio S., (T), 17 April 1976.

71. Izzo, *Popolazione calabrese,* pp. 56-57; Conforti, *Risposta,* p. 17.

72. Social class profiles in their studies of contemporary communities have been presented by, among others, Moss and Cappannari, "Estate and Class," pp. 287-300; A.L. Maraspini, *The Study of an Italian Village* (Paris 1968), pp. 88-97; Edward C. Banfield, *The Moral Basis of a Backward Society* (New York 1958), ch. 4.

73. Joseph Lopreato, *Peasants No More: Social Class and Social Change in an Underdeveloped Society* (Scranton, Penn. 1967), pp. 197-99.

74. Eugenio S., 17 April 1976; Antonio S., 20 April 1976; Gaspare C., 2 November 1976; Franco G., 25 September 1976. See Fedele Fonte, *Rende nella sua cronistoria* (Chiaravalle Centrale, Italy 1976), p. 246ff.

75. Manlio Rossi-Doria, *Dieci anni di politica agraria nel mezzogiorno* (Bari 1958), p. 20.

76. Rosario P., 29 May 1974; interviews.

77. Writing of the widespread nature of investment in land by the urban petit bourgeoisie in the Italian South after Unification, Rossi-Doria has observed: "Every doctor, storekeeper, public official, up to the last *carabiniere,* felt that with the purchase of a piece of land, he could make his own economic position more stable, and in any case raise himself a grade on the social scale." Rossi-Doria, *Dieci anni,* p. 22.

78. Cf. Silverman, *Three Bells of Civilization,* pp. 24, 75, 95, 105-12; J. Davis, *Land and Family in Pisticci* (London 1973) pp. 9-10. Aside from living in communal capitals, some wealthy landed proprietors from the Rende area also lived in the city of Cosenza. See Karl Baedeker, *Southern Italy and Sicily: Handbook for Travellers,* 15th rev. ed. (Leipzig 1908), p. 250.

79. Shepherds, while relatively few within the Rende area, were sometimes placed by the informants alongside the *affittuario* and sometimes not. This apparently depended on the size of one's herd. But even those who placed the shepherd as equal to the tenant farmer qualified this by saying that he was less civil or "educated."

80. See N.T. Colclough, "Social Mobility and Social Control in a Southern Italian Village," in *Gifts and Poison,* ed. Bailey, pp. 218-25.

81. Interviews.

82. Santo St., 20 March 1976; Ernesto S., 25 April 1974; Caspare C., 22 January 1977.

83. Interviews; Conforti, *Risposta,* pp. 13, 35-36, 40-42, 61. Also see Alain Morel, "Power and Ideology in the Village Community of Picardy: Past and Present," in *Rural Society in France: Selections from the Annales; Economies, Sociétés, Civilisations,* ed. Robert Forster and Orest Ranum (Baltimore 1977), pp. 118-25.

84. Interviews.

85. See Moss and Cappannari, "Estate and Class," p. 292.

86. Conforti, *Risposta,* pp. 5-6, 13, 49, 61. Also see Anton Blok, *The Mafia of a Sicilian Village, 1860–1960* (New York 1974), pp. 91ff., 18ff; Mack Smith, *Italy,* p. 73.

87. Francesco G., 27 September 1976; Geraldo Sa., 7 November 1976.

88. Francesco M., (N), 25 September 1976.

89. Francesco G., (N), 25 September 1976.

90. Conforti, *Risposta,* pp. 21-30, 66-67; Grisfisi, *Una provincia,* pp. 19-20.

91. Taruffi et al., *Questione agraria,* pp. 810-11. Francesco M., (N), 25 September 1976.

92. Interviews. Interestingly, communes, as administrative units, originated from the early feudal grants vassals received from an overlord. See Silverman, *Three Bells of Civilization,* pp. 114-15; Maraspini, *Italian Village,* pp. 101-3.

93. Santo St., 16 November 1975; Michele St., 24 January 1976. The *paesani*'s accounts of the brigands were reminiscent of that given by Carlo Levi, referring to the peasants of Basilicata with whom he stayed while exiled from the North by the fascist regime: "When I talked to the peasants I could be sure that, whatever was the subject of our conversation, we should in one way or another slip into mention of the brigands. Their traces are everywhere; there is not a mountain, gully, wood, fountain, cave, or stone that is not linked with one of their adventures or that did not serve them as a refuge or hideout; not a dark corner that was not their meeting-place; not a country chapel where they did not leave threatening letters or wait for ransom money. Many places, like the Fossa del Bersagliere, were named for their deeds. Every family was at one time for or against them: one of its members was an outlaw, or they took in and hid a brigand, or a wandering band killed some relative, or set fire to their crops. The peasants, with a few exceptions, were all on the side of the brigands and, with the passing of time, the deeds which so struck their fancy became bound up with the familiar sites of the village, entered into their everyday speech." Carlo Levi, *Christ Stopped at Eboli* (New York 1947), pp. 138-39.

94. Conforti, *Risposta,* pp. 47-49. Among the more famous brigands of Cosenza in the late nineteenth century were Palma, Romanello, Catalano and Faccione See G. Orioli, *Moving Along* (London 1934), pp. 82-87; Ernesto S., 2 March 1977.

95. Giovanni So., (T), 29 May 1976. Cf. E.J. Hobsbawm, *Primitive Rebels: Studies in Archaic Forms of Social Movement in the Nineteenth and Twentieth Centuries* (New York 1965), ch. 2.

96. Adolfo Rossi, "Vantaggi e danni dell'emigrazione nel mezzogiorno d'Italia (Note di un viaggo fatto in Basilicata e in Calabria)," *Bollettino dell'emigrazione,* anno 1908, no. 13 (Ministero degli Affari Esteri, Commissariato dell'Emigrazione; Rome 1908), p. 42.

97. Santo St., (T), 16 November 1975.

98. Michele St., (T), 16 November 1975.

99. Rosario P., (T), 29 May 1974; Giovanni So., (T), 29 May 1976.

100. See Morel, "Power and Ideology," pp. 107-8.

101. Giovanni So., (T), 29 May 1976.

102. Italy, Ministero di Agricoltura, Industria e Commercio, Direzione Generale della Statistica, *Censimento della popolazione del Regno d'Italia al 31 dicembre 1881, relazione generale* (Rome 1885), Table. If the capital of Cosenza is omitted from the calculations, the figure is 87%.

103. Taruffi et al., *Questione agraria,* pp. 106, 823. In the late nineteenth century the illiteracy rate of the *mezzogiorno* along with those of the Iberian peninsula and the eastern Balkans were among the highest in Europe. Izzo, *Popolazione calabrese,* p. 146.
104. *Censimento 1881, relazione generale,* p. 133; Izzo, *Popolazione calabrese,* p. 153; In 1881 no province north of Rome, except for nearby Terano in Apulia had an illiteracy rate in excess of 84%, which was the norm in the South. In the North the illiteracy rate was generally half this and even in the depressed northeast it was 10 to 20% lower (*Censimento 1881, relazione generale,* Map).
105. Concetta Sm., (T), June 1976.
106. Taruffi et al., *Questione agraria,* pp. 800, 813-14.
107. Isnardi points out that of Italian funds going to the construction of new schools between 1879 and 1922, Calabria received 6,278,100 lire compared to 52,600,943 lire for Lombardy and 42,561,737 for Veneto or even 25,758,813 for Sicily. The amount spent per capita in Calabria was the lowest in Italy: 4 lire compared to 16 lire in Emilia or 10.7 lire for the nation as a whole. Giuseppe Isnardi, "L'edilizia scolastica," *Almanacco calabrese,* anno 6, no. 6 (1956), pp. 159-60.
108. Villari, *Italian Life,* p. 221, outlined the responsibility of the Italian *comune:* "It keeps the streets and municipal roads in order, it exercises a control over the markets, the lighting of the town, the burial grounds, and various sanitary matters. The elementary schools and certain secondary schools are wholly managed by it, and many charities are under its supervision." See also Isnardi, "L'edilizia scolastica," pp. 158-60.
109. Mack Smith, *Italy,* p. 236; Taruffi et al., *Questione agraria,* pp. 801, 816.
110. Grisfsi, *Una provincia,* pp. 20, 24. In this connection, Villari wrote in 1902: "Many communes, especially in Sicily and in the Neapolitan provinces, throw away large sums in fireworks, illuminations, festivities, centenaries, and bad municipal bands, while there is not enough for necessary purposes. In Palermo a new opera house was built at the expense of the commune, while the hospital was left in a most disgraceful condition, and necessary repairs had to be suspended for want of funds. Other communes are practically run by some local clique or family, who administer them entirely to their own advantage." (*Italian Life,* p. 221).
111. Quoted in Taruffi et al., *Questione agraria,* pp. 810, 803 (translation mine).
112. Ibid., pp. 800-3; See also, Isnardi, "L'edilizia scolastica," p. 158.
113. It can be noted from American sources that the illiteracy rate of Southern Italians in the United States was lower than the rate for Southern Italy. In particular, in Calabria, which had the gravest illiteracy problem of any region, 79 per cent of the population was illiterate in 1901. In comparison, the proportion of Southern Italians illiterate in the United States a few years later was calculated by the Congressional Immigration Commission to be about 65 per cent, though the early sociologist, Henry Fairchild, placed the figure as low as 54 per cent. In Canada, J.S. Woodsworth, writing in 1909 in his capacity as a Methodist minister, estimated that 60 per cent of Italians were illiterate, and, moreover, that 80 per cent were from the South. Such estimates indicate that there can be little doubt that emigration was educationally selective and, by extension, selective of the more enterprising. See *Censimento 1911,* 3: 230; Peter Roberts, *The New Immigration: A Study of the Industrial and Social Life of Southeastern Europeans in America* (New York 1913), p. 370; Henry Pratt Fairchild, *Immigration: A World Movement and Its American Significance,* rev. ed. (New York 1933), p. 201; and James S. Woodsworth, *Strangers within Our Gates* (Toronto 1909), pp. 133-35.

114. Interviews. It was in 1911 that Rome nationalized and centralized education, taking the matter out of the inept hands of the *comuni.* U.S., Department of Health, Education, and Welfare, Office of Education, *Progress and Trends in Italian Education,* by Anthony A. Scarangello, Bulletin 1964, no. 21 (Washington 1964), p. 5.

115. See Jan Vansina, "Once Upon a Time: Oral Traditions as History in Africa," in *Historical Studies Today,* ed. Felix Gilbert and Stephen R. Graubard (New York 1971), pp. 415-23, or Jan Vansina, *Oral Tradition: A Study in Historical Methodology* (London 1965), ch. 3. A good collection of Calabrian oral tradition is contained in Francesco Antonio Angarano, *Vita tradizionale dei contadini e pastori calabrese* (Florence 1973).

116. Ida Sp., (N), 22 January 1977; Ida S., (N), 22 January 1977.

117. Ida S., (N), 19 February 1977; Maria Ca., (N), 19 February 1977. For an account of carnival customs in the Kingdom of Naples, see MacFarlane, *Popular Customs,* pp. 46-47, 130-34, 152ff.

118. Giovanni G., (N), 22 September 1976. Since the Rende area was located along the main seismic fault of Italy, earthquakes were a major scourge of the locality and very much a part of the everyday talk and lore of its people. See Giuseppe Rinaldi, "L'attraversamento stabile della stretto," *Almanacco calabrese,* anno 14, no. 14 (1964): 148-49. A contemporary account of the equally disastrous earthquake of 1783 which hit western Calabria is given in Henry Swinburne, *Travels in the Two Sicilies in the Years 1777, 1778, 1779, and 1780* (London 1785), 1: 418-24.

119. *Dreadful Newes: or, A True Relation of the Great, Violent and the Late Earthquake, Hapned the 27 day of March, Stilo Romano last, at Callabria, in the Kingdom of Naples, about the houres of 3 and foure in the after-noone, to the over-throw and ruin of many Cities, Townes, and Castles, and the death of above 50,000 persons* (London 1638), pp. 12-13.

120. Ernesto S., 16 September 1976; Fonte, *Rende,* pp. 289-91.

121. Michele F., 27 September 1977.

122. Fonte, *Rende,* pp. 289-91. A number of knowledgeable travelogues written by British (as well as French and German) observers provide entertaining accounts of the history and culture of Calabria. On the Jewish presence, for example, see Crawfurd Tait Ramage, *The Nooks and Biways of Italy: Wanderings in Search of Its Ancient Remains and Modern Superstitions* (Liverpool 1868), pp. 75-76; and the classic volume (first published in 1915) by Norman Douglas, *Old Calabria* (Oxford 1938), p. 52.

123. Banfield, *Moral Basis,* p. 83ff. Banfield's view is also held by Joseph Lopreato, "How would you like to be a peasant?" *Human Organization* 24, no. 4 (1965): 300-1. Also Johan Galtung, *Members of Two Worlds: A Development Study of Three Villages in Western Sicily* (Oslo 1971), ch. 5.

124. Jan Brögger, *Montevarese: A Study of Peasant Society and Culture in Southern Italy* (Oslo 1971), pp. 41-52, 82-86, 117-23; Davis, *Land and Family,* chs. 4 and 6. See also Frank Cancian, "The Southern Italian Peasant: World View and Political Behaviour," *Anthropological Quarterly* 34, no. 1 (1961): 1-18, for a critique of Banfield. One of the most interesting of such studies on Southern Italy is that of Donald S. Pitkin, "Land Tenure and Family Organization in an Italian Village," *Human Organization* 18, no. 4 (1959-60): 169-73. Pitkin makes the point that the type of "property ownership (especially land) is an important determinant of family organization" (pp. 172-73). He maintains that the nuclear family household was predominant in the peasant village proper he studied, though for peasants who lived on the land the majority lived in an extended family arrangement. Though it is tempting to utilize his findings to explain

the familism of Banfield as opposed to the co-operation of Davis and Brögger discussed below, the implicit correlation does not seem to hold true. Banfield, for example, notes that three-quarters of the peasants of the village he studied lived on their farms, and similar mixed types of village/land settlements were reported by Brögger and Davis. My own study further found little correlation between peasants living in the village proper and familism. Rather kinship coherence cut across such boundaries.

125. Constance Cronin, *The Sting of Change: Sicilians in Sicily and Australia* (Chicago 1970), pp. 184-202; Jeremy Boissevain, *The Italians of Montreal: Social Adjustment in a Plural Society* (Ottawa 1970), ch. 3.

126. Interviews; see Leonard W. Moss and Walter H. Thomson, "The South Italian Family: Literature and Observation," *Human Organization* 18, no. 1 (1959): 38-39; and Leonard Covello, *The Social Background of the Italo-American School Child: A Study of the Southern Italian Family Mores and Their Effect in the School Situation in Italy and America* (Leiden, Netherlands 1967), p. 99.

127. Interviews. See Davis, *Land and Family*, pp. 43-49; Maraspini, *Italian Village*, p. 183.

128. Interviews. See Covello, *Social Background*, pp. 173-74, 196-98.

129. Interviews. See Maraspini, *Italian Village*, pp. 158-59; Davis, *Land and Family*, pp. 34-36; Covello, *Social Background*, pp. 200-2.

130. Ida S., (N), 12 March 1977.

131. Michele St., (T), 16 November 1975.

132. Ida S., (N), 12 March 1977.

133. The celebration around the posting of the banns was also reported by Covello in his study of the social background of Southern Italians. Though the specific description given by him was not wholly applicable to the Rende area, it is nonetheless noteworthy: "On the day of the first announcement in the Church of an intended marriage, there was held a party at the girl's house. Among those present was the groom and his relatives. The former, according to tradition and as part of a ritual, brought raw meat – usually in the form of a slain lamb – thus symbolically indicating the responsibility of the husband to provide victuals. Likewise, this act symbolized the girl's future role as a preparer of the raw food." Covell, *Social Background*, p. 205.

134. Interviews; see Leonard W. Moss and Stephen C. Cappannari, "Patterns of Kinship, Comparaggio and Community in a Southern Italian Village," *Anthropological Quarterly* 33 (1960): 30-31; Fortunata Piselli, *Parentele ed Emigrazione: Mutamenti e Continuità in una Comunità Calabrese* (Turin 1981), pp. 48-53, 210-17.

CHAPTER 2. CAUSATION AND CONTOURS OF EMIGRATION

1. Any discussion of the "causes" of emigration is likely to seem somewhat presumptuous because of the matrix of factors that converged to "cause" any one individual to emigrate. The number and complexity of factors – economic, social, and psychological – as well as their specific combination that influenced any individual or set of individuals was often so varied and indeterminate that any effort to discuss causation is bound to seem incomplete.

At the same time, reading the accounts of *meridionalisti* such as Francesco Nitti, Giuseppe Scalise, and Taruffi and his associates, one is struck by the litany of factors said to lie behind the emigration from Calabria.

Though these authors took account of the importance of distinguishing initial causes from those arising from the influence of the emigration process itself, beyond this, little order is presented which can give one a sense of what was primary. Both Nitti and Taruffi, De Nobili and Lori, for example, documented through the collection of contemporary testimony the ingredients of *miseria:* unstable working conditions, low wages, poor diet and health care, and so on. Scalise, for his part, diverged from this and offered a classification of causes under the categories of psychological (for example, fantasy, vanity), economic (usury, poor crops, and such), and socio-political (taxation, immigration laws, etc.). For Scalise, these groups of causes accounted for the steady increase in emigration as the first type of motivation gave way to the second which gave way to the third. All recognized the complex of causative factors that grew out of emigration itself: the support of overseas kin, the example of returned emigrants, the "contagion" of stories of success. While all this is valuable, one rarely gets the sense of moving beyond the trees to view the forest as a whole. As contemporaries of the movement they were attempting to explain, however, one can hardly fault the *meridionalisti* for not providing a model of migratory causation that weeded out the primary from secondary factors, which only the distance of time could adequately provide.

See Francesco Nitti, *Scritti sulla questione meridionale,* vol. 1: *Saggi sulla storia del mezzogiorno, emigrazione e lavoro* [1888-1908] (Bari 1952), pp. 349-64; *Scritti sulla questione meridionale,* vol. 4, Pt. 1: *Inchiesta sulle condizioni dei contadini in Basilicata e in Calabria (1910)* (Bari 1968), pp. 153-206; D. Taruffi, L. De Nobili, C. Lori, *La questione agraria e l'emigrazione in Calabria* (Florence 1908), pp. 137-38, 841-80; Giuseppe Scalise, *L'emigrazione dalla Calabria: Saggio di economia sociale* (Naples 1905), pp. 27-39.

2. For the Italian peninsula as a whole, Cipolla points out that from the advent of reasonably reliable demographic figures around 1500 the population fluctuated considerably but never surpassed 12 million until after the mid-seventeenth century. From 1660 to 1820 the peninsula experienced an annual rate of increase of about 3 per thousand and thenceforth to 1870 a further increase to about 7 per thousand. This translated itself into a population increase of from 20.4 million in 1820 to 28 million in 1870. Carlo M. Cipolla, "Four Centuries of Italian Demographic Development," in *Population in History: Essays in Historical Demography* (London 1969), pp. 570-87.

3. Luigi Izzo, *La popolazione calabrese nel secolo XIX: Demografia e economia* (Naples 1965), pp. 167, 170 (calculation mine). After 1870 the annual rate of increase for Italy rose sharply, reaching 11 per thousand at the turn of the century. Rates of infant mortality which had fluctuated between 200 and 300 per thousand in the first part of the nineteenth century were cut to 160 by 1901-10. This improvement in the death rate made possible by improved medical and hygienic practices took place in Southern as well as Northern Italy. By the turn of the century the peninsula as a whole had started to adjust its birth rate downward to offset the improvement in infant mortality. However, relative to the North, this adjustment lagged behind in the agricultural South, thus progressively widening the demographic gap between the two areas. Cipolla, "Italian Demographic Development," pp. 570-87.

4. Izzo, *Popolazione calabrese,* p. 167. Of the three regions in Calabria, Cosenza experienced a relatively greater population increase, especially in the

decades 1871-90. This was due to a higher birth rate on the one hand and a generally lower death rate on the other, which gave the province a rate of increase of 10.4 per thousand in 1881 compared to 9.6 for the region generally. For Calabria as a whole, the population increased from 792,600 in the early nineteenth century (1813) to 1,370,200 at the turn of the century (1901). Ibid., 163, 166-67, 187.

5. Aside from smallpox, another main cause of death in Calabria prior to Unification was cholera, especially the epidemics which hit the region during 1836-37 and 1853-54. (Ibid., p. 164.) In 1820 and 1901 the population density for Calabria as a whole was 56 and 90.6 inhabitants per square kilometre respectively. For Italy it was 57 and 106 inhabitants per square kilometre at the two dates. See Cipolla, "Italian Demographic Development," p. 573.

6. Cipolla, "Italian Demographic Development," p. 584. Between 1880 and 1887 the price of soft wheat in Italy dropped from 32.3 to 21.4 lire per quintal and that of corn from 24.2 to 13.4. Ibid., Gaetano Cingari, *Storia della Calabria dall' Unità a Oggi* (Bari 1982), p. 80.

7. Izzo, *Popolazione calabrese,* p. 41; Cingari, *Storia della Calabria,* p. 80.

8. Denis Mack Smith, *Italy: A Modern History,* rev. ed. (Ann Arbor 1959), p. 159.

9. The importance of France in the economic health of Cosenza is illustrated by the fact that the province had its own agricultural representatives in the republic to promote its interests. The provincial Catholic co-operative, for example, at the turn of the century had representatives in Marseilles to promote the important dried fig trade to France. See Taruffi et al., *Questione agraria,* pp. 432-33.

10. Ibid., pp. 168-69, 363; Izzo, *Popolazione calabrese,* pp. 40-41, 50, 79; Mack Smith, *Italy,* p. 152.

11. The position that levels of living in Cosenza deteriorated during the latter part of the nineteenth century is best developed by Scalise, *Emigrazione della Calabria,* p. 44ff. This is confirmed by Cipolla, "Italian Demographic Development," pp. 582, 585. Also see Cingari, *Storia della Calabria,* chap. 4.

Izzo, comparing the results of the first serious investigation into the socio-economic conditions of Calabria ordered in 1811 by Joachim Murat to those of the *Inchiesta agraria* of 1883, shows the similarity between conditions reported by the two inquiries and concludes that levels of living remained essentially unchanged throughout the century. Similarly, Taruffi, De Nobili and Lori quote extensively from both Rotondo's study of 1834 and Franchetti's report of 1875 to argue the same point. Further, they draw parallels between the socio-economic conditions reported by earlier investigators and their own 1906 observations. Izzo, *Popolazione calabrese,* pp. 63-72. The third and fourth sections of the 1811 inquiry dealing with socio-economic conditions have been published by U. Caldora, *La statistica murattiana del Regno di Napoli: Le relazioni sulla Calabria* (Messina 1960). The 1883 study cited was published under the title, *Atti della giunta per la inchiesta agraria e sulle condizioni della classe agricola,* vol. 9 (Rome 1883). See also Taruffi et al., *Questione agraria,* pp. 762-94. The works referred to by Taruffi, De Nobili, and Lori are: M.L. Rotondo, *Saggio politico su la popolazione e le pubbiche contribuzioni del Regno delle Due Sicilie al di qua del Faro* (Naples 1834), and Leopoldo Franchetti, *Condizioni economiche ed amministrative delle provincie napoletane: Abruzzi e Molise, Calabria e Basilicata* (Florence 1875).

12. An indication of the regional levels of living around the time of the *Inchiesta* is given by the fact that the yearly per capita consumption of meat in Calabria stood at 8.1 kilograms compared to the national average of 16.0 kilograms. This national average was the lowest in Europe, less than half the average per capita consumption in France of 35.6 kilograms and 44.8 kilograms in Germany. The corresponding ratio in the United States was even higher at 54.4 kilograms of meat consumed per person. Eggs and milk were also less commonly available in Southern Italy vis-à-vis the North and considerably less plentiful among the peasantry as compared to the *galantuomini*. Taruffi et al., *Questione agraria*, pp. 775-76.

13. Ibid., pp. 772-73; Izzo, *Popolazione calabrese*, pp. 64-65. Cingari, *Storia della Calabria*, pp. 90-91. Interviews. The diet of agricultural labourers was less varied and poorer than the peasants' and in times of high unemployment they were reduced to gleaning and subsisting on weeds and wild plants, even the cheaper breads being beyond their means.

14. Taruffi et al., *Questione agraria*, pp. 192-94; Izzo, *Popolazione calabrese*, pp. 63-64. Also interviews.

15. Izzo, *Popolazione calabrese*, pp. 65, 116, 197.

16. Benedetto Croce, *History of the Kingdom of Naples* (Chicago 1970), pp. 212-13 (originally published as *Storia del Regno di Napoli* [Bari 1925]); Izzo, *Popolazione calabrese*, pp. 65-66; Taruffi et al., *Questione agraria*, pp. 815-16.

17. Croce, *History of Naples*, p. 240. The author cites the observations of the Swiss writer, Marc Monnier.

18. Santo St., 16 November 1976; Caspare C., 2 November 1976. Cingari makes the point that in the late nineteenth century, the problem of *polverizzazione* was more acute in Calabria than other regions, and more pronounced in Cosenza than the other two provinces of Calabria. Fragmentation is seen as related to concentration in landholding, and inter-related to de-industrialization and concomitant ruralization. Moreover, these trends are connected to the increased feminization of the peasant workforce. See Cingari, *Storia della Calabria*, pp. 84-89, 95-99.

19. Demarco, *La Calabria*, p. 81; interviews. Also see J. Davis, *Land and Family in Pisticci* (London 1973), pp. 108-12, 117.

20. Demarco, *La Calabria*, p. 77.

21. Luigi Conforti, *Risposta all'opuscolo "Una provincia fuori legge"* (Cosenza 1881), pp. 66-68. Mack Smith's account of the effect of Unification on land distribution is apt here:

    The landowners no longer had a paternalistic government to keep them in check. One result of the risorgimento was that the landholding classes became more powerful than ever: they were the electors; they controlled local government; their wishes decided the appointment to jobs, the appointment of local taxes and public works' contracts. They could now ignore Bourbon social legislation and enclose the common lands in each village to their exclusive advantage, with the result that peasant families were deprived of grazing lands which for centuries had been the basis of their livelihood.

    Denis Mack Smith, *The Making of Italy, 1796-1870* (New York 1968), p. 369.

22. Nitti, *Questione meridionale*, vol. 1: 261; Cingari, *Storia della Calabria*, p. 20ff. Also see Anton Blok, *The Mafia of a Sicilian Village, 1860-1960* (New York 1974), pp. 118-20.

23. Adolfo Rossi, "Vantaggi e danni dell'emigrazione nel mezzogiorno d'Italia (note di un viaggio fatto in Basilicata e in Calabria)," *Bollettino dell'emigrazione,* anno 1908, no. 13 (Ministero degli Affari Esteri, Commissariato dell'Emigrazione; Rome 1908), p. 46 (my translation).

24. Nitti, *Questione meridionale,* vol. 1: 265.

25. Scalise, *Emigrazione della Calabria,* pp. 44, 47-48. Taruffi, De Nobili and Lori in their 1908 report expressed their belief that in many instances through the nineteenth century wage rates were actually lower than those obtained in the 1790s. (Taruffi et al., *Questione agraria,* p. 788.)

26. Demarco, *La Calabria,* pp. 92-94. In the province of Reggio, on the other hand, where out-migration was still insignificant, the maximum wage level reached was only 1.50 lire per day.

27. "Tassa sul macinato," *La provincia di Reggio Calabria, giornale politico amministrativo,* anno 3, no. 43 (22 June 1879), cited in Demarco, *La Calabria,* p. 97 (my translation). Fortunato noted that at the turn of the century Italy, along with Russia, was the most heavily taxed country in Europe. About one-quarter of its national income was derived from taxation whereas for Germany the proportion was 10% and for France 15%. Further, the South paid disproportionately more than the North. Whereas the South paid 28% of its income into the national treasury, the North only paid 23%. See Giustino Fortunato, *Il mezzogiorno e lo stato italiano,* 2 (Bari 1911): 348.

28. Cingari, *Storia della Calabria,* pp. 81, 98. Land rents were from 25 lire per hectare prior to Unification to 32 lire in the 1870s.

29. According to Scalise, the worst decades of the century were the two following Unification, which barely allowed the subsistence upkeep of one's family. At the turn of the century he cited the oral testimony of old *contadini* who attested to the relative comfort of the Bourbon decades compared to those following Unification. "The Calabrian peasant had never been in more desperate conditions than in the years that preceded the full development of emigration," he concluded. Scalise, *Emigrazione dalla Calabria,* p. 47.

30. Robert F. Foerster, *The Italian Emigration of Our Times* (Cambridge, Mass. 1919), p. 416.

31. Izzo, *Popolazione calabrese,* pp. 171-72.

32. Ibid.; Demarco, *La Calabria,* p. 93; Taruffi et al., *Questione agraria,* pp. 137-38; interviews.

33. In being issued the *nulla osta,* emigrants were to declare whether they intended to emigrate "temporarily" or "permanently." The term "permanent" was actually a misnomer for emigration of "indefinite duration" whereas "temporary" denoted short-term seasonal migration. Hence nineteenth-century emigration figures show "permanent" emigration being of much greater magnitude than the "temporary" stream. At any rate, students of Southern emigration have long recognized the artificiality of the categories, which the Italian government acknowledged by dropping the labels in the early twentieth century. Hence, I have dealt through this chapter with the total emigration count, omitting the two misleading categories the official statistics often utilized.

34. Taruffi et al., *Questione agraria,* pp. 699, 734. Construction of the Suez Canal lasted from 1859 to 1869.

35. Izzo, *Popolazione calabrese,* p. 175.

36. Italy, Ministero di Agricoltura, Industria e Commercio, Direzione Generale della Statistica, *Statistica della emigrazione italiana per gli anni 1884 e 1885* (Rome 1886), pp. 50, 64; Italy, Commissariato Generale

dell'Emigrazione, *Annuario statistico della emigrazione italiana dal 1876 al 1925* (Rome 1926), p. 182 (my calculations).

37. Scalise, *Emigrazione della Calabria*, pp. 6-7.

38. Taruffi et al., *Questione agraria*, p. 710.

39. Indeed, according to Arlacchi, in the Cortone Plain of Catanzaro, proletarians only made one-quarter the return of Cosenza peasants in the Crati River valley area. See Pino Arlacchi, "Perche si emigrazia dalla società contadina e non dal latifondo," in *L'emigrazione calabrese dell'unita ad oggi,* ed., Pietro Borzomati (Rome 1982), p. 159.

40. Ibid., pp. 157-60. Also see Taruffi, *Questione agraria,* p. 708ff., and Pino Arlacchi, *Mafia, contadini e latifondo nella Calabria tradizionale* (Bologna 1980).

41. Scalise, *Emigrazione dalla Calabria,* pp. 132-33 (Table E).

42. Many emigrants gravitated either to the expanding coffee plantations of southern Brazil or the grain and flax farms of eastern Argentina. Others were drawn to city pursuits and construction projects reflective of the commercial, industrial, and urban growth that was both based on, and concomitant to, the agricultural expansion of the two republics. During these early years, emigration to South America allowed men to do what had already become familiar in the old world – seasonal or short-term labour after which they could return home. Many left Italy during the idle winter months (often in October) and arrived on the new world plantations or farms for the harvest and threshing bottlenecks, after which they would return home in time to engage in the spring harvest. Others would remain for longer periods in urban industrial jobs before returning. Samuel L. Baily, "Italians and Organized Labor in the United States and Argentina, 1880-1910," in *The Italian Experience in the United States,* ed. Silvano M. Tomasi and Madeline H. Engel (New York 1970), pp. 113-14; Ralph Della Cava, "The Italian Immigrant Experience: Views of a Latinamericanist," in *Perspectives in Italian Immigration and Ethnicity,* ed. S[ilvano] M. Tomasi (New York 1977), pp. 188-89; Foerster, *Italian Emigration,* pp. 243-44.

43. An indication of the opportunities offered outside of agriculture is given by the fact that the city of Buenos Aires expanded its population from 180,000 in 1869 to half a million by the First World War, the nation as a whole more than tripling its population in the same period. Baily, "Italians and Organized Labor," pp. 113-15, 121.

44. One interesting reason given by informants for the early emigration to Argentina was the ease with which *paesani* could learn to speak Spanish and the cultural affinity between the South American republic and the home country. Hence *paesani* were said to feel more at home in Argentina than in North America, in a similar way that Germans, it was said, found it easier to blend into "English" society than Italians. While the consideration of cultural affinity was a factor behind the early migration to Argentina, the radical shift in emigration from South to North America after 1900 implies that it was not a primary or enduring motivation for *paesani.*

45. Taruffi et al., *Questione agraria,* p. 708; *Statistica della emigrazione, 1884 e 1885,* pp. 50, 175; *Statistica della emigrazione, 1888,* p. 8; Italy, Ministero di Agricoltura, Industria e Commercio, Direzione Generale della Statistica, *Statistica della emigrazione italiana avvenuta nell'anno 1890* (Rome 1891), p. 63; Italy, Ministero di Agricoltura, Industria e Commercio, Direzione Generale della Statistica, *Statistica della emigrazione italiana avvenuta nel 1894, 1895* (Rome 1896), p. 67; Italy, Ministero di Agricoltura, Industria

e Commercio, Direzione Generale della Statistica, *Statistica della emigrazione italiana avvenuta nel 1897 e confronti coll'emigrazione dagli altri stati d'Europa per l'America* (Rome 1899), p. 97 (my calculations).

46. Scalise, *Emigrazione dalla Calabria,* pp. 132-33 (Table E).

47. Ibid., Taruffi et al., *Questione agraria,* p. 744 (Table 3) (my calculations).

48. *Statistica della emigrazione, 1888,* pp. 140-42. For Cosenza district, it was found that its 54 mayors mentioned the United States as a destination 33 times as opposed to 31 times for Argentina and 24 for Brazil. This is in opposition to what would be expected from provincial emigration rates which, until the advent of mass emigration after 1900, show a greater volume of emigration toward Argentina than the United States. As can be seen from Table 7, a similar pattern holds true for the Rende area. It would appear, then, that the United States was relatively more important as a destination for Cosenza district and the Rende area particularly than for the province as a whole.

49. Rossi, "Vantaggi e danni dell'emigrazione," pp. 32, 52; Taruffi et al., *Questione agraria,* pp. 702, 703-4, 756-57; Foerster, *Italian Emigration,* pp. 417, 460; Scalise, *Emigrazione dalla Calabria,* pp. 32-33, 23.

50. Taruffi et al., p. 708. Taking statistics derived from the 1911 census, it is of interest to note that for Calabria as a whole the natural increase in population was almost offset by emigration. In 1911 the population of the region numbered 1,402,000. While this represented an increase of 173,000 over the previous census, 82% of this natural increase was matched by out-migration (i.e., 141,000 emigrants between the two census dates). In comparison, emigration offset 61% of the natural increase in 1901 and only 35% in 1881 over the respective previous decades.

Calabria's 1911 emigration rate of 82% of natural increase was higher than the average for the South generally at 62% of natural increase, though not as high as Basilicata and Abruzzi-Molise, both of which experienced net population losses after 1900. The 1911 emigration rate for Italy as a whole was 43% of natural increase and that of the North 32%.

Between 1911 and 1914, Calabria had a birth rate of 34.6 per 1,000 compared to the national rate of 31.7 per 1,000, and the region had a death rate of 19.7 per 1,000, almost identical to the national rate of 19.1. Further, in 1911, the population density of Calabria was 93 people per square kilometre. This was an increase over 91 people per square kilometre in 1901, 83 in 1881, 80 in 1871, and 76 in 1861. This density compared to the rest of Italy showed an increasing divergence from the national average. Whereas the regional density was 89% of the national in 1861, it was 88% in 1871, 86% in 1881, 83% in 1901, and 79% in 1911. Obviously the high rate of out-migration from Calabria played a significant role in this trend.

Italy, Associazione per lo Sviluppo dell'Industria nel Mezzogiorno (SVIMEZ), *Statistiche sul mezzogiorno d'Italia 1861-1953* (Rome 1954), pp. 14, 61, 116.

51. *Statistica della emigrazione, 1890,* pp. 70-75; Taruffi et al., *Questione agraria,* pp. 731-32; Izzo, *Popolazione calabrese,* p. 179 (my calculations); interviews.

52. *Statistica della emigrazione, 1884-1885,* p. 175; *Statistica della emigrazione, 1886,* pp. 50-175; *Statistica della emigrazione, 1888,* p. 8; *Statistica della emigrazione, 1890,* p. 63; *Statistica della emigrazione, 1894 & 1895,* p. 67; *Statistica della emigrazione, 1897,* p. 67; *Annuario della emigrazione, 1876-1925,* p. 182; (my calculations). Interestingly, the emigration figures

indicate that families with a surplus of male minors were more likely to be involved in family resettlement in the new world than those with a predominance of females. Hence, before 1890 male minors from Calabria were double the number of female minors. In 1905 the gap was less pronounced so that 3,537 minor males emigrated compared with 2,088 minor females. (Taruffi et al., *Questione agraria*, p. 747.) There were two reasons which can contribute to an explanation of this pattern. First, families with a predominance of males over females would have more productive hands to help accumulate the capital necessary for emigration and subsequent family resettlement. Secondly, the code of virginity and female seclusion may have made families with a predominance of females more reluctant to embark upon family resettlement than those with a predominance of males since these values were seen to be more likely of attainment in the village as opposed to the more unpredictable environment of the new world.

53. *Annuario della emigrazione, 1876-1925*, p. 41; Taruffi et al., *Questione agraria*, pp. 751-52 (Table 10, my calculation). For Calabria as a whole, the period of mass emigration witnessed a voluminous outflow of about 572,400: approximately 326,700 (57%) of whom were destined for the United States, 130,900 (22%) for Argentina, and 61,300 (11%) for Brazil. This was equivalent to an annual regional emigration of about 44,000 during the period.

   Emigration from Calabria between 1876 and 1900 totalled 275,926, of which 90,681 went to Argentina, 81,230 to the United States, and 61,514 to Brazil. In these years the annual rate of emigration averaged 11,037. *Statistiche sul mezzogiorno*, p. 117; my calculations.

54. Rossi, "Vantaggi e danni dell'emigrazione," p. 95.

55. An indication of American industrial expansion in these years is given by the fact that in 1913 the productive capacity of the United States was five times that of 1875. While the population of the United States had doubled between these dates, non-agricultural workers increased four times over 1875. Whereas in 1875 the non-agricultural sector employed 7 million people and roughly the same number were farm labourers, in 1913 the sector employed 27 million (11 million of these in manufacturing and mining), as opposed to fewer than 12 million in agriculture. Rowland Berthoff, *An Unsettled People: Social Order and Disorder in American History* (New York 1971), pp. 316-17.

56. Foerster, *Italian Emigration*, pp. 249-51. A particularly damning account of exploitation was given by Rossi in 1902 who described the indebtedness and harsh treatment of migrants on the *fazendas* of Brazil, likening their position to that of native black workers. Later, when travelling through Cosenza district in 1908 as royal commissioner of emigration, he cited evidence from returned emigrants showing disillusionment with Brazil and preference for the United States. Many Italian observers held the opinion that only in the United States could the Italian immigrant escape exploitation and find peace and honest profit. See Adolfo Rossi, "Condizioni dei coloni italiani nello stato di S. Paolo del Brasile," *Bollettino dell'emigrazione*, anno 1902, no. 10 (Ministero degli Affari Esteri, Commissariato dell' Emigrazione; Rome 1902); Rossi, "Vantaggi e danni dell'emigrazione," p. 44, and Taruffi et al., *Questione agraria*, p. 736.

57. Taylor, citing studies prepared for the National Bureau of Economic Research covering the late nineteenth century and the early twentieth to the First World War, concludes of the general position of the working man in the United States at the turn of the century: "the latest view is

that living costs rose more slowly than used to be thought, and that over the whole period, and for industry as a whole, real wages may have risen more than one-third." See Philip Taylor, *The Distant Magnet: European Emigration to the U.S.A.* (New York 1972), p. 207.
58. See Table 5. Again in these years, as in the previous periods, almost the entire overseas emigration (98%) was destined for the Americas, *Annuario della emigrazione, 1876-1925*, p. 41.
59. Ibid., pp. 182, 546-48, 595, 1,191, 1,322, 1,468 (my calculation).
60. John Higham, *Strangers in the Land: Patterns of American Nativism, 1860-1925* (New York 1963), pp. 202-3, 308-11, 319; Joseph Lopreato, *Italian Americans* (New York 1970), pp. 13-16; Humbert S. Nelli, "Italians," in *Harvard Encyclopedia of American Ethnic Groups*, ed. Stephan Thernstrom (Cambridge, Mass. 1980), p. 547 (Table 1). The high point of Italian immigration to the United States was reached in 1907 when 286,000 landed. This flow alone approached the total European quota. See Nelli, "Italians," p. 547.
61. Higham, *Strangers in the Land*, pp. 319-24; *Annuario della emigrazione, 1876-1925*, p. 1410ff.
62. John J. Baxevanis, *Economy and Population Movements in the Peloponnesos of Greece* (Athens 1972), p. 60. There are two salient factors which help both to describe and to explain the relationship between levels and standards of living. First, expectations or standards of a better life presuppose the existence of a social system fluid enough to allow a certain degree of upward mobility. In a completely closed system with no possibility of upward movement, levels and standards of living are one and the same. The second factor relates to the fact that peasant society is not a static entity in opposition to a dynamic urban one, but rather that it incorporates elements of the latter while maintaining local distinctiveness. Standards of living are essentially borrowed from the general culture peasants have contact with and from the living levels of the better-off among them. The example of well-to-do relatives, the influence of education, local travel, or military service are all capable of raising people's standards.
63. Taruffi et al., *Questione agraria*, p. 757 (my translation).
64. Interviews.
65. Scalise, *Emigrazione dalla Calabria*, pp. 29-30 (my translation).
66. Taruffi et al., *Questione agraria*, p. 835 (my translation).
67. Eugenio U., (T), 25 April 1974. Ida S., (N), 23 September 1976.
68. Like other *meridionalisti*, Taruffi and his partners believed that there was at least some exaggeration in the returned emigrants' praise of America. They wrote, for example:
   The *americano* took me to his home to introduce me to his wife and daughter. We entered, coffee was brought, a woman dressed like a *signora*, the hair thick and brown, the accent *castigliano* [i.e., from Castiglione], the manner gloomy and coarse: she was followed by a girl dressed with refinement, the hair styled with city coquetry. I break the ice, and make myself ask something of her life in the village .... I should never have done it! Mother and daughter got upset with complaints and imprecations against the village ... against the father that had brought them amongst these savages .... Then she started to magnify America: everything beautiful, from the shoes to the hat ... you find everything fresh, all English goods. My daughter had a magnificent piano ... German ... you can't even find one that nice in Naples!
   Here, added her daughter, there's nothing.... (pp. 871-72: my translation).

69. Nitti, *Questione meridionale,* vol. 4, part 1, p. 161 (my translation).
70. Giovanni So., 29 May 1976; Francesco G., 30 July 1975.
71. Nitti, *Questione meridionale,* vol. 4, part 1, p. 160.
72. Rossi, "Vantaggi e danni dell'emigrazione," p. 42; Nitti, *Questione meridionale,* vol. 4, part 1, p. 164 (my translations).
73. Rossi, "Vantaggi e danni dell'emigrazione," pp. 36, 45, 48, 52, 59, 61; Nitti, *Questione meridionale,* vol. 4, part 1, p. 181.
74. Scalise, *Emigrazione dalla Calabria,* p. 57; Taruffi et al., *Questione agraria,* pp. 852-56; interviews.
75. Scalise, *Emigrazione dalla Calabria,* pp. 53-56; Taruffi et al., *Questione agraria,* p. 853. In 1905, Cosenza's deposits in postal banks at 16,832,700 lire were far above those of Catanzaro's at 10,229,005 lire and of Reggio's at 4,308,905 lire. Taking the three fiscal years from 1901 to 1903 shows that Cosenza was also the richest province with a total wealth estimated at 598,000,000 lire or 1,285 lire per inhabitant. This compared favourably with Catanzano's wealth of 578,500,000 lire or 1,214 lire per capita and Reggio's income of 455,000,000 lire or 1,061 lire per inhabitant. Here again the position of Cosenza was very likely influenced by its earlier and more voluminous emigration.
76. Nitti, *Questione meridionale,* vol. 4, part 2, pp. 187-89.
77. Ernesto S., (T), 14 March 1976.
78. Michele P., (N), 6 September 1976. Also see Rossi, "Vantaggi e danni dell'emigrazione," pp. 39, 41, 44, 48-49, 53-54, 60, 62.
79. Alberto S., (T), 14 March 1976.
80. Santo St., 7 November 1976; Giovanni So., 29 May 1976.
81. Eugenio S., (T), 17 April 1976.
82. Vincenzo S., (T), 25 April 1974. It should be noted that for the years immediately following the First World War informants mentioned factors of a push as well as pull nature. This reflected the economic dislocations of the war, which contributed to the decision to emigrate. Specifically, postwar inflation and unemployment resulting from demobilization were mentioned as causes of emigration.
83. Although it is my position that it was the influence of returned emigrants that led to the raising of communal expectations, it is realized that other interrelated factors were also operative. Both the increasing incorporation of the peasant village into the higher living standards of an urbanizing, industrializing nation and the general economic prosperity experienced by Italy after 1896 played significant roles here. See Alexander Gershenkron, "Notes on the Rate of Industrial Growth in Italy, 1881-1913," *Journal of Economic History,* 15, no. 4 (Dec. 1955): 364 and passim.
84. Foerster, *Italian Emigration,* pp. 455-56.
85. Taruffi et al., *Questione agraria,* p. 822 (my translation).
86. Rossi, "Vantaggi e danni dell'emigrazione," pp. 40, 50, 53, 59, 64-65; also interviews.
87. Taruffi et al., *Questione agraria,* p. 309; Rossi, "Vantaggi e danni dell'emigrazione," p. 44 (my translation). The new-found pride of *americani* was also eloquently noted by Foerster, who wrote: "They do often assume abroad, and manifest at home, a certain self-assurance, a challenging disposition, even a sort of vainglory, which contrasts sharply with their former servility and has among its many consequences, some good, some ill, one of sterling, epochal value: a more resolute attitude toward the employing landlord" (*Italian Emigration,* p. 459).
88. Scalise, *Emigrazione dalla Calabria,* pp. 116-18; Taruffi et al., *Questione agraria,* pp. 846-47; Foerster, *Italian Emigration,* pp. 45-51.

89. Interviews. See Rossi, "Vantaggi e danni dell'emigrazione," p. 34. Not surprisingly, informants related how in a few cases the "social capital" of *americani* had the negative result of having a young woman's parents pressure her into an unwanted marriage, though, it was added, such arrangements born of expediency were hardly unique with respect to *americani*. Nor were cases unknown of men being pressured by their parents to marry undesired women for purely material reasons.

90. Though I have attempted to cover here the main socio-economic effects of the returned emigrants which contributed to the raising of expectations and sparking of further out-migration, there were several other, less conspicuous changes that accompanied the return. For example, returned emigrants were more likely to pay their taxes on time, which while motivated by the desire to escape interest charges, nevertheless helped introduce new standards of civil-mindedness. As a further example, through acting as a safety valve and by adding to the prosperity of the province, emigration contributed to the general lowering of crime and to public safety. See Scalise, *Emigrazione dalla Calabria*, pp. 72-84.

91. Ibid., pp. 47-51; Taruffi et al., *Questione agraria*, pp. 844-45. Not surprisingly, land near town and irrigable land were most in demand. In some isolated localities where land was poor, especially in the marshy coastal plains or rugged mountains, there was less of a demand. Hence, the high emigration rates in such zones actually resulted in land prices dropping rather than rising as they did through most of the province. Where a labour shortage occurred, land was turned over to pasturage if possible. See also Rossi, "Vantaggi e danni dell'emigrazione," pp. 32, 38, 51, 62-63.

92. Cingari, *Storia dalla Calabria*, p. 19; Demarco, *La Calabria*, p. 93.

93. Scalise, *Emigrazione della Calabria*, pp. 39-43; Taruffi et al., *Questione agraria*, pp. 338, 841-42. The wages within the Rende area were slightly higher than the provincial average, which ranged from 1.25 to 2.70 lire per day. For the region as a whole the wage spread for men averaged from 1.50 to 2.50 lire per day. For women wages ranged from 0.60 to 1.25 lire and for children from 0.70 to 0.90 lire per day. In any case, agricultural wages as a whole within the Rende area and Calabria generally more than doubled over pre-emigration rates (*Questione agraria*, pp. 787-88; *Emigrazione della Calabria*, p. 48.).

    Interestingly, Rossi noted that in some communes of heavy out-migration and high labour shortage, landowners resorted to imported peasants from Northern Italy to work their land. In one case, for example, a landlord in Castrovillari (Cosenza) imported four families from Ferrara under a *mezzadria* contract with a view to further importations if they proved successful, though, not surprisingly, it was not an easy task finding willing colonizers from the North ("Vantaggi e danni dell'emigrazione," p. 37).

94. Izzo, *Popolazione calabrese*, p. 77. Scalise points out that once the wave of emigration descended upon an area, the subsequent increase in wages was very rapid, in some cases doubling in the space of two to three years. (*Emigrazione della Calabria*, p. 44).

95. Taruffi et al., *Questione agraria*, pp. 789-90.

CHAPTER 3. THE PROCESS OF MIGRATION

1. Robert F. Harney, "The Commerce of Migration," *Canadian Ethnic Studies* 9, no. 1 (1977): 42-53; Robert F. Harney, "Ambiente and Social Class

in North American Little Italies," *Canadian Review of Studies in Nationalism* 2, no. 2 (Spring 1975): 208-24; Grazia Dore, "Some Social and Historical Aspects of Italian Emigration to America," *Journal of Social History* 2, no. 2 (Winter 1968): 95-122.

2. Francesco Nitti, *Scritti sulla questione meridionale*, vol. 1: *Saggi sulla storia del mezzogiorno, emigrazione e lavoro* (Bari 1952), pp. 409ff.; D. Taruffi, L. De Nobili, C. Lori, *La questione agraria e l'emigrazione in Calabria* (Florence 1908), pp. 827-32, 836. Information provided by the Commissariato in 1907 showed that Calabria had 246 emigration committees: 138 in Catanzano, 56 in Reggio, and 52 in Cosenza. But, as Taruffi discovered in this investigation through Calabria, these were hollow figures for, "even if these figures are reliable, they have no importance, since all agree in the absolutely negative function of those Comitati" (p. 833; my translation).

3. Ibid., p. 833.

4. Nitti, *Questione meridionale*, 1: 417.

5. Rosario P., (T), 29 May 1974.

6. Interviews. See Bailey, "The Peasant View of the Bad Life," in *Peasants and Peasant Societies*, ed. Teodor Shanin (Harmondsworth, England 1971), pp. 300-4.

7. Trentina C., (N), 21 January 1978.

8. Interviews. See Robert Wade, "Political Behaviour and World View in a Central Italian Village," in *Gifts and Poison*, ed. Bailey, pp. 254-62; also Stanley H. Brandes, *Migration, Kinship, and Community: Tradition and Transition in a Spanish Village* (New York, 1975), pp. 151-54.

9. Adolfo Rossi, "Vantaggi e danni dell'emigrazione nel mezzogiorno d'Italia (note di un viaggio fatto in Basilicata e in Calabria del R. Commissario dell'emigrazione)," *Bollettino dell'emigrazione*, 1908, no. 13 (Ministero degli Affari Esteri, Commissariato dell'Emigrazione; Rome 1908), p. 45; my translation. Interviews.

10. Interviews.

11. Nitti, *Questione meridionale*, vol. 4, pt. 1, pp. 182-83. Interviews.

12. Domenico F., (N), 16 January 1978.

13. See Brandes, *Migration, Kinship and Community*, pp. 127-29.

14. Eugenio S., (T), 17 April 1976.

15. Alberto S., (T), 14 March 1976.

16. Ernesto S., 8 September 1974.

17. Ida So., 21 January 1977.

18. Nitti, *Questione meridionale*, vol. 4, pt. 1, p. 160.

19. Giovanni So., (T), 29 May 1976.

20. Nitti, *Questione meridionale*, vol. 4, pt. 1, p. 190.

21. The *nulla osta* had indicated on it the emigrant's destination, motive for emigration, personal characteristics, family status, occupation, education, conscription status, identifying features, and the date, municipality, and province of birth (*Touring Club Italiano, Annuario Generale 1922*, anno 28, no. 22 [Milan 1922], p. 197).

22. Interviews. It is interesting to note that although emigrants going overseas to work did not have to pay a tax on their passport, tourists paid up to 12 lire – a fact which sustains the view questioning the Italian government's commitment to restricting emigration. See *Touring Club Italiano, Annuario Generale 1912*, anno 17, no. 187 (Milan 1912), p. 127.

23. Ibid. Aside from those with a criminal record or in the military, others who were prohibited from obtaining a passport included: a) minors (those under eighteen years) without their guardian's consent if trav-

elling alone; b) those leaving dependants alone without assuring for their care; c) minors under sixteen without proof of vaccination; d) minors under fifteen or minor females suspected of going abroad to engage in dangerous, unhealthy, or immoral work; e) bankrupt merchants, leaving without judicial approval; f) those under special vigilance, leaving without approval; g) those suspected of being rejected at destination; h) those who, because of other special provisions were forbidden to emigrate (p. 198, my translation).

24. Broughton Brandenburg, *Imported Americans: The Story of the Experiences of a Disguised American and His Wife Studying the Immigration Question* (New York 1904), pp. 116, 152.
25. Interviews.
26. Eugenio U., (T), 25 April 1974.
27. Interviews. Karl Baedeker, *Southern Italy and Sicily*, 15th rev. ed. (Leipzig 1908), p. 251.
28. See Mauro Francesco Minervino, *L'Ultima Cremagliera: La ferrovia Paola-Cosenza, 1915-1987, Ricerche, immagini e testi originali* (Cosenza 1988).
29. Vincenzo S., (T), 25 April 1974.
30. Karl Baedeker, *Southern Italy and Sicily*, 16th rev. ed. (Leipzig 1912), p. 275; Baedeker, *Southern Italy* (1908), pp. 252-54. Emigrants also had the option of taking steamers from Paola to Naples three times weekly. Up until about 1900 steamers of the Navigazione Generale Italiana touched at the chief ports on the Calabrian coast on the Naples to Reggio/Messina run, taking about one-and-a-half to two days. Apparently lack of a passenger trade due to rail competition led to cessation of the service in the early part of the century, except for a direct Naples to Reggio/Messina route which took approximately half a day.

    Of this journey through the "Deep" South, well travelled by *paesani*, Baedeker gave an accurate, albeit tourist's, account:
    > The railway along the Western coast of Calabria is very striking and is notable both for the boldness of the construction, and the beauty of its scenery. The Neapolitan and Calabrian mountains abut so closely and so abruptly on the Tyrrhenian Sea that the railway has often to burrow its way through the cliffs by means of tunnels. The ancient towns, with their ruined castles, lie picturesquely on the mountain sides. The inhabitants, many of whom still wear their quaint and many-coloured local costumes, are mostly fishermen or cultivators of grain and wine, agrumi, figs, and olives. The fields are often enclosed by prickly hedges of the Opuntia cactus. Many short-coursed streams fall into the sea, generally with but a scanty supply of water, but wild and devastating torrents during the rainy season. The railway crosses these and their gorges by lofty viaducts, affording grand and ever-changing views. (*Southern Italy* [1908], pp. 252-53).
31. Before 1861 Naples had been the capital of a kingdom of 8 million people and was the largest port on the Italian peninsula. The Neapolitan kingdom as a whole possessed four times the merchant shipping of Piedmont. For the city of Naples, its maritime supremacy was quickly lost after Unification put an end to its governmental functions and the protectionism that had nurtured its industry. Conversely, the "natural" economic advantages of the North just as quickly projected Milan and Turin to the forefront of Italian industrial activity and helped nearby Genoa to overtake Naples as the main Italian port. Denis Mack Smith, *Italy: A Modern History*, rev. ed. (Ann Arbor 1959), p. 49; Grazia Dore, *La democrazia italiana e l'emigrazione in America* (Brescia 1964), pp. 80-81.

32. Dore, "Italian Emigration," p. 117; Camera di Commercio e Industria di Napoli, *I Grandi Porti Commerciali de Nord: Rotterdam, Amsterdam, Anversa, con note sul Porto di Napoli* (Naples 1914), pp. 187-93; Baedeker, *Southern Italy* (1912), pp. xi, 40.

33. Interviews; Baedeker, *Southern Italy* (1896), pp. 19, 23-24; Baedeker, *Southern Italy* (1908), p. 20.

34. Again I quote from Baedeker who presented a picture of Neapolitan street life around 1900:

    The life of the people of Naples is carried on with greater freedom and more careless indifference to publicity than in any other town in Europe. From morning till night the streets resound with the cries of the vendors of edibles and other articles. Strangers especially are usually besieged by swarms of hawkers, pushing their wares, and all eager and able to take full advantage of the inexperience of their victims. The most medley throng is seen in the Toledo, especially towards evening and after the lamps are lit. At fixed hours the importunate tribe of *Giornalisti* or newsvendors makes itself heard, and late in the evening appear the lanterns of the *Trovatori* (scavengers) hunting for cigar-ends and similar unconsidered trifles. The narrow side-streets between the new Corso Re di Italia and the harbour as far as the Piazza del Mercato, especially in the afternoon, also afford most characteristic studies of the humbler city life. Here itinerant cooks set up their stoves in the open air or under awnings and drive a brisk trade in fish, meat, or maccaroni, while other dealers tempt the crowd with fragments from the trattorie or trays of carefully assorted cigar-ends....

    Quack Doctors extol their nostrums in interminable harangues, which they punctuate by drawing teeth....

    Shoe-blacks ("lustrini" or "lustrascarpe"), whose knocking is intended to attract passers-by, [charge] 10 c[entesmi]....

    Vendors of Iced Water ("acquaiuoli") in summer are usually provided with two large tubs filled with snow, in which the water is cooled, and a supply of lemons, etc. (2-10 c). (*Southern Italy* [1896], pp. 27-28).

    A word about some of the place names and other terms used in the excerpt: the Toledo was the main street of Naples, renamed Via Roma after Unification. It divided the city into two main parts, west and east, the latter being the older section containing the business quarter (and within this, the port area). The Corso (Avenue) Re di Italia ran roughly east-west through the downtown area to the market-square (Piazza del Mercato) located between the Central Station to the north and the main port area to the south-west. The *centesimo* above refers to 1/100 of a lire, a lire being roughly equal to 20c in the first decade of the century (*Southern Italy* [1912], [front chart]).

35. Eugenio S., (T), 17 April 1976; Brandenburg, *Imported Americans*, p. 138.

36. Vincenzo S., (T), 25 April 1974.

37. Eugenio U., (T) 25 April 1974. The Galleria Umberto I referred to was a 160-yard long commercial complex adorned with statues stretching from the Toledo eastward to the Municipio (or city hall). Built during 1887-90, at a cost of 22 million lire, it incorporated two churches and private houses alongside commercial establishments. Located in the downtown area just a short walk from the harbour, it was a major attraction for travellers. Baedeker, *Southern Italy* (1896), p. 36.

38. According to a brochure put out by the Thomson Line, which in 1910 commenced service between Naples and Halifax/Montreal/Portland, steerage passengers (i.e., third class) were allowed ten cubic feet of baggage space gratis, for which 25¢ per cubic foot was charged. Such may have been a consideration in some *paesani*'s "travelling light," though in any

case, most, as sojourners, did not travel with hold baggage. Canada, Immigration Branch, Public Archives of Canada, RG76, file 28885 (Immigration from Italy), vol. 129, pt. 4 (1910).

39. Brandenburg, *Imported Americans,* p. 169.

40. Vicenzo S., (T), 25 April 1974.

41. Despite the impression of Naples given by informants and contemporary observers as a city abounding with swindlers, the 1903 report of the American Special Immigrant Inspector indicated that regulations were not evaded here more than elsewhere. With regard to the screening of the diseased and those with a criminal record, the procedures at Naples, when compared to other European ports, were judged as among the most efficient. Hence Braun, the immigration inspector charged by Washington to investigate the recruitment and processing of European emigrants, reported in 1903: "I find upon investigation that the steamship companies carrying emigrants from Naples, Hamburg, and Rotterdam are subjecting such emigrants to a strict medical examination for the purpose of ascertaining whether or not they are afflicted with any dangerous contagious disease which might prevent their landing in the United States; this can be said of almost all European ports, but is more strictly enforced at the three ports enumerated." ("Report of Special Immigrant Inspector," cited in Brandenburg, *Imported Americans,* pp. 273-74.)

42. Interviews; ibid., pp. 162-67. Regarding the emigrant's anxiety of being debarred, Brandenburg observed: "A few times before, I had seen evidences of this fear among others of our party, and I soon realized that what makes the emigrant so meek in the face of outrageous brutalities, so open to the wiles of sharpers, so thoroughly disconcerted and bewildered in the face of an examination, is his terrible dread of not being allowed to enter America. He would as soon think of cutting off a hand as doing anything that 'would get him into trouble'" (p. 142).

43. Interviews. See Edward Corsi, *In the Shadow of Liberty: The Chronicle of Ellis Island* (New York 1935), pp. 283-84, 287-89.

44. Philip Taylor, *The Distant Magnet: European Emigration to the U.S.A.* (New York 1971), pp. 150-62. For an informative pictorial account, see Robert Wall, *Ocean Liners* (London 1977).

45. A listing of emigration vessels according to the Commissariato's classification is given in the *Decree of the Commissioner-General of Emigration, Dated April 5th, 1923, Fixing the Maximum Rates for the Transport of Emigrants from the Ports of Genoa, Naples and Palermo* (Gazzetta Officiale no. 79, 27 April 1923), RG76, pt. 6. After the First World War ships were classed into four categories: superior, first, second, and third, the great majority being in the first and second classes.

46. After 1900 the general practice was for steamship lines increasingly to designate the categories of ship conditions, as first, second, and third class, the latter of these corresponding to real improvement made in the "new-type steerage," described in the text. However, as was noted by Fairchild, "old and new steerages are sometimes found on the same vessel," in which case the "steerage" category was maintained as a sort of "fourth" class. Henry Pratt Fairchild, *Immigration: A World Movement and Its American Significance,* rev. ed. (New York 1933), p. 183. See also Taylor, *The Distant Magnet,* pp. 156-67.

47. See *Reports and Abstracts of the U.S. Immigration Commission* (Washington 1911), vol. 37, "Steerage Conditions," cited in Lawrence Guy Brown, *Immigration: Cultural Conflicts and Social Adjustments* (New York 1933), pp. 188-89.

48. Vincenzo S., (T), 25 April 1974. The picture presented of strict segregation between the sexes contrasts with the "air of immorality" reported by a female investigator of steerage conditions to the United States Immigration Commission. Here a discrepancy between the "refined taste" of the investigator and the peasant's account of the situation did exist. (Cited in Brown, *Immigration*, p. 188).
49. Vincenzo S., (T), 25 April 1974.
50. Ibid.
51. Eugenio S., (T), 17 April 1976.
52. Brandenburg noted the day before landing: "Happy, excited, enthusiastic as they were, there was still that dread among the people of the 'Batteria,' the name used to sum up all that pertains to Ellis Island. I saw more than one man with a little slip of notes in his hand carefully rehearsing his group in all that they were to say when they came up for examination .... Many, many persons whose entry into the country would be in no way hindered by even the strictest enforcement of the letter of the emigration laws, were trembling in their shoes" (p. 200).
53. Ibid., p. 201. Writing in 1913, Roberts noted the psychological and emotional dilemma the contract labour legislation caused the emigrant: "But of all the legal causes of deportation, that of the Contract Labor Law is the most sweeping. Men who come with an assurance of work, or in other words a sure means of subsistence, cannot enter; if, on the other hand, the authorities see that they have no visible means of support, they are deported .... This law works great hardships to many poor people" (Roberts, *The New Immigration: A Study of the Industrial and Social Life of Southeastern Europeans in America* [New York 1913], p. 26).
54. Brandenburg, *Imported Americans*, p. 203; Ann Novotny, *Strangers at the Door: Ellis Island, Castle Garden, and the Great Migration to America* (New York 1974), p. 8.
55. Charles A. Bailey, "The Medical Inspection of Immigrants," *Public Health Journal* 3, no. 8 (August 1912): 435. Dr. Bailey of the United States Public Health Service wrote thus of the preliminary check given the immigrant at ports of entry: "To the casual spectator the medical inspection and examination of immigrants doubtless seems hasty and superficial, but the trained examiner with a definite formulated method of scrutiny, beginning at the aliens' feet, when he is about ten feet away and marching toward the examiner ... cultivate an ability of rapidly 'sizing up' and detecting physical and mental defectiveness .... The primary inspection is principally for the segregation of suspects and the obviously diseased and defective...." (p. 435).
56. Eugenio U., (T), 25 April 1974.
57. Vincenzo S., (T), 25 April 1974. It is interesting to compare this description to that of the U.S. Commissioner General of Immigration in 1905: "Favus is another name for the disease known as ring worm. It is a vegetable parasite which attacks the hair, causing it to become dry, brittle, dull and easily pulled out. Favus is also susceptible to temporary 'cures' " (cited in Fairchild, *Immigration and Its American Significance*, p. 211).
58. The last medical procedure involved checking the emigrant's eyelid linings for trachoma, the contagious blinding disease common at the time. Trachoma, probably more than any other disease, was a source of constant consternation for immigration doctors because its similarity to the relatively harmless, but highly contagious and widespread condition of conjunctivitis (inflammation of the inner eyelids) made detection difficult and particularly contentious, especially since trachoma itself was quite unfamiliar to North American medical men. See "Trachoma and

Immigration – Our Detention Hospitals," *Dominion Medical Monthly* 25, no. 6 (Dec. 1905): 303-12.

59. Roberts, *The New Immigration*, pp. 26, 250; Novotny, *Strangers at the Door*, p. 29.
60. Eugenio U., (T), 25 April 1974.
61. Ibid.

CHAPTER 4. THE SOJOURN PHASE OF MIGRATION

1. Giovanni So., (T), 29 May 1976.
2. Henceforth, with the discussion moving to the new world side of the *paesani's* migration experience, I shall employ the terms "village" and "villagers" to refer to the setting of the Rende area in the former case and as a synonym for *paesani* in the latter. Both terms are employed to emphasize a contrast with the new world reality. The word "village" is used to connote the peasant, rural settlements of the Rende area in contradistinction to the industrial, urban city of North America. The word "villager," while it is employed to imply a member of the traditionalist, small-scale community bound by the Rende area, is also used in the sense of "urban villagers" to refer to members of the Rende area colonies in North American cities; in either case, "villager" is used as opposed to modern urban dwellers who have been integrated into a mass society.

   Moreover, depending on the context I shall also at times use the two terms to refer to Southern Italian peasant society or to Southerners generally. As well, especially when referring to the work of other students, I use the words "village" and "villager" in their literal sense to mean a small nucleated settlement and the inhabitants of such.
3. W.D. Scott, Superintendent of Immigration, Department of the Interior, to Donald Sutherland, Director of Colonization (Toronto), 20 December 1910, Canada, Immigration Branch, Public Archives of Canada, RG76, file 28885 (Immigration from Italy), vol. 129, pt. 4.
4. The bulk of Italians in Chicago were from the Deep South: from the three Calabrian provinces; the provinces of Trapani, Palermo, and Arigento in Sicily; the provinces of Aquila and Campobasso in the region of Abruzzi-Molise; the province of Potenza in Basilicata; and Bari in Publia. See Humbert S. Nelli, *The Italians in Chicago, 1880-1930: A Study in Ethnic Mobility* (New York 1970), p. xiii.
5. Thomas Lee Philpott, *The Slum and the Ghetto: Neighbourhood Deterioration and Middle-Class Reform, Chicago, 1880-1930* (New York 1978), pp. 6-7. Howard B. Furer, ed., *Chicago: A Documentary History*, American Cities Chronology series (New York 1974), pp. 3-21, 31; Nelli, *Italians in Chicago*, p. 9.
6. William T. Stead, *If Christ Came to Chicago: A Plea for the Union of All Who Love the Service of All Who Suffer* (London 1894), p. 413; Furer, *Chicago*, pp. 23-32, 39.
7. Philpott, *The Slum and the Ghetto*, p. 7.
8. Carl W. Condit, *Chicago, 1910-29: Building, Planning, and Urban Technology* (Chicago 1973), pp. 5-6; Furer, *Chicago*, pp. 22-23.
9. Nelli, *Italians of Chicago*, p. 59.
10. John S. and Leatrice D. MacDonald, "Chain Migration, Ethnic Neighbourhood Formation, and Social Networks," *Milbank Memorial Fund Quarterly* 42 (1964): 82-83; ibid., "Urbanization, Ethnic Groups, and Social Segmentation," *Social Research* 29, no. 4 (Winter 1962): 439-40, 442-43.

11. Beniamino Co., Alberto S., and Eugenio S., 3 June 1979.
12. Interviews; *Bollettino dell'emigrazione,* anno 13 (Ministero degli Affari Esteri, Commissariato dell'Emigrazione; Rome 1914), pp. 39-40.
13. For example, see Robert F. Foerster, *The Italian Emigration of Our Times* (Cambridge, Mass. 1919), p. 326.
14. The labour agent's role in linking the migrant to work far from home, the prolonged duration of the sojourn, being connected much more intimately with a cash economy and industrialism, the size, bustle, and foreignness of Chicago and other cities, as well as the fact that the agent himself was of a different social class to the traditional intermediaries of the village, all impressed upon the *paesani* a departure from past patterns, that is to say, the "American-ness" of their experience.
15. Interviews.
16. Regarding the use of intermediaries, see Amy A. Bernardy, *America Vissuta* (Turin 1911), p. 318.
17. W.B. Bailey, "The Bird of Passage," *American Journal of Sociology* 18, no. 3 (Nov. 1912): 391, 395-96.
18. Interviews.
19. Domenico F., (N), 18 January 1978; see Charles B. Phipard, "The Philanthropist-Padrone," *Charities: A Weekly Review of Local and General Philanthropy* 12 (1904): 470.
20. Alain Morel, "Power and Ideology in the Village Community of Picardy: Past and Present," in *Rural Society in France: Selections from the Annales; Economies, Sociétés, Civilisations,* ed. Robert Forster and Orest Ranum (Baltimore 1977), p. 113.
21. Santo St., (N), 7 November 1976.
22. See Bernardo Attolico, "L'agricoltura e l'immigrazione nel Canada," *Bollettino dell'emigrazione,* anno 12, no. 6 (Ministero degli Affari Esteri, Commissariato dell'Emigrazione; Rome 1912), p. 35; Alessandro Mastro-Valerio, "Remarks upon the Italian Colony in Chicago," in *Hull-House Maps and Papers: A Presentation of Nationalities and Wages in a Congested District of Chicago. Together with Comments and Essays on Problems Growing Out of the Social Conditions* (Boston 1895; rpt., New York 1970), p. 132.
23. Francesco L., (T), 15 September 1976.
24. Interviews. In addition, since marriage in some instances was primarily a utilitarian and implicitly contractual arrangement rather than a love match, separation in such cases was more a matter of practical calculation rather than an emotionally distressing affair.
25. Maraspini has noted in his ethnographic study of an Italian village: "On the other hand, the [sexual] norm requires that a man be virile, strong, manly, and all these qualities are understood on the sexual point of view. But a man cannot prove himself virile, if he is deprived of all contacts with the opposite sex. We thus find that in spite of the rigid norm imposing chastity on women, certain relationships whose chastity is extremely doubtful are allowed." A.L. Maraspini, *The Study of an Italian Village* (Paris 1968), p. 150.
26. Foerster, *Italian Emigration,* p. 357.
27. Egisto Rossi, "Della condizioni del Canada respetto all' immigrazione italiana," *Bollettino dell'emigrazione,* anno 1903, no. 3 (Ministero degli Affari Esteri, Commissariato dell'Emigrazione; Rome 1903), p. 6 (translation mine); see also *Bollettino dell'emigrazione,* anno 13, p. 43.
28. Arthur F. Burns, *The Frontiers of Economic Knowledge,* National Bureau of Economic Research, General Series no. 57 (New York 1965), p. 199.
29. Again to quote Burns: "Whereas additions to road mileage in the United States reached a peak in 1887, additions to auxiliary track reached a

peak in 1904; additions in total track mileage were about as large in 1904 as in 1887; the peak in rail consumption came in 1906, in additions to leading types of equipment between 1907 and 1911, in additions to book value of investment around 1910. Thus the peak in railroad investment expenditures came after the turn of the century, or some 20 years after the building of new mileage had passed its maximum" (p. 199).

30. Giovanni So., (T), 29 May 1976.
31. Ibid.; Michele P., 6 September 1976; Alberto S., 14 March 1976; Caspare C., 2 November 1976; Domenico F., 18 January 1978.

    Foerster pointed out that the 1905 United States census showed 311,000 track workers employed on American railroads. Of these he estimated that the states of New York, Pennsylvania, New Jersey, Delaware, and Maryland contained 60,547 railroad workers who were "largely Italian"; those of Ohio, Indiana, and Michigan contained 42,530, and those of Illinois, Wisconsin, Minnesota, and Iowa, 59,265 – both groupings containing "largely Italians and Slavs." With respect to other states, Italians did not figure as significantly. Foerster, *Italian Emigration*, pp. 357-58.

32. Salvatore S., 18 April 1977. Regarding a number of these roads and other lines *paesani* worked on, Foerster in 1919 presented estimates as to the number of Italians employed:
    In the new century the utilization of Italian labor has continued apace. A few years ago, the Union Pacific was employing with some constancy 500-1000 Italians, the Great Northern 1500, and the Pennsylvania 10,000. The Wabash reported that it had employed at one time over 800, the Chicago, Milwaukee, and Puget Sound 1500, the Union Pacific 1500-2000, the Great Northern 9000, the New York, New Haven and Hartford 10,000, the Pennsylvania 13,500. These are samples only. On the other Eastern Central and Western roads the scale has been similar; but on the Southern roads Italians have been fewer. Even the most distant parts of Canada have received a great supply of Italian railroad labor, sometimes importing it directly through Italian employment houses, sometimes receiving it from the United States. In 1902, consular agents claimed that the Canadian roads were employing 6000 Italians. In 1903 the Canadian Pacific alone employed over 3000, and the Grand Trunk Pacific has in recent years used large numbers in its extensive construction work (Foerster, *Italian Emigration*, p. 359).

33. Peter Roberts, *The New Immigration: A Study of the Industrial and Social Life of Southeastern Europeans in America* (New York 1913), pp. 113-14.
34. See Nelli, *Italians of Chicago*, pp. 60-61; Phipard, "The Philanthropist-Padrone"; Gino C. Speranza, "The Italian Foreman as a Social Agent: Labour Unrest in West Virginia and Their Consequences to the Community," *Charities: A Weekly Review of Local and General Philanthropy*, 2 (1903): 26-28. A few observers, however, disagreed with the negative evaluation of camp life. Bradwin reported on camp conditions in Canada between 1903 and 1914 and although admitting deficiencies, characterized the box-car housing as relatively clean, comfortable, and well heated. See Edmund Bradwin, *The Bunkhouse Man: A Study of Work and Pay in the Camps of Canada, 1903-1914* (New York 1928; rpt. Toronto 1972), p. 172.
35. Thomas Shaughnessy, cited in Donald Avery, "Canadian Immigration Policy and the 'Foreign' Navvy 1896-1914," Canadian Historical Association, *Historical Papers* (1972): 137-38.
36. Eugenio De., (T), 22 August 1983.
37. Foerster, *Italian Emigration*, p. 362.

38. Ibid., pp. 362, 385; Stead, *If Christ Came to Chicago,* p. 147; Luciano J. Iorizzo, "The Padrone and Immigrant Distribution," in *The Italian Experience in the United States,* ed. Silvano M. Tomasi and Madelaine H. Engel (Staten Island, N.Y. 1970), p. 56. Such evidence indicates that only seven to eight dollars per month was spent by Southerners for camp accommodation and food.

39. Carroll D. Wright, *The Italians in Chicago: Ninth Special Report of the Commissioner of Labor* (Washington 1897), p. 50. See Phipard, "The Philanthropist-Padrone," pp. 100-1.

40. Interviews; Abbott, "Chicago Employment Agency," p. 292. Edmund Bradwin calculated that the Southern labourers' purchasing power in North America compared to Italy was consonant with my own conclusions based on the *paesani*'s testimony: "Many of these ... men were remitting money to families in Italy. Its purchasing power in southern Italy at that time, when the price of many necessaries and general living conditions were compared, was five to one. The Italian navvy was no fool! He was living, in his own way, on the same plane as the higher-paid machine men and officials on the line. The Italian as an individual profited most from his work as a navvy" (*The Bunkhouse Man,* p. 134).

41. Wright, *Ninth Special Report,* pp. 44-47, 59; Phipard, "The Philanthropist-Padrone," p. 101. Even on the basis of the *Special Report*'s own sample diets of Italian workmen in Chicago (p. 47), which include much meat and protein, it is difficult to see how – on a common-sense level, at least – the conclusion regarding a dietary "deficiency" can be reached.

42. Nelli, *Italians of Chicago,* p. 62. Quotation from Ministero degli Affari Esteri, Commissariato dell'Emigrazione, *Emigrazione e colonie,* 3 (Rome 1908): 122.

43. Bernardo Attolico, "Sui campi di lavoro della nuova ferrovia transcontinentale canadese," *Bollettino dell'emigrazione,* anno 13, no. 1 (Ministero degli Affari Esteri, Commissariato dell'Emigrazione; Rome 1913), p. 36 (my translation).

44. Iorizzo, "The Padrone and Immigrant Distribution," pp. 56-57; Bradwin, *The Bunkhouse Man,* p. 134.

45. Domenico F., (N), 18 January 1978. Iorizzo has also noted that Italian track labourers were known to bake their own bread ("The Padrone and Immigrant Distribution," p. 56).

46. Eugenio De, (T), 22 August 1983.

47. Roberts, *The New Immigration,* p. 114.

48. Bradwin, *Bunkhouse Man,* p. 92.

49. Regarding the "Anglo" affiliation of work bosses, Richard Juliani's research on Philadelphia's Italians substantiated the picture drawn by *paesani:* "informants who had worked in the construction industry noted that the crews of unskilled labourers who toiled in the building of streets, homes, and subways of the city were often entirely Italian or Polish, but the owners, supervisors, and foremen – the hated bosses – were frequently Irish." Richard Juliani, "The Social Organization of Immigration: The Italians of Philadelphia," (Diss., Pennsylvania 1971, p. 187).

50. Speranza, "The Italian Foreman as a Social Agent," p. 27.

51. Vincenzo S., (T), 25 April 1974.

52. Caspare C., (N), 2 November 1976. See *Bollettino dell'emigrazione,* anno 1914, no. 7, p. 225.

53. Interviews. This negative aspect of the American experience was observed by Amy A. Bernardy in her second book on America, *Italia randagia attraverso gli Stati Uniti* (Turin 1913), pp. 164-69.

54. See "Labour Abuses Among Italians" (editorial), *Charities: A Weekly Review of Local and General Philanthropy* 12 (1904): 448-49.
55. Vincenzo S., (T), 25 April 1974.
56. See "The Italian Problem," *Harper's Weekly,* 3 July 1909.
57. Michele St., (T), 20 March 1976.
58. Speranza, "The Italian Foreman as a Social Agent," pp. 188-89; also see *Bollettino dell'emigrazione,* anno 1914, p. 224.
59. Concerning the radical stereotype Rudolph Vecoli has noted: "Diametrically opposed to the padrone slave image is that of the Italian immigrant as a primitive rebel. Ironically its source can also be found in the rhetoric of conservative labor leaders. Now they complained that the Italian immigrants were rebellious and uncontrollable, prone to radicalism and violence" ("Italian American Workers, 1880-1920: Padrone Slaves or Primitive Rebels?" in *Perspectives in Italian Immigration and Ethnicity: Proceedings of the Symposium held at Casa Italiana, Columbia University, 1976* [New York 1977], p. 28).
60. In this regard, Harney has concluded: "To suggest that the 'victims' of padronism approved of and in some ways created the system because they were fundamentally migrant, concerned with temporary work, cash income, hostile to the North American environment, and anxious to return to their villages, alters the easy moral tale in which the padrone was a slaver and the worker a slave. It suggests that America did not appeal only to the uprooted who wished to immigrate but also to sojourners ... deeply committed to returning and improving the family's status in the Old World" ("The Padrone and the Immigrant," *Canadian Review of American Studies* 5, no. 2 [Fall 1974]: 112). See also Robert F. Harney, "Montreal's King of Italian Labour: A Case Study of Padronism," *Labour: Journal of Canadian Labour Studies* 4 (1979): 83-84.

CHAPTER 5. THE CITY EXPERIENCE

1. D. Taruffi, L. De Nobili, C. Lori, *La questione agraria e l'emigrazione in Calabria* (Florence 1908), p. 876; interviews.
2. Federico Chabod, *L'Italia contemporanea, 1918-1948* (Turin 1961), pp. 28-34.
3. Carlo M. Cipolla, "Four Centuries of Italian Demographic Development," in *Population in History: Essays in Historical Demography* (London 1969), p. 580. Because of the effect of the Great War, I am referring specifically here to the years 1921-25 regarding population growth.
4. Francesco L., (T), 29 September 1976.
5. Cf. Giovanni E. Schiavo, *The Italians in Chicago: A Study in Americanization* (Chicago 1928), p. 44.
6. Interviews. This profile regarding the role played by the war in promoting settlement and derived from oral testimony substantiates to a large degree the work of Juliani, who also utilized oral evidence, on the Italians of Philadelphia: "Italy could barely have offered comparable opportunities for wealth and respect to so many of her native sons. Furthermore, any prolonged stay in urban America probably raised the level of expectations and aspirations of many Italians in regard to material standards of living .... Consequently, the opportunities extended to the immigrant in Philadelphia became more valuable than whatever amenities and rewards a return to the Old World country offered" ("The Origin and Development of the Italian Community in Philadelphia," in

The Ethnic Experience in Pennsylvania, ed. J.E. Bodnar [Lewisburg, Penn. 1973], p. 258).

7. Rudolph J. Vecoli, "Italian American Workers, 1880-1920: Padrone Slaves or Primitive Rebels?" in *Perspectives in Italian Immigration and Ethnicity*, ed. S[ilvano] M. Tomasi (New York 1977) p. 25.

8. The Southerner's early concentration in the construction sector of the city's labour market was noted by Foerster who remarked with some humour that "Italians were claimed (with superfine precision!) to be doing '99 per cent' of the street work of Chicago. When natural gas was discovered in [nearby] Indiana the labor of laying 250 miles of pipe for its conduction was performed by Italians ... and many were employed on the grounds of the Chicago Exposition [of 1893]" (*The Italian Emigration of Our Times* [Cambridge, Mass. 1919], p. 354).

9. Rosario P., 29 May 1974; Michele St., 24 January 1976; Alberto S., 14 March 1976; Domenico F., 18 January 1978; Luigi A., 28 June 1983; Eugenio De., 22 August 1983.

10. Thomas Lee Philpott, *The Slum and the Ghetto: Neighborhood Deterioration and Middle-Class Reform, Chicago, 1880-1930* (New York 1978), pp. 13-14; Robert F. Harney, "Chiaroscuro: Italians in Toronto, 1885-1915," *Italian Americana* 1, no. 1 (Spring 1975): 152-53.

11. Francesco L., (T), 29 September 1976.

12. Luigi A., (T), 28 June 1983.

13. Pietro DiDonato, *Christ in Concrete* (London 1939).

14. Michele St., (T), 24 January 1976.

15. Interviews.

16. William T. Stead, *If Christ Came to Chicago: A Plea for the Union of All Who Love the Service of All Who Suffer* (London 1894), pp. 44-45, 159-64, 457-58. Regarding city patronage jobs, the Chicago reformer, John Palmer Gravit, who was intimately involved in local politics in the heavily Italian Seventeenth Ward, noted that: "Not only the petty employments in saloons and even brothels have been at the disposal of the local leaders [but also] places for unskilled labor with street-railroad corporations and other public utilities needing the franchises and privileges in the public streets, have been utilized as the coin-current of local political traffic" (*Americans by Choice* [New York 1922], pp. 32-33).

17. Sam S., (T), 24 August 1983.

18. Ida S., (N), 8 January 1977.

19. Stead, *If Christ Came to Chicago*, pp. 457-58. Cf. Richard N. Juliani, "The Social Organization of Immigration: The Italians of Philadelphia" (Diss. Pennsylvania 1971), p. 192; and Gerd Korman, *Industrialization, Immigrants and Americanizers: The View from Milwaukee, 1866-1921* (Madison, Wisc. 1967), pp. 65-68.

20. Eugenio U., (T), 25 April 1974.

21. Eugenio De., (T), 22 August 1983.

22. Giovanni So., (T), 29 May 1976.

23. Domenico F., (N), 18 January 1978.

24. Melvin G. Holli, "The Great War Sinks Chicago's German *Kultur*," in *Ethnic Chicago*, eds. Peter d'A. Jones and Melvin G. Holli (Grand Rapids, Mich. 1981), pp. 301, 308; Howard B. Furer, ed., *Chicago: A Documentary History*, American Chronology series (New York 1974), pp. 40-41.

25. For an excellent local history of Kenosha and its immigrants, particularly the Italian community, see John D. Buenker, "Immigration and Ethnic Groups," in *Kenosha County in the Twentieth Century: A Topical History*, ed. John A. Neuenschwander (Kenosha, Wisc. 1976), pp. 1-45. This work

is augmented by an interesting case study: John D. Buenker, "George Molinaro: Labor-Ethnic Politicians," in *Kenosha Retrospective: A Biographical approach*, eds. Nicholas C. Burckel and John A. Neuenschwander (Kenosha, Wisc. 1981), pp. 242-91. It is noteworthy that a large proportion, perhaps the great majority, of Italians in the Kenosha-Racine area derive from Cosenza province.

26. Irving Cutler, *The Chicago-Milwaukee Corridor: A Geographic Study of Inter-metropolitan Coalescence* (Evanston, Ill. 1965), p. 212; Moody's Investors Service, *Moody's Industrial Manual*, vol. 1: *A-I* (New York 1976), pp. 96-97. In 1922 the American Brass Company was bought out by the Anaconda Mining Company, a major corporation with holdings throughout the United States and South America.

27. Vincenzo S., (T), 25 April 1974.

28. Eugenio De., (T), 22 August 1983.

29. Domenico F., 18 January 1978; Francesco B., 19 July 1979.

30. Interviews.

31. Also writing of Southern Italians, a similar diminution in the role of labour agents has been noted by the MacDonalds: "Although many new arrivals first worked on railroad gangs in relatively rural areas, they tended sooner or later to settle in cities. Eventually they were able to move from temporary or seasonal employment as common labourers to factory work. This broadening and stabilizing of employment which was particularly marked at the beginning of this century, decreased the power of the *padroni*. Many American industries did have Southern Italian foremen who functioned as middlemen, but factories did not offer the same opportunities for the exploitation of dependency as the subcontracting and straw boss systems in railroad and construction work" ("Urbanization, Ethnic Groups, and Social Segmentation," *Social Research* 29, no. 4 [Winter 1962]: 444).

32. Korman, *Industrialization*, p. 66.

33. Humbert S. Nelli, *The Italians in Chicago, 1880-1930: A Study in Ethnic Mobility* (New York 1970), p. 209.

34. Ibid.; Schiavo, *The Italians in Chicago*, p. 196.

35. Interviews.

36. Domenico F., (N), 18 January 1978.

37. Herbert G. Gutman, "Work, Culture, and Society in Industrializing America, 1815-1919," *American Historical Review* 78, no. 3 (June 1973): 540-41). On the concept of "chain occupations," see John S. and Leatrice D. MacDonald, "Chain Migration, Ethnic Neighbourhood Formation, and Social Networks," *Milbank Memorial Fund Quaterly* 42 (1964): 95.

38. Alberto S., (T), 14 March 1976.

39. Bruce Laurie, Theodore Hershberg, George Alter, "Immigrants and Industry: The Philadelphia Experience, 1850-1880," in *Immigrants in Industrial America*, ed. Richard L. Ehrlich (Charlottesville, Va. 1977), p. 148. More fully the authors write on this point: "All too often we treat skill as an absolute and assume that an occupation is either skilled or it is not, that a man who calls himself a tailor, carpenter, or butcher is a skilled worker. It should be clear, however, that skill is relative in that one skilled occupation may require more skill than another, though we hasten to add that measuring the differences is extremely difficult. It should also be evident that the skill of an occupation changes over time, as do wage rates and the immediate environment of the workplace."

40. Interviews.

41. Concetta Sm., (T), 9 June 1976. See also Robert F. Harney, "Ambiente and Social Class in North America Little Italies," *Canadian Review of Studies in Nationalism* 2, no. 2 (Spring 1975): 208-24.

42. Cf. Samuel Sidlofsky, "Post-War Immigrants in the Changing Metropolis – with Special Reference to Toronto's Italian Population" (Diss. Toronto 1969), p. 42.

43. Interviews.

44. Nelli, *Italians in Chicago,* pp. 28, 36-37; Harney, "Italians in Toronto," p. 151.

45. Agnes Sinclair Holbrook, "Map Notes and Comments," in *Hull-House Maps and Papers: A Presentation of Nationalities and Wages in a Congested District of Chicago, Together with Comments and Essays in Problems Growing Out of the Social Conditions* (Boston 1895; facs. rpt. New York 1970), pp. 4-5.

46. Bureau of Municipal Research, *What Is the "Ward" Going to Do with Toronto?* (Toronto 1918), p. 23.

47. Carroll D. Wright, *Seventh Special Report of the Commissioner of Labour: The Slums of Baltimore, Chicago, New York, and Philadelphia* (Washington 1894; facs. rpt. New York 1970), p. 13. Regarding the association made in the public mind between slums and criminality, a resident of the Central Neighbourhood House settlement in Toronto wrote a description of the Ward, which, while composed in a satirical vein, probably well reflected prevailing attitudes: "The district that lies between College and Queen Streets, Yonge Street and University Avenue is generally regarded by the respectable citizens of Toronto as a strange and fearful place into which it is unwise to enter even in daylight, which after dark – no sane person would dream of running such a risk! The danger that lurks in these crowded streets is not always clearly formulated in the minds of those who fear it, perhaps it is the dagger of an Italian desperado of which they dream – perhaps the bearded faces of the 'Sheenies' are sufficient in themselves to inspire terror – but at any rate the fear remains and probably it could best be analyzed as Fear of the Unknown." Central Neighbourhood House (City of Toronto Archives, subsequently CNH, Records, "Life in the Ward," Toronto, 28 October 1915).

48. Charles J.C.O. Hastings, *Report of the Toronto Medical Health Officer Dealing with the Recent Investigation of Slum Conditions in Toronto, Embodying Recommendations for the Amelioration of the Same* (Toronto 1911). The same association was made by the Ward's social settlement. For example, CNH, Records, "Annual Report of the Central Neighbourhood House," Toronto, October 1919–October 1920.

49. Holbrook, "Map Notes and Comments," pp. 5-6.

50. Margaret Bell, "Toronto's Melting Pot," *Canadian Magazine* 4, no. 3 (July 1913): 236, 242.

51. Foerster, *Italian Emigration,* p. 386; I.W. Howerth, "Are the Italians the Dangerous Class?," *The Charities Review: A Journal of Practical Sociology* 4, no. 24, (1894): 36; P.H. Bryce, "Immigration in Relation to the Public Health," *Canadian Journal of Medicine and Surgery* 19, no. 4 (April 1906): 32.

52. Philpott, *The Slum and the Ghetto,* p. 16; Charles J.C.O. Hastings, "Medical Inspection of Public Schools," *Canadian Journal of Medicine and Surgery* 21 (1907): 73.

53. Chicago Department of Public Welfare, "Housing Survey in the Italian District of the Seventeenth Ward," *First Semi-Annual Report of Department of Public Welfare* (Chicago 1915), cited in Schiavo, *The Italians in Chicago,*

pp. 36-37. Also of interest are CNH, Records, "Annual Report of Italian and Slavic Work," Toronto, 1919-1920.

54. The connection between sojourning, boarding, and urban congestion was noted by the early sociologist, W.B. Bailey, one of the more acute observers of the new immigration: "The 'bird of passage' is a male. He may be married or single, but as far as this country is concerned he is single. The industrial unit in this country has been the family. We have gone on the assumption that the head of the household should, with his earnings, be able to support a household. The 'bird of passage' has no obligation resting upon him. He wants to save a maximum amount of money. He is, therefore, anxious at all times to increase his earnings, but greater attention is given to the problem of reducing his expenditure. A group of these individuals will unite in hiring rooms and purchasing food with someone to do the cooking and care for the establishment. There is overcrowding and unsanitary living but the cost is reduced to a minimum" ("The Bird of Passage," *American Journal of Sociology* 18, no. 3 [November 1912]: 396).

55. Interviews.

56. Giovanni So., (T), 29 May 1976.

57. Francesco L., (T), 29 September 1976.

58. Of these important motivations behind boarding, Foerster observed: "An immigration so mobile as the Italian and containing so many men either without families or separated from them must often be unconventional in its housing. Partly because of expense but more because of the human desire for the sociability, or at least presence, of a normally constituted family, the single man avoids a hotel and becomes a lodger. He pays, maybe, $3 per month for a bed, the necessary personal laundry, and the use of the kitchen. He buys his food, but may pay the *padrona* to cook it" (*Italian Emigration*, pp. 384-85).

59. Carroll D. Wright, *Ninth Special Report of the Commissioner of Labor: The Italians in Chicago* (Washington, D.C. 1897), pp. 11-12. Besides the normal or "private" family classification used by the commissioner, two others were distinguished: "cooperative families" composed of households in which a number of men shared all expenses, and boarding or lodging houses. The commissioner found that only 5.1% of housing arrangements were cooperative and 1.1% of the latter type. While this scheme may be somewhat inadequate because of the confounding between kinship and household type (for example, in what might be considered a "lodging house," where the owner was a relative, the household could be placed in the "normal family" classification), nevertheless, the report leaves little doubt as to the importance of kinship in boarding arrangements (p. 20). See also G. La Piana, *The Italians and Milwaukee, Wisconsin: A General Survey Prepared under the Direction of the Associated Charities* (Milwaukee 1915), pp. 4-5, 16.17.

60. Howerth, "Are Italians Dangerous?", p. 38. Also see Holbrook, "Map Notes and Comments," p. 20.

61. Interviews.

62. Ibid.; see Schiavo, *The Italians of Chicago*, p. 37 and Robert F. Harney, "Men without Women: Italian Migrants in Canada, 1885-1930," in *The Italian Immigrant Woman in North America*, eds. Betty Boyd Caroli, Robert F. Harney, Lydio F. Tomasi (Toronto 1978), pp. 91-92.

63. Francesco L., (T), 29 September 1976. Robert F. Harney, "Boarding and Belonging: Thoughts on Sojourner Institutions," *Urban History Review*, no. 2 (1978): 13.

64. Interviews.

65. J[ohn] S. and L[eatrice] D. MacDonald, "Italian Migration to Australia: Manifest Functions of Bureaucracy versus Latent Functions of Informal Networks," *Journal of Social History* 3, no. 3 (Spring 1970): 257.

66. Interviews; Schiavo, *The Italians in Chicago,* p. 143; John E. Zucchi, "Italian Hometown Settlements and the Development of an Italian Community in Toronto, 1875-1935," in *Gathering Place: Peoples and Neighbourhoods of Toronto,* ed. Robert F. Harney (Toronto 1985), pp. 128-31.

67. Schiavo, *The Italians in Chicago,* p. 143; Egisto Rossi, "Delle condizioni del Canada: rispetto all'immigrazione italiana," *Bollettino dell'emigrazione,* anno 1903, no. 3 (Ministero degli Affari Esteri, Commissariato dell'Emigrazione; Roma 1903), p. 9. Similarly, around a decade later the *Toronto Star* estimated that only one in four of the city's Italians were permanently established, which again suggests that the census figures greatly underestimated the number of actual residents in the colony. See Sidlofsky, "Post-War Immigrants in the Changing Metropolis," p. 31.

68. Interviews.

69. Domenico F., (N), 18 January 1978.

70. Schiavo, *The Italians in Chicago,* p. 33.

71. Nelli, *Italians in Chicago,* pp. 37, 194-95.

72. Interviews. See Nelli, *Italians in Chicago,* pp. 36-37; Philpott, *The Slum and the Ghetto,* p. 22.

73. Alesandro Mastro-Valerio, "Remarks upon the Italian Colony in Chicago," in *Hull-House Maps and Papers,* p. 135.

74. Interviews.

75. Schiavo, *The Italians in Chicago,* pp. 56-57; Nelli, *Italians in Chicago,* p. 173.

76. Italy, Ministero di Agricoltura, Industria e Commercio, Direzione Generale della Statistica, *Statistica della Società de mutuo soccorso e delle istituzioni cooperative annesse alle medesime,* anno 1885 (Rome 1888), pp. 2-3. Cf. John W. Briggs, *An Italian Passage: Immigrants to Three American Cities, 1890-1930* (New Haven 1978), p. 29.

77. Interviews; Schiavo, *The Italians in Chicago,* p. 55-56; Nelli, *Italians in Chicago,* p. 177.

78. *Statistica della Società di mutuo soccorso,* pp. 2-3; Schiavo, *The Italians in Chicago,* p. 65.

79. Eugenio De., (T), 22 August 1983.

80. Zucchi, "Italian Hometown Settlements," p. 142.

81. Interviews; Vecoli, "Chicago's Italians," pp. 199, 202-3.

82. Interviews.

83. Holbrook, "Map Notes and Comments," p. 9; Brian J.L. Berry, *Chicago: Transformations of an Urban System* (Cambridge, Mass. 1976), pp. 6-7.

84. *Hull-House Maps and Papers,* pp. vii-viii.

85. Interviews.

CHAPTER 6. THE DIVERSION OF CHAIN MIGRATION

1. Francesco L., (T), 29 September 1976.

2. I.W. Howerth, "Are the Italians a Dangerous Class?," *The Charities Review* 4, (1894): 24, reprinted in *The Italian in America: The Progressive View, 1891-1914,* ed. Lydio F. Tomasi (New York 1972), p. 135.

3. Francesco Nitti, *Scritti sulla questione meridionale,* vol. 1: *Saggi sulla storia del mezzogiorno, emigrazione e lavoro* (Bari 1952), pp. 389-95.

4. D. Taruffi, L. De Nobili, C. Lori, *La questione agraria e l'emigrazione in Calabria* (Florence 1908), p. 824. Taruffi, De Nobili and Lori cite a speech

made by Nitti in the Chamber of Deputies regarding these proposals and lent their support to them. Francesco Nitti, "Discorso pronunciato il 15 febbraio 1907 alla Camera dei Deputati," in ibid., pp. 824-25.

5. Ibid., pp. 822-23.

6. United States, Department of Health, Education and Welfare, *Progress and Trends in Italian Education,* by Anthony A. Scarangello, Studies in Comparative Education, no. 21 (Washington, D.C. 1964), pp. 4-5. The Coppino Law of 1877 made education obligatory for all children between the ages of six and nine and the Orlando Law of 1904 extended compulsory attendance from three to four years of school. This latter law also made provision for communes to provide instruction to adult illiterates. In any case, as was documented earlier, gross infringement of the legislation took place within the Rende area and the South generally at least until the 1911 nationalization of communal schools.

After the First World War over half the male population in the Rende area was literate and hence could gain acceptance into the United States. Since American legislation allowed such individuals to sponsor the immigration of wives and children, it made possible the entry of illiterate women (or children). Then, too, the fact that emigration was a selective process acting to draw out the most able, energetic, and educated of the peasantry contributed to the ineffectiveness of the literacy legislation. (See Chapter 1, section on education.)

7. Broughton Brandenburg, *Imported Americans: The Story of the Experiences of a Disguised American and His Wife Studying the Immigration Question* (New York 1904), pp. 71-72.

8. Vincenzo S., (T), 25 April 1974.

9. Carmina S., (T), 25 April 1974.

10. Giovanni So., (T), 29 May 1976.

11. Israel Zangwill, "Some American Impressions," *Proceedings of the Canadian Club of Toronto* 21 (1923-24): 206.

12. Italy, Istituto Centrale di Statistica, *Annuario statistico italiano, 1944-48,* Serie V, 1 (Rome 1949), calculations mine; League of Nations, International Labour Office, *World Statistics of Aliens: A Comparative Study of Census Returns, 1910-1920-1930,* Studies and Reports, Series O (Migration), no. 6 (Geneva 1936), table 8, p. 46.

13. From 1921 to 1925 between 9,000 to 14,000 emigrants from Cosenza departed for the United States. See Italy, Commissariato Generale dell'Emigrazione, *Annuario statistico della emigrazione italiana dal 1876 al 1925,* Parte seconda: *Movimento dell'emigrazione italiana negli anni 1902-1925* (Roma 1926), pp. 897-913.

14. Censuses of Canada and the United States for 1930; John E. Zucchi, "Italian Hometown Settlements and the Development of an Italian Community in Toronto, 1875-1935," in *Gathering Place: Peoples and Neighbourhoods of Toronto,* ed. Robert F. Harney (Toronto 1985), p. 130; Rudolph J. Vecoli, "Chicago's Italians Prior to World War I: A Study of their Social and Economic Adjustment" (Ph.D. diss., University of Wisconsin 1963), p. 80 (calculations mine).

15. Estimated from interviews and 1935 Toronto Italian directory: Italian Information Bureau, *Annuario italiano* (Toronto 1935).

16. W.G. Smith, *A Study of Canadian Immigration* (Toronto 1920), pp. 72-73, 93, 97, 341-42; Donald Avery, "Canadian Immigration Policy and the 'Foreign' Navvy, 1896-1914," Canadian Historical Association, *Historical Papers* (1972): 142.

17. In a 1903 report to his Washington superior, the American Commissioner of Immigration at Montreal, Robert Watchorn, revealed: "One year ago I had occasion to report that an act of Parliament had been passed at Ottawa, to wit, Bill 111, passed by House of Commons May, 1902, designed to prevent "the landing at Canadian ports of any immigrant or other passenger who is suffering from a loathsome, dangerous, infectious disease or malady, whether such immigrant intents to settle in Canada, *or only intends to pass through Canada to settle in some other country* ...the above mentioned Canadian legislation is due solely to revelations made by United States immigrant inspectors on the Canadian frontier" ("Report of [U.S. Immigration] Commissioner for Canada" [Montreal 1903], cited in Brandenburg, *Imported Americans,* p. 249-50).
18. "Report of Special [U.S.] Immigrant-Inspector" (New York, Aug. 24, 1903), by Marcus Braun, cited in Brandenburg, *Imported Americans,* p. 292.
19. Smith, *Canadian Immigration,* pp. 72-73.
20. Brandenburg, *Imported Americans,* pp. 39, 102-03, 107, 167.
21. Smith, *Canadian Immigration,* pp. 357-58; See Tony Cyriax, *Among Italian Peasants* (London 1919), pp. 81-82, 232.
22. Avery, "Canadian Immigration Policy," pp. 136, 141-45. By the beginning of the war much of Canada's infrastructure had been laid. Though construction activity increased sharply after 1918, it was not much more than half the value of construction in 1912. This had a major dampening effect on Canada's open door towards unskilled, and in particular railway, workers after the war. W.A. Mackintosh, *The Economic Background of Dominion-Provincial Relations* (Ottawa 1939; rpt. Toronto 1964), p. 71.
23. Instituto Centrale di Statistica, *Annuario Statistico Italiano, Anno 1936,* Serie 4, vol. 3 (Rome 1936), chart B.
24. Francesco L., (T), 29 September 1976.
25. Domenico F., 18 January 1978; Salvatore S., 18 April 1977; Caspare C., 2 November 1976; Santo St., 23 September 1976.
26. Robert F. Harney, "Chiaroscuro: Italians in Toronto, 1885-1915," *Italian Americana* 1, no. 1 (Spring 1975): 144. See also Samuel Sidlofsky, "Post-War Immigrants in the Changing Metropolis – with Special Reference to Toronto's Italian Population" (Ph.D. diss., Toronto 1969), p. 32.
27. Zucchi, "Italian Hometown Settlements," pp. 123-32; interviews.
28. Francesco L., (T), 29 September 1976.
29. Salvatore S., 18 April 1977; Domenico F., 18 January 1978; Alberto S., 14 March 1976; Michele F., 27 September 1977.
30. F.C. Blair, Secretary of the Department of Immigration and Colonization (hereafter DIC), to F.A. Harrison, Canadian Government Agent (Harrisburg, Pa.), 3 February 1923, Canada, Immigration Branch, Public Archives of Canada, RG76, file 28885 (Immigration from Italy), vol. 130, pt. 6.
31. W.R. Little, Commissioner of Immigration (DIC), Eastern Division (Ottawa) to W.M. German, Barrister (Welland, Ont.), 19 November 1923, RG76, pt. 6.
32. Mackintosh, *Economic Background,* pp. 71-73, 94-98; Jacob Spelt, *Urban Development in South-Central Ontario* (Toronto 1972), pp. 152-54, 191-94. See also George C. Creelman, "Some Rural Problems," *Proceedings of the Canadian Club of Toronto* 11 (1913-14): 292-304; John MacDougall, *Rural Life in Canada, Its Trend and Tasks* (Toronto 1913), ch. 1.
33. W.R. Little, Secretary, DIC, to F.J. McGue, Algoma Steel Corporation (Sault Ste. Marie, Ont.), 20 September 1920, RG76, pt. 5; David C. Corbett, *Canada's Immigration Policy: a Critique* (Toronto 1957), pp. 4-6.

34. Regarding the growth of secondary and tertiary industries through the twenties relative to most primary ones, especially agriculture, the Canadian economist W.A. Mackintosh found:

    During the decade, and particularly during the last half of it, there had been important shifts in the sources of the national income. In general, agriculture had declined relatively in importance.... Contributing 41 per cent of the national net production in 1920, it contributed... 26 per cent with the poor yields of 1929.... The construction industry increased its relative importance, as measured by net value of production, from 4 per cent in 1920... to 10 per cent in 1929. The change in manufacturing was most marked; from 33 per cent in 1920... it rose to 40 per cent in 1929....

    Still further shifts in the Canadian economy can be discerned in the census records of occupations. Between 1921 and 1931 there were striking relative increases in the numbers gainfully occupied as unskilled workers, in the service industries... in transportation, and in construction. Neither manufacturing nor agriculture kept pace with these industries.... These changes were associated with increased urbanization, the growing importance of the tourist industries, and of occupations related to the increasing use of the automobile and truck, and to the heavy investment in fixed capital particularly in the latter part of the period (*Economic Background,* pp. 81-82).

35. For example, MacDougall, *Rural Life in Canada,* pp. 19-23; James S. Woodsworth, *Strangers within our Gates* (Toronto 1909), pp. 210-20.

36. F.C. Blair, Secretary, DIC, to L.S. Tobin, Manager, Passenger Department, White Star–Dominion Line (Montreal), 2 June 1923, RG76, pt. 6; Blair to P.M. Buttler, General Agent, Canadian National-Grand Trunk Railways (Ottawa), 17 September 1923.

37. J.S. Graham, Inspectional Branch, DIC (Ottawa), to F.C. Blair, Secretary, DIC, 15 June 1926, RG76, pt. 7.

38. J.S. Fraser, Division Commissioner (DIC) to Sacca Financial Agency (Montreal), 11 May 1928, RG76, pt. 9. Italy, *Bollettino dell'emigrazione,* anno 26, no. 1 (May 1927) (Ministero degli Affari Esteri, Commissariato dell'Emigrazione), p. 652.

39. John S. and Leatrice D. MacDonald, "Italian Migration to Australia: Manifest Functions of Bureaucracy versus Latent Functions of Informal Networks," *Journal of Social History* 3, no. 3 (Spring 1970): 267.

40. See J. Davis, *Land and Family in Pisticci* (London 1973), pp. 64-65.

41. Cf. Stanley H. Brandes, *Migration, Kinship and Community: Tradition and Transition in a Spanish Village* (New York 1975), pp. 13-14.

42. MacDonald, "Italian Migration to Australia," pp. 249-56; Grazia Dore, "Some Social and Historical Aspects of Italian Emigration to America," *Journal of Social History* 2, no. 2 (Winter 1968): 96.

43. Vincenzo S., (T), 25 April 1974.

44. In a variation of the farm labour system, a few villagers entered Canada under similar contractual arrangements to work as woodcutters in northern Ontario.

45. *Bollettino dell'emigrazione,* anno 26, p. 652.

46. Vincenzo S., (T), 25 April 1974.

47. W.R. Little, Commissioner of Immigration (DIC), Eastern Division (Ottawa), to W.J. Black, deputy minister, DIC, 22 September 1923, RG76, pt. 6.

48. Vincenzo S., (T), 25 April 1974.

49. Letter quoted in W.R. Little (DIC), to Hon. C. Steward, acting minister, DIC, 16 April 1923, RG76, pt. 6.

50. F.C. Blair to J.A. McGill, general agent, Canadian Pacific Railways Co. (Ottawa), 21 November 1923, RG76, pt. 6; E. Bonardelli, Royal Italian Commissioner of Emigration (Ottawa), to Hon. J.A. Robb, Minister of Immigration (DIC), 6 February 1924, RG76, pt. 7.
51. F.C. Blair, assistant deputy minister, DIC, to W.J. Egan, deputy minister (DIC), 17 March 1927, RG76, pt. 8.
52. Alberto S., (T), 14 March 1976.
53. Smith, *Canadian Immigration,* pp. 102-3.
54. E. Bonardelli, Royal Consul General of Italy, to W.J. Egan, deputy minister, DIC, 2 September 1927, RG76, pt. 8. Regarding the failure of the government's permits of entry to stem the farm labour system the assistant deputy minister admitted in 1927: "I may say that it has been apparent for several years that individuals in Canada have been profiting out of letters or permits so-called, issued by the Department for the admission of individuals. Before the permit letter was adopted, they were making money out of a system of affidavits of employment which grew out of some steamship activities. I think it is pretty generally known by those who are familiar with the conditions of Italian immigration that a great deal of money is being made by a few unscrupulous rascals in this country, who use any and every person they can for the purpose of getting permit letters" (Blair to Egan, 17 March 1927).
55. F.C. Blair, Memorandum, 25 October 1927, RG76, pt. 8.
56. P. Margotti, Royal Consul General of Italy (Montreal), to W.J. Egan, deputy minister, DIC, 2 November 1927, RG76, pt. 8; DIC, Memorandum, "Immigration from Italy," 13 January 1928, RG76, pt. 9.
57. Passenger Managers for Cunard, Anchor, White Star and Canadian Pacific Steamship Lines (Montreal) to W.J. Egan, 4 April 1928, RG76, pt. 9; Denis Mack Smith, *Italy: A Modern History,* rev. ed. (Ann Arbor 1959), pp. 402, 446.
58. Margotti to Egan, 2 November 1927.
59. W.J. Egan to J.B. Walker, director, DIC (London, England), 22 December 1927, RG76, pt. 8; P. Margotti, Royal Consul General of Italy (Montreal), to A.L. Joliffe, Commissioner of Immigration (DIC), 24 January 1929, RG76, pt. 9.
60. Vincenzo S., (T), 25 April 1974.
61. F.C. Blair to A. Ferrante, Royal Consul General for Italy (Ottawa), 17 March 1930; A. Ferrante, to F.C. Blair, 12 March 1930, RG76, pt. 9.
62. Cf. Sidlofsky, "Post-War Immigrants," p. 52.
63. Eugenio S., 17 April 1976; Domenico F., 18 January 1978; Ida So., 23 September 1976.
64. W.R. Little, to W.J. Black, 8 October 1923, RG76, pt. 6; DIC, Memorandum, "International Emigration and Immigration Conference – to be held at Rome in 1924: Notes of Meeting at Board of Trade, 15th November, 1923, with Representatives of Overseas Dominions, Colonial Office, and British Steamship Lines," RG76, pt. 7.
65. Gaspare M. Cusumano, Manager, the Society for Italian Immigrants (New York), to Hon. J.A. Robb, Minister, DIC, 21 November 1923, RG76, pt. 6.
66. J.H. Spence (Toronto) to Hon. J.A. Robb, 21 November 1923, RG76, pt. 6; W.J. Egan, deputy minister, DIC, to E. Bonardelli, Royal Italian Commissioner of Emigration, 7 December 1923, RG76, pt. 6.
67. Mabel Sutherland, director, Nicholas County Welfare Work, Richwood Community Service, Richwood, West Virginia, to (Canadian) Bureau of Colonization (Summer 1927), RG76, pt. 8.

68. Carmina S., (N), 18 January 1978.
69. Domenico F., (N), 18 January 1978.
70. See G.E. Jackson, "Emigration of Canadians to the United States," *The Annals of the American Academy of Political and Social Science,* vol. 57: *Social and Economic Conditions in the Dominion of Canada* (May 1923), pp. 26-28.
71. Vincenzo S., (T), 25 April 1974.
72. Smith, *Canadian Immigration,* pp. 152-53; John Higham, *Strangers in the Land: Patterns of American Nativism, 1860-1925* (New York 1963), p. 118.
73. Domenico F., (N), 18 January 1978.
74. F.C. Blair, to Hon. C. Stewart, minister of interior (DIC), 30 December 1925, RG76, pt. 7.
75. Ibid.
76. Sidlofsky, "Post-War Immigrants," pp. 52-53.
77. W.R. Little, to W.J. Cullen, secretary, DIC, 22 November 1923, RG76, pt. 6.
78. T. Gelley, Division Commissioner of Immigration (DIC, (Winnipeg), to W.J. Egan, 9 September 1926, RG76, pt. 7.
79. Windsor *Border City Star* (summer 1925), clipping in RG76, pt. 7.
80. Cusumano to Robb, 21 November 1923.
81. Vincenzo S., (T), 25 April 1974.
82. Domenico F., (N), 18 January 1978.
83. Alfredo C., (N), 25 September 1976. In this connection, it is interesting to note that the *Montreal Star* on 19 December 1923, reported that farmers within a thirty-mile radius of Montreal were availing themselves of Italian labourers for $10 to $15 per month while the sons of these employers were being sent to the United States to work for $30 to $50 per week.
84. Carmina S., (T), 25 April 1974. Francesco M., 25 September 1976.
85. MacDougall, *Rural Life in Canada,* p. 129.
86. Creelman, "Some Rural Problems," p. 299.
87. Blair to Stewart, 30 December 1925.
88. Vincenzo S., 21 March 1976; Salvatore S., 18 April 1977; Michele F., 27 September 1977.
89. Alberto S., (T) 14 March 1976.
90. W.R. Little to E. Bonardelli, 2 October 1923, RG76, pt. 6; Blair to McGill, 21 November 1923.

CHAPTER 7. SETTLER PATTERNS IN TORONTO

1. Canada, *Censuses of Canada,* 1911, vol. 1, pp. 352-53; 1921, vol. 1, pp. 488-89; 1931, vol. 2, pp. 430-31 (calculations mine). Reporting on Toronto's Italian community within which the *paesani* moved, the *Bollettino dell'emigrazione* in 1915 gave the following revealing summary:
   In Toronto (with a population of 425,000 inhabitants) there are 1,200 industrial establishments, employing 78,000 people.
   It is the seat of a Royal Vice Consulate of Italy: the colony is composed of about 6,000 fellow countrymen... the majority are from Calabria, Sicily, Venezia, Latium, Piedmont, etc.
   Our compatriots possess four wholesale companies, 200 stores selling food products, a pasta factory, restaurants, tailor shops, and small retail outlets selling sweets, fruit and vegetables.
   There is only one professional, a doctor. The principal trades exercised by our compatriots are those of tailor, barber, shoemaker, musician, waiters, woodworkers, boot-blacks, etc.

> There are four mutual aid societies: the Società di mutuo soccorso italiana founded in 1890 with 120 members; the "Vittorio Emanuelle III" founded in 1905, with 44 members; the "Umberto I" founded in 1908 with 100 members, and the "Trinacria" founded in 1913 with 250 members, all from Sicily.
>
> The property owned by the colony amounts to $2 million.
>
> In Toronto there is an Italian Catholic Church, a school, and there is published a weekly paper "La tribuna canadiana."
>
> A few Italians own or rent truck-farms in Mt. St. Dennis, in West Toronto and in Long Branch, making a moderate profit. (*Bollettino dell'emigrazione*, anno 1914 [Ministero degli Affari Esteri, Commissariato dell'Emigrazione; Rome 1915], p. 75).

2. Central Neighbourhood House (hereafter CNH), *"The" Central Neighbourhood House* (Toronto 1911). As well, in 1911 a new playground was responsible for the destruction of forty homes, and factories and businesses for fifty. At the same time the Ward's population increased by 2,000 over the decade. See also CNH, *"The" House by the Side of the Road* (Toronto June 1913), p. 2.

3. Samuel Sidlofsky, "Post-War Immigrants in the Changing Metropolis — with Special Reference to Toronto's Italian Population" (Diss. Toronto 1969), pp. 34-35, 41-43.

4. John E. Zucchi, "Italian Hometown Settlements and the Development of an Italian Community in Toronto, 1875-1935," in *Gathering Place: Peoples and Neighbourhoods of Toronto*, ed. Robert F. Harney (Toronto 1985), pp. 131-35. For an expanded version of Zucchi's work, see his recently published *Italians in Toronto: Development of a National Identity 1875-1935* (Kingston and Montreal 1988).

5. Robert F. Harney, "Toronto's Little Italy, 1885-1945," in *Little Italies in North America*, ed. Robert F. Harney and J. Vincenza Scarpaci (Toronto 1981), pp. 49-52; Robert F. Harney, "The Italian Community in Toronto," in *Two Nations, Many Cultures: Ethnic Groups in Canada*, ed. Jean Leonard Elliott (Scarborough, Ont. 1979), p. 226.

6. Canada, Department of the Secretary of State, Canadian Citizenship Branch, Ethnic Press Analysis Section, *The Italians in Canada*, by Ladislas Hudak (Ottawa 1967), p. 16.

7. Sidlofsky, "Post-War Immigrants," pp. 39-40, 45-57; St. Christopher House, *St. Christopher House Silver Jubilee, 1912-1937: 25 Years of Achievement* (Toronto 1937), p. 3; Harney, "Toronto's Little Italy," pp. 50-51.

8. Zucchi, "Italian Hometown Settlements," pp. 131-32.

9. Interviews; Italian Information Bureau, *Annuario italiano* (Toronto 1935), also referred to as the 1935 Toronto Italian directory.

10. Vincenzo S., (T), 25 April 1974.

11. Interviews; Sidlofsky, "Post-War Immigrants," pp. 39, 54. Commenting on the causes of resettlement of Toronto's Italians outward from the Ward, Harney has observed: "While the location of the first clusters of Italian immigrants near train yards and then in the Ward behind the business district could be explained simply enough, the history of secondary colonies in the city is more complex. Churches, the proximity of work, new public-transit routes, and cheap housing drew people to new areas but so did accident and, of course, chain or family migration patterns within the city itself" ("Italians in Toronto," p. 155).

12. Zucchi, "Italian Hometown Settlements," pp. 137-40.

13. Ibid., pp. 131-35. Also see Zucchi, *Italians in Toronto*, p. 42 (calculation mine).

14. *Annuario italiano* (1935); *Might's Toronto City Directory* (Toronto, 1925 to 1935) (calculation mine). By 1935, ethnic concentrations surrounding Little Italy were clearly discernible. North of the colony between College and Bloor the population was predominantly Jewish; and north again between Bloor and Dupont Anglo-Canadians predominated. South of Little Italy between Dundas and Queen Streets the population was an amalgam of poorer Anglo-Canadians, Slavs, and Jews.

15. Concetta Sm., (T), 9 June 1976.

16. Francesco L., (T), 29 September 1976.

17. Ibid. See Francesco M. Gualtieri, *We Italians: A Study of Italian Immigration in Canada* (Toronto 1928), pp. 52-55.

18. Harney, "Italian Community in Toronto," pp. 222-23, 227; see also, for example, John S. and Leatrice D. MacDonald, "Chain Migration, Ethnic Neighbourhood Formation, and Social Networks," *Milbank Memorial Fund Quarterly* 42 (1964): 82-87.

19. Francesco Grisfsi, *Una provincia fuori legge: con documenti* (Roma 1881), pp. 49-52; Chiesa della Pietà, "Chiesa della pietà" (pamphlet listing donations from Canada for 1979) (Rende 1979); *Annuario italiano* (1935).

20. Harney has put forward the suggestion that "subcolonization" of Italians outward from the original Ward settlement may have followed the early movement of small nuclei of track maintenance and related workers who found it convenient to live near the railway depots, warehouses, and yards at which they worked: "One sort of distribution that may have been... important... was that promoted by the street railway development and by the construction of sheds and warehouses in the train yards of greater Toronto. Just as the railroads played a key role in the settlement of various ethnic groups across the continent, so the substations and junctions created little groups of foreign labourers and later of their dependants in various outlying parts of the city. Track maintenance in the severe winters further attenuated the pattern of settlement. In the city itself the street railway and the radial trolleys served to disperse the original Italian community. Track workers, motormen, and ultimately drivers who worked the long and often split twelve-hour shifts on the street railway found it logical to reside at different turns and junctions on the line" ("Toronto's Little Italy," pp. 49-50).

    In this connection, it is interesting to note that aside from the Junction area's proximity to the strategic intersection of the Canadian National and Canadian Pacific railways, the Brockton concentration was located a ten-minute walk from the Canadian National Railway's Parkdale substation on Queen Street, and the Brandon settlement was located just north of the Canadian Pacific line and just east of another intersection point.

21. For example, Stanley Lieberson, "Residential Segregation and Ethnic Assimilation," *Social Forces* 40 (1961): 52.

22. Interviews.

23. Ibid.; cf. Harney, "Italian Community in Toronto," p. 225.

24. Of the economic tasks of the "family circle" in the Rende area (discussed in chapter 1), obviously the harvests and hog slaughter ended with immigration to Toronto. But groups of *familiari* still formed for the annual making of wine and preserved meats. These tasks, which usually involved the pressing of grapes and processing of carcasses, still required a cooperative effort among *paesani,* though the work parties that formed were often smaller than in the village. The economic necessity in the village for work parties to contribute to a yearly food supply was largely elim-

inated in Toronto. Now it became the *paesani*'s cultural preference for traditional village foods and the opportunity that work parties provided for a social get-together that accounted for their survival in the New World.

The importance of home ownership in Toronto as *the* form of property ownership brought into prominence a variation of the work party that had had relatively little importance in the village. This was the building work party. As home owners in the older sections of the city, *paesani* were continually improving, finishing, or adding to their homes. Some, who were in the building trades, built their own. The home rather than the land became the major focus of property ownership, and just as work parties concerned with the land were of prime importance in the village, work parties concerned with the home became such in the city.

25. *Annuario italiano* (1935); *Toronto City Directory* (1925 to 1935); interviews.
26. Cf. Jeremy Boissevain, *The Italians of Montreal: Social Adjustment in a Plural Society* (Ottawa 1970), pp. 10-11.
27. Interviews.
28. Maria C., 26 September 1977; Julio S., 30 November 1975; Michele F., 27 September 1977.
29. Interviews.
30. Francesco L., (T), 29 September 1976.
31. Cf. Boissevain, *The Italians of Montreal,* p. 17.
32. Michele F., 27 September 1977; Concetta Sm., June 9, 1976.
33. Pietro D., (T), 5 July 1976.
34. Interviews.
35. Ibid.
36. Cf. Boissevain, *The Italians of Montreal,* p. 17 and Suzanne Ziegler, *Characteristics of Italian Householders in Metropolitan Toronto* (Toronto 1972), pp. 58-62, 73.
37. Interviews.
38. Ibid. Cf. Constance Cronin, *The Sting of Change: Sicilians in Sicily and Australia* (Chicago 1970), pp. 210-11, 215.
39. Anna Pe., 13 December 1979; Ernesto S., 2 March 1977; Francesco G., 25 September 1976. See also Judith E. Smith, "Italian Mothers, American Daughters: Changes in Work and Family Roles," in *The Italian Immigrant Woman in North America,* Proceedings of the Tenth Annual Conference of the American Italian Historical Association, 1977 (Toronto 1978), p. 211.
40. Ibid., pp. 211-12, looks at the prevalence of industrial homework among Italian women in Providence, R.I. Colomba M. Furio, "The Cultural Background of the Italian Immigrant Woman and Its Impact on Her Unionization in the New York City Garment Industry, 1880-1919," in *Pane e Lavoro: The Italian American Working Class,* ed. George E. Pozzetta (Toronto 1980), pp. 88-89, notes that government surveys in 1910 showed that up to 98% of all garment industry homework in New York was done by Italians; in finishing or homesewing tasks — the principal form of such homework — in 1916 they made up 46% of all workers. Also see Florence Kelley, "The Sweating-System," in *Hull-House Maps and Papers: A Presentation of Nationalities and Wages in a Congested District of Chicago, Together with Comments and Essays on Problems Growing out of the Social Conditions* (Boston 1895; facs. rpt. New York 1970), p. 33.
41. Yolanda St., 23 September 1976; Ida S., 27 November 1976; Ida Sp., 30 November 1975. Carmina S., 21 March 1976.

42. Interviews; *Toronto City Directory* (1925-1935). Harney indicates that as early as the late 1880s Italians had established the reputation of doing industrial homework and running "sweat shops" in their homes ("Italian Community in Toronto," pp. 222-23). See also Franca Iacovetta, "From *Contadina* to Worker: Southern Italian Immigrant Working Women in Toronto, 1947-62," in *Looking into My Sister's Eyes: An Exploration in Women's History,* ed. Jean Burnet (Toronto 1986), pp. 209-13.

43. See Furio, "Cultural Background of the Italian Immigrant Woman," pp. 83-84. A synoptic critique of the "emancipating" role played by women's work outside the home is presented by Joan W. Scott and Louise A. Tilly, "Woman's Work and the Family in Nineteenth-Century Europe," *Comparative Studies in Society and History* 25 (January 1975): 55.

44. In a provocative analysis of the housewife's work, Wally Secombe has written of its covert value: "The housewife's labour cannot assert itself nor assert her because its value is hidden, and she receives no paycheck to signify its presence. The fact that the product of her labour is embodied in another person does not allow for a clear perception of its appropriation by capital, and consequently of her relation to capital" ("The Housewife and Her Labour under Capitalism," *New Left Review* 83 [1974]: 20).

45. See Ruth Schwartz Cowan, "The 'Industrial Revolution' in the Home: Household Technology and Social Change in the 20th Century," *Technology and Culture* 17, no. 1 (1976): 1-5.

46. Maria Sm., (T), 9 June 1976.

47. Hans Medick, "The Proto-industrial Family Economy: The Structural Function of Household and Family during the Transition from Peasant Society to Industrial Capitalism," *Journal of Social History* 9, no. 3 (1976): 311.

48. Trentina C., 27 November 1976; Yolanda St., 23 September 1976; Ida S., 27 November 1976; Maria Co., 19 February 1977.

49. Cf. Robert F. Harney, "Boarding and Belonging: Thoughts on Sojourner Institutions," *Urban History Review* (1978), pp. 27-30.

50. Interestingly, it was also reported that the part-time *paesani* farmers supplied Rende area grocers in the city with produce, this trade sometimes taking on the characteristics of a barter arrangement.

51. Interviews. In this connection, writing of Southern Italians in the new world at the turn of the century, Harney has noted how gleaning, the keeping of gardens, and certain part-time occupations reflected the immigrants' pre-industrial roots, and in particular the primacy of family economy: "willingness to engage in a large variety of semi-occupations from the gathering of wild greens and mushrooms to weekend ice-cream vending and knife-sharpening fit the pre-modern world view... the almost feudal sense of demesne held by Italian immigrants. The vestigial attempt at family self-sufficiency also appears in the maintenance of a goat or some chickens in the backyard and in the small rented vegetable patches along railway rights of way on the outskirts of industrial cities. Family endeavours such as rag-picking and scavenging were not only an aspect of this world view but also assumed, in the face of liberal and industrial society, that the family was a single economic unit" ("Ambiente and Social Class in North American Little Italies," *Canadian Review of Studies in Nationalism* 2, no. 2 [Spring 1975]: 212-13).

    For a moving account drawn from extensive interviews of how the poor of Sicily as late as the mid-fifties had to make use of gleaning to subsist, see Danilo Dolci, *Report from Palermo,* trans. P.D. Cummins (New York 1959), pp. 202-4, 253-70.

52. Interviews.

53. Ibid.; see also Florence Kelley and Alzina P. Stevens, "Wage-Earning Children," in *Hull-House Maps and Papers*, p. 213 passim.

54. Interviews; see also Leonard Covello, *The Social Background of the Italo-American School Child: A Study of the Southern Italian Family Mores and Their Effect on the School Situation in Italy and America* (Leiden, Neth. 1967), pp. 256, 265, 292, 307.

55. Interviews; see also Smith, "Italian Mothers, American Daughters," p. 213; Cronin, *Sting of Change*, pp. 231-32.

56. W. Lloyd Warner and Leo Srole, *The Social Systems of American Ethnic Groups*, Yankee City Series, vol. 3 (New Haven 1945), p. 108; Oscar Handlin, *The Uprooted: The Epic Story of the Great Migrations That Made the American People* (New York 1951), pp. 227-29, 235, 244; and Covello, *Italo-American School Child*, p. 296.

57. Virginia Yans McLaughlin, "Patterns of Work and Family Organization: Buffalo's Italians," in *The Family in History: Interdisciplinary Essays*, ed. Theodore K. Rabb and Robert I. Rotberg (New York 1973), p. 113. See also Virginia Yans McLaughlin, "A Flexible Tradition: South Italian Immigrants Confront a New World Experience," in *Immigrants in Industrial America*, ed. Ehrlich, pp. 67-84; and R.J. Vecoli, "Contadini in Chicago: A Critique of the Uprooted," *Journal of American History* 51 (December 1964): 407, 409.

58. See Karl Marx, *Pre-Capitalist Economic Formations*, ed. and introd. Eric J. Hobsbawm, trans. Jack Cohen (New York, 1965), p. 116.

59. Interviews.

60. Handlin, *The Uprooted*, p. 235.

61. For example, Sidney M. Greenfield, "Industrialization and the Family in Sociological Theory," *American Journal of Sociology* 67 (1961): 312-14; William J. Goode, "The Family as an Element in the World Revolution," in *The Study of Society: An Integrated Anthology*, ed. Peter I. Rose (New York 1967), pp. 536-38. Also Lydio F. Tomasi, "The Italian American Family: The Southern Italian Family's Process of Adjustment to an Urban America," Center for Migration Studies paper (New York 1972), pp. 22-24.

62. McLaughlin, "Patterns of Work and Family Organization," p. 117.

63. Ibid., 118-22; Furio, "Cultural Background of the Italian Immigrant Woman," pp. 88-89; McLaughlin, "A Flexible Tradition," pp. 71, 81-82.

64. McLaughlin, "Patterns of Work and Family Organization," p. 118; Tomasi, "Italian-American Family," pp. 12, 25. For suggestive alternate views, see Teodor Shanin, "The Peasantry as a Political Factor," *Sociological Review* 14, no. 1 [1966]: 8-10; and J.G. Peristiany, ed., *Honour and Shame: The Values of a Mediterranean Society* (Chicago 1966), introduction.

65. For the genesis of the relationship between female fidelity and small property, see F[riedrich] Engels, *The Origin of the Family, Private Property and the State* (Moscow 1948; English ed.), p. 58 passim. Cf. Shanin, "Peasantry as a Political Factor," pp. 13-14.

66. Interviews; see also A.L. Maraspini, *The Study of an Italian Village* (Paris 1968), p. 180.

67. Germaine Greer pointed out after observing Calabrian and similar peasant women that they did not experience the pervasive emphasis on female honour as something forced upon them by men — any more than men experienced their roles as providers as forced (*Sex and Destiny: The Politics of Human Fertility* [London 1984], pp. 95-97).

68. Interviews; cf. Furio, "Cultural Background of the Italian Immigrant Women," p. 84.

69. Interviews; cf. McLaughlin, "Patterns of Work and Family Organization," pp. 118-20. In her study of Providence's Southern Italians, Smith calculated that 60% of the daughters in her sample of 160 families in 1915 employed in factories and offices were working with a brother or sister, a proportion that decreased only slightly to 56% by 1935. Moreover, many of the daughters' jobs were acquired through kin connections ("Italian Mothers, American Daughters," pp. 212-13).
70. Interviews; cf. Covello, *Social Background of the Italo-American School Child*, p. 196 passim. Regarding antagonism between the sexes, Engels has made the provocative statement that "The first class antagonism which appears in history coincides with the development of the antagonism between man and woman in monogamous marriage, and the first class oppression with that of the female sex by the male" (*Origin of the Family*, p. 66).
71. Ida Sp., 30 November 1975; Ida S., 12 June 1978; Anna Pe., 22 January 1977.
72. Interviews.

APPENDIX

1. See Alan Macfarlane, "History, Anthropology and the Study of Communities," *Journal of Social History* 10, no. 5 (May 1977): 650-51.
2. Pierre Goubert, "Local History," in *Historical Studies Today*, ed. Felix Gilbert and Stephen R. Graubard (New York 1972), p. 217.
3. George Ewart Evans, "I Am a Tape Recorder: 'Oral History,'" *Encounter* 42, no. 5 (Nov., 1976): 75.
4. For example, Robert F. Harney, "Oral Testimony and Ethnic Studies," *Polyphony: The Bulletin of the Multicultural History Society of Ontario* 1, no. 2 (Summer 1978): 44-45; Richard N. Juliani, "Field Research in the Study of Ethnic Communities: The Italians in Philadelphia," unpublished paper, Temple University, Oct. 1972, p. 6.
5. I am referring here to informants for whom a record of the discussion was kept. Besides these, many other *paesani* as well as Italians generally and relevant individuals such as social workers, teachers, and immigration officials were consulted in unrecorded casual conversations, both in personal and group situations, to throw light on the immigrant experience.
6. Andrei Simić, *The Peasant Urbanites: A Study of Rural-Urban Mobility in Serbia* (New York 1973), p. 26.
7. William Foote Whyte, *Street Corner Society: The Social Structure of an Italian Slum* (Chicago 1955), p. 303.
8. Bronislaw Malinowski, *Argonauts of the Western Pacific* (London 1922), p. 23.
9. In the synthesizing of these diverse sources, one of my aims was to attempt to follow the advice given over four decades ago by Lucien Febvre: "Methodology: move from the material, concrete, and carefully observed *fact* to the duly analyzed *state of mind*. And then move back from the *state of mind* to the *fact*, which then becomes clear and assumes its [true] meaning" ("Man or Productivity," in *Rural Society in France: Selections from the Annales: Economies, Sociétés, Civilisations*, ed. Robert Forster and Orest Ranum [Baltimore 1977], p. 4).

Table 1. Population of Rende Area, 1881

Commune and settlements	Altitude of capital (metres above sea level)*	Population Present			Legally resident population
		Nucleated settlement	Dispersed settlement	Total	
Castiglione Cosentino	335	943	504	1,447	1,510
Castrolibero	548	424	1,038	1,462	1,456
Cerisano	620	1,444	841	2,285	2,376
Marano Marchesato	550				
Sant'Anna		234	1,221	1,455	1,564
Curcio		326	976	1,302	1,443
Total		560	2,197	2,757	3,007
Marano Principato	—				
Annuciata		219	241	460	463
Moretti		45	418	463	466
Savagli		132	310	442	449
Total		396	969	1,365	1,378
Montalto Uffugo	468				
Montalto Uffugo		2,226	952	3,178	3,231
Vaccarizzo		987	33	1,020	1,090
Parantoro		733	—	733	760
Santa Maria la Castagna		236	70	306	305
Cardopiano		577	—	577	599
Berarda		166	83	199	201
Total		4,875	1,138	6,013	6,186

Table 1. (cont'd)

Rende	482				
Rende		1,715	466	2,181	2,171
Nogiano		422	772	1,194	1,195
Arcavacata		622	507	1,129	1,127
Surdo		–	746	746	746
Total		2,759	2,491	5,250	5,239
San Fili	550				
San Fili		2,642	274	2,916	3,430
Bucita		780	64	844	1,034
Total		3,442	338	3,760	4,464
San Vincenzo la Costa	470				
San Vincenzo		543	38	581	629
Palazzo		47	69	116	121
San Sisto		473	239	712	728
Gesuitie Giranda		520	196	716	796
Total		1,583	542	2,125	2,274
Cosenza†	383	13,463	3,223	16,686	16,253
Total of Circondario of Cosenza	–	133,460	41,131	174,591	187,319

SOURCE: Ministero di Agricoltura, Industria e Commercio, Direzione Generale della Statistica, *Censimento della popolazione del Regno d'Italia al 31 dicembre 1881*, Vol. 1, Part 1: *Popolazione dei comuni e dei mandamenti* (Roma, 1883), pp. 120-23.

*Altitude of municipal capitals from Map of Cosenza (Sheet 23 – First Edition) prepared in 1943 by the U.S. Army, *Army Map Service, M[ap] 592* (Washington, D.C., 1943). Altitude of Marano Principato not available.

†Though Cosenza *comune* containing the provincial capital appears in this and following tables, it did not form an integral part of the local area. It is included here because of its proximity and concomitant importance in the lives of Rende area inhabitants.

Table 2. Rural Industrial Sector of Rende Area, 1911

Commune* and Population†	Industries processing Agricultural products			Metallurgical industries			Construction			Textiles			Chemical industries			Service industries			Total		
	a	b	c	a	b	c	a	b	c	a	b	c	a	b	c	a	b	c	a	b	c
	a) Number of enterprises at 1911 census									*b) Number of people employed*									*c) Force in horsepower*		
Castrolibero (1,817)	25	55	–	–	–	–	–	–	–	–	2	–	–	–	–	–	–	–	27	57	–
Cerisano (2,236)	8	21	14	2	6	–	–	–	–	–	14	–	–	–	–	–	–	–	13	41	14
Marano Marchesato (2,689)	–	–	–	–	–	–	–	–	–	2	132	20	–	–	–	–	–	–	2	132	20
Marano Principato (1,398)	4	8	9	–	–	–	–	–	–	2	5	–	–	–	–	–	–	–	6	13	9
Montalto Uffugo (6,900)	7	21	10	2	6	–	–	–	–	1	28	5	–	–	–	–	–	–	10	55	15
Rende (7,170)	22	164	77	3	9	–	10	134	40	7	26	–	–	–	–	–	–	–	42	333	117
San Fili (3,811)	27	87	70	6	19	–	–	–	–	5	23	–	1	100‡	–	1	3	20	39	232	90

Table 2. (cont'd.)

Commune* and Population	Industries processing Agricultural products			Metallurgical industries			Construction			Textiles			Chemical industries			Service industries			Total		
	a	b	c	a	b	c	a	b	c	a	b	c	a	b	c	a	b	c	a	b	c
	a) Number of enterprises at 1911 census									b) Number of people employed						c) Force in horsepower					
San Vincenzo la Costa (2,038)	5	16	16	–	–	–	–	–	–	–	–	–	1	71	150	–	–	–	6	87	166
Cosenza (24,177)	103	620	110	33	89	–	11	87	–	33	440	58	5	67	150	13	80	573	198	1,343	891
Total of Circondario of Cosenza	678	2,388	1,044	145	378	–	50	337	65	221	1,509	194	9	147	301	15	86	728	1,119	4,847	2,332

SOURCE: Ministero di Agricoltura, Industria e Commercio, Direzione Generale della Statistica e del Lavoro, Ufficio del Censimento, *Censimento degli opifici e della imprese industriali al 10 giugno 1911*, Vol. 1: *Dati riassuntivi concernenti il numero, il personale e la forza motrice delle imprese censite* (Rome, 1913), pp. 82-83, 240.

*Castiglione Cosentino has been omitted since no information on industrial activity there was reported by the census.

†Population of communes from Ministero Agricoltura, Industria e Commercio, Direzione Generale della Statistica e del Lavoro, Ufficio del Censimento, *Censimento della popolazione del Regno d'Italia al 10 giugno 1911*, Vol. 1: *Popolazione presente, popolazione temporaneamente assente, popolazione residente* (Roma, 1913), pp. 179-83, 570.

‡Cited in a report by Adolfo Rossi, Italian Royal Commissioner of Emigration, 1908: Adolfo Rossi, "Vantaggi e danni dell'emigrazione nel mezzogiorno d'Italia (note di un viaggio fatto in Basilicata et in Calabria)," *Bollettino dell'emigrazione*, anno 1908, no. 13 (Ministero degli Affari Esteri, Commissariato dell'Emigrazione; Roma, 1908), p. 40.

Table 3. Illiteracy Rate of Rende Area, 1911

Commune	Population 6 years of age and over	Number illiterate			Percentage illiterate		
		Male	*Female*	*Total*	*Male*	*Female*	*Total*
Castiglione Consentino	1,226	307	556	863	56	82	70
Castrolibero	1,460	246	699	945	39	85	65
Cerisano	1,880	362	738	1,100	45	74*	59
Marano Marchesato	2,401	548	1,227	1,775	57	85	74
Marano Principato	1,184	284	613	897	57	89	76
Montalto Uffugo	5,826	1,313	2,447	3,760	51	75	65
Rende	6,023	1,996	2,734	4,730	70	87	79
San Fili	3,239	571	1,221	1,792	41	66	55
San Vincenzo la Costa	1,694	394	730	1,124	52	78	66
Cosenza	20,417	4,049	6,188	10,237	41	59	50
Total: Circondario Cosenza	159,745	39,081	65,680	104,761	55	74	66

SOURCE: Ministero di Agricoltura, Industria e Commercio, Direzione Generale della Statistica e del Lavoro, Ufficio del Censimento, *Censimento della popolazione del Regno d'Italia al 10 giugno 1911*, Vol. 3: *L'alfabetismo della popolazione presente* (Roma, 1914), pp. 84-85, 223.

*Proportion omitted by census (calculation mine).

Table 4. Population Increase of Rende Area, 1820-1881

Commune	Area in sq.km.*	Population 1820†	Population density 1820 (inhabitants per sq.km.)	Population 1881‡	Population density 1881 (inhabitants per sq.km.)	% increase in population density (inhabitants per sq. km.)
Castiglione Cosentino	15.15	934	61.65	1,447	95.51	54.93
Castrolibero	18.94	1,100	58.08	1,462	77.19	32.91
Rende	48.06	3,592	74.74	5,250	109.23	46.15
San Fili	18.45	2,914	157.94	3,760	203.79	29.03
Cosenza	40.73	8,856	217.43	16,686	409.67	88.41

SOURCES:

*Commune area from Ministero di Agricoltura, Industria e Commercio, Direzione Generale della Statistica e del Lavoro, Ufficio del Censimento, *Censimento degli opifici e della imprese industriali al 10 giugno 1911*, Vol. 1: *Dati riassuntivi concernenti il numero, il personale e la forza motrice delle imprese censite* (Rome, 1913), pp. 180, 182. Calculations mine.

†Census population from Luigi Izzo, *La popolazione calabrese nel secolo XIX: Demografia e economia* (Napoli, 1965), pp. 294, 301, 307, 309.

‡See Table 1.

Table 5. Destination of Emigrants from Cosenza, 1876-1925

Date	Emigration from Cosenza Province*		Total emigration Cosenza District†
	To North & South America	*World total*	
1876	674	774	98
77	983	1,073	104
78	1,862	2,038	436
79	3,188	3,525	889
80	2,430	2,752	500
81	3,336	4,022	1,083
82	6,423	8,453	3,918
83	5,882	7,362	3,137
84	3,590	4,290	1,363
85	7,034	9,168	3,387
86	6,163	7,091	2,712
87	7,798	8,472	2,537
88	9,118	9,662	2,968
89	6,990	7,366	2,178
90	7,480	7,757	2,918
91	5,970	6,208	2,179
92	5,435	5,799	1,702
93	8,448	8,812	2,950
94	6,441	6,753	1,592
95	8,671	9,304	2,682
96	7,439	8,270	1,930
97	6,191	6,893	1,576
98	6,295	7,021	1,890
99	6,447	7,116	1,418
1900	6,328	7,103	1,471
01	8,908	9,817	2,413
02	8,173	9,031	2,092
03	7,265	7,856	1,637
04	14,016	14,246	5,997
05	21,799	22,103	9,052
06	20,854	21,531	7,944
07	17,328	17,520	7,281
08	13,194	13,345	
09	19,836	20,111	
10	19,504	19,777	
11	13,543	13,819	
12	16,824	17,076	
13	18,393	18,565	

Table 5. (cont'd.)

Date	Emigration from Cosenza Province*		Total emigration Cosenza District†
	To North & South America	World total	
1914	8,527	8,655	
15	2,624	2,710	
16	2,639	3,123	
17	427	555	
18	235	279	
19	5,711	6,088	
20	21,547	21,996	
21	8,027	8,147	
22	7,903	7,995	
23	9,458	9,598	
24	6,735	6,930	
25	6,870	6,976	

SOURCES:

*(for 1876-1905), Giuseppe Scalise, *L'emigrazione dalla Calabria: Saggio di economia sociale* (Napoli, 1905), pp. 132-33 (Table E); (for 1906-25), Commissariato Generale dell'Emigrazione, *Annuario statistico della emigrazione italiana dal 1876 al 1925* (Roma, 1926), p. 62.

†(for 1876-1903), D. Taruffi, L. De Nobili, C. Lori, *La questione agraria e l'emigrazione in Calabria* (Firenze, 1908), p. 744 (Table 3); (for 1904-7), Adolfo Rossi, "Vantaggi e danni dell'emigrazione nel mezzogiorno d'Italia (note di un viaggio fatto in Basilicata e in Calabria)," *Bollettino dell'emigrazione*, anno 1908, no. 13 (Ministero degli Affari Esteri, Commissariato dell'Emigrazione: Roma, 1908), p. 95.

Table 6. Emigration from Rende Area, 1881-97

Commune	Population present 1881	Emigration												Total emigration (excl. 1888 & 1893)	Total emigrants as % of 1881 Pop.
		1884	1885	1886	1887	1889	1890	1891	1892	1894	1895	1896	1897		
Castiglione Cosentino	1,447	37	5	58	–	52	38	51	69	29	51	33	–	423	29.2
Castrolibero*	1,462	11	–	–	–	–	–	12	–	–	–	–	–	23	1.6
Cerisano	2,285	14	40	46	41	41	34	25	70	63	12	33	41	460	20.1
Marano Marchesato	2,757	17	47	20	34	16	40	29	34	21	16	67	16	357	13.0
Marano Principato*	1,365	–	–	–	–	17	–	–	–	–	–	21	–	38	2.8
Montalto Uffugo	6,013	152	183	95	–	220	49	43	67	57	123	26	–	1,015	16.9
Rende	5,250	83	102	86	51	77	42	35	92	70	70	120	94	922	17.6
San Fili	3,760	83	175	110	144	105	118	102	143	55	68	68	44	1,215	32.3
San Vincenzo la Costa	2,125	32	82	72	109	36	48	46	37	93	88	59	–	702	33.0
Cosenza*	16,686	99	141	176	97	236	110	54	–	–	–	–	–	922	5.5
Total for Rende area	43,150	528	775	663	475	800	479	397	512	388	428	427	195	6,067	14.1
Total for Circondaric of Cosenza	174,591	1433	3386	2712	2607	2178	2919	2199	1707	1592	2682	1930	1576	21,763	12.5

SOURCES: Ministero di Agricoltura, Industria e Commercio, Direzione Generale della Statistica, *Statistica della emigrazione italiana* for the years 1886 (p. 54), 1887 (p. 48), 1888 (p. 142), 1890 (p. 52), 1892 (p. 56), 1894-95 (p. 55), 1897 (p. 56).

*Emigration figures incomplete.

Table 7. Causes and Destination of Emigration from Rende Area: Results of Survey of Mayors, 1888

Commune	Principal causes of emigration	Whether immigrants Successful	Destination	Principal employment
Castiglione Cosentino	– Miseria – Desire for betterment	Yes	– Chicago – New York – Buenos Aires	– Railroad work – Factory work
Castrolibero	–	–	–	–
Cerisano	– Desire for betterment – Shortage of work	Almost all	– Denver – Washington – Buenos Aires – Porto Allegre	– Railroad work – Shopowners/artisans
Marano Marchesato	–	–	–	–
Marano Principato	– Miseria – Desire for betterment – Poor Harvests	Some	– Chicago – New York – Buenos Aires – Montevideo	– Railroad work
Montalto Uffugo*	– Miseria – Desire for betterment – Poor harvests & crop prices	Yes	– New York – Pennsylvania – Buenos Aires – Rio de Janeiro	– Railroad work
Rende*	– Desire for betterment – Shortage of work – Poor pay	Almost all	– Chicago – New York – Pittsburgh – Colorado	– Railroad work

Table 7. (cont'd)

Commune	Principal causes of emigration	Whether immigrants Successful	Destination	Principal employment
San Fili†	– Desire for betterment – Shortage of work	Yes	– Chicago – Pennsylvania – Argentina – Brazil	–
San Vincenzo la Costa	– Miseria – Desire for betterment – Poor harvests	Some	– North America – Argentina – Brazil	– Railroad work – Peddling
Cosenza	– Miseria – Shortage of work – Poor pay	Almost all	– Buenos Aires – Sao Paolo	– Artisans

SOURCE: Ministero di Agricoltura, Industria e Commercio, Direzione Generale della Statistica, *Statistica della emigrazione italiana avvenuta nell anno 1888* (Roma, 1889), pp. 140-42.

*Some of information for destination and employment added from interviews.

†Some of information for destination derived from Adolfo Rossi, "Vantaggi e danni dell'emigrazione nel mezzogiorno d'Italia (note di un viaggio fatto in Basilicata e in Calabria)," *Bollettino dell'emigrazione*, anno 1908, no. 13 (Ministero degli Affari Esteri, Commissariato dell'Emigrazione: Roma, 1908), p. 41.

Table 8. Italian Population of Chicago and Toronto, 1840-1930

Decades	Chicago			Toronto‡	
	Number of Italian-born	*Italian origin*	*†Total population*	*Number of Italian origin*	*Total population*
1840	–	–	4,470	–	13,092
1850	30	–	29,963	–	30,775
1860	100	–	109,260	24	44,821
1870	552	–	298,977	40	56,092
1880	1,357	–	503,185	121	86,415
1890	5,591	8,219	1,099,850	500	144,023
1190	16,008	26,046	1,698,575	1,098	208,040
1910	45,169	74,943	2,185,283	4,873	376,471
1920	59,215	124,284	2,701,705	8,987	521,893
1930	80,000	200,000	3,376,438	15,623	631,207

SOURCES:

*United States Census figures cited in Giovanni E. Schiavo, *The Italians in Chicago: A Study in Americanization* (Chicago, 1928), Table 3 (p. 143). Figures for 1840 and 1930 estimated.

†United States Census figures cited in Thomas Lee Philpott, *The Slum and the Ghetto: Neighbourhood Deterioration and Middle-Class Reform, Chicago, 1880-1930* (New York, 1978), p. 116.

‡*Censuses of Canada 1665 to 1871*, vol. 4 (Ottawa, 1876), pp. 128, 180. Beyond this early volume the sources utilized are the standard decennial Census of Canada for the following years: 1870-71, vol. 1, pp. 16, 266-67; 1880-81, vol. 1, pp. 73, 276-77; 1890-91, vol. 1, pp. 66, 348-51; 1901, vol. 1, pp. 84-5, 344-45; 1911, vol. 1, pp. 352-53 and vol. 2, pp. 248-49; 1921, vol. 1, pp. 488-89; 1931, vol. 2, pp. 430-31. Figure for number of Italians for 1860 estimated from Toronto *Mail and Empire*, October 2, 1897.

Select Bibliography of Published Sources

Sources Relating to the Italian Setting

Alvaro, Corrado. "Aspetti della società calabrese." *Almanacco Calabrese* 2, no. 2 (1952): 117-22.

Angarano, Francesco Antonio. *Vita tradizionale dei contadini e pastori calabresi.* Firenze: Leo S. Olschki Editore, 1973.

Arlacchi, Pino. *Mafia, contadini e latifondo nella Calabria tradizionale.* Bologna: Il Mulino, 1980.

Baedeker, Karl. *Southern Italy and Sicily.* 12th, 15th and 16th revised editions. Leipzig: Karl Baedeker, 1896, 1908 and 1912.

Bailey, F.G., ed. *Gifts and Poison: The Politics of Reputation.* Oxford: Basil Blackwell, 1971.

Baldacci, Osvaldo. "Osservazioni sull'emigrazione calabrese." *Almanacco Calabrese* 22-23, no. 23 (1973): 131-37.

Banfield, Edward C. *The Moral Basis of a Backward Society.* New York: Free Press, 1958.

Baxevanis, John J. *Economy and Population Movements in the Peloponnesos of Greece.* Athens: National Centre of Social Research, 1972.

Bell, Rudolph M. *Fate and Honor, Family and Village: Demographic and Cultural Change in Rural Italy since 1880.* Chicago: University of Chicago Press, 1979.

Bloch, Marc. *Feudal Society.* Vol. 1: *The Growth of the Ties of Dependence.* Chicago: University of Chicago Press, 1961.

Blok, Anton. *The Mafia of a Sicilian Village, 1860-1960: A Study of Violent Peasant Entrepreneurs.* New York: Harper and Row, 1975; Harper Torchbooks, 1975.

Borzomati, Pietro. *L'emigrazione calabrese dall'unità ad oggi.* Roma: Centro Studi Emigrazione, 1982.

Brandes, Stanley H. *Migration, Kinship, and Community: Tradition and Transition in a Spanish Village.* New York: Academic Press, 1975.

Brögger, Jan. *Montevarese: A Study of Peasant Society and Culture in Southern Italy.* Oslo: Scandinavian University Books, 1971.

Campbell, J.K. *Honour, Family and Patronage: A Study of Institutions and Moral Values in a Greek Mountain Community.* Oxford: Clarendon Press, 1964.

Cancian, Frank. "The Southern Italian Peasant: World View and Political Behavior." *Anthropological Quarterly* 34, no. 1 (January 1961): 1-18.

Chabod, Federico. *L'Italia contemporanea, 1918-48.* Torino: Piccola Biblioteca Einaudi, 1961.

Chiva, I. "Social organization, traditional economy and customary law in Corsica: Outline of a plan of analysis." In *Mediterranean Countrymen,* pp. 97-112. Edited by J.K. Campbell. Paris: Mouton & Co., 1963.

Ciasca, Raffaele. "Le transformazioni agrarie in Calabria dopo l'unità." *Archivo storico per la Calabria e la Lucania* 25 (1956): 83-100.

Cingari, Gaetano. *Storia della Calabria dall'unità a Oggi.* Bari: Editori Laterza, 1982.

Cipolla, Carlo M. "Four Centuries of Italian Demographic Development." In *Population in History: Essays in Historical Demography*, pp. 570-87. Edited by D.V. Glass and D.E.C. Eversley. London: Edward Arnold, 1965.

Cole, John W. and Eric R. Wolf. *The Hidden Frontier: Ecology and Ethnicity in an Alpine Valley.* New York: Academic Press, 1975.

Conforti, Luigi. *Risposta all'opuscolo "Una provincia fuori legge: con documenti."* Cosenza: Ospizio Vittoria Emanuelle, 1881.

Corso, Raffaele. "Il folklore agricolo." *Almanacco Calabrese* 10, no. 10 (1960): 23-31.

Croce, Benedetto. *History of the Kingdom of Naples.* Chicago: University of Chicago, 1970.

Cyriax, Tony. *Among Italian Peasants.* London: W. Collins Sons, 1919.

Davis, J(ohn). *Land and Family in Pisticci.* London: London School of Economics, 1973.

de Giorgio, Domenico. *Figure e momenti del Risorgimento in Calabria.* Messina: Peloritana Editrice, 1971.

Demarco, Domenico. *La Calabria: Economia e società.* Napoli: Edizioni Scientifiche Italiane, 1966.

di Caparelli, Filippo. "Calabresi nel mondo." *Almanacco Calabrese* 2, no. 2 (1952): 145-50.

Dickinson, Robert E. *The Population Problem of Southern Italy: An Essay in Social Geography.* Syracuse: Syracuse University Press, 1955.

Dolci, Danilo. *Report from Palermo.* New York: Orion, 1959.

Douglas, Norman. *Old Calabria.* London: M. Secker, 1915; Oxford University Press, 1938.

Douglass, William A. *Emigration in a South Italian Town: An Anthropological History.* New Brunswick, New Jersey: Rutgers University Press, 1984.

Fonte, Fedele. *Rende nella sua cronistoria.* Chiaravalle Centrale, Cosenza: Frama Sud, 1976.

Forster, Robert and Orest Ranum, eds., *Rural Society in France: Selections from the Annales: Economies, Sociétés, Civilisations.* Baltimore: Johns Hopkins University Press, 1977.

Fortunato, Giustino. *Il mezzogiorno e lo stato italiano.* Vol. 2: *Discorsi politici, 1890-1910.* Bari: Giuseppe Laterza e figli, 1911.

Foster, George M. "Interpersonal Relations in Peasant Society." *Human Organization* 19, no. 4 (Winter 1960-61): 174-83.

Galtung, Johan. *Members of Two Worlds: A Development Study of Three Villages in Western Sicily.* Oslo: International Peace Research Institute, 1971.

Gerschenkron, Alexander. "Notes on the Rate of Industrial Growth in Italy, 1881-1913." *Journal of Economic History* 15, no. 4 (1955): 360-75.

Giorgetti, Giorgio. *Contadini e proprietari nell'Italia moderna.* Torino: Piccola Biblioteca Einaudi, 1974.

Gramsci, Antonio. *La questione meridionale.* Roma: Editori Riuniti, 1966.

Grisfsi, Francesco. *Una provincia fuori legge: con documenti.* Roma: Barbèra, 1881.

Grisolìa, Luigi. *Dizionario dei Calabresi nel mondo.* Roma: Edisud, 1965.

Gross, Feliks. *Il Paese: Values and Social Change in an Italian Village.* New York: New York University Press, 1973.

Guerrieri, Michele. "Passato e presente di un comune meridionale." *Nord e Sud* 19, no. 149 (March 1972): 95-103.

Gunnell, Bryn. *Calabrian Summer.* London: Rupert-Hart Davis, 1965.

Hare, Augustus J.C. *Cities of Southern Italy.* New York: E.P. Dutton, 1911.

Hobsbawn, Eric J. *Primitive Rebels: Studies in Archaic Forms of Social Movement in the 19th and 20th Centuries.* New York: W.W. Norton, 1965.

Isnardi, Giuseppe. "La Calabria e la Questione Meridionale," *Almanacco Calabrese* 1, no. 1 (1951): 157-62.

Izzo, Luigi. *La popolazione Calabrese nel secolo XIX: Demografia e economia.* Napoli: Edizioni Scientifiche Italiane, 1965.

Jones, Emrys. *Towns and Cities.* Oxford: Oxford University Press, 1966.

King, Russell. *The "Questione Meridionale" in Southern Italy.* Durham: University of Durham, 1971.

La Stella Degli Emigranti (Anno 1904): Polistena, Calabria, 1904; facsimile reprint as special supplement of *la Regione Calabria – Emigrazione,* nos. 11-12, (November-December 1989).

Lear, Edward. *Journals of a Landscape Painter in Southern Calabria.* London: Richard Bentley, 1852.

Lopreato, Joseph. *Peasants No More: Social Class and Social Change in an Under-developed Society.* Scranton, Pennsylvania: Chandler Publications, 1967.

MacFarlane, Charles. *Popular Customs, Sports, and Recollections of the South of Italy.* London. W. Clowes and Sons, 1846.

Mack Smith, Denis. *Italy: A Modern History,* revised ed. Ann Arbor: The University of Michigan Press, 1959.

Maraspini, A.L. *The Study of an Italian Village.* Paris: Mouton, 1968.

Medick, Hans, "The Proto-industrial Family Economy: The Structural Function of Household and Family during the Transition from Peasant Society to Industrial Capitalism." *Journal of Social History* 9, no. 3 (October 1976): 291-315.

Morel, Alain, "L'espace social d'un village picard." *Études Rurales* 45, no. 73 (January-March 1972): 62-80.

Moss, Leonard W. and Walter H. Thomson. "The South Italian Family: Literature and Observation." *Human Organization* 18, no. 1 (Spring 1959): 35-41.

Moss, Leonard W. and Stephen C. Cappannari. "Patterns of Kinship, Comparaggio and Community in a South Italian Village." *Anthropological Quarterly* 33 (January 1960): 24-32.

————. "Estate and Class in a Southern Italian Hill Village." *American Anthropologist* 64, no. 2 (April 1962): 287-300.

Nitti, Francesco Saverio. *Scritti sulla questione meridionale.* Vol. 1: *Saggi sulla storia del mezzogiorno, emigrazione e lavoro (1888-1908).* Bari: Editori Laterza, 1958.

————. *Scritti sulla questione meridionale.* Vol. 2: *Il bilancio dello stato dal 1862 al 1896-97: Nord e Sud (1900).* Bari: Editori Laterza, 1958.

————. *Scritti sulla questione meridionale.* Vol. 4: *Inchiesta sulle condizioni dei contadini in Basilicata e in Calabria (1910).* Bari: Editori Laterza, 1968.

Pitkin, Donald S. "Land Tenure and Family Organization in an Italian Village." *Human Organization* 18, no. 4 (Winter 1959-60): 169-73.

————. "Marital Property Considerations Among Peasants: An Italian Example." *Anthropological Quarterly* 33, no. 1 (January 1960): 33-39.

Pitto, Cesare. *Al di la dell'emigrazione: Elementi per una antropologia dei processi migratori.* Cassano All'Jonio, Calabria: Ionica Editrice, 1988.

Pitt-Rivers, J.A. *The People of the Sierra.* Chicago: University of Chicago Press, 1961.

Prezzolini, Giuseppe. *The Legacy of Italy.* New York: S.F. Vanni, 1948.

Principe, Ilario. *La Calabria.* Firenze: Istituto Geografico Militare, 1968.

Ramage, Craufurd Tait. *The Nooks and Bi-ways of Italy: Wanderings in Search of its Ancient Remains and Modern Superstitions.* Liverpool: Edward Howell, 1868.

Rohlfs, Gerardo. "Le due Calabrie." *Almanacco Calabrese* 12 (1962): 59-71.

Rosoli, Gianfausto, ed., *Un Secolo di Emigrazione Italiana, 1876-1976.* Roma: Centro Studi Emigrazione, 1978.

Rossi, Adolfo. "Vantaggi e danni dell'emigrazione nel mezzogiorno d'Italia (Note di un viaggio fatto in Basilicata e in Calabria)". *Bollettino dell'emigrazione*, no. 13 (1908): 3-99.

Rossi-Doria, Manlio. *Dieci anni di politica agraria nel mezzogiorno*. Bari: Editori Laterza, 1958.

Scalise, Giuseppe. *L'emigrazione dalla Calabria: Saggio di economia sociale*. Napoli: Luigi Pierro Editore, 1905.

Schachter, Gustus. *The Italian South: Economic Development in Mediterranean Europe*. New York: Random House, 1965.

Scott, Joan W. and Louise A. Tilly. "Women's Work and the Family in Nineteenth-Century Europe." *Comparative Studies in Society and History* 25, no. 42 (January 1975): 36-64.

Sereni, Emilio. *La questione agraria nella rinascita nazionale italiana*. Torino: Piccola Biblioteca Einaudi, 1975.

Shanin, Teodor, ed. *Peasants and Peasant Societies*. Harmondsworth, England: Penguin, 1971.

Silverman, Sydel. *Three Bells of Civilization: The Life of an Italian Hill Town*. New York: Columbia University Press, 1975.

Simíc, Andrei. *The Peasant Urbanites: A Study of Rural-Urban Mobility in Serbia*. New York: Seminar Press, 1973.

Sjoberg, Gideon. "Folk and 'Feudal' Societies." *American Journal of Sociology* 58 (November 1952): 231-39.

Swinburne, Henry. *Travels in the Two Sicilies: in the years 1777, 1778, 1779 and 1780*. 2 vols. London: P. Emsly, 1783.

Tarrow, Sidney G. *Peasant Communism in Southern Italy*. New Haven: Yale University Press, 1967.

Taruffi, D., L. DeNobili, and C. Lori. *La questione agraria e l'emigrazione in Calabria*. Firenze: G. Barbèra, 1908.

Toor, Frances. *Festivals and Folkways of Italy*. New York: Crown, 1953.

Touring Club Italiano. *Annuario Generale*. 1912 (anno 17), 1922 (anno 28), and 1923-24 (anno 30). Milano: Stamperia Mondaini, 1912, 1922, and 1924.

———. *Basilicata e Calabria*. 3rd ed. Milano: n.p., 1965.

Villari, Luigi. *Italian Life in Town and Country*. New York: Knickerbocker Press, 1902.

Vincelli, Guido. *Una comunità meridionale: preliminari ad un'indagine sociologico-culturale*. Torino: Taylor Torino, 1958.

Wheaton, Robert. "Family and Kinship in Western Europe: The Problem of the Joint Family Household." *Journal of Interdisciplinary History* 4 (Spring 1975): 601-28.

Williams, Herbert H. and Judith R. Williams. "The Extended Family as a Vehicle of Culture Change." *Human Organization* 24, no. 1 (Spring 1965): 59-64.

Zimmern, Helen. *Italy and the Italians*. London: Pitman & Sons, 1907.

Sources Relating to the New World Experience

Abbott, Edith. "Grace Abbott and Hull-House, 1908-1921." *Social Service Review* (September 1950): 378-85.

Abbott, Grace. "The Chicago Employment Agency and the Immigrant Worker." *American Journal of Sociology* 14, no. 3 (November 1908): 289-305.

Annals of the American Academy of Political and Social Science. Vol. 57: *Social and Economic Conditions in the Dominion of Canada* (May 1923).

Annuario Italiano, 1935. Toronto: Italian Information Bureau, 1935.

Avery, Donald. "Canadian Immigration Policy and the 'Foreign' Navvy 1896-1914." Canadian Historical Association *Historical Papers* (1972): 135-36.

Bagnell, Kenneth. *Canadese: A Portrait of the Italian Canadians.* Toronto: Macmillan, 1989.

Baily, Samuel L. "Chain Migration of Italians to Argentina: case studies of the Aghonesi and the Lirolesi." *Studi Emigrazione* 19, no. 65 (March 1982): 73-91.

Bailey, W.B. "The Bird of Passage." *American Journal of Sociology* 18, no. 3 (November 1912): 391-97.

Barton, Josef J. *Peasants and Strangers: Italians, Rumanians, and Slovaks in an American City, 1890-1950.* Cambridge: Harvard University Press, 1975.

Bell, Margaret. "Toronto's Melting-Pot." *Canadian Magazine* 41, no. 3 (July 1913): 234-42.

Bernardy, Amy A. *America vissuta.* Torino: Fratelli Bocco, 1911.

————. *Italia randaglia attraverso gli Stati Uniti.* Torino: Fratelli Bocco, 1913.

Bianco, Carla. *The Two Rosetos.* Bloomington; Indiana: Indiana University Press, 1974.

Boissevain, Jeremy. *The Italians of Montreal: Social Adjustment in a Plural Society.* Ottawa: Information Canada, 1970.

Bradwin, Edmund. *The Bunkhouse Man: A Study of Work and Pay in the Camps of Canada, 1903-1914.* New York: Columbia University Press, 1928; facsimile reprint, Toronto: University of Toronto Press, 1972.

Brandenburg, Broughton. *Imported Americans: The Story of the Experiences of a Disguised American and his wife studying the Immigration Question.* New York: Frederick A. Stokes, 1904.

Breton, Raymond. "Institutional Completeness of Ethnic Communities and the Personal Relations of Immigrants." *American Journal of Sociology* 70, no. 2 (September 1964): pp. 193-205.

Bridle, Augustus. "The Drama of the 'Ward'." *The Canadian Magazine* 34, no. 1 (November 1909): 3-8.

Briggs, John W. *An Italian Passage: Immigrants to Three American Cities, 1890-1930.* New Haven: Yale University Press, 1978.

Brown, Lawrence Guy. *Immigration: Cultural Conflicts and Social Adjustments.* New York: Longmans, Green, 1933; facsimile reprint, New York: Arno Press & The New York Times, 1969.

Bryce, P.H. "Immigration in Relation to the Public Health." *Canadian Journal of Medicine and Surgery* 19, no. 4 (April 1906): 203-10.

Bureau of Municipal Research. *What Is the "Ward" Going to Do with Toronto?* Toronto: Bureau of Municipal Research, 1918.

Burnley, J.H. "Italian Migration and Settlement in New Zealand, 1874-1968." *International Migration* 9, nos. 3-4 (1971): 139-55.

Campisi, Paul J. "Ethnic Family Patterns: The Italian Family in the United States." *American Journal of Sociology* 53, no. 6 (May 1948): 443-49.

Caroli, Betty Boyd, Robert F. Harney, and Lydio F. Tomasi, eds. *The Italian Immigrant Woman in North America.* Toronto: Multicultural History Society of Ontario, 1978.

Carr, John Foster. "The Coming of the Italian." In *Immigration and Americanization*, pp. 141-54. Edited by Philip Davis and Bertha Schwartz. Boston: Ginn, 1920.

Choldin, Harvey M. "Kinship Networks in the Migration Process." *International Migration Review* 7, no. 2 (Summer 1973): 163-75.

Corbett, David C. *Canada's Immigration Policy: A Critique.* Toronto: University of Toronto Press, 1957.

Corsi, Edward. *In the Shadow of Liberty: The Chronicle of Ellis Island.* New York: Macmillan, 1935.

Covello, Leonard. *The Social Background of the Italo-American School Child: A Study of the Southern Italian Family Mores and Their Effect in the School Situation in Italy and America.* Leiden, Netherlands: E.J. Brill, 1967.

Cronin, Constance. *The Sting of Change: Sicilians in Sicily and Australia.* Chicago: University of Chicago Press, 1970.

d'A. Jones and Melvin G. Holli, eds., *Ethnic Chicago.* Grand Rapids, Michigan: William B. Eerdmans, 1981.

Danziger, Kurt. "The Acculturation of Italian Immigrant Girls." In *The Canadian Family,* revised ed., Edited by K. Ishwaran. Toronto: Holt, Rinehart and Winston, pp. 200-12. 1976.

Dore, Grazia. *La democrazia Italiana e l'emigrazione in America.* Brescia: Marcellina, 1964.

______ . "Some Social and Historical Aspects of Italian Emigration to America." *Journal of Social History* 2, no. 2 (Winter 1968): 95-122.

Erickson, Charlotte, ed. *Emigration from Europe 1815-1914: Select Documents.* London: Adam and Charles Black, 1976.

Ets, Marie Hall. *Rosa: The Life of an Immigrant.* Minneapolis: University of Minnesota Press, 1970.

Fairchild, Henry Pratt. *Immigration: A World Movement and its American Significance,* rev. ed. New York: Macmillan, 1933.

Fenton, Edwin. *Immigrants and Unions, a Case Study: Italians and American Labor, 1870-1920.* Ph.D. dissertation. Harvard University, 1957; facsimile reprint, New York: Arno Press and The New York Times, 1975.

______ . "Italians in the Labor Movement." *Pennsylvania History* 26, no. 2 (April 1959): 133-48.

Foerster, Robert F. *The Italian Emigration of Our Times.* Cambridge: Harvard University Press, 1919.

Furio, Colomba M. "The Cultural Background of the Italian Immigrant woman and Its Impact on Her Unionization in the New York City Garment Industry, 1880-1919." In *Pane e Lavoro: the Italian American Working Class,* pp. 81-98. Edited by George E. Pozzetta. Toronto: Multicultural History Society of Ontario, 1980.

Gans, Herbert J. *The Urban Villagers: Group and Class in the Life of Italian-Americans.* New York: Free Press, 1962.

Gibbon, J. Murray. "The Foreign Born." *Queen's Quarterly* 27, no. 4 (April-June 1920): 331-51.

Gordon, Milton M. *Assimilation in American Life: The Role of Race, Religion and National Origins.* New York: Oxford University Press, 1964.

Greenfield, Sidney M. "Industrialization and the Family in Sociological Theory." *American Journal of Sociology* 67 (1961): 312-314.

Gualtieri, Francesco M. *We Italians: A Study in Italian Immigration in Canada.* Toronto: Italian World War Veterans' Association, 1928.

Gutman, Herbert G. "Work, Culture, and Society in Industrializing America, 1815-1919." *American History Review* 78, no. 3 (June 1973): 531-87.

Handlin, Oscar. *The Uprooted: The Epic Story of the Great Migrations that Made the American People.* New York: Grosset and Dunlap, 1951.

Harney, Robert F. "The Padrone and the Immigrant." *Canadian Review of American Studies* 5, no. 2 (Fall 1974): 101-18.

______ . "Ambiente and Social Class in North American Little Italies." *Canadian Review of Studies in Nationalism* 2, no. 2 (Spring 1975): 208-24.

______ . "Chiaroscuro: Italians in Toronto, 1885-1915." *Italian Americana* 1, no. 1 (Spring 1975): 143-67.

______ . "The Commerce of Migration." *Canadian Ethnic Studies* 9, no. 1 (1977): 42-53.

______ . "Boarding and Belonging: Thoughts on Sojourner Institutions." *Urban History Review* 2, no. 78 (October 1978): 8-37.

______ . "Montreal's King of Italian Labour: A Case Study of Padronism." *Labour: Journal of Canadian Labour Studies* 4 (1979): 57-84.

______ . "Toronto's Little Italy, 1885-1945." In *Little Italies in North America*, pp. 41-62. Edited by Robert F. Harney and J. Vincenza Scarpaci. Toronto: Multicultural History Society of Ontario, 1981.

Hastings, J.C.O. *Report of the Toronto Medical Health Officer Dealing with the Recent Investigation of Slum Conditions in Toronto, Embodying Recommendations for the Amelioration of the Same.* Toronto: 1911.

Higham, John. *Strangers in the Land: Patterns of American Nativism, 1860-1925.* New York: Atheneum, 1963.

Howerth, I.W. "Are the Italians a Dangerous Class?" *The Charities Review: A Journal of Practical Sociology* 4, no. 24 (1894): 17-40.

Hurd, W. Burton, "The Case for a Quota." *Queen's Quarterly* 36 (Winter 1929): 145-59.

Iacovetta, Franca. "From *Contadina* to Worker: Southern Italian Immigrant Working Women in Toronto, 1947-62." In *Looking into My Sister's Eyes: an Exploration in Women's History*, pp. 195-222. Edited by Jean Burnet. Toronto: Multicultural History Society of Ontario, 1986.

Italian Information Bureau. *Annuario italiano.* Toronto: Italian Information Bureau, 1935.

Juliani, Richard N. "The Origin and Development of the Italian Community in Philadelphia." In *The Ethnic Experience in Pennsylvania*, pp. 233-62. Lewisburg, Pennsylvania: Bucknell University Press, 1973.

Korman, Gerd. *Industrialization, Immigrants, and Americanizers: The View from Milwaukee, 1866-1921.* Madison: State Historical Society of Wisconsin, 1967.

LaGumina, Salvatore J., ed. *Wop! A Documentary History of Anti-Italian Discrimination in the United States.* New York: Straight Arrow Books, 1973.

LaPiana, G. *The Italians of Milwaukee, Wisconsin: A General Survey under the Direction of the Associated Charities.* Milwaukee: Associated Charities, 1915; facsimile reprint, San Francisco: Robert D. Reed, 1970.

Lee, Trevor R. "The role of the Ethnic Community as a Reception Area for Italian Immigrants in Melbourne, Australia." *International Migration* 8, nos. 1-2 (1970): 50-63.

Lieberson, Stanley. "Residential Segregation and Ethnic Assimilation." *Social Forces* 40 (1961): 52-57.

Lopreato, Joseph. *Italian Americans.* New York: Random House, 1970.

McDonald, J(ohn) S. "Italy's Rural Social Structure and Migration." *Occidente* 12, no. 5 (September 1956): 437-456.

______ . "Agricultural Organization, Migration and Labour Militancy in Rural Italy." *Economic History Review* 16, no. 1-3 (1963-64): 61-75.

MacDonald, John S. and Leatrice D. MacDonald. "Urbanization, Ethnic Groups, and Social Segmentation." *Social Research* 29, no. 4 (Winter 1962): 433-48.

______ . "Chain Migration, Ethnic Neithbourhood Formation, and Social Networks." *Milbank Memorial Fund Quarterly* 42 (1964): 82-97.

______ . "Italian Migration to Australia: Manifest Functions of Bureaucracy versus Latent Functions of Informal Networks." *Journal of Social History* 3, no. 3 (Spring 1970): 249-75.

McLaughlin, Virginia Yans. "Patterns of Work and Family Organization: Buffalo's Italians." In *The Family in History: Interdisciplinary Essays*, pp. 111-26. Edited by Theodore K. Rabb and Robert I. Rotberg. New York: Harper and Row, 1973.

________ . "A Flexible Tradition: South Italian Immigrants Confront a New Work Experience." In *Immigrants in Industrial America, 1850-1920*, pp. 67-84. Edited by Richard L. Ehrlich. Charlottesville, Virginia: University of Virginia Press, 1977.

Modell, John and Hareven, Tamara K. "Urbanization and the Malleable Household: An Examination of Boarding and Lodging in American Families." *Journal of Marriage and the Family* 35 (August 1973): 467-79.

Nelli, Humbert S. *The Italian in Chicago, 1880-1930: A Study in Ethnic Mobility.* New York, Oxford University Press, 1970.

Novotny, Ann. *Strangers at the Door: Ellis Island, Castle Garden, and the Great Migration to America.* Riverside, Connecticut; Chatham, 1972; New York: Bantam Books, 1974.

Park, Robert T. and Miller, Herbert A. *Old World Traits Transplanted.* New York: Harper and Brothers, 1921.

Perin, Roberto and Franc Sturino, eds. *Arrangiarsi: The Italian Immigration Experience in Canada.* Montreal: Guernica, 1989.

Philpott, Thomas Lee. *The Slum and the Ghetto: Neighbourhood Deterioration and Middle-Class Reform: Chicago, 1880-1930.* New York: Oxford University Press, 1978.

Phipard, Charles B. "The Philanthropist-Padrone." *Charities: A Weekly Review of Local and General Philanthropy* 12 (1904): 470-72.

Price, Charles. "Southern Europeans in Australia: Problems of Assimilation." *International Migration Review* 2, no. 3 (Summer 1968): 3-24.

Potestio, John, ed. *The Memoirs of Giovanni Veltri.* Toronto: Multicultural History Society of Ontario, 1987.

Pozzeta, George E. "Immigrants and Ethnics: The State of Italian-American Historiography." *Journal of American Ethnic History* 9, no. 1 (Fall 1989): 67-95.

Ramirez, Bruno. *Les Premiers Italiens de Montréal: L'origine de la Petite Italie du Québec.* Montreal: Boréal Express, 1984.

________ . *The Italians in Canada.* Canada's Ethnic Groups Series, Booklet no. 14. Ottawa: Canadian Historical Association, 1989.

Ratti, Anna Maria. "Italian Migration Movements, 1876 to 1926." In *International Migrations.* vol. 2: *Interpretations*, pp. 440-70. Edited by Walter F. Willcox. New York: National Bureau of Economic Research, 1931.

Residents of Hull-House, a Social Settlement. *Hull-House Maps and Papers: A Presentation of Nationalities and Wages in a Congested District of Chicago, Together with Comments and Essays on Problems Growing Out of the Social Conditions.* Boston: Thomas Y. Crowell, 1895; facsimile reprint, New York: Arno Press and The New York Times, 1970.

Roberts, Peter. *The New Immigration: A Study of the Industrial and Social Life of Southeastern Europeans in America.* New York: Macmillan, 1913.

Rossi, Egisto. "Delle condizioni del Canada rispetto all'immigrazione italiana." *Bollettino dell'emigrazione* 4 (1903): 3-28.

Saloutos, Theodore. "Exodus U.S.A." In *In the Trek of the Immigrants*, pp. 197-215. Edited by D. Fritiof Ander. Rock Island, Illinois: Augustana College Publications, 1964.

Schiavo, Giovanni E. *The Italians in Chicago: A Study in Americanization.* Chicago: Italian American Publishing, 1928; facsimile reprint, New York: Arno Press & The New York Times, 1975.

Smith, Timothy L. "New Approaches to the History of Immigration in Twentieth Century America." *American Historical Review* 71, no. 4 (July 1966): 1265-79.

Smith, W.G. *A Study in Canadian Immigration.* Toronto: Ryerson Press, 1920.

Spada, A.V. *The Italians in Canada*. Ottawa: Riviera Publishers, 1969.

Speranza, Gino C. "The Italian Foreman as a Social Agent: Labour Unrest in West Virginia and Their Consequences to the Community." *Charities: A Weekly Review of Local and General Philanthropy* 11 (1903): pp. 26-28.

Stead, William T. *If Christ Came to Chicago: A Plea for the Union of All Who Love the Service of All Who Suffer*. London: Review of Reviews, 1894.

Steiner, Edward. *On the Trail of the Immigrant*. New York: F.H. Revell, 1906.

Stella, Antonio. *Some Aspects of Italian Immigration to the United States: Statistical Data and General Considerations Based Chiefly upon United States Censuses and other Official Publications*. New York: G.P. Putnam's & Sons, 1924.

Stephenson, F.C. "Mission Work among Italians in Canada." In *Religious Work among Italians in America: A Survey for the Home Missions Council*. Edited by Antonio Mangano. Philadelphia: Board of the Home Missions and Church Extension of the Methodist Episcopal Church, 1917; facsimile reprint in *Protestant Evangelism among Italians in America*, pp. 5-45. Edited by Francesco Cordasco. New York: Arno Press & The New York Times, 1975.

Sturino, Franc. "Italian immigration to Canada and the farm labour system through the 1920's." *Studi Emigrazione* 22, no. 77 (March 1985): 81-97.

______ . *Italian-Canadian Studies: A Select Bibliography*. Toronto: Mariano A. Elia Chair in Italian-Canadian Studies, York University and Multicultural History Society of Ontario, 1988.

Taschereau, Sylvie. *Pays et Patries: Mariages et lieux d'origine des Italiens de Montréal, 1906-1930*. Montreal: Université de Montréal, 1987.

Taylor, Philip. *The Distant Magnet: European Emigration to the U.S.A.* New York: Harper & Row, 1972.

Thernstrom, Stephan. "Immigrants and Wasps: Ethnic Difference in Occupational Mobility in Boston, 1890-1940." In *Nineteenth-Century Cities: Essays in The New Urban History*, pp. 125-64. Edited by Stephan Thernstrom and Richard Sennett. New Haven: Yale University Press, 1969.

Thistlewaite, Frank. "Migration from Europe Overseas in the Nineteenth and Twentieth Centuries." In *Population Movements in Modern European History*, pp. 73-92. Edited by Herbert Moller. New York: Macmillan, 1964.

Tilly, Charles and Brown, C. Harold. "On Uprooting, Kinship, and the Auspices of Migration." In *An Urban World*, pp. 108-33. Edited by Charles Tilly. Boston: Little, Brown, 1974.

Timlin, Mabel F. "Canada's Immigration Policy, 1896-1910." *Canadian Journal of Economics and Political Science* 26, no. 4 (November 1960): 517-32.

Tomasi, Silvano M. and Madeline H. Engel, eds. *The Italian Experience in the United States*. New York: Center for Migration Studies, 1970.

Vangelisti, P. Guglielmo. *Gli Italiani in Canada*. Montreal: Chiesa della Difesa, 1958.

Vecoli, Rudolph J. "Contadini in Chicago: A Critique of the Uprooted." *Journal of American History* 51 (December 1964): 404-17.

______ . "European Americans: From Immigrants to Ethnics." *International Migration Review* 6, no. 4 (Winter 1972): 403-36.

______ . "Emigration Historiography in Italy." *Immigration History Newsletter* 6, no. 2 (November 1974): 1-5.

______ . "Italian American Workers, 1880-1920: Padrone Slaves or Primitive Rebels." In *Perspectives in Italian Immigration and Ethnicity*, pp. 25-43. Edited by S(ilvano) M. Tomasi. New York: Center for Migration Studies, 1977.

Warner, W. Lloyd and Leo Srole. *The Social Systems of American Ethnic Groups*. Yankee City Series, vol. 3. New Haven: Yale University Press, 1945.

Whyte, William Foote. *Street Corner Society: The Social Structure of an Italian Slum*. Chicago: University of Chicago Press, 1955.

Woodsworth, J.S. *Strangers within Our Gates: Coming Canadians.* Toronto: F.C. Stephenson, 1909. (Young People's Forward Movement Department of the Methodist Church, 1909.)

Zangwill, Israel. "Some American Impressions." *Proceedings of the Canadian Club of Toronto* 21 (1923-24): 198-207.

Zorbaugh, Harvey W. *Gold Coast and Slum.* Chicago: University of Chicago Press, 1929.

Zucchi, John E. "Italian Hometown Settlements and the Development of an Italian Community in Toronto, 1875-1935." In *Gathering Place: Peoples and Neighbourhoods of Toronto*, pp. 121-46. Edited by Robert F. Harney. Toronto: Multicultural History Society of Ontario, 1985.

______ . *Italians in Toronto: Development of a National Identity, 1875-1935.* Kingston and Montreal: McGill-Queen's Press, 1988.

Index